DUNGEONS & DRAGONS®

ADVENTURER'S VAULT™
Arms and Equipment for All Classes

ROLEPLAYING GAME SUPPLEMENT

Logan Bonner • Eytan Bernstein • Chris Sims

CREDITS

Design
Logan Bonner (lead),
Eytan Bernstein, Chris Sims

Additional Design
Kolja Raven Liquette, Owen K.C. Stephens

Development
Stephen Schubert (lead),
Andy Collins, Peter Schaefer

Editing
Greg Bilsland (lead),
Scott Fitzgerald Gray, Alex Jurkat, Gwendolyn F.M. Kestrel

Managing Editing
Christopher Perkins

Director of R&D, Roleplaying Games/Book Publishing
Bill Slavicsek

D&D Story Design and Development Manager
Christopher Perkins

D&D System Design and Development Manager
Andy Collins

Art Directors
Stacy Longstreet, Jon Schindehette

Cover Illustration
David Griffith (front), **William O'Connor** (back)

Graphic Designers
Kevin Smith, Leon Cortez

Interior Illustrations
Drew Baker, Ryan Barger, Ed Cox, Thomas Denmark, Wayne England, Jason A. Engle, Randy Gallegos, David Griffith, Howard Lyon, Lee Moyer, William O'Connor, Darrell Riche, Marc Sasso, Chris Seaman, Anne Stokes, Franz Vohwinkel, James Zhang

D&D Script Design
Daniel Reeve

Publishing Production Specialist
Christopher Tardiff

Prepress Manager
Jefferson Dunlap

Imaging Technicians
Travis Adams, Bob Jordan, Sven Bolen

Production Manager
Cynda Callaway

This product requires the 4th Edition DUNGEONS & DRAGONS® game rules, which are based on previous DUNGEONS & DRAGONS game rules designed by **E. Gary Gygax, Dave Arneson** (1st Edition and earlier); **David "Zeb" Cook** (2nd Edition); **Jonathan Tweet, Monte Cook, Skip Williams, Richard Baker,** and **Peter Adkison** (3rd Edition).

620-21783720-001 HB
9 8 7 6 5 4 3 2 1
First Printing: September 2008
ISBN: 978-0-7869-4978-6

U.S., CANADA, ASIA, PACIFIC, & LATIN AMERICA
Wizards of the Coast, Inc.
P.O. Box 707
Renton WA 98057-0707
+1-800-324-6496

EUROPEAN HEADQUARTERS
Hasbro UK Ltd
Caswell Way
Newport, Gwent NP9 0YH
GREAT BRITAIN
Please keep this address for your records

WIZARDS OF THE COAST, BELGIUM
't Hofveld 6D
1702 Groot-Bijgaarden
Belgium
+32 2 467 3360

VISIT OUR WEBSITE AT WWW.WIZARDS.COM/DND

INTRODUCTION

Equipment and magic items are essential to the survival of any D&D® character. Treasure is vital to any adventure. As a player outfitting a character or a DM filling hoards with shiny baubles, the more options you have the better.

That's where *Adventurer's Vault* comes in. It expands on the rules for using equipment found in the *Player's Handbook®*. These pages are full of options for the PC with gold or *residuum* burning a hole in his pouch, and the DM looking for that enticing reward. *Adventurer's Vault* also expands the D&D® game with new tricks for normal tasks.

Open *Adventurer's Vault* and find out . . .

WHAT'S INSIDE

This book has two chapters—Equipment and Magic Items—followed by appendices designed to aid in using the rest of the contents. Use it to equip your PC or your NPCs, or to stock your adventures with interesting stuff.

✦ **Chapter 1: Equipment:** This chapter focuses on nonmagical items—masterwork armor, new weapons, alchemical substances, mounts, and vehicles—and presents rules for using them in your game. Vehicles can add action to encounters and overland travel. An alchemy system allows you to add some bang to your game without having to rely on the wizard or magic items.

✦ **Chapter 2: Magic Items:** Vastly expanding on the items found in the *Player's Handbook,* this chapter is divided by item slot. You'll find a vast array of new items for every slot, as well as the expanded ranks of wondrous items and consumables. Even companion beasts and mounts have their own items now, allowing you to make more of your pets.

✦ **Appendix 1:** This section gives you, the DM or player, ideas and tools for making magic items seem unique in your campaign and world. Give your items a story. Learn how to give items levels as treasure or to move magic from one item to another.

✦ **Appendix 2:** To help parcel treasure, all the magic items in this book are listed alphabetically by level.

CONTENTS

CHAPTER 1

EQUIPMENT

BEING PREPARED means having what you need in any situation. The adventurer's life is nothing if not unpredictable, so the savvy explorer takes unusual paths even when it comes to finding or making equipment. While wandering the markets in unusual locales, you can find all sorts of exotic and useful gear. The right training can grant you access to such equipment, giving you an edge that just might save your life.

In this chapter, you'll find:

✦ **Masterwork Armor:** Techniques and magic from across the cosmos allow master craftsfolk to make strange and amazing armor. Choosing the right kind of armor is a matter of need and taste. Shore up your soft spots with the items in this section.

✦ **Weapons:** Weapons are as varied as the reasons to do battle in the darkening world. Nonhuman cultures have also produced a few variations on typical weapon forms. Herein you'll find several new simple, military, and superior weapons comparable to yet different from those presented in the *Player's Handbook*®.

✦ **Mounts:** The right mount can get you where you want to go faster, and many able creatures can be trained to serve in this capacity. In this section, you'll find mounts that expand on those presented in the *Monster Manual*®. You'll also find gear to make your mount a better ally.

✦ **Vehicles:** Some tasks and terrain demand more than a mount. When that's true, then it's time to learn to drive. This section provides sample vehicles and the rules required to use them.

✦ **Alchemy:** With a little special training, you can combine arcane reagents according to mystic formulas to produce fell poisons, bizarre powders, and wondrous concoctions. For those unskilled in the alchemical arts, such items can also be procured from the right merchant with a little coin.

WILLIAM O'CONNOR

This section describes several new kinds of masterwork armor. These special suits of masterwork armor are sometimes used in the creation of magic armor. Just as adventurers are likely to be dealing in different currencies as they attain higher levels, so too are they likely to be acquiring new kinds of armor materials.

Masterwork armor always has an enhancement bonus, and the price of the masterwork armor material is incorporated into the overall cost of the magic armor. For example, +4 *crysteel mail armor* costs 45,000 gp–the same as nonmasterwork +4 *chain armor*. Thus, an adventurer of higher level is generally better off shopping for masterwork armors than the armors he or she used at lower levels.

A magic armor's enhancement bonus is still added to the armor bonus to determine a character's overall armor bonus. For example, +4 *stormscale armor* provides a +13 bonus to the wearer's AC, +9 for the armor bonus and +4 for the enhancement bonus.

An armor entry on the Masterwork Armor table contains the following information.

Armor Bonus: Armor provides this bonus to AC.

Minimum Enhancement Bonus: Masterwork armor requires a minimum enhancement bonus, as shown in this entry.

Check: You take this penalty to all Strength-, Dexterity-, and Constitution-based skill checks when you wear the armor. You don't take the penalty to ability checks (such as a Strength check to break down a door or a Dexterity check to determine initiative in combat).

Speed: You take this penalty to your speed (in squares) when wearing the armor.

Price: The item's price in gold pieces (gp). The cost of masterwork armor is included in the cost of magic armor.

Weight: The armor's weight in pounds.

Special: Some masterwork armors have additional properties, such as a defense boost or additional resistance. A bonus received from the special property of a masterwork armor is an armor bonus.

ARMOR TYPES

Cloth: Githzerai weavers first taught other peoples the methods of making githweave. It's clear that the githzerai took these techniques from their erstwhile masters, the mind flayers. Patterns taken from captured mind flayer garments led to mindweave and mindpatterned armor. All these armors infuse some form of crystal into textiles, channeling mind energy to fortify the body. Efreetweave seems to be similar, but uses rare reagents and metallic threads from the Elemental Chaos.

Leather: Drowmesh uses strands of leather woven together in a fine lattice for maximum flexibility. Yuan-ti overlap fine "scales" of leather to produce the incredibly supple snakeskin armor, and they weave stands of this with shadow magic to produce anathema armor. Swordwing leather mimics the way swordwings make their paper spires, creating a light, flexible, and hard leather.

Hide: Dwarves use earth energy to fortify earthhide, mimicking the strange living-earth skin of creatures such as the galeb duhr and the earth titan. Feyhide armor is treated with an elven process that gives resilience akin to the hide of tough fey beasts. Astral stalker preservation techniques yield stalkerhide. Voidhide armor comes from similar methods used by the sorrowsworn to preserve their grisly trophies.

Chain: Weavemail is an exquisite armor made according to an advanced technique perfected in the eladrin courts of the Feywild, consisting of closely linked chains that provide few openings for enemy attacks. Finemail is a more common eladrin derivative of this method, while braidmail is a similar armor made according to elven tradition. Genasi mix steel with magic volcanic glass to create resilient crysteel armor. Pitmail is derived from an infernal technique used to armor great commanders in the days of the tiefling empire of Bael Turath.

FRANZ VOHWINKEL

MASTERWORK ARMOR

Cloth Armor (Light)	Armor Bonus	Minimum Enhancement Bonus	Check	Speed	Price	Weight	Special
Githweave armor	+0	+3	–	–	special	2 lb.	+1 Will
Mindweave armor	+0	+4	–	–	special	2 lb.	+2 Will
Efreetweave armor	+1	+5	–	–	special	2 lb.	+1 Will
Mindpatterned armor	+1	+6	–	–	special	2 lb.	+2 Will

Leather Armor (Light)	Armor Bonus	Minimum Enhancement Bonus	Check	Speed	Price	Weight	Special
Drowmesh armor	+2	+3	–	–	special	10 lb.	+1 Reflex
Snakeskin armor	+2	+4	–	–	special	10 lb.	+2 Reflex
Anathema armor	+3	+5	–	–	special	10 lb.	+1 Reflex
Swordwing armor	+3	+6	–	–	special	10 lb.	+2 Reflex

Hide Armor (Light)	Armor Bonus	Minimum Enhancement Bonus	Check	Speed	Price	Weight	Special
Earthhide armor	+3	+3	-1	–	special	25 lb.	+1 Fortitude
Feyhide armor	+3	+4	-1	–	special	25 lb.	+2 Fortitude
Stalkerhide armor	+4	+5	-1	–	special	25 lb.	+1 Fortitude
Voidhide armor	+4	+6	-1	–	special	25 lb.	+2 Fortitude

Chainmail (Heavy)	Armor Bonus	Minimum Enhancement Bonus	Check	Speed	Price	Weight	Special
Finemail armor	+7	+2	-1	-1	special	40 lb.	–
Braidmail armor	+8	+3	-1	-1	special	40 lb.	–
Crysteel armor	+8	+4	-1	-1	special	40 lb.	+2 Will
Weavemail armor	+10	+5	-1	-1	special	40 lb.	+1 Will
Pitmail armor	+11	+6	-1	-1	special	40 lb.	+2 Will

Scale Armor (Heavy)	Armor Bonus	Minimum Enhancement Bonus	Check	Speed	Price	Weight	Special
Drakescale armor	+8	+2	–	-1	special	45 lb.	–
Wyvernscale armor	+9	+3	–	-1	special	45 lb.	–
Stormscale armor	+9	+4	–	-1	special	45 lb.	+2 Fortitude
Nagascale armor	+11	+5	–	-1	special	45 lb.	+1 Fortitude
Titanscale armor	+12	+6	–	-1	special	45 lb.	+2 Fortitude

Plate Armor (Heavy)	Armor Bonus	Minimum Enhancement Bonus	Check	Speed	Price	Weight	Special
Rimefire plate armor	+8	+2	-2	-1	special	50 lb.	Resist 1 all
Layered plate armor	+9	+2	-2	-1	special	50 lb.	–
Gith plate armor	+10	+3	-2	-1	special	50 lb.	–
Specter plate armor	+10	+4	-2	-1	special	50 lb.	Resist 2 all
Legion plate armor	+12	+5	-2	-1	special	50 lb.	–
Tarrasque plate armor	+12	+6	-2	-1	special	50 lb.	Resist 5 all

Scale: Drakescale armor mimics the small, close scales of rage drakes to stave off attacks, while wyvernscale uses larger scales in a similar pattern. Stormscale armor resembles the storm gorgon's hardened plating and incorporates elemental magic. Ancient yuan-ti crafting techniques infuse metal plates with elemental power to produce nagascale armor. Dwarves took the primordial methods of producing titanscale armor from the titans and giants.

Plate: Rimefire plate is bathed in elemental frost and fire to infuse it with hardness. Humans developed the process of layering steel several dozen times to create layered plate. Gith plate is hardened with psionic techniques originating with either the mind flayers or the first generation of escaped githyanki slaves. Specter plate is infused with energy from the Shadowfell. Legion plate mimics the forging techniques used in the Nine Hells to armor legion devils. Tarrasque plate, designed to emulate the tarrasque's impenetrable hide, has hundreds of nodules packed between very thin metal layers, each treated with a different process.

WEAPONS

The *Player's Handbook* covers a broad range of commonly used weapons. This section describes a range of more unusual weapons, which provide a host of new combinations and benefits.

A weapon entry on the Melee Weapons table or Ranged Weapons table contains the following information.

Weapon: The weapon's name.

Prof.: Proficiency with a weapon gives you a proficiency bonus to attack rolls, which appears in this column if applicable. If you're not proficient with the weapon, you don't gain this bonus.

Damage: The weapon's damage die or dice.

Range: Weapons that can be thrown or have ammunition that can be shot have a range. The number before the slash indicates the normal range distance (in squares) for an attack. The number after the slash indicates the long-range distance for an attack. An entry of "–" indicates that the weapon can't be used at range.

Price: The weapon's cost in gold pieces.

Weight: The weapon's weight in pounds.

Category, Group, and Properties: Weapon categories, groups, and properties are explained in Chapter 7 of the *Player's Handbook*. In addition, two new weapon properties are described below.

Brutal: A brutal weapon's minimum damage is higher than that of a normal weapon. When rolling the weapon's damage, reroll any die that displays a value equal to or lower than the brutal value given for the weapon. Reroll the die until the value shown exceeds the weapon's brutal value, and then use the new value.

For example, the execution axe has a property of brutal 2. If a fighter wielding this weapon hits with *steel serpent strike* (a 2[W] power), the player rolls 2d12 for the weapon damage, rerolling a die result of 1 or 2 until the die shows 3 or higher.

Defensive: A defensive weapon grants you a +1 bonus to AC while you wield the defensive weapon in one hand and wield another melee weapon in your other hand. Wielding more than one defensive weapon does not increase this bonus. To gain this benefit, you need not attack with the defensive weapon, but you must be proficient with it.

WEAPON TYPES

Broadsword: This stout, wide-bladed weapon lacks the accuracy of a longsword, but what it lacks in accuracy, it redeems with deadliness.

Craghammer: This dwarven hammer has a heavily weighted head, making it resemble a one-handed maul backed by a deadly spike.

Double Axe: Fitted with an axe head at each end, a double axe offers increased offensive and defensive capabilities.

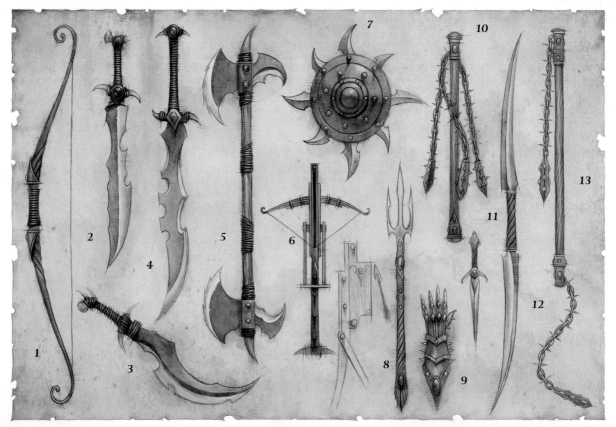

1. Greatbow; 2. Broadsword; 3. Khopesh; 4. Fullblade; 5. Double axe; 6. Repeating crossbow; 7. Spiked shield;
8. Trident; 9. Spiked gauntlet; 10. Triple-headed flail; 11. Parrying dagger; 12. Double sword; 13. Double flail.

MELEE WEAPONS (ILLUSTRATED ON PAGES 8 AND 63)

SIMPLE MELEE WEAPONS

One-Handed

Weapon	Prof.	Damage	Range	Price	Weight	Group	Properties
Spiked gauntlet[1]	+2	d6	–	5 gp	1 lb.	Unarmed	Off-hand

MILITARY MELEE WEAPONS

One-Handed

Weapon	Prof.	Damage	Range	Price	Weight	Group	Properties
Broadsword	+2	d10	–	20 gp	5 lb.	Heavy blade	Versatile
Khopesh	+2	d8	–	20 gp	8 lb.	Axe, heavy blade	Brutal 1, versatile
Light war pick	+2	d6	–	10 gp	4 lb.	Pick	High crit, off-hand
Scourge	+2	d8	–	3 gp	2 lb.	Flail	Off-hand
Trident	+2	d8	3/6	10 gp	4 lb.	Spear	Heavy thrown, versatile

Two-Handed

Weapon	Prof.	Damage	Range	Price	Weight	Group	Properties
Heavy war pick	+2	d12	–	20 gp	8 lb.	Pick	High crit

SUPERIOR MELEE WEAPONS

One-Handed

Weapon	Prof.	Damage	Range	Price	Weight	Group	Properties
Craghammer	+2	d10	–	20 gp	6 lb.	Hammer	Brutal 2, versatile
Kukri	+2	d6	–	10 gp	2 lb.	Light blade	Brutal 1, off-hand
Parrying dagger[2]	+2	d4	–	5 gp	1 lb.	Light blade	Defensive, off-hand
Spiked shield[3]	+2	d6	–	10 gp	7 lb.	Light blade	Off-hand
Tratnyr	+2	d8	10/20	10 gp	5 lb.	Spear	Heavy thrown, versatile
Triple-headed flail	+3	d10	–	15 gp	6 lb.	Flail	Versatile
Waraxe	+2	d12	–	30 gp	10 lb.	Axe	Versatile

Two-Handed

Weapon	Prof.	Damage	Range	Price	Weight	Group	Properties
Execution axe	+2	d12	–	30 gp	14 lb.	Axe	Brutal 2, high crit
Fullblade	+3	d12	–	30 gp	10 lb.	Heavy blade	High crit
Greatspear	+3	d10	–	25 gp	8 lb.	Polearm, spear	Reach
Mordenkrad	+2	2d6	–	30 gp	12 lb.	Hammer	Brutal 1

Double Weapons

Weapon	Prof.	Damage	Range	Price	Weight	Group	Properties
Double axe[4]	+2	d10/d10	–	40 gp	15 lb.	Axe	Defensive, off-hand
Double flail[4]	+2	d10/d10	–	30 gp	11 lb.	Flail	Defensive, off-hand
Double sword[4]	+3	d8/d8	–	40 gp	9 lb.	Heavy blade, light blade	Defensive, off-hand
Urgrosh[4]	+2	d12/d8	–	30 gp	12 lb.	Axe, spear	Defensive, off-hand

[1] This weapon also occupies the magic item hands slot. See description.

[2] A rogue proficient with this weapon can treat it as a dagger for the purpose of the Rogue Weapon Talent class feature.

[3] This weapon is combined with a light shield. See description.

[4] Double weapon (see page 10).

Double Flail: This weapon has a spiked flail head at either end to maximize attack and damage.

Double Sword: This well-balanced weapon combines the deadliness of two longswords with increased defensive capability.

Execution Axe: This broad-bladed axe is heavily weighted for greater hewing power.

Fullblade: This enormous, two-handed sword is favored by fighters and paladins.

RANGED WEAPONS (ILLUSTRATED ON PAGES 8 AND 63)

SIMPLE RANGED WEAPONS

Two-Handed

Weapon	Prof.	Damage	Range	Price	Weight	Group	Properties
Repeating crossbow	+2	d8	10/20	35 gp	6 lb.	Crossbow	Load free*

Ammunition

Weapon	Prof.	Damage	Range	Price	Weight	Group	Properties
Magazine	–	–	–	1 gp	1 lb.	–	–

SUPERIOR RANGED WEAPONS

Two-Handed

Weapon	Prof.	Damage	Range	Price	Weight	Group	Properties
Greatbow	+2	d12	25/50	30 gp	5 lb.	Bow	Load free
Superior crossbow	+3	d10	20/40	30 gp	6 lb.	Crossbow	Load minor

*See weapon description.

Greatbow: This massive, recurved bow stands as tall as a human when strung, and it fires arrows with greater power than a traditional longbow.

Greatspear: This reach weapon resembles a longspear, but its broad head and strong haft allow it to strike with increased force.

Heavy War Pick: This larger version of the light war pick delivers devastating strikes.

Khopesh: This sturdy weapon is identified by the crescent-shaped curve at the end of its blade.

Kukri: The blade of this heavy knife curves forward for greater potency. A rogue proficient with the kukri can treat it as a dagger for the purpose of the Rogue Weapon Talent class feature.

Light War Pick: This smaller version of the war pick is suitable as an off-hand weapon.

Mordenkrad: First used by dwarf shock troops in battle against giants, this oversized two-handed hammer has a massive head studded with spikes.

Parrying Dagger: This narrow dagger features a specially designed guard that can deflect attacks. A rogue proficient with the parrying dagger can treat it as a dagger for the purpose of the Rogue Weapon Talent class feature.

Repeating Crossbow: A rectangular magazine attaches to the top of this crossbow. A double-action lever drops a bolt into place as a free action, then fires it as a standard action. A repeating crossbow does not need to be reloaded as long as it has ammunition in its magazine. A magazine costs 1 gp and holds 10 bolts. It takes a standard action to remove an empty magazine and load a new one.

Spiked Gauntlet: These gauntlets are specially fitted with metal spikes. Unlike other weapons, the spiked gauntlet occupies your magic item hands slot while enchanted.

Scourge: This lightweight flail has leather thongs inlaid with sharpened bits of metal or bone.

Spiked Shield: This light shield is constructed with a sharpened spike at its center. A spiked shield can be enchanted as a magic shield or a magic weapon, but not both. A spiked shield enchanted as a magic weapon does not occupy a character's magic item arms slot. Although a character cannot use two shields at the same time, a character wielding a spiked shield enchanted as a weapon can employ arms slot items such as bracers.

Superior Crossbow: This crossbow appears similar to a traditional crossbow, but it has knobs and dials that allow the weapon to be fine-tuned for greater accuracy.

Tratnyr: Also known as the wingspear, this weapon was first crafted by the dragonborn for maximum efficiency in melee and ranged combat.

Trident: This three-tined spear is weighted for throwing over short distances.

Triple-headed Flail: This oversized flail has three heads for more potent attacks.

Urgrosh: Originally of dwarven make, this weapon has a heavy axe head at one end (dealing d12 damage) and a sharp spear point at the base of the haft (dealing d8 damage).

Waraxe: This weapon's superior balance allows it to be wielded in one hand.

DOUBLE WEAPONS

Wielding a double weapon is like wielding a weapon in each hand. The first die given in the damage column of the table for a double weapon is for the primary (or main) end of the weapon; the second damage die is for the secondary (or off-hand) end. You can use either end of a double weapon to deliver an attack unless a power specifies a main or off-hand weapon attack.

An enchanted double weapon receives an enhancement bonus on both ends, but weapon properties or powers conferred by the enchantment affect only the primary end of the weapon.

Like two-handed weapons, double weapons cannot normally be wielded by Small creatures unless the weapon has the small property.

MOUNTS

At some point in their careers, adventurers may trade their walking sticks for mounts. Mounts allow characters to move quickly from one location to another, crossing untamed frontiers to reach the next dungeon or some distant city.

A city or town usually has one or more kinds of creatures that can be purchased as mounts. Unusual settings require special mounts. PCs might be setting out across a desert, in which case a camel or riding lizard might be appropriate. Conversely, characters might be exploring the undersea depths of a fallen empire, allowing them to use sharks or sea horses as mounts. Regardless of where the PCs are, most mounts have a speed that exceeds that of a PC, allowing for faster passage between places.

Many mounts are also useful in combat. Pages 46–47 of the *Dungeon Master's Guide* describe how to use a mount in combat and how a mount can take advantage of any natural attacks it might have.

The table below lists mounts from *Adventurer's Vault* and from the *Monster Manual* (MM).

Price: The cost of the mount in gold pieces.

Speed: The creature's best speed in squares.

Per Hour/Per Day: How far, in miles, the creature can travel in an hour and in a 10-hour day of travel.

Normal/Heavy/Push/Drag: The normal load, heavy load, and push/drag load for the creature (in pounds). Like characters, mounts exceeding their normal load take a reduction in speed.

Camel		Level 1 Brute
Large natural beast		XP 100
Initiative +1	**Senses** Perception +0	
HP 38; **Bloodied** 19		
AC 13; **Fortitude** 13, **Reflex** 10, **Will** 9		
Speed 9		
⊕ **Kick** (standard; at-will)		
+4 vs. AC; 1d10 + 4 damage.		
Alignment Unaligned	**Languages** —	
Skills Endurance +9		
Str 19 (+4)	**Dex** 13 (+1)	**Wis** 11 (+0)
Con 18 (+4)	**Int** 2 (−4)	**Cha** 8 (−1)

MOUNTS

Mount	Price (gp)	Speed[1]	Per Hour[1]	Per Day[1]	Normal (lb.)	Heavy (lb.)	Push/Drag (lb.)
Blade spider[MM]	13,000	6	3 miles	30 miles	250	500	1,250
Camel	75	9	4-1/2 miles	45 miles	237	475	1,187
Dire boar[MM]	1,800	8	4 miles	40 miles	237	475	1,187
Elephant	3,400	8	4 miles	40 miles	312	625	1,562
Giant ant	1,800	9	4-1/2 miles	45 miles	237	475	1,187
Giant lizard, draft	200	7	3-1/2 miles	35 miles	237	475	1,187
Giant lizard, riding	1,800	9	4-1/2 miles	45 miles	250	500	1,250
Griffon[MM]	9,000	fly 10	5 miles	50 miles	250	500	1,250
Griffon, rimefire[MM]	525,000	fly 10	5 miles	50 miles	300	600	1,500
Hippogriff[MM]	4,200	fly 10	5 miles	50 miles	237	475	1,187
Hippogriff dreadmount[MM]	4,200	fly 10	5 miles	50 miles	262	525	1,312
Horse, celestial charger[MM]	13,000	8	4 miles	40 miles	287	575	1,437
Horse, riding[MM]	75	8	4 miles	40 miles	237	475	1,187
Horse, sea	1,800	swim 10	5 miles	50 miles	225	450	1,125
Horse, skeletal	17,000	10	5 miles	50 miles	250	500	1,250
Horse, warhorse[MM]	200	8	4 miles	40 miles	262	525	1,312
Manticore[MM]	45,000	fly 8	4 miles	40 miles	262	525	1,312
Nightmare[MM]	25,000	fly 10	5 miles	50 miles	287	575	1,437
Rage drake[MM]	2,600	8	4 miles	40 miles	237	475	1,187
Rhinoceros	2,600	6	3 miles	30 miles	262	525	1,312
Shark, dire	21,000	swim 11	5-1/2 miles	55 miles	210	420	1,050
Shark, riding	3,400	swim 11	5-1/2 miles	55 miles	190	380	950
Trihorn behemoth	21,000	6	3 miles	30 miles	325	650	1,625
Wolf, dire[MM]	1,000	8	4 miles	40 miles	237	475	1,187
Wyvern[MM]	21,000	fly 8	4 miles	40 miles	300	600	1,500

[MM] This monster's statistics can be found in the *Monster Manual*.

[1] A flying mount ignores distance multipliers for difficult terrain. Distances for an aquatic mount assume it is traveling in water.

Elephant — Level 8 Brute
Huge natural beast (mount) — XP 350

Initiative +4   **Senses** Perception +7
HP 111; **Bloodied** 55
AC 20; **Fortitude** 22, **Reflex** 15, **Will** 18
Speed 8

⊕ **Tusk Slam** (standard; at-will)
    Reach 2; +11 vs. AC; 2d6 + 7 damage.

⦀ **Stamp** (standard; at-will)
    +11 vs. AC; 1d10 + 7 damage, and the target is knocked prone.

Trampling Charge (while mounted by a friendly rider of 8th level or higher; at-will) ✦ **Mount**
    When charging, the elephant can move through one Medium or smaller creature's space and make a stamp attack against that creature. The elephant must end its move in an unoccupied space. The rider still attacks at the end of the mount's movement.

Alignment Unaligned   **Languages** —
Str 25 (+11)	**Dex** 11 (+4)	**Wis** 16 (+7)
Con 21 (+9)	**Int** 2 (+0)	**Cha** 9 (+3)

Giant Ant — Level 4 Skirmisher
Large natural beast (mount) — XP 175

Initiative +8   **Senses** Perception +8
HP 54; **Bloodied** 27
AC 18; **Fortitude** 17, **Reflex** 17, **Will** 14
Speed 9

⊕ **Bite** (standard; at-will)
    +9 vs. AC; 1d10 + 4 damage, and the target is knocked prone.

Skitter (while mounted by a friendly rider of 4th level or higher; at-will) ✦ **Mount**
    The giant ant shifts 2 squares instead of 1 square when it shifts.

Alignment Unaligned   **Languages** —
Str 19 (+6)	**Dex** 19 (+6)	**Wis** 12 (+3)
Con 14 (+4)	**Int** 1 (−3)	**Cha** 7 (+0)

Giant Lizard, Draft — Level 4 Brute
Large natural beast — XP 175

Initiative +4   **Senses** Perception +1
HP 69; **Bloodied** 34
AC 16; **Fortitude** 18, **Reflex** 16, **Will** 13
Speed 7 (swamp walk), climb 2

⊕ **Bite** (standard; at-will)
    +7 vs. AC; 2d6 + 4 damage.

Alignment Unaligned   **Languages** —
Str 19 (+6)	**Dex** 14 (+4)	**Wis** 9 (+1)
Con 19 (+6)	**Int** 2 (−2)	**Cha** 7 (+0)

Giant Lizard, Riding — Level 6 Brute
Large natural beast (mount) — XP 250

Initiative +6   **Senses** Perception +2
HP 90; **Bloodied** 45
AC 18; **Fortitude** 20, **Reflex** 18, **Will** 14
Speed 9 (swamp walk), climb 4

⊕ **Bite** (standard; at-will)
    +9 vs. AC; 2d8 + 5 damage.

⦀ **Claw** (standard; at-will)
    +10 vs. AC; 2d6 + 5 damage.

Combined Attack (while mounted by a friendly rider of 6th level or higher; at-will) ✦ **Mount**
    When the giant lizard's rider makes a melee attack against a target, the lizard can make a claw attack against the same target.

Alignment Unaligned   **Languages** —
Str 20 (+8)	**Dex** 17 (+6)	**Wis** 9 (+2)
Con 20 (+8)	**Int** 2 (−1)	**Cha** 7 (+1)

Horse, Sea — Level 5 Brute
Large natural beast (aquatic, mount) — XP 200

Initiative +4   **Senses** Perception +2
HP 80; **Bloodied** 40
AC 17; **Fortitude** 19, **Reflex** 17, **Will** 15
Speed swim 10

(+) **Tail Slap** (standard; at-will)
Reach 2; +8 vs. AC; 2d8 + 4 damage; see also *waterborn*.

Aquatic Charge (while mounted by a friendly rider of 5th level or higher; at-will) ✦ **Mount**
The sea horse's rider deals an extra 1d10 damage when he or she attacks after the sea horse charges. While in water, the rider also gains a +2 bonus to attack rolls against creatures without a swim speed.

Waterborn
While in water, the sea horse gains a +2 bonus to attack rolls against creatures without a swim speed.

Alignment Unaligned   **Languages** —
Str 18 (+6)   **Dex** 15 (+4)   **Wis** 10 (+2)
Con 20 (+7)   **Int** 2 (−2)   **Cha** 9 (+1)

Horse, Skeletal — Level 11 Brute
Large natural animate (mount, undead) — XP 600

Initiative +9   **Senses** Perception +6
HP 143; **Bloodied** 71
AC 23; **Fortitude** 24, **Reflex** 23, **Will** 20
Immune poison; **Resist** 20 necrotic
Speed 10

(+) **Kick** (standard; at-will)
+14 vs. AC; 3d6 + 5 damage.

Shadow Symbiosis (while mounted by a friendly rider of 11th level or higher; at-will) ✦ **Mount**
The horse's rider gains resist 20 necrotic.

Alignment Unaligned   **Languages** —
Str 20 (+10)   **Dex** 18 (+9)   **Wis** 13 (+6)
Con 23 (+11)   **Int** 2 (+1)   **Cha** 7 (+3)

Rhinoceros — Level 7 Soldier
Large natural beast (mount) — XP 300

Initiative +8   **Senses** Perception +3
HP 83; **Bloodied** 41
AC 23; **Fortitude** 23, **Reflex** 21, **Will** 18
Speed 6

(+) **Gore** (standard; at-will)
+13 vs. AC; 2d6 + 5 damage.

Crushing Charge (while mounted by a friendly rider of 7th level or higher; at-will) ✦ **Mount**
When charging, the rhinoceros can make a gore attack in addition to its rider's charge attack.

Alignment Unaligned   **Languages** —
Str 21 (+8)   **Dex** 16 (+6)   **Wis** 11 (+3)
Con 19 (+7)   **Int** 2 (−1)   **Cha** 8 (+2)

Shark, Dire — Level 14 Skirmisher
Huge natural beast (aquatic, mount) — XP 1,000

Initiative +16   **Senses** Perception +9
HP 139; **Bloodied** 69
AC 28; **Fortitude** 26, **Reflex** 28, **Will** 23
Speed swim 11

(+) **Bite** (standard; at-will)
+17 vs. AC; 3d6 + 5 damage; see also *waterborn*.

Deft Swimmer (while mounted by a friendly rider of 14th level or higher; at-will) ✦ **Mount**
The dire shark's rider gains a +2 bonus to AC against opportunity attacks. While in water, the rider also gains a +2 bonus to attack rolls against creatures without a swim speed.

Waterborn
While in water, the dire shark gains a +2 bonus to attack rolls against creatures without a swim speed.

Alignment Unaligned   **Languages** —
Str 21 (+12)   **Dex** 24 (+14)   **Wis** 14 (+9)
Con 19 (+11)   **Int** 2 (+3)   **Cha** 9 (+6)

Shark, Riding — Level 8 Skirmisher
Large natural beast (aquatic, mount) — XP 350

Initiative +11   **Senses** Perception +4
HP 88; **Bloodied** 44
AC 22; **Fortitude** 21, **Reflex** 22, **Will** 17
Speed swim 11

(+) **Bite** (standard; at-will)
+13 vs. AC; 2d6 + 4 damage; see also *waterborn*.

Deft Swimmer (while mounted by a friendly rider of 8th level or higher; at-will) ✦ **Mount**
The shark's rider gains a +2 bonus to AC against opportunity attacks. While in water, the rider also gains a +2 bonus to attack rolls against creatures without a swim speed.

Waterborn
While in water, the shark gains a +2 bonus to attack rolls against creatures without a swim speed.

Alignment Unaligned   **Languages** —
Str 19 (+8)   **Dex** 21 (+9)   **Wis** 11 (+4)
Con 16 (+7)   **Int** 2 (+0)   **Cha** 7 (+2)

Trihorn Behemoth — Level 12 Soldier
Huge natural beast (mount) — XP 700

Initiative +12   **Senses** Perception +7
HP 127; **Bloodied** 63
AC 28; **Fortitude** 30, **Reflex** 26, **Will** 23
Speed 6

(+) **Gore** (standard; at-will)
+17 vs. AC; 2d8 + 8 damage.

Protective Crest (while mounted by a friendly rider of 12th level or higher; at-will) ✦ **Mount**
The trihorn behemoth's rider gains a +1 shield bonus to AC and Reflex defense.

Alignment Unaligned   **Languages** —
Str 26 (+14)   **Dex** 18 (+10)   **Wis** 13 (+7)
Con 23 (+12)   **Int** 2 (+2)   **Cha** 10 (+6)

BARDING

Type	Armor Bonus*	Check	Speed	Price (gp)	Weight
Light barding	+1	–	–	75	40 lb.
Huge creature	+1	–	–	75	60 lb.
Heavy barding	+2	-2	-1	150	80 lb.
Huge creature	+2	-2	-1	150	120 lb.

*Reduce the armor bonus by 1 for creatures with the soldier role.

Mount Equipment

Mounts acquired by the PCs are assumed to have basic gear, such as a saddle, a saddle blanket, a bridle, and reins. Although mounts are mainly used as basic transportation, others (especially warhorses and other combat-trained mounts) might take advantage of specialized gear such as barding (described below) and mount magic items (described in Chapter 2). These items enhance a mount's abilities in combat, generally by augmenting its speed, increasing its defenses, or allowing the mount to bypass certain terrain features.

Barding

Barding is armor for your mount. It adds to a mount's Armor Class just as armor does to a character's. Barding also has similar check penalties and speed penalties. The barding's armor bonus is added to a creature's existing AC. Unlike heavy armor, heavy barding does not negate a mount's Dexterity or Intelligence bonus to AC. Creatures that fill the soldier role already have additional armor (natural or otherwise) factored into their AC. As such, barding is less effective for them (as shown in the accompanying table).

Magic barding can be crafted with its own unique properties. However, magic barding cannot be enchanted with an enhancement bonus like normal armor. Most creatures already benefit from natural defenses that exceed those of a typical PC.

VEHICLES

A wizard stands on the deck of a storm-tossed ship, his spells blasting the raiding party of sahuagin climbing over the rails. A rogue clambers up a tree to leap upon the goblin king's chariot as it thunders beneath her. A warlock sets an airship on a collision course toward the lich's castle, abandoning the massive craft as it crashes into the topmost tower.

The DUNGEONS & DRAGONS® game is built around fast-moving, dynamic combat, but adding vehicles into the mix can take a combat encounter to a new level. Whether the PCs battle from the backs of chariots, fight off goblin wolf riders while racing a supply wagon through a treacherous mountain pass, or leap aboard a longship to seize it from gnoll pirates, vehicles can serve as the centerpiece for any number of memorable confrontations.

This section provides the rules for managing vehicles in your game. Vehicles function much like mounts, in that a character takes control of a vehicle, uses it to move, and can take advantage of its special features. Most vehicles carry more passengers and cargo than a mount, but their lack of maneuverability creates unique challenges on the battlefield.

The Basics

Vehicles have statistics, some of which are similar to a creature's and others of which are not. Vehicles are considered objects, so the rules in Chapter 4 of the *Dungeon Master's Guide* apply to them unless otherwise noted.

Size: Vehicles have a size just like creatures.

Hit Points: A vehicle's hit points indicate the amount of punishment it can take. A vehicle reduced to 0 hit points or fewer is destroyed, and creatures on board the destroyed vehicle are knocked prone in their current squares. The vehicle's wreckage occupies its space, making it difficult terrain.

Space: Unlike creatures, which can move around within a space and squeeze into smaller spaces, vehicles occupy all the space within its dimensions. As a result, vehicles cannot squeeze. For example, a wagon takes up a full 2 squares by 3 squares, meaning it can't fit through a narrow chasm that is only 1 square wide.

Vehicles pulled by creatures indicate only the vehicle's space. The creatures pulling it occupy their normal space on the battle grid.

Defenses: Like all objects, vehicles have an Armor Class, a Fortitude defense, and a Reflex defense. They do not have a Will defense.

Speed: A vehicle's speed (given in squares) determines how far it travels when a driver or pilot uses a move action. A driver or pilot who uses two move actions can move a vehicle twice its speed.

The speed of a creature-drawn vehicle is determined by the speed of the creature(s) moving it.

For long-distance movement, most creature-drawn vehicles can travel no more than 10 hours in a day. However, sailing ships and magically propelled crafts are not limited in this way and can travel all day and night if properly crewed.

Load: A vehicle's load is expressed as the number of Medium creatures (both crew and passengers) that can ride within it, plus the amount of cargo it carries (in pounds or tons). In general, one Large creature is equivalent to four Medium creatures, a Huge creature equals nine Medium creatures, and a Gargantuan creature equals sixteen Medium creatures. These comparisons assume that the vehicle has basically one horizontal surface upon which these creatures can stand. For covered vehicles or vehicles with multiple decks or levels, the number and size of creatures that can fit inside may vary. Regardless, a creature's size cannot exceed the available space in the vehicle.

Driver or Pilot: This entry describes the position a vehicle's driver or pilot occupies and any requirements of the vehicle's driver or pilot. Vehicles larger than Medium size usually require a driver or pilot to direct the vehicle from the front or rear. Thus, when placing a vehicle on the battle grid, you should decide which side is the front and which side is the rear.

Crew: This entry describes any crew needed to control a vehicle, and describes the effect on a vehicle's movement if the crew members are not present.

Out of Control: If a driver or pilot loses control of a vehicle, this entry describes what happens.

Special Features: If a vehicle has any attacks or special features, they are noted at the bottom of its statistics block.

Initiative: Vehicles never roll for initiative. A vehicle acts on the initiative of the creature controlling it.

If you need to know when an out-of-control vehicle acts (for example, to determine when a driverless wagon moves across the battle grid), the vehicle has an initiative check result of 1 lower than the last creature in the initiative order. If the encounter involves multiple out-of-control vehicles, the vehicles act in order of which has been out of control longest, with the most recently out-of-control vehicle acting last.

VEHICLE AND MOUNT SPEEDS

Speed	Per Hour	Per 10-hour Day	Per 24-hour Day
2 squares	1 mile	10 miles	24 miles
3 squares	1-1/2 miles	15 miles	36 miles
4 squares	2 miles	20 miles	48 miles
5 squares	2-1/2 miles	25 miles	60 miles
6 squares	3 miles	30 miles	72 miles
7 squares	3-1/2 miles	35 miles	84 miles
8 squares	4 miles	40 miles	96 miles
9 squares	4-1/2 miles	45 miles	108 miles
10 squares	5 miles	50 miles	120 miles
20 squares	10 miles	100 miles	240 miles

VEHICLES IN COMBAT

Most of the time, you use a vehicle's per-day and per-hour speed. If the PCs travel from one city to another by wagon, the wagon's speed determines the length of their journey. However, if kobold bandits ambush the wagon en route, it becomes important to keep track of how the wagon moves during the fight and what the NPCs or PCs can do to control it.

A vehicle needs a driver or a pilot—a character or creature that spends actions to control the vehicle. This character must meet the conditions described under the vehicle's driver or pilot entry. A vehicle with no controller goes out of control, typically continuing on its course and crashing into the first obstacle it encounters or else grinding to a halt.

Only one character can control a vehicle during a round, though any number of characters can attempt to take control until one is successful. A character can yield control of a vehicle to another character as a free action, but the character assuming control of the vehicle (a free action) can take no other action with the vehicle during that turn. If a character does not move into the driver or pilot position and assume control when control is yielded to him or her, then the vehicle might go out of control. If no character has taken control of the vehicle by the end of the yielder's next turn, then the vehicle acts at the end of the initiative order according to its out-of-control rules.

A vehicle's movement does not provoke opportunity attacks against the vehicle or the creatures occupying it. Creatures moving within a vehicle still provoke opportunity attacks from other creatures in the same vehicle, as normal.

CONDITIONS

Vehicles can be attacked just like other objects. Some conditions (such as being knocked prone) have special rules when applied to a vehicle. Any conditions from the *Player's Handbook* excluded from this section have no effect on vehicles. If an effect allows a saving throw to end a condition, a vehicle makes one at the end of its controller's turn (or at the end of the vehicle's turn if it is out of control.) A driver or pilot can use a move action to allow a vehicle to make an additional saving throw during his or her turn.

Immobilized: An immobilized vehicle cannot move except by a pull, a push, or a slide effect.

Prone: A vehicle subject to an effect that would knock it prone instead takes 1d10 damage and is slowed (see below) until the end of the next round.

Restrained: A vehicle that is restrained is immobilized and cannot be forced to move by a pull, a push, or a slide effect. If the restrained condition is ended by the escape action, the vehicle uses the driver's or pilot's relevant skill modifier.

Slowed: A slowed vehicle uses the standard rules for this condition (PH 277).

OUT OF CONTROL

Creatures can move, change direction, and come to a stop whenever they choose. Vehicles don't have that luxury. When a vehicle starts moving, it requires effort to keep it moving and on course. Otherwise, it goes out of control.

A driver or pilot must use specific actions to steer, move, or stop a vehicle if he or she doesn't want the vehicle to go out of control. In any round in which no character uses actions to control it, a vehicle acts according to the "Out of Control" section of its statistics block. Some out-of-control vehicles—most commonly those pulled by creatures—come to a stop automatically. Some vehicles, such as ships, continue to move ahead until they collide with something. Other vehicles—especially flying crafts—can crash quickly.

CRASHING AND RAMMING

Though most vehicles are meant for long-distance transportation, some are designed for combat. If a vehicle tries to move into a space occupied by an object, a creature, or another vehicle, it crashes. The vehicle, any creatures pulling it, and whatever it hits take 1d10 damage per square the vehicle moved in its previous turn. Creatures on board the vehicle (and those on the vehicle or object it hits) take half damage.

If the target of the crash is more than one size category smaller than the out-of-control vehicle, the vehicle continues to move regardless of how much damage it dealt during the crash. The space that the target occupies is treated as difficult terrain for the vehicle's movement.

Against targets of equal or greater size, the vehicle continues to move only if the target is destroyed. If the target is not destroyed, the vehicle's move ends immediately.

TURNING AND HEADING

Creatures on a battle grid can change direction at any point during movement. The rules do not make a distinction between a creature's front, back, and sides because it is assumed that a creature can turn around in its space. However, you cannot simply turn a speeding vehicle in the opposite direction, and thus vehicle combat is more complicated.

Every vehicle has a **heading**—the direction in which it currently moves. To track a vehicle's heading, place a coin or similar marker along the front edge of the vehicle's space on the battle grid. When a vehicle moves, use the small marker to count off squares in the direction the vehicle is moving. Then move the larger vehicle counter or miniature to catch up.

DRIVE

Vehicles are designed to move in one direction only. You direct a vehicle forward, pushing it ahead. However, vehicles typically lack the maneuverability of a walking creature, and turning them can be slow and difficult.

DRIVE

- ✦ **Action:** Move.
- ✦ **Movement:** Move the vehicle a distance up to its speed.
- ✦ **Direction:** When you move the vehicle, it must move in the direction of its heading marker. The vehicle can move directly forward or it can move along either forward diagonal adjacent to its heading marker (a 45-degree adjustment). It cannot move in other directions without making a turn.
- ✦ **Opportunity Attacks:** A vehicle's movement does not provoke opportunity attacks against the vehicle or the creatures on it.
- ✦ **Terrain:** Terrain affects a vehicle in the way it affects creatures. If a terrain feature requires a skill or ability check, the driver or pilot must make that check for any vehicle that is not drawn by creatures. In the case of a creature-drawn vehicle, the creature pulling or pushing the vehicle makes the appropriate check(s). For vehicles pulled by multiple creatures, choose one creature to make the check and have the other creatures use the aid another action. If a vehicle does not have the appropriate mode of movement to traverse a terrain, then it cannot move on that terrain.

TURN

You turn a vehicle to speed around corners, avoid obstacles, or make a sudden change in its current heading.

TURN

- ✦ **Action:** Move
- ✦ **Movement:** Move the vehicle a distance equal to half its speed.
- ✦ **Direction:** When you move the vehicle, it must move in the direction of its heading marker. The vehicle can move directly forward or it can move along either forward diagonal adjacent to its heading marker (a 45-degree adjustment).
- ✦ **Heading Marker:** At any point during the vehicle's movement, move its heading marker from its current position to either side of the vehicle (a 90-degree turn). Reorient the vehicle's counter or miniature accordingly at the end of the move.

- ✦ **Opportunity Attacks:** A vehicle's movement does not provoke opportunity attacks against the vehicle or the creatures on it.
- ✦ **Terrain:** Terrain affects a vehicle in the way it affects creatures. If a terrain feature requires a skill or ability check, the driver or pilot must make that check for any vehicle that is not drawn by creatures. In the case of a creature-drawn vehicle, the creature pulling or pushing the vehicle makes the appropriate check(s). In the case of vehicles pulled by multiple creatures, choose one creature to make the check and have the other creatures use the aid another action. If a vehicle does not have the appropriate mode of movement to traverse a terrain, then it cannot move on that terrain.

STOP

When a vehicle is moving, it takes effort to stop it.

STOP

- ✦ **Action:** Move
- ✦ **Movement:** Move the vehicle forward a number of squares equal to the distance it moved in the previous round. At the end of the move, the vehicle is motionless. A vehicle begins moving again when its driver or pilot uses the drive action. A stopped vehicle does not go out of control while motionless unless otherwise noted in its description.
- ✦ **Direction:** The vehicle's heading marker remains in place. If and when the vehicle moves again, it must initially move in this direction.

SAMPLE VEHICLES

Apparatus of Kwalish
Large vehicle

HP 200   **Space** 2 squares by 2 squares   **Cost** 5,000 gp

AC 22; **Fortitude** 20, **Reflex** 4

Speed 6, swim 6

Pilot
The pilot must occupy the front seat in the apparatus and have both hands free to manipulate its ten control levers.

Load
Two Medium creatures; 200 pounds of gear.

Out of Control
An out-of-control *apparatus of Kwalish* comes to a stop at the beginning of its turn. At the DM's discretion, it might move in the direction of a strong current at half speed.

☩ Rending Claws (standard; at-will)
The pilot can use the apparatus's claws to attack a single creature: Reach 2; +5 vs. AC; 2d6 + 5 damage. The pilot adds half his or her level as a bonus to the claw's attack rolls.

Sealed
Creatures inside the *apparatus of Kwalish* cannot gain line of effect to those outside (and vice versa), though they have line of sight to each other through portholes.

Submersible
An *apparatus of Kwalish* can travel underwater. It holds enough air to support two creatures for five hours or one creature for ten hours.

VEHICLE MOVEMENT

The creature pulling the chariot is always in an adjacent square.	Creature moves so it's not adjacent. The chariot moves 1 to stay adjacent. Do this after every 1 square the creature moves.	Creature is still adjacent. The chariot doesn't move.	The creature can "cut the corner" of the chariot, but can't move through it.

Airship
Gargantuan vehicle

HP 400   Space 4 squares by 8 squares   Cost 85,000 gp
AC 4; Fortitude 20, Reflex 2
Speed 0, fly 12 (hover), overland flight 15

Pilot

The pilot must stand at a control wheel, typically at the front of the topmost deck of the airship cabin.

Crew

In addition to the pilot, an airship requires a crew of five, all of whom use a standard action each round to help control the vessel. Reduce the ship's speed by 4 for each missing crew member. At fly speed 0, the ship is unable to travel and flies out of control.

Load

Thirty Medium creatures; twenty tons of cargo.

Out of Control

An out-of-control airship moves forward at half speed. Each round, it has a 50% chance of descending. It descends 5 squares for the first 10 rounds it is out of control. After 10 rounds, it descends 10 squares per round. An out-of-control airship that hits the ground after descending more than 20 squares is destroyed.

Decks

The airship's cabin has four decks: an exterior observation platform, the topmost crew deck, a middle deck for passengers, and a lower cargo hold.

Fragile Propulsion

For every 50 damage the airship takes, its speed is reduced by 2 squares. At fly speed 0, the ship is unable to travel and floats out of control.

Chariot, Heavy
Large vehicle

HP 60   Space 2 squares by 2 squares   Cost 840 gp
AC 4; Fortitude 12, Reflex 4
Speed creature's speed – 2

Creature-Drawn

A heavy chariot is pulled by two Large creatures or one Huge creature. A heavy chariot takes a –2 penalty to its speed if only one Large creature pulls it.

Driver

A heavy chariot's driver stands at the front of the chariot. He or she must hold the reins in at least one hand or else the chariot goes out of control.

Load

Four Medium creatures; 400 pounds of gear.

Out of Control

An out-of-control chariot comes to a stop at the beginning of its turn. At the DM's discretion, the chariot might move in a random direction if the creatures that pull it are panicked or attacked.

Cover

A heavy chariot provides cover to its driver and passengers.

Chariot, Light
Medium vehicle

HP 30   Space 1 square   Cost 520 gp
AC 5; Fortitude 10, Reflex 5
Speed Creature's speed – 2

Creature-Drawn

A light chariot is pulled by one Large creature.

Driver

A light chariot's driver must hold the reins in at least one hand or else the chariot goes out of control.

Load

One Medium creature; 100 pounds of gear.

Out of Control

An out-of-control chariot comes to a stop at the beginning of its turn. At the DM's discretion, the chariot might move in a random direction if the creatures that pull it are panicked or attacked.

Cover

A heavy chariot provides cover to its driver and passengers.

Greatship
Gargantuan vehicle

HP 400   Space 8 squares by 20 squares   Cost 13,000 gp
AC 4; Fortitude 20, Reflex 2
Speed swim 6

Pilot

The pilot must stand at the ship's wheel, typically at the rear of the topmost deck.

Crew

In addition to the pilot, a greatship requires a crew of twenty, all of whom use a standard action each round to help control the ship. Reduce the ship's speed by 2 for every 5 missing crew members. At swim speed 0, the ship sails out of control.

Load

Two hundred Medium creatures; five hundred tons of cargo.

Out of Control

An out-of-control greatship moves forward at half speed. At the DM's discretion, it can move in the same direction as a strong wind at up to full speed.

Decks

The greatship has four decks: the topmost open deck (which incudes the upper deck and quarter deck), two middle decks for crew and passengers, and a cargo hold.

Sails

At the DM's discretion, a greatship can take a penalty or bonus to its speed of –4 to +4 depending on the strength and direction of the wind.

Longship
Gargantuan vehicle

HP 300   **Space** 4 squares by 14 squares   **Cost** 5,000 gp
AC 3; **Fortitude** 20, **Reflex** 2
Speed swim 5

Pilot

The pilot must stand at the stern of the longship and operate the rudder.

Crew

In addition to the pilot, a longship requires a crew of three, all of whom use a standard action each round to control the ship. Reduce the ship's speed by 2 squares for each missing crew member. At swim speed 0, the ship sails out of control.

Load

Fifty Medium creatures; three tons of cargo.

Out of Control

An out-of-control longship moves forward at half speed. At the DM's discretion, it can move in the same direction as a strong wind at up to full speed.

Sails

At the DM's discretion, a longship can take a penalty or bonus to its speed of –4 to +4, depending on the strength and direction of the wind.

Ornithopter
Large vehicle

HP 40   **Space** 2 squares by 2 squares   **Cost** 3,400 gp
AC 4; **Fortitude** 12, **Reflex** 4
Speed fly 5

Pilot

The pilot must work the ornithopter's control stick with both hands.

Load

One Medium creature; 100 pounds of cargo.

Out of Control

An out-of-control ornithopter comes to a stop at the beginning of its turn. This ends its horizontal movement, but its wings initially prevent it from falling until the end of its next turn. Its pilot can attempt a DC 20 Strength check as a move action to regain control. If the pilot fails, the ornithopter falls to the ground.

An ornithopter falling from a height of more than 100 squares does not impact the ground until the end of its second turn, granting the pilot a second turn to attempt to regain control.

Pinnace
Gargantuan vehicle

HP 250   **Space** 2 squares by 6 squares   **Cost** 1,800 gp
AC 2; **Fortitude** 20, **Reflex** 2
Speed swim 8

Pilot

The pilot must stand at the ship's wheel, typically at the rear of the topmost deck.

Crew

In addition to the pilot, a pinnace requires a crew of four, all of whom use a standard action each round to help control the ship. Reduce the ship's speed by 2 squares for each missing crew member. At swim speed 0, the ship sails out of control.

Load

Twenty Medium creatures; thirty tons of cargo.

Out of Control

An out-of-control pinnace moves forward at half speed. At the DM's discretion, it can move in the same direction as a strong wind at up to full speed.

Decks

The pinnace has three decks: the topmost open deck, a middle deck for crew and passengers, and a cargo hold.

Sails

At the DM's discretion, a pinnace can take a penalty or bonus to its speed of –4 to +4, depending on the strength and direction of the wind.

Wagon
Large vehicle

HP 100   **Space** 2 squares by 2 squares   **Cost** 20 gp
AC 3; **Fortitude** 10, **Reflex** 3
Speed creature's speed – 4

Creature-Drawn

A wagon is typically pulled by two Large creatures or one Huge creature. The wagon takes an additional –2 penalty to its speed if only one Large creature pulls it. A wagon built to accommodate a team of four Large creatures gains an additional 2 squares of movement when drawn by all four creatures.

Driver

A wagon's driver sits at the front of the wagon. The rider must hold the reins in at least one hand or else the wagon goes out of control.

Load

Four Medium creatures; four tons of cargo.

Out of Control

An out-of-control wagon comes to a stop at the beginning of its turn. At the DM's discretion, the wagon might continue in a random direction if the creatures that pull it are panicked or attacked.

Cover

An uncovered wagon provides cover to its passengers and driver. A covered wagon or carriage provides superior cover to passengers inside it.

VEHICLE DESCRIPTIONS

Game statistics for these vehicles are presented above.

Apparatus of Kwalish: This vehicle resembles a huge metal lobster. Kwalish, a wizard skilled in architecture and arcane engineering, built the original apparatus to explore the ocean depths and establish ties with sentient aquatic races.

A hatch situated beneath the apparatus's tail opens into its hollow central torso. This space holds two chairs for a driver and a passenger. The apparatus is propelled magically through water of any depth or current. It can traverse the swiftest rivers and descend to the depths of the ocean floor.

Airship: This vessel floats above the ground, held aloft by a balloon filled with magic gas. The balloon sits within a wooden or metal frame, beneath which is a boat-shaped cabin that holds the crew, the passengers, and the cargo.

Although most airships are powered a magic propeller, some resemble sailing ships and are driven by magically created winds. An airship requires a crew of five (in addition to the pilot) to fly effectively. Including the gas balloon, this vessel is 8 squares long, 4 squares wide, and 6 squares tall.

Chariot: This two-wheeled conveyance is designed for combat and typically drawn by horses. A light chariot carries a single driver and is pulled by one creature. A heavy chariot can carry up to three passengers plus a driver, and it is pulled by two creatures.

Greatship: This enormous ship has four masts and can carry up to two hundred Medium creatures. Greatships are often used in war to carry soldiers. In addition to the pilot, it requires a crew of twenty to

sail effectively. The vessel is 20 squares long and 8 squares wide, and it has a deck that rises 4 squares above the waterline.

Longship: This single-mast ship has a shallow draft, allowing it to travel up rivers or onto beaches. In addition to the pilot, it needs a crew of three to sail effectively. The vessel is 14 squares long and 4 squares wide, and it has a deck that rises 1 square above the waterline.

Ornithopter: This magical flying craft was designed by dwarves and is used for reconnaissance and solo travel. Its flapping wings provide both lift and steering.

Pinnace: This two-mast ship functions equally well close to shore and on the high seas. In addition to the pilot, it requires a crew of four to sail effectively. The vessel is 6 squares long and 2 squares wide, and it has a deck that rises 2 squares above the waterline.

Wagon: The most common vehicle used for transporting goods overland, a wagon is typically pulled by two horses. They can have open or closed tops. A carriage is a wagon with a self-contained passenger cabin.

ALCHEMY

The crafting of magic items is an expensive endeavor. For those unwilling or unable to devote the resources to crafting magic items, alchemy provides a powerful alternative. A ranger might use alchemy to craft a poultice that aids an ally's healing. A rogue can create an alchemical chalk to destroy a lock beyond the limits of his Thievery skill. A cleric can use alchemy to make his or her weapons more potent against insubstantial creatures.

Magic is unnecessary to create alchemical items, but arcane ingredients are required. These items are rare and expensive, so alchemists commonly have adventuring backgrounds.

Applying an alchemical substance or administering an alchemical item is a standard action. Imbibing an alchemical substance or drawing an alchemical item out of your pack is a minor action.

USING ALCHEMY

The process of creating alchemical items is similar to the process of casting rituals (see Chapter 10 of the *Player's Handbook*). As with casting rituals, a character using alchemy must first take a special feat that allows them to understand and use alchemical formulas.

GETTING THERE IS HALF THE FUN

The primary purpose of most vehicles and mounts is to allow a party to move from place to place. However, the PCs' travel plans can also provide a way to bring the game setting to life. Characters on their way to an ancient mountain keep might seek to borrow or buy horses from a nearby clan of elves. Instead, the elves might offer them use of several ornithopters to help the characters ascend the steep slopes. If the PCs need to reach an underwater ruin, having to procure riding sharks or an *apparatus of Kwalish* makes for a colorful mini-quest and offers the promise of dynamic, underwater battles.

Larger vehicles can serve as a base of operations, or they can be used as adventure locations. A sailing ship or an airship under attack makes for an exciting encounter. The PCs might have to repel invaders even as others work to keep the vessel from careening out of control. A fight on board a greatship might span several decks and half a dozen different encounters.

ALCHEMIST

Heroic Tier

Benefit: You can make alchemical items of your level or lower. You must have the correct formula and an appropriate skill.

Special: If you receive the Ritual Caster feat as a class feature, you can take the Alchemist feat instead.

GAINING AND USING ALCHEMICAL FORMULAS

Alchemical formulas are like rituals; they are usually written down in a book or on a scroll. Unlike rituals, though, formulas are nonmagical and recorded with normal materials. As a result, alchemical formulas are generally less expensive than rituals. They also cannot be performed from a scroll like rituals. A character wishing to use a formula must buy the formula and learn it or else pay someone to teach it to him or her (the same market price).

Alchemical formulas have a cost and creation time that the character creating an alchemical item must spend. The components used in alchemical formulas are the same as those used for rituals (PH 300).

ALCHEMICAL FORMULAS

Name	Market Price (gp)	Key Skills
Alchemical silver	200	Nature, Religion, Thievery
Alchemist's acid	70	Arcana, Thievery
Alchemist's fire	70	Arcana, Thievery
Alchemist's frost	70	Arcana, Thievery
Antivenom	70	Heal, Nature
Beastbane	160	Heal, Nature
Blastpatch	120	Arcana, Thievery
Blinding bomb	120	Arcana, Thievery
Bloodstinger poison	120	Nature, Thievery
Clearsense powder	80	Heal, Nature
Clearwater solution	100	Arcana, Nature, Religion
Dragonfire tar	120	Nature, Thievery
Ghoststrike oil	500	Nature, Religion, Thievery
Goodnight tincture	150	Nature, Thievery
Herbal poultice	90	Nature
Jolt flask	800	Arcana, Thievery
Lockbust chalk	160	Arcana, Thievery
Salve of slipperiness	375	Nature, Thievery
Slow-step oil	120	Arcana, Nature, Thievery
Smokestick	450	Arcana, Thievery
Sovereign glue	375	Arcana, Thievery
Tanglefoot bag	100	Arcana, Thievery
Thunderstone	200	Arcana, Nature, Thievery
Tracking dust	160	Nature, Thievery
Universal solvent	600	Arcana, Thievery

CATEGORY

Each alchemical formula has a category that defines the type of item it creates.

Oil: Oils are applied to items (typically weapons), granting them temporary properties or powers.

Volatile: An item of this type explodes or expands when shattered or broken, often dealing damage by the creation of a specific type of energy, such as acid, cold, fire, or lightning.

Curative: These items aid in healing or in overcoming adverse and debilitating effects.

Poison: A poison is a toxin that hampers or harms a creature.

Other: Some items create miscellaneous effects that don't fall into the other alchemical categories.

MODIFICATIONS

Some alchemical items can be modified to change some aspect of the item's function, such as turning an item that is normally thrown into ammunition. Changing an item's function typically increases the item's level and cost.

CONSUMABLE

Like potions and elixirs, alchemical items are consumable items. They contain one-time powers that are expended when you use them, rendering the items inert or destroying them.

ALCHEMICAL ITEMS

The items presented below represent but a sampling of the kinds of things alchemists can craft when they put their minds to it.

ALCHEMICAL ITEMS

Lvl	Name	Component Cost (gp)
1	Alchemist's acid	20
1	Alchemist's fire	20
1	Alchemist's frost	20
1	Antivenom	20
1	Clearsense powder	20
1	Clearwater solution	20
2	Alchemist's acid (ammunition)	25
2	Alchemist's fire (ammunition)	25
2	Alchemist's frost (ammunition)	25
2	Tanglefoot bag	25
3	Blinding bomb	30
3	Bloodstinger poison	30
3	Dragonfire tar	30
3	Ghoststrike oil	30
3	Herbal poultice	30
3	Slow-step oil	30
4	Beastbane	160
4	Blastpatch	40
4	Lockbust chalk	40
4	Tracking dust	40

ALCHEMICAL ITEMS (CONTINUED)

Lvl	Name	Component Cost (gp)
5	Alchemical silver	50
5	Thunderstone	50
6	Alchemist's acid	75
6	Alchemist's fire	75
6	Alchemist's frost	75
6	Clearsense powder	75
6	Goodnight tincture	150
6	Smokestick	150
7	Alchemist's acid (ammunition)	100
7	Alchemist's fire (ammunition)	100
7	Alchemist's frost (ammunition)	100
7	Tanglefoot bag	100
8	Blinding bomb	125
8	Bloodstinger poison	125
8	Dragonfire tar	125
8	Ghoststrike oil	125
8	Herbal poultice	125
8	Salve of slipperiness	125
8	Slow-step oil	125
8	Sovereign glue	125
9	Beastbane	320
9	Blastpatch	160
9	Lockbust chalk	160
9	Tracking dust	160
10	Jolt flask	200
10	Thunderstone	200
10	Universal solvent	200
11	Alchemist's acid	350
11	Alchemist's fire	350
11	Alchemist's frost	350
11	Antivenom	350
11	Clearsense powder	350
11	Goodnight tincture	700
12	Alchemist's acid (ammunition)	500
12	Alchemist's fire (ammunition)	500
12	Alchemist's frost (ammunition)	500
12	Tanglefoot bag	500
13	Blinding bomb	650
13	Bloodstinger poison	650
13	Dragonfire tar	650
13	Ghoststrike oil	650
13	Herbal poultice	650
13	Salve of slipperiness	650
13	Slow-step oil	650
14	Beastbane	1,600
14	Blastpatch	800
14	Lockbust chalk	800
14	Tracking dust	800
15	Alchemical silver	1,000
15	Jolt flask	1,000
15	Thunderstone	1,000
16	Alchemist's acid	1,800
16	Alchemist's fire	1,800
16	Alchemist's frost	1,800

ALCHEMICAL ITEMS (CONTINUED)

Lvl	Name	Component Cost (gp)
16	Clearsense powder	1,800
16	Goodnight tincture	3,600
17	Alchemist's acid (ammunition)	2,600
17	Alchemist's fire (ammunition)	2,600
17	Alchemist's frost (ammunition)	2,600
17	Tanglefoot bag	2,600
18	Blinding bomb	3,400
18	Bloodstinger poison	3,400
18	Dragonfire tar	3,400
18	Ghoststrike oil	3,400
18	Herbal poultice	3,400
18	Salve of slipperiness	3,400
18	Slow-step oil	3,400
18	Sovereign glue	3,400
19	Beastbane	9,400
19	Blastpatch	4,200
19	Lockbust chalk	4,200
19	Tracking dust	4,200
20	Jolt flask	5,000
20	Thunderstone	5,000
21	Alchemist's acid	9,000
21	Alchemist's fire	9,000
21	Alchemist's frost	9,000
21	Antivenom	9,000
21	Clearsense powder	9,000
21	Goodnight tincture	18,000
22	Alchemist's acid (ammunition)	13,000
22	Alchemist's fire (ammunition)	13,000
22	Alchemist's frost (ammunition)	13,000
22	Tanglefoot bag	13,000
23	Blinding bomb	17,000
23	Bloodstinger poison	17,000
23	Dragonfire tar	17,000
23	Ghoststrike oil	17,000
23	Herbal poultice	17,000
23	Salve of slipperiness	17,000
23	Slow-step oil	17,000
24	Beastbane	42,000
24	Blastpatch	21,000
24	Lockbust chalk	21,000
24	Tracking dust	21,000
25	Alchemical silver	25,000
25	Jolt flask	25,000
25	Thunderstone	25,000
26	Alchemist's acid	45,000
26	Alchemist's fire	45,000
26	Alchemist's frost	45,000
26	Clearsense powder	45,000
26	Goodnight tincture	90,000
27	Alchemist's acid (ammunition)	65,000
27	Alchemist's fire (ammunition)	65,000
27	Alchemist's frost (ammunition)	65,000
27	Tanglefoot bag	65,000
28	Blinding bomb	85,000

ALCHEMICAL ITEMS (CONTINUED)

Lvl	Name	Component Cost (gp)
28	Bloodstinger poison	85,000
28	Dragonfire tar	85,000
28	Ghoststrike oil	85,000
28	Herbal poultice	85,000
28	Salve of slipperiness	85,000
28	Slow-step oil	85,000
28	Sovereign glue	85,000
29	Beastbane	210,000
29	Blastpatch	105,000
29	Lockbust chalk	105,000
29	Tracking dust	105,000
30	Jolt flask	125,000
30	Thunderstone	125,000

1. Alchemist's acid; 2. Alchemist's frost; 3. Alchemist's fire

ALCHEMICAL SILVER

Level: 5
Category: Oil
Time: 15 minutes
Component Cost: See below
Market Price: 200 gp
Key Skill: Nature, Religion, or Thievery (no check)

You can apply this silver liquid to a weapon to give it the silvered property, allowing the wielder to take advantage of certain creatures' weaknesses.

Alchemical Silver		Level 5+

This shimmering liquid clings to a weapon, giving it the appearance of brightly polished silver.

Lvl 5	50 gp	Lvl 25	25,000 gp
Lvl 15	1,000 gp		

Alchemical Item

Power (Consumable): Standard Action. Your weapon or one group of ammunition (30 arrows, 10 crossbow bolts, 20 sling bullets, or 5 shuriken) attacks as a silvered weapon until the end of the encounter or for the next 5 minutes. Alchemical silver can be applied to nonmagical weapons and to magic weapons of 14th level or lower.

Level 15: The weapon deals an extra 1d6 damage against creatures that are vulnerable to silvered weapons or to creatures that suffer other detrimental effects from silvered weapons, such as a werewolf's inability to regenerate. Alchemical silver can be applied to nonmagical weapons and to magic weapons of 24th level or lower.

Level 25: The weapon deals an extra 2d6 damage against creatures that are vulnerable to silvered weapons or to creatures that suffer other detrimental effects from silvered weapons, such as a werewolf's inability to regenerate. Alchemical silver can be applied to nonmagical weapons and to magic weapons of 34th level or lower.

ALCHEMIST'S ACID

Level: 1
Category: Volatile
Time: 30 minutes
Component Cost: See below
Market Price: 70 gp
Key Skill: Arcana or Thievery (no check)

The glass vial containing alchemist's acid can withstand the corrosive liquid but easily shatters upon impact. The volatile acid explodes when the flask is broken, corroding anything in its way.

Alchemist's Acid — Level 1+

When shattered, this glass vial releases a spray of acid.

Lvl 1	20 gp	Lvl 16	1,800 gp
Lvl 6	75 gp	Lvl 21	9,000 gp
Lvl 11	350 gp	Lvl 26	45,000 gp

Alchemical Item

Power (Consumable ✦ Acid): Standard Action. Make an attack: Ranged 5/10; +4 vs. Reflex; on a hit, the attack deals 1d10 acid damage and ongoing 5 acid damage (save ends); on miss, half damage and no ongoing acid damage.
Level 6: +9 vs. Reflex; 1d10 acid damage and ongoing 5 acid damage (save ends).
Level 11: +14 vs. Reflex; 2d10 acid damage and ongoing 5 acid damage (save ends).
Level 16: +19 vs. Reflex; 2d10 acid damage and ongoing 10 acid damage (save ends).
Level 21: +24 vs. Reflex; 3d10 acid damage and ongoing 10 acid damage (save ends).
Level 26: +29 vs. Reflex; 3d10 acid damage and ongoing 15 acid damage (save ends).

Modification: Ammunition (level + 1). You create this item for use with a ranged weapon such as a bow, a crossbow, or a sling. Item's range becomes the range of the weapon but continues to use the indicated attack modifier. You do not include a weapon's proficiency bonus or enhancement bonus in the attack. The item's component cost corresponds to the table below.

Level	Component Cost (gp)
2	25
7	100
12	500
17	2,600
22	13,000
27	65,000

ALCHEMIST'S FIRE

Level: 1
Category: Volatile
Time: 30 minutes
Component Cost: See below
Market Price: 70 gp
Key Skill: Arcana or Thievery (no check)

This explosive substance is sealed in a specially treated clay flask. A thrown flask shatters when it hits a solid object, igniting the liquid within.

Alchemist's Fire — Level 1+

When shattered, this flask fills an area with alchemical flame.

Lvl 1	20 gp	Lvl 16	1,800 gp
Lvl 6	75 gp	Lvl 21	9,000 gp
Lvl 11	350 gp	Lvl 26	45,000 gp

Alchemical Item

Power (Consumable ✦ Fire): Standard Action. Make an attack: Area burst 1 within 10; +4 vs. Reflex; on a hit, deal 1d6 fire damage; on miss, deal half damage.
Level 6: +9 vs. Reflex; 2d6 fire damage.
Level 11: +14 vs. Reflex; 3d6 fire damage.
Level 16: +19 vs. Reflex; 3d6 fire damage.
Level 21: +24 vs. Reflex; 4d6 fire damage.
Level 26: +29 vs. Reflex; 4d6 fire damage.

Modification: Ammunition (level + 1). You create this item for use with a ranged weapon such as a bow, a crossbow, or a sling. Item's range becomes the range of the weapon but continues to use the indicated attack modifier. The burst area remains unchanged. You do not include a weapon's proficiency bonus or enhancement bonus in the attack. The item's component cost corresponds to the table below.

Level	Component Cost (gp)
2	25
7	100
12	500
17	2,600
22	13,000
27	65,000

ALCHEMIST'S FROST

Level: 1
Category: Volatile
Time: 30 minutes
Component Cost: See below
Market Price: 70 gp
Key Skill: Arcana or Thievery (no check)

Alchemist's frost is sealed in an insulated ceramic vial. When it shatters, the sudden exposure to air causes the alchemist's frost to expand and freeze.

Alchemist's Frost — Level 1+

This ceramic flask explodes in an icy haze when it hits, crippling its target with numbing cold.

Lvl 1	20 gp	Lvl 16	1,800 gp
Lvl 6	75 gp	Lvl 21	9,000 gp
Lvl 11	350 gp	Lvl 26	45,000 gp

Alchemical Item

Power (Consumable ✦ Cold): Standard Action. Make an attack: Ranged 5/10; +4 vs. Reflex; on a hit, the target takes 1d10 cold damage and is slowed until the end of your next turn; on miss, the target takes half damage and is not slowed.
Level 6: +9 vs. Reflex; 1d10 cold damage.
Level 11: +14 vs. Reflex; 2d10 cold damage.
Level 16: +19 vs. Reflex; 2d10 cold damage.
Level 21: +24 vs. Reflex; 3d10 cold damage.
Level 26: +29 vs. Reflex; 3d10 cold damage.

Modification: Ammunition (level + 1). You create this item for use with a ranged weapon such as a bow, a crossbow, or a sling. Item's range becomes the range of the weapon but continues to use the indicated attack modifier. You do not include a weapon's proficiency bonus or enhancement bonus in the attack. The item's component cost corresponds to the table below.

Level	Component Cost (gp)
2	25
7	100
12	500
17	2,600
22	13,000
27	65,000

ANTIVENOM

Level: 1
Category: Curative
Time: 15 minutes
Component Cost: See below
Market Price: 70 gp
Key Skill: Heal or Nature (no check)

Antivenom is contained in a small vial. Consuming the liquid provides additional resistance against poison.

Antivenom — Level 1+

This thick tonic can help counter the effects of most poisons.

Lvl 1	20 gp	Lvl 21	9,000 gp
Lvl 11	350 gp		

Alchemical Item

Power (Consumable): Minor Action. Gain a +2 bonus to saving throws against poisons from a source of 10th level or lower. This effect lasts until the end of the encounter or for the next 5 minutes.
Level 11: Poisons of 20th level or lower.
Level 21: Poisons of 30th level or lower.

BEASTBANE

Level: 4
Category: Other
Time: 30 minutes
Component Cost: See below
Market Price: 160 gp
Key Skill: Heal or Nature (no check)

You can ignite this item by breaking it, which creates an area that has an aroma offensive to beasts.

Beastbane — Level 4+

This rod of fast-burning incense creates a haze of smoke that holds beasts at bay.

Lvl 4	160 gp	Lvl 19	9,400 gp
Lvl 9	320 gp	Lvl 24	42,000 gp
Lvl 14	1,600 gp	Lvl 29	210,000 gp

Alchemical Item

Power (Consumable ✦ Zone): Standard Action. Make an attack: Close burst 1; targets beasts only; +10 vs. Fortitude; the burst creates a zone, and targets that are hit slide to the closest square outside the zone. The zone lasts until the end of the encounter, and beasts that move into an affected square or begin their turn in an affected square are subject to the same attack from the beastbane.
Level 9: +15 vs. Fortitude.
Level 14: +20 vs. Fortitude.
Level 19: +25 vs. Fortitude.
Level 24: +30 vs. Fortitude.
Level 29: +35 vs. Fortitude.

BLASTPATCH

Level: 4
Category: Volatile
Time: 30 minutes
Component Cost: See below
Market Price: 120 gp
Key Skill: Arcana or Thievery (no check)

A collection of small crystals comprise blastpatch, and when applied carefully to the ground, these can become a dangerous trap that explodes when tread upon. Blastpatch comes in three varieties, and the type is determined when the blastpatch is made.

Blastpatch — Level 4+

These granular crystals explode when they are stepped upon.

Lvl 4	120 gp	Lvl 19	4,200 gp
Lvl 9	160 gp	Lvl 24	21,000 gp
Lvl 14	800 gp	Lvl 29	105,000 gp

Alchemical Item

Power (Consumable ✦ Cold, Fire, or Lightning): Standard Action. You apply blastpatch to an adjacent unoccupied square. When a creature moves into that square, the blastpatch makes an attack against the creature as an immediate reaction: +7 vs. Reflex; on a hit, the target takes damage and suffers effects depending on the blastpatch:
Firepatch—2d8 fire damage, and the target is immobilized until the beginning of its next turn.
Icepatch—1d8 cold damage, and the target is immobilized until the end of its next turn.
Shockpatch—1d8 lightning damage, the target is immobilized until the beginning of its next turn, and the target grants combat advantage until the end of its next turn.
Blastpatch can be detected with a DC 20 Perception check. A creature that flies or jumps over the square does not trigger the blastpatch.
Level 9: +12 vs. Reflex.
Level 14: +17 vs. Reflex; +1d8 damage; Perception DC 25.
Level 19: +22 vs. Reflex; +1d8 damage; Perception DC 25.
Level 24: +27 vs. Reflex; +2d8 damage; Perception DC 30.
Level 29: +32 vs. Reflex; +2d8 damage; Perception DC 30.

Blinding Bomb

Level: 3
Category: Volatile
Time: 30 minutes
Component Cost: See below
Market Price: 120 gp
Key Skill: Arcana or Thievery (no check)

This ceramic sphere contain reagents that combine and ignite in a brilliant flash when the sphere shatters.

Blinding Bomb — Level 3+

When thrown, this fist-sized ceramic sphere explodes in a blinding flash.

Lvl 3	30 gp	Lvl 18	3,400 gp
Lvl 8	125 gp	Lvl 23	17,000 gp
Lvl 13	650 gp	Lvl 28	85,000 gp

Alchemical Item

Power (Consumable): Standard Action. Make an attack: Area burst 1 within 10; +6 vs. Fortitude; on a hit, the target treats all nonadjacent creatures as having concealment until the end of your next turn. Creatures that do not rely on sight to detect other creatures are immune to this effect.
Level 8: +11 vs. Fortitude.
Level 13: +16 vs. Fortitude.
Level 18: +21 vs. Fortitude.
Level 23: +26 vs. Fortitude.
Level 28: +31 vs. Fortitude.

BLOODSTINGER POISON

Level: 3
Category: Poison
Time: 30 minutes
Component Cost: See below
Market Price: 120 gp
Key Skill: Nature or Thievery (no check)

This black poison comes from the chemically enhanced poisons of spiders, centipedes, and scorpions.

Bloodstinger Poison — Level 3+

This inky toxin inflicts wounds that burn long after the initial blow is struck.

Lvl 3	30 gp	Lvl 18	3,400 gp
Lvl 8	125 gp	Lvl 23	17,000 gp
Lvl 13	650 gp	Lvl 28	85,000 gp

Alchemical Item

Power (Consumable ✦ Poison): Standard Action. Apply the bloodstinger poison to your weapon or one piece of ammunition. Make a secondary attack against the next target you hit with the coated weapon or ammunition: +6 vs. Fortitude; on a hit, the target takes ongoing 5 poison damage (save ends).
Level 8: +11 vs. Fortitude.
Level 13: +16 vs. Fortitude.
Level 18: +21 vs. Fortitude.
Level 23: +26 vs. Fortitude.
Level 28: +31 vs. Fortitude.

CLEARSENSE POWDER

Level: 1
Category: Curative
Time: 30 minutes
Component Cost: See below
Market Price: 80 gp
Key Skill: Heal or Nature (no check)

This white powder is usually kept in a small vial that can be placed under a subject's nose. When inhaled, the powder can remove the blinded or deafened conditions.

Clearsense Powder — Level 1+

This fine, silvery powder can restore lost senses.

Lvl 1	20 gp	Lvl 16	1,800 gp
Lvl 6	75 gp	Lvl 21	9,000 gp
Lvl 11	350 gp	Lvl 26	45,000 gp

Alchemical Item

Power (Consumable): Minor Action. You or an adjacent ally can make a saving throw against a blinded or deafened condition that a save can end. The source of the condition must be 5th level or lower.
Level 6: 10th level or lower.
Level 11: 15th level or lower.
Level 16: 20th level or lower.
Level 21: 25th level or lower.
Level 26: 30th level or lower.

CLEARWATER SOLUTION

Level: 1
Category: Other
Time: 30 minutes
Component Cost: See below
Market Price: 100 gp
Key Skill: Arcana, Nature, or Religion (no check)

Clearwater solution makes stagnant water drinkable and cleanses even the deadliest liquids.

Clearwater Solution	Level 1

This small glob of white jelly purifies even the most toxic liquids, from poisons to dwarven spirits.

Alchemical Item 20 gp

Power (Consumable): Minor Action. Apply clearwater solution to a volume of liquid filling a cube 1 square on a side (5 feet by 5 feet by 5 feet; approximately 935 gallons). The solution removes any poison or disease present in the liquid after 1 minute.

Clearwater solution cannot remove poison or disease from water already in a creature's system, and it has no adverse effect on creatures with the aquatic or water keyword. If it's applied to a volume of liquid larger than the amount specified above, the clearwater solution has no effect.

DRAGONFIRE TAR

Level: 3
Category: Volatile
Time: 30 minutes
Component Cost: See below
Market Price: 120 gp
Key Skill: Nature or Thievery (no check)

This green tar is wrapped in a protective covering that splits when it strikes a solid target. Dragonfire tar clings to a target and burns with alchemical flame.

Dragonfire Tar			Level 3+

This sticky substance sears the target with ongoing flames.

Lvl 3	30 gp	Lvl 18	3,400 gp
Lvl 8	125 gp	Lvl 23	17,000 gp
Lvl 13	650 gp	Lvl 28	85,000 gp

Alchemical Item

Power (Consumable ✦ Fire): Standard Action. Make an attack: Ranged 5/10; +6 vs. Reflex; on a hit, the target takes ongoing 5 fire damage (save ends).
Level 8: +11 vs. Reflex; ongoing 5 fire damage (save ends).
Level 13: +16 vs. Reflex; ongoing 10 fire damage (save ends).
Level 18: +21 vs. Reflex; ongoing 10 fire damage (save ends).
Level 23: +26 vs. Reflex; ongoing 15 fire damage (save ends).
Level 28: +31 vs. Reflex; ongoing 15 fire damage (save ends).

Ghoststrike Oil

Level: 3
Category: Oil
Time: 15 minutes
Component Cost: See below
Market Price: 500 gp
Key Skill: Nature, Religion, or Thievery (no check)

This clear oil is applied to a weapon and is the bane of ghosts, wraiths, and other insubstantial creatures.

Ghoststrike Oil			Level 3+
A weapon coated with this murky oil exudes a ghostly yellow mist.			
Lvl 3	30 gp	Lvl 18	3,400 gp
Lvl 8	125 gp	Lvl 23	17,000 gp
Lvl 13	650 gp	Lvl 28	85,000 gp
Alchemical Item			

Power (Consumable): Standard Action. Apply ghoststrike oil to your weapon or one piece of ammunition. Make a secondary attack against the next undead creature with resist insubstantial that you hit with the coated weapon or ammunition: +6 vs. Fortitude; on a hit, you ignore the creature's resist insubstantial when determining damage for the attack.
Level 8: +11 vs. Fortitude.
Level 13: +16 vs. Fortitude.
Level 18: +21 vs. Fortitude.
Level 23: +26 vs. Fortitude.
Level 28: +31 vs. Fortitude.

Goodnight Tincture

Level: 6
Category: Poison
Time: 1 hour
Component Cost: See below
Market Price: 750 gp
Key Skill: Nature or Thievery (no check)

This liquid is dissolved into the food or drink of an unsuspecting victim to knock the subject unconscious.

1. Goodnight tincture; 2. Jolt flask; 3. Herbal poultice

Goodnight Tincture

Goodnight Tincture			Level 6+
This sweet elixir can incapacitate a foe without ever harming it.			
Lvl 6	150 gp	Lvl 21	18,000 gp
Lvl 11	700 gp	Lvl 26	90,000 gp
Lvl 16	3,600 gp		
Alchemical Item			

Power (Consumable ✦ Sleep): Minor Action. You apply goodnight tincture to an adjacent food or drink. A creature that consumes that food or drink is subject to an attack after 1 minute: +12 vs. Fortitude; on a hit, that creature becomes unconscious for 1 hour or until it is subject to an attack or violent motion.
Level 11: +17 vs. Fortitude.
Level 16: +22 vs. Fortitude.
Level 21: +27 vs. Fortitude.
Level 26: +32 vs. Fortitude.

Herbal Poultice

Level: 3
Category: Curative
Time: 30 minutes
Component Cost: See below
Market Price: 90 gp
Key Skill: Nature (no check)

This collection of medicinal herbs grants the subject extra hit points when it spends a healing surge after a short rest.

Herbal Poultice			Level 3+
This pack of specially prepared medicinal herbs increases one's natural recuperative ability.			
Lvl 3	30 gp	Lvl 18	3,400 gp
Lvl 8	125 gp	Lvl 23	17,000 gp
Lvl 13	650 gp	Lvl 28	85,000 gp
Alchemical Item			

Power (Consumable ✦ Healing): Standard Action. Use before you or an ally takes a short rest. The target of the herbal poultice regains an additional 2 hit points when he or she spends a healing surge at the end of the short rest.
Level 8: Regain an additional 4 hit points.
Level 13: Regain an additional 6 hit points.
Level 18: Regain an additional 8 hit points.
Level 23: Regain an additional 10 hit points.
Level 28: Regain an additional 12 hit points.

Jolt Flask

Level: 10
Category: Volatile
Time: 1 hour
Component Cost: See below
Market Price: 800 gp
Key Skill: Arcana or Thievery (no check)

Specially prepared reagents create a concussive explosion when this sealed flask shatters.

Jolt Flask — Level 10+

When it bursts, this flask creates a concussive wave that dazes your enemies.

Lvl 10	200 gp	Lvl 25	25,000 gp
Lvl 15	1,000 gp	Lvl 30	125,000 gp
Lvl 20	5,000 gp		

Alchemical Item

Power (Consumable): Standard Action. Make an attack: Area burst 1 within 10; +13 vs. Fortitude; on a hit, the target is dazed until the end of your next turn.
Level 15: +18 vs. Fortitude.
Level 20: +23 vs. Fortitude.
Level 25: +28 vs. Fortitude.
Level 30: +33 vs. Fortitude.

LOCKBUST CHALK

Level: 4
Category: Other
Time: 30 minutes
Component Cost: See below
Market Price: 160 gp
Key Skill: Arcana or Thievery (no check)

This narrow chalk rod is made of special reagents that expand when the end of the chalk is snapped off.

Lockbust Chalk — Level 4+

When fitted within a keyhole, this thin stick of gray chalk can force open the most complicated locks.

Lvl 4	40 gp	Lvl 19	4,200 gp
Lvl 9	160 gp	Lvl 24	21,000 gp
Lvl 14	800 gp	Lvl 29	105,000 gp

Alchemical Item

Power (Consumable): Standard Action. Make a Thievery check on an adjacent locked object or a locked object you are holding, gaining a +7 bonus to the check instead of your normal check modifiers. A successful check destroys the lock; a failed check does not damage it.
Level 9: +9 bonus.
Level 14: +12 bonus.
Level 19: +14 bonus.
Level 24: +17 bonus.
Level 29: +19 bonus.

SALVE OF SLIPPERINESS

Level: 8
Category: Other
Time: 1 hour
Component Cost: See below
Market Price: 375 gp
Key Skill: Nature or Thievery (no check)

This greenish-black oil allows a creature to escape from a grab or slip out of restraints.

Salve of Slipperiness — Level 8+

This oily gel makes it easy to escape restraint.

Lvl 8	125 gp	Lvl 23	17,000 gp
Lvl 13	650 gp	Lvl 28	85,000 gp
Lvl 18	3,400 gp		

Alchemical Item

Power (Consumable): Standard Action. You or an adjacent ally gains a +14 bonus on Acrobatics checks against the DC of a restraint or the Reflex defense of a grabbing creature for 5 minutes or until the end of the encounter; use this modifier instead of your normal check modifiers.
Level 13: +16 bonus.
Level 18: +19 bonus.
Level 23: +21 bonus.
Level 28: +24 bonus.

SLOW-STEP OIL

Level: 3
Category: Oil
Time: 1 hour
Component Cost: See below
Market Price: 120 gp
Key Skill: Arcana, Nature, or Thievery (no check)

This paralyzing oil is applied to a weapon to make your attacks slow your enemies' advances.

Slow-Step Oil — Level 3+

A weapon coated with this white oil has the power to slow the movement of a foe.

Lvl 3	30 gp	Lvl 18	3,400 gp
Lvl 8	125 gp	Lvl 23	17,000 gp
Lvl 13	650 gp	Lvl 28	85,000 gp

Alchemical Item

Power (Consumable): Standard Action. Apply slow-step oil to your weapon or one piece of ammunition. Make a secondary attack against the next creature you hit with the coated weapon or ammunition: +6 vs. Fortitude; on a hit, the target is slowed (save ends).
Level 8: +11 vs. Fortitude.
Level 13: +16 vs. Fortitude.
Level 18: +21 vs. Fortitude.
Level 23: +26 vs. Fortitude.
Level 28: +31 vs. Fortitude.

SMOKESTICK

Level: 6
Category: Volatile
Time: 1 hour
Component Cost: See below
Market Price: 450 gp
Key Skill: Arcana or Thievery (no check)

A smokestick contains reagents that mix and ignite when it is cracked, creating an area of smoke.

TANGLEFOOT BAG

Level: 2
Category: Other
Time: 1 hour
Component Cost: See below
Market Price: 100 gp
Key Skill: Arcana or Thievery (no check)

A tanglefoot bag contains a sticky gel that expands and hardens when exposed to air. The bag containing the gel is specially sealed to explode on impact.

Tanglefoot Bag			Level 2+
This small leather bag or satchel contains a sticky gel that can immobilize foes.			
Lvl 2	25 gp	Lvl 17	2,600 gp
Lvl 7	100 gp	Lvl 22	13,000 gp
Lvl 12	500 gp	Lvl 27	65,000 gp
Alchemical Item			

Power (Consumable): Standard Action. Make an attack: Ranged 5/10; +5 vs. Reflex; on a hit, the target is immobilized until the end of your next turn, at which point the creature is then slowed until the end of its next turn.
Level 7: +10 vs. Reflex.
Level 12: +15 vs. Reflex.
Level 17: +20 vs. Reflex.
Level 22: +25 vs. Reflex.
Level 27: +30 vs. Reflex.

Smokestick	Level 6
This rod of alchemical clay ignites to release a haze of obscuring smoke.	

Alchemical Item 150 gp

Power (Consumable ✦ Zone): Standard Action. The smokestick creates smoke within an area burst 1 within 5 squares. The burst creates a zone, and all squares within the zone are considered lightly obscured. The zone lasts until the end of your next turn.

SOVEREIGN GLUE

Level: 8
Category: Other
Time: 2 hours
Component Cost: See below
Market Price: 375 gp
Key Skill: Arcana or Thievery

Sovereign glue is stored in a special vial that keeps it viscous until it is exposed to air, at which point it creates an adhesive bond between two objects.

Sovereign Glue			Level 8+
This gray paste creates a virtually unbreakable bond between the objects it glues together.			
Lvl 8	125 gp	Lvl 28	85,000 gp
Lvl 18	3,400 gp		
Alchemical Item			

Power (Consumable): Standard Action. Apply this glue to an object, and affix that object to another object in reach. The two objects must remain affixed to one another until the end of your next turn. After the end of your next turn, the items are adhered, and separating them requires a DC 29 Strength check. A successful Strength check deals 2d10 damage to each adhered object.
Level 18: DC 35 Strength check.
Level 28: DC 42 Strength check.

THUNDERSTONE

Level: 5
Category: Volatile
Time: 1 hour
Component Cost: See below
Market Price: 200 gp
Key Skill: Arcana, Nature, or Thievery (no check)

A thunderstone splits when it is strikes a hard surface, mixing the powerful reagents to create a deafening boom.

Thunderstone			Level 5+
On impact, this clay sphere unleashes a clap of thunder that can deafen creatures and knock them back.			
Lvl 5	50 gp	Lvl 20	5,000 gp
Lvl 10	200 gp	Lvl 25	25,000 gp
Lvl 15	1,000 gp	Lvl 30	125,000 gp
Alchemical Item			

Power (Consumable ✦ Thunder): Standard Action. Make an attack: Area burst 1 within 10; +8 vs. Fortitude; on a hit, the target takes 1d4 thunder damage, is pushed 1 square from the center of the burst, and deafened (save ends).
Level 10: +13 vs. Fortitude.
Level 15: +18 vs. Fortitude; 2d4 thunder damage.
Level 20: +23 vs. Fortitude; 2d4 thunder damage.
Level 25: +28 vs. Fortitude; 3d4 thunder damage.
Level 30: +33 vs. Fortitude; 3d4 thunder damage.

TRACKING DUST

Level: 4
Category: Other
Time: 1 hour
Component Cost: See below
Market Price: 160 gp
Key Skill: Nature or Thievery (no check)

This fine dust is typically applied in areas where you are searching for existing tracks or where you want to detect a creature passing through at a later time.

Tracking Dust			Level 4+
The fine grains of this silvery powder can reveal the subtlest tracks.			
Lvl 4	40 gp	Lvl 19	4,200 gp
Lvl 9	160 gp	Lvl 24	21,000 gp
Lvl 14	800 gp	Lvl 29	105,000 gp
Alchemical Item			

Power (Consumable ✦ Zone): Standard Action. The tracking dust creates a zone of 5 contiguous squares. In areas where the dust is spread, Perception checks to track can be made with a total +7 bonus; use this modifier instead of your normal check modifiers. Tracking dust can be detected with a DC 20 Perception check, and its effects lasts for 1 hour.
Level 9: +9 bonus.
Level 14: +12 bonus.
Level 19: +14 bonus.
Level 24: +17 bonus.
Level 29: +19 bonus.

UNIVERSAL SOLVENT

Level: 10
Category: Other
Time: 30 minutes
Component Cost: See below
Market Price: 600 gp
Key Skill: Arcana or Thievery (no check)

This transparent liquid has an odor similar to that of butterscotch. It is often stored near vials of sovereign glue (see above).

Universal Solvent	Level 10
This clear solution can dissolve almost any adhesive.	
Alchemical Item 200 gp	

Power (Consumable): Standard Action. Apply this substance to a creature or object. Destroy any type of mundane bonding agent (including sovereign glue) affecting you, an object in your possession, or in a square adjacent to you.
Universal solvent allows a creature immobilized by mundane agents such as a kobold slinger's gluepot or an aboleth slime mage's *slime burst* power to immediately save against the effect. It does not affect the aftereffects of those substances (such as *slime burst's* slow effect), nor does it have any affect on creatures immobilized by other effects (for example, a ghoul's claw attack).

MAGIC ITEMS

FROM THE TIME of the clash between the gods and the primordials, magic has been funneled into items. This practice started as a way to store magical effects for later use in battle. That practice has continued through the modern age, producing objects of mundane pleasure and fantastic prowess.

This chapter is a catalog of treasures, for purchase or reward. In it, you'll find:

✦ **Armor:** Magic, materials, and armorcraft combine to bring you more choices for saving your skin.

✦ **Weapons:** Expand your armory with a host of new simple, military, and superior weapons.

✦ **Implements:** Holy symbols, orbs, rods, staffs, and wands—each with its own twist.

✦ **Arm Slot Items:** Bracers and shields to bolster your defenses. Some give you new attack options, too.

✦ **Companion Items:** Your companion can wear a magic item to enhance its abilities and strengthen its bond with you.

✦ **Feet Slot Items:** When moving, or not, is key, a solution might be as easy as changing your shoes.

✦ **Hand Slot Items:** It's your hands you depend on combat. Help them help you.

✦ **Head Slot Items:** A host of new headgear to boost your skills, perception, and reactions.

✦ **Neck Slot Items:** Merely shoring up your defenses isn't enough. Flashier magic goes on your neck.

✦ **Rings:** Who knows what a magic ring might do? The most unpredictable magic lives in magic rings.

✦ **Waist Slot Items:** Physical power and health find their root in your middle. Gird up!

✦ **Wondrous Items:** Magic tools and bizarre objects reward ingenious use and prepare you for anything.

✦ **Consumables:** Sometimes a single use is all you need. Elixirs, reagents, and more are catalogued here.

RANDY GALLEGOS

ARMOR

Weapons will not cut me, spells will not sear me. Behind this coat of steel, I am invincible.

Each piece of armor, from the heaviest plate armor to the thinnest of robes, has a level and a corresponding enhancement bonus. The enhancement bonus represents the magical defenses of the armor. It could be an invisible field that deflects attacks, or an enchantment that fortifies the armor's material.

An armor's enhancement bonus scales with level, enabling adventurers to face deadlier threats as they advance. At the highest levels, this bonus represents the thin line between being mauled by a red dragon and slipping safely out of its grasp.

MAGIC ARMOR

Lvl	Name	Price (gp)	Categories
2	Armor of resistance +1	520	Any
2	Immunizing +1	520	Scale, Plate
2	Martyr's +1	520	Scale, Plate
2	Repulsion +1	520	Cloth, Leather
2	Robe of eyes +1	520	Cloth
2	Robe of scintillation +1	520	Cloth
2	Screaming +1	520	Hide, Scale, Plate
2	Slick +1	520	Chain, Scale, Plate
2	Veteran's +1	520	Any
3	Addergrass +1	680	Leather, Hide
3	Armor of cleansing +1	680	Any
3	Armor of exploits +1	680	Any
3	Bestial +1	680	Leather, Hide
3	Breaching +1	680	Any
3	Heartening +1	680	Scale, Plate
3	Lifegiving +1	680	Plate
3	Meliorating +1	680	Chain, Scale, Plate
3	Robe of quills +1	680	Cloth
3	Serpentskin +1	680	Leather, Hide
3	Stoneborn +1	680	Plate
3	Stoneskin robes +1	680	Cloth
3	Versatile +1	680	Chain, Plate
3	Whiteflame +1	680	Chain, Scale, Plate
4	Armor of durability +1	840	Hide, Chain, Scale, Plate
4	Crystal +1	840	Scale, Plate
4	Fortification +1	840	Scale, Plate
4	Frozen +1	840	Scale, Plate
4	Mithral +1	840	Chain, Scale, Plate
4	Pelaurum +1	840	Chain, Scale, Plate
4	Reinforcing +1	840	Scale, Plate
4	Robe of contingency +1	840	Cloth

MAGIC ARMOR (CONTINUED)

Lvl	Name	Price (gp)	Categories
4	Salubrious +1	840	Scale, Plate
4	Shimmering +1	840	Any
4	Verve +1	840	Scale, Plate
5	Agile +1	1,000	Chain, Scale, Plate
5	Armor of sacrifice +1	1,000	Chain, Scale, Plate
5	Shared suffering +1	1,000	Any
5	Skybound +1	1,000	Cloth, Leather
5	Tactician's +1	1,000	Chain, Scale, Plate
6	Imposter's +2	1,800	Chain, Scale, Plate
6	Summoned +2	1,800	Any
7	Armor of resistance +2	2,600	Any
7	Immunizing +2	2,600	Scale, Plate
7	Irrefutable +2	2,600	Scale, Plate
7	Martyr's +2	2,600	Scale, Plate
7	Repulsion +2	2,600	Cloth, Leather
7	Robe of eyes +2	2,600	Cloth
7	Robe of scintillation +2	2,600	Cloth
7	Screaming +2	2,600	Hide, Scale, Plate
7	Slick +2	2,600	Chain, Scale, Plate
7	Veteran's +2	2,600	Any
8	Addergrass +2	3,400	Leather, Hide
8	Armor of cleansing +2	3,400	Any
8	Armor of exploits +2	3,400	Any
8	Beastlord +2	3,400	Leather, Hide
8	Bestial +2	3,400	Leather, Hide
8	Bloodiron +2	3,400	Scale, Plate
8	Breaching +2	3,400	Any
8	Briartwine +2	3,400	Chain, Scale, Plate
8	Heartening +2	3,400	Scale, Plate
8	Lifegiving +2	3,400	Plate
8	Meliorating +2	3,400	Chain, Scale, Plate
8	Rat form +2	3,400	Leather
8	Robe of quills +2	3,400	Cloth
8	Serpentskin +2	3,400	Leather, Hide
8	Snakefang +2	3,400	Leather, Hide
8	Stoneborn +2	3,400	Plate
8	Stoneskin robes +2	3,400	Cloth
8	Versatile +2	3,400	Chain, Plate
8	Whiteflame +2	3,400	Chain, Scale, Plate
9	Armor of durability +2	4,200	Hide, Chain, Scale, Plate
9	Champion's +2	4,200	Scale, Plate
9	Crystal +2	4,200	Scale, Plate
9	Fortification +2	4,200	Scale, Plate
9	Frozen +2	4,200	Scale, Plate
9	Laughing death +2	4,200	Cloth, Leather, Hide

MAGIC ARMOR (CONTINUED)

Lvl	Name	Price (gp)	Categories
9	Loamweave +2	4,200	Cloth
9	Mirrorsheen coat +2	4,200	Cloth, Leather, Hide
9	Mithral +2	4,200	Chain, Scale, Plate
9	Pelaurum +2	4,200	Chain, Scale, Plate
9	Reflexive +2	4,200	Chain, Scale, Plate
9	Reinforcing +2	4,200	Scale, Plate
9	Righteous +2	4,200	Plate
9	Robe of contingency +2	4,200	Cloth
9	Salubrious +2	4,200	Scale, Plate
9	Shimmering +2	4,200	Any
9	Solar +2	4,200	Scale, Plate
9	Survivor's +2	4,200	Cloth, Leather, Hide
9	Thunderhead +2	4,200	Chain, Scale, Plate
9	Verve +2	4,200	Scale, Plate
10	Agile +2	5,000	Chain, Scale, Plate
10	Armor of sacrifice +2	5,000	Chain, Scale, Plate
10	Shared suffering +2	5,000	Any
10	Skybound +2	5,000	Cloth, Leather
10	Tactician's +2	5,000	Chain, Scale, Plate
10	Warsheath +2	5,000	Plate
11	Imposter's +3	9,000	Chain, Scale, Plate
11	Summoned +3	9,000	Any
12	Armor of resistance +3	13,000	Any
12	Darkforged +3	13,000	Chain, Scale, Plate
12	Flickersight +3	13,000	Cloth, Leather, Hide
12	Immunizing +3	13,000	Scale, Plate
12	Irrefutable +3	13,000	Scale, Plate
12	Martyr's +3	13,000	Scale, Plate
12	Repulsion +3	13,000	Cloth, Leather
12	Robe of eyes +3	13,000	Cloth
12	Robe of scintillation +3	13,000	Cloth
12	Screaming +3	13,000	Hide, Scale, Plate
12	Slick +3	13,000	Chain, Scale, Plate
12	Veteran's +3	13,000	Any
13	Addergrass +3	17,000	Leather, Hide
13	Armor of cleansing +3	17,000	Any
13	Armor of exploits +3	17,000	Any
13	Armor of starlight +3	17,000	Cloth
13	Beastlord +3	17,000	Leather, Hide
13	Bestial +3	17,000	Leather, Hide
13	Bloodfire +3	17,000	Chain, Scale, Plate

MAGIC ARMOR (CONTINUED)

Lvl	Name	Price (gp)	Categories
13	Bloodiron +3	17,000	Scale, Plate
13	Breaching +3	17,000	Any
13	Briartwine +3	17,000	Chain, Scale, Plate
13	Coral +3	17,000	Scale, Plate
13	Elukian clay +3	17,000	Chain, Scale, Plate
13	Giantdodger +3	17,000	Leather
13	Heartening +3	17,000	Scale, Plate
13	Lifegiving +3	17,000	Plate
13	Meliorating +3	17,000	Chain, Scale, Plate
13	Rat form +3	17,000	Leather
13	Robe of defying flames +3	17,000	Cloth
13	Robe of defying frost +3	17,000	Cloth
13	Robe of quills +3	17,000	Cloth
13	Robe of stars +3	17,000	Cloth
13	Serpentskin +3	17,000	Lethaer, Hide
13	Snakefang +3	17,000	Leather, Hide
13	Stoneborn +3	17,000	Plate
13	Stoneskin robes +3	17,000	Cloth
13	Surge +3	17,000	Any
13	Versatile +3	17,000	Chain, Plate
13	Whiteflame +3	17,000	Chain, Scale, Plate
14	Aqueous +3	21,000	Cloth, Leather, Hide
14	Armor of attraction +3	21,000	Scale, Plate
14	Armor of durability +3	21,000	Hide, Chain, Scale, Plate
14	Armor of night +3	21,000	Cloth, Leather
14	Bonegrim +3	21,000	Plate
14	Champion's +3	21,000	Scale, Plate
14	Chaos weave +3	21,000	Any
14	Crystal +3	21,000	Scale, Plate
14	Displacer +3	21,000	Cloth, Leather, Hide
14	Feymind +3	21,000	Cloth, Leather
14	Fortification +3	21,000	Scale, Plate
14	Frostburn +3	21,000	Plate
14	Frozen +3	21,000	Scale, Plate
14	Laughing death +3	21,000	Cloth, Leather, Hide
14	Loamweave +3	21,000	Cloth
14	Mirrorsheen coat +3	21,000	Cloth, Leather, Hide
14	Mithral +3	21,000	Chain, Scale, Plate
14	Pelaurum +3	21,000	Chain, Scale, Plate
14	Reflexive +3	21,000	Chain, Scale, Plate
14	Reinforcing +3	21,000	Scale, Plate
14	Righteous +3	21,000	Plate
14	Robe of contingency +3	21,000	Cloth
14	Salubrious +3	21,000	Scale, Plate

Lvl	Name	Price (gp)	Categories
14	Shimmering +3	21,000	Any
14	Solar +3	21,000	Scale, Plate
14	Survivor's +3	21,000	Cloth, Leather, Hide
14	Thunderhead +3	21,000	Chain, Scale, Plate
14	Verve +3	21,000	Scale, Plate
14	Voidcrystal +3	21,000	Any
15	Agile +3	25,000	Chain, Scale, Plate
15	Armor of negation +3	25,000	Any
15	Armor of sacrifice +3	25,000	Chain, Scale, Plate
15	Assassinbane +3	25,000	Any
15	Illithid robes +3	25,000	Cloth
15	Robe of defying storms +3	25,000	Cloth
15	Shared suffering +3	25,000	Any
15	Skybound +3	25,000	Cloth, Leather
15	Spiritlink +3	25,000	Chain
15	Stormlord +3	25,000	Chain, Scale, Plate
15	Tactician's +3	25,000	Chain, Scale, Plate
15	Warsheath +3	25,000	Plate
15	Zealot's +3	25,000	Cloth
16	Imposter's +4	45,000	Chain, Scale, Plate
16	Summoned +4	45,000	Any
17	Armor of resistance +4	65,000	Any
17	Darkforged +4	65,000	Chain, Scale, Plate
17	Flickersight +4	65,000	Cloth, Leather, Hide
17	Immunizing +4	65,000	Scale, Plate
17	Irrefutable +4	65,000	Scale, Plate
17	Martyr's +4	65,000	Scale, Plate
17	Repulsion +4	65,000	Cloth, Leather
17	Robe of bloodwalking +4	65,000	Cloth
17	Robe of eyes +4	65,000	Cloth
17	Robe of sapping +4	65,000	Cloth
17	Robe of scintillation +4	65,000	Cloth
17	Screaming +4	65,000	Hide, Scale, Plate
17	Slick +4	65,000	Chain, Scale, Plate
17	Veteran's +4	65,000	Any
17	Wildleaf +4	65,000	Cloth, Leather, Hide
18	Addergrass +4	85,000	Leather, Hide
18	Armor of cleansing +4	85,000	Any
18	Armor of exploits +4	85,000	Any
18	Armor of starlight +4	85,000	Cloth
18	Beastlord +4	85,000	Leather, Hide
18	Bestial +4	85,000	Leather, Hide
18	Bloodfire +4	85,000	Chain, Scale, Plate

Lvl	Name	Price (gp)	Categories
18	Bloodiron +4	85,000	Scale, Plate
18	Breaching +4	85,000	Any
18	Briartwine +4	85,000	Chain, Scale, Plate
18	Coral +4	85,000	Scale, Plate
18	Dragonscale, black +4	85,000	Scale
18	Dragonscale, white +4	85,000	Scale
18	Elukian clay +4	85,000	Chain, Scale, Plate
18	Giantdodger +4	85,000	Leather
18	Heartening +4	85,000	Scale, Plate
18	Lifegiving +4	85,000	Plate
18	Meliorating +4	85,000	Chain, Scale, Plate
18	Rat form +4	85,000	Leather
18	Robe of defying flames +4	85,000	Cloth
18	Robe of defying frost +4	85,000	Cloth
18	Robe of quills +4	85,000	Cloth
18	Robe of stars +4	85,000	Cloth
18	Serpentskin +4	85,000	Leather, Hide
18	Snakefang +4	85,000	Leather, Hide
18	Stalker's +4	85,000	Leather, Hide
18	Stoneborn +4	85,000	Plate
18	Stoneskin robes +4	85,000	Cloth
18	Surge +4	85,000	Any
18	Versatile +4	85,000	Chain, Plate
18	Whiteflame +4	85,000	Chain, Scale, Plate
19	Aqueous +4	105,000	Cloth, Leather, Hide
19	Armor of attraction +4	105,000	Scale, Plate
19	Armor of durability +4	105,000	Hide, Chain, Scale, Plate
19	Armor of night +4	105,000	Cloth, Leather
19	Bloodtheft +4	105,000	Leather
19	Bonegrim +4	105,000	Plate
19	Champion's +4	105,000	Scale, Plate
19	Chaos weave +4	105,000	Any
19	Crystal +4	105,000	Scale, Plate
19	Displacer +4	105,000	Cloth, Leather, Hide
19	Dragonscale, blue +4	105,000	Scale
19	Dragonscale, green +4	105,000	Scale
19	Feymind +4	105,000	Cloth, Leather
19	Fortification +4	105,000	Scale, Plate
19	Frostburn +4	105,000	Plate
19	Frozen +4	105,000	Scale, Plate
19	Laughing death +4	105,000	Cloth, Leather, Hide
19	Loamweave +4	105,000	Cloth
19	Mirrorsheen coat +4	105,000	Cloth, Leather, Hide
19	Mithral +4	105,000	Chain, Scale, Plate
19	Pelaurum +4	105,000	Chain, Scale, Plate

Lvl	Name	Price (gp)	Categories
19	Prismatic robe +4	105,000	Cloth
19	Reflexive +4	105,000	Chain, Scale, Plate
19	Reinforcing +4	105,000	Scale, Plate
19	Righteous +4	105,000	Plate
19	Robe of contingency +4	105,000	Cloth
19	Salubrious +4	105,000	Scale, Plate
19	Shimmering +4	105,000	Any
19	Skeletal +4	105,000	Chain, Scale, Plate
19	Solar +4	105,000	Scale, Plate
19	Survivor's +4	105,000	Cloth, Leather, Hide
19	Thunderhead +4	105,000	Chain, Scale, Plate
19	Vaporform +4	105,000	Cloth, Leather, Hide
19	Verve +4	105,000	Scale, Plate
19	Voidcrystal +4	105,000	Any
20	Agile +4	125,000	Chain, Scale, Plate
20	Armor of negation +4	125,000	Any
20	Armor of sacrifice +4	125,000	Chain, Scale, Plate
20	Assassinbane +4	125,000	Any
20	Dragonscale, red +4	125,000	Scale
20	Illithid robes +4	125,000	Cloth
20	Robe of defying storms +4	125,000	Cloth
20	Robe of the archfiend +4	125,000	Cloth
20	Shared suffering +4	125,000	Any
20	Skybound +4	125,000	Cloth, Leather
20	Spiritlink +4	125,000	Chain
20	Stormlord +4	125,000	Chain, Scale, Plate
20	Tactician's +4	125,000	Chain, Scale, Plate
20	Warsheath +4	125,000	Plate
20	Zealot's +4	125,000	Cloth
21	Imposter's +5	225,000	Chain, Scale, Plate
21	Summoned +5	225,000	Any
22	Armor of resistance +5	325,000	Any
22	Darkforged +5	325,000	Chain, Scale, Plate
22	Deflection +5	325,000	Chain, Scale, Plate
22	Flickersight +5	325,000	Cloth, Leather, Hide
22	Immunizing +5	325,000	Scale, Plate
22	Irrefutable +5	325,000	Scale, Plate
22	Martyr's +5	325,000	Scale, Plate
22	Repulsion +5	325,000	Cloth, Leather
22	Robe of bloodwalking +5	325,000	Cloth
22	Robe of eyes +5	325,000	Cloth
22	Robe of sapping +5	325,000	Cloth
22	Robe of scintillation +5	325,000	Cloth

Lvl	Name	Price (gp)	Categories
22	Screaming +5	325,000	Hide, Scale, Plate
22	Slick +5	325,000	Chain, Scale, Plate
22	Veteran's +5	325,000	Any
22	Wildleaf +5	325,000	Cloth, Leather, Hide
23	Addergrass +5	425,000	Leather, Hide
23	Armor of cleansing +5	425,000	Any
23	Armor of exploits +5	425,000	Any
23	Armor of starlight +5	425,000	Cloth
23	Beastlord +5	425,000	Leather, Hide
23	Bestial +5	425,000	Leather, Hide
23	Bloodfire +5	425,000	Chain, Scale, Plate
23	Bloodiron +5	425,000	Scale, Plate
23	Breaching +5	425,000	Any
23	Briartwine +5	425,000	Chain, Scale, Plate
23	Coral +5	425,000	Scale, Plate
23	Dragonscale, black +5	425,000	Scale
23	Dragonscale, white +5	425,000	Scale
23	Elukian clay +5	425,000	Chain, Scale, Plate
23	Giantdodger +5	425,000	Leather
23	Heartening +5	425,000	Scale, Plate
23	Lifegiving +5	425,000	Plate
23	Meliorating +5	425,000	Chain, Scale, Plate
23	Rat form +5	425,000	Leather
23	Robe of defying flames +5	425,000	Cloth
23	Robe of defying frost +5	425,000	Cloth
23	Robe of quills +5	425,000	Cloth
23	Robe of stars +5	425,000	Cloth
23	Serpentskin +5	425,000	Leather, Hide
23	Snakefang +5	425,000	Leather, Hide
23	Stalker's +5	425,000	Leather, Hide
23	Stoneborn +5	425,000	Plate
23	Stoneskin robes +5	425,000	Cloth
23	Surge +5	425,000	Any
23	Versatile +5	425,000	Chain, Plate
23	Whiteflame +5	425,000	Chain, Scale, Plate
24	Aqueous +5	525,000	Cloth, Leather, Hide
24	Armor of attraction +5	525,000	Scale, Plate
24	Armor of durability +5	525,000	Hide, Chain, Scale, Plate
24	Armor of night +5	525,000	Cloth, Leather
24	Bloodtheft +5	525,000	Leather
24	Bonegrim +5	525,000	Plate
24	Champion's +5	525,000	Scale, Plate
24	Chaos weave +5	525,000	Any
24	Crystal +5	525,000	Scale, Plate
24	Displacer +5	525,000	Cloth, Leather, Hide

ARMOR

2

Lvl	Name	Price (gp)	Categories
24	Dragonscale, blue +5	525,000	Scale
24	Dragonscale, green +5	525,000	Scale
24	Feymind +5	525,000	Cloth, Leather
24	Fortification +5	525,000	Scale, Plate
24	Frostburn +5	525,000	Plate
24	Frozen +5	525,000	Scale, Plate
24	Laughing death +5	525,000	Cloth, Leather, Hide
24	Loamweave +5	525,000	Cloth
24	Mirrorsheen coat +5	525,000	Cloth, Leather, Hide
24	Mithral +5	525,000	Chain, Scale, Plate
24	Pelaurum +5	525,000	Chain, Scale, Plate
24	Prismatic robe +5	525,000	Cloth
24	Reflexive +5	525,000	Chain, Scale, Plate
24	Reinforcing +5	525,000	Scale, Plate
24	Righteous +5	525,000	Plate
24	Robe of contingency +5	525,000	Cloth
24	Robe of forbearance +5	525,000	Cloth
24	Salubrious +5	525,000	Scale, Plate
24	Shimmering +5	525,000	Any
24	Skeletal +5	525,000	Chain, Scale, Plate
24	Solar +5	525,000	Scale, Plate
24	Soulwarding +5	525,000	Chain, Scale, Plate
24	Survivor's +5	525,000	Cloth, Leather, Hide
24	Thunderhead +5	525,000	Chain, Scale, Plate
24	Vaporform +5	525,000	Cloth, Leather, Hide
24	Verve +5	525,000	Scale, Plate
24	Voidcrystal +5	525,000	Any
25	Agile +5	625,000	Chain, Scale, Plate
25	Armor of negation +5	625,000	Any
25	Armor of sacrifice +5	625,000	Chain, Scale, Plate
25	Assassinbane +5	625,000	Any
25	Bolstering +5	625,000	Leather
25	Dragonscale, red +5	625,000	Scale
25	Illithid robes +5	625,000	Cloth
25	Robe of defying storms +5	625,000	Cloth
25	Robe of the archfiend +5	625,000	Cloth
25	Shared suffering +5	625,000	Any
25	Skybound +5	625,000	Cloth, Leather
25	Spiritlink +5	625,000	Chain
25	Stormlord +5	625,000	Chain, Scale, Plate
25	Tactician's +5	625,000	Chain, Scale, Plate

Lvl	Name	Price (gp)	Categories
25	Warsheath +5	625,000	Plate
25	Zealot's +5	625,000	Cloth
26	Imposter's +6	1,125,000	Chain, Scale, Plate
26	Summoned +6	1,125,000	Any
27	Armor of resistance +6	1,625,000	Any
27	Darkforged +6	1,625,000	Chain, Scale, Plate
27	Deflection +6	1,625,000	Chain, Scale, Plate
27	Flickersight +6	1,625,000	Cloth, Leather, Hide
27	Immunizing +6	1,625,000	Scale, Plate
27	Irrefutable +6	1,625,000	Scale, Plate
27	Martyr's +6	1,625,000	Scale, Plate
27	Repulsion +6	1,625,000	Cloth, Leather
27	Robe of bloodwalking +6	1,625,000	Cloth
27	Robe of eyes +6	1,625,000	Cloth
27	Robe of sapping +6	1,625,000	Cloth
27	Robe of scintillation +6	1,625,000	Cloth
27	Screaming +6	1,625,000	Hide, Scale, Plate
27	Shocking +6	1,625,000	Chain, Scale, Plate
27	Slick +6	1,625,000	Chain, Scale, Plate
27	Veteran's +6	1,625,000	Any
27	Wildleaf +6	1,625,000	Cloth, Leather, Hide
28	Addergrass +6	2,125,000	Leather, Hide
28	Armor of cleansing +6	2,125,000	Any
28	Armor of exploits +6	2,125,000	Any
28	Armor of starlight +6	2,125,000	Cloth
28	Beastlord +6	2,125,000	Leather, Hide
28	Bestial +6	2,125,000	Leather, Hide
28	Bloodfire +6	2,125,000	Chain, Scale, Plate
28	Bloodiron +6	2,125,000	Scale, Plate
28	Breaching +6	2,125,000	Any
28	Briartwine +6	2,125,000	Chain, Scale, Plate
28	Coral +6	2,125,000	Scale, Plate
28	Dragonscale, black +6	2,125,000	Scale
28	Dragonscale, white +6	2,125,000	Scale
28	Elukian clay +6	2,125,000	Chain, Scale, Plate
28	Giantdodger +6	2,125,000	Leather
28	Heartening +6	2,125,000	Scale, Plate
28	Lifegiving +6	2,125,000	Plate
28	Meliorating +6	2,125,000	Chain, Scale, Plate
28	Rat form +6	2,125,000	Leather
28	Robe of defying flames +6	2,125,000	Cloth
28	Robe of defying frost +6	2,125,000	Cloth
28	Robe of quills +6	2,125,000	Cloth

CHAPTER 2 | *Magic Items*

MAGIC ARMOR (CONTINUED)

Lvl	Name	Price (gp)	Categories
28	Robe of stars +6	2,125,000	Cloth
28	Serpentskin +6	2,125,000	Leather, Hide
28	Snakefang +6	2,125,000	Leather, Hide
28	Stalker's +6	2,125,000	Leather, Hide
28	Stoneborn +6	2,125,000	Plate
28	Stoneskin robes +6	2,125,000	Cloth
28	Surge +6	2,125,000	Any
28	Versatile +6	2,125,000	Chain, Plate
28	Whiteflame +6	2,125,000	Chain, Scale, Plate
29	Aqueous +6	2,625,000	Cloth, Leather, Hide
29	Armor of attraction +6	2,625,000	Scale, Plate
29	Armor of durability +6	2,625,000	Hide, Chain, Scale, Plate
29	Armor of night +6	2,625,000	Cloth, Leather
29	Bloodtheft +6	2,625,000	Leather
29	Bonegrim +6	2,625,000	Plate
29	Champion's +6	2,625,000	Scale, Plate
29	Chaos weave +6	2,625,000	Any
29	Crystal +6	2,625,000	Scale, Plate
29	Displacer +6	2,625,000	Cloth, Leather, Hide
29	Dragonscale, blue +6	2,625,000	Scale
29	Dragonscale, green +6	2,625,000	Scale
29	Feymind +6	2,625,000	Cloth, Leather
29	Fortification +6	2,625,000	Scale, Plate
29	Frostburn +6	2,625,000	Plate
29	Frozen +6	2,625,000	Scale, Plate
29	Laughing death +6	2,625,000	Cloth, Leather, Hide
29	Loamweave +6	2,625,000	Cloth
29	Mirrorsheen coat +6	2,625,000	Cloth, Leather, Hide
29	Mithral +6	2,625,000	Chain, Scale, Plate
29	Pelaurum +6	2,625,000	Chain, Scale, Plate
29	Prismatic robe +6	2,625,000	Cloth
29	Reflexive +6	2,625,000	Chain, Scale, Plate
29	Reinforcing +6	2,625,000	Scale, Plate
29	Righteous +6	2,625,000	Plate
29	Robe of contingency +6	2,625,000	Cloth
29	Robe of forbearance +6	2,625,000	Cloth
29	Salubrious +6	2,625,000	Scale, Plate
29	Shimmering +6	2,625,000	Any
29	Skeletal +6	2,625,000	Chain, Scale, Plate
29	Solar +6	2,625,000	Scale, Plate
29	Soulwarding +6	2,625,000	Chain, Scale, Plate
29	Survivor's +6	2,625,000	Cloth, Leather, Hide
29	Thunderhead +6	2,625,000	Chain, Scale, Plate

MAGIC ARMOR (CONTINUED)

Lvl	Name	Price (gp)	Categories
29	Vaporform +6	2,625,000	Cloth, Leather, Hide
29	Verve +6	2,625,000	Scale, Plate
29	Voidcrystal +6	2,625,000	Any
30	Agile +6	3,125,000	Chain, Scale, Plate
30	Armor of negation +6	3,125,000	Any
30	Armor of sacrifice +6	3,125,000	Chain, Scale, Plate
30	Assassinbane +6	3,125,000	Any
30	Bolstering +6	3,125,000	Leather
30	Dragonscale, red +6	3,125,000	Scale
30	Illithid robes +6	3,125,000	Cloth
30	Robe of defying storms +6	3,125,000	Cloth
30	Robe of the archfiend +6	3,125,000	Cloth
30	Shared suffering +6	3,125,000	Any
30	Skybound +6	3,125,000	Cloth, Leather
30	Spiritlink +6	3,125,000	Chain
30	Stormlord +6	3,125,000	Chain, Scale, Plate
30	Tactician's +6	3,125,000	Chain, Scale, Plate
30	Warsheath +6	3,125,000	Plate
30	Zealot's +6	3,125,000	Cloth

Addergrease Armor — Level 3+

The worn leather of this armor gleams with toxic grease.

Lvl 3	+1	680 gp	Lvl 18	+4	85,000 gp
Lvl 8	+2	3,400 gp	Lvl 23	+5	425,000 gp
Lvl 13	+3	17,000 gp	Lvl 28	+6	2,125,000 gp

Armor: Leather, Hide

Enhancement: AC

Power (Daily ✦ Poison): Immediate Reaction. Use this power when an enemy misses you with a melee attack. The attacker takes ongoing 5 poison damage (save ends), and you shift a number of squares equal to this item's enhancement bonus.

Level 13 or 18: Ongoing 10 poison.

Level 23 or 29: Ongoing 15 poison.

Agile Armor — Level 5+

This armor's flexibility allows its wearer much greater freedom of movement.

Lvl 5	+1	1,000 gp	Lvl 20	+4	125,000 gp
Lvl 10	+2	5,000 gp	Lvl 25	+5	625,000 gp
Lvl 15	+3	25,000 gp	Lvl 30	+6	3,125,000 gp

Armor: Chain, Scale, Plate

Enhancement: AC

Property: While you are not bloodied, you gain an item bonus to AC equal to your Dexterity modifier up to a maximum of +1.

Level 15 or 20: Maximum of +2.

Level 25 or 30: Maximum of +3.

Armor of Attraction
Level 14+

This stout armor can attract projectiles, allowing you to better protect your allies.

Lvl 14	+3	21,000 gp	Lvl 24	+5	525,000 gp
Lvl 19	+4	105,000 gp	Lvl 29	+6	2,625,000 gp

Armor: Scale, Plate

Enhancement: AC

Power (Encounter): Immediate Interrupt. Use this power when an attack against AC or Reflex targets an adjacent ally, or when a ranged attack against an ally within 5 squares of you targets AC or Reflex. You become the target of the attack.

Armor of Cleansing
Level 3+

The exterior of this armor is covered with symbols of healing, while the interior has many silken bands that cradle you comfortably and move to ease your suffering.

Lvl 3	+1	680 gp	Lvl 18	+4	85,000 gp
Lvl 8	+2	3,400 gp	Lvl 23	+5	425,000 gp
Lvl 13	+3	17,000 gp	Lvl 28	+6	2,125,000 gp

Armor: Any

Enhancement: AC

Property: Add a +2 item bonus to your saving throws against ongoing damage.

Aqueous Armor
Level 14+

Cold to the touch, this armor always appears damp. A person wearing the armor can transform into water, but at a cost.

Lvl 14	+3	21,000 gp	Lvl 24	+5	525,000 gp
Lvl 19	+4	105,000 gp	Lvl 29	+6	2,625,000 gp

Armor: Cloth, Leather, Hide

Enhancement: AC

Power (Daily ✦ Polymorph): Move Action. You transform into a flood of rushing water and move up to your speed. You can move through small cracks and tight spaces with no difficulty. You automatically escape a grab or free yourself from bonds or shackles. You can only take move actions until you return to your natural form, which you can do as a free action. While in watery form, you take 5 damage at the start of each of your turns until you return to your natural form.

Armor of Durability
Level 4+

When your allies rely on you to keep fighting, this armor helps keep you in the fray.

Lvl 4	+1	840 gp	Lvl 19	+4	105,000 gp
Lvl 9	+2	4,200 gp	Lvl 24	+5	525,000 gp
Lvl 14	+3	21,000 gp	Lvl 29	+6	2,625,000 gp

Armor: Hide, Chain, Scale, Plate

Enhancement: AC

Property: When you spend a healing surge to regain hit points, you regain additional hit points equal to the armor's enhancement bonus.

THOMAS DENMARK, RANDY GALLEGOS

Armor of Exploits — Level 3+

The arcane symbols etched into this armor's surface glow brightly as the item unleashes a previously stored power.

Lvl 3	+1	680 gp	Lvl 18	+4	85,000 gp
Lvl 8	+2	3,400 gp	Lvl 23	+5	425,000 gp
Lvl 13	+3	17,000 gp	Lvl 28	+6	2,125,000 gp

Armor: Any

Enhancement: AC

Property: During a short rest or an extended rest, you can store one at-will or encounter martial power in your armor that you or an ally has. You can have only one power stored in the armor at a time.

Armor of exploits cannot store a power of higher level than the armor. You cannot use a power stored in the armor if the power's level is higher than yours.

Once the power is used, another power must be stored in the armor before it can be used again. If a new power is stored before the old one is used, the old exploit is lost.

Power (Daily): Standard Action. Use the power stored in your armor. If it is an encounter power, you must spend 1 action point to use it.

Armor of Negation — Level 15+

A wearer of this armor need not fear suffering the adverse effects of an enemy's missed attack.

| Lvl 15 | +3 | 25,000 gp | Lvl 25 | +5 | 625,000 gp |
| Lvl 20 | +4 | 125,000 gp | Lvl 30 | +6 | 3,125,000 gp |

Armor: Any

Enhancement: AC

Power (Daily): Immediate Interrupt. Use this power when an attack misses you and deals half damage. You take no damage.

Armor of Night — Level 14+

In this armor, you can drown the light and conceal yourself in roiling clouds of shadow.

| Lvl 14 | +3 | 21,000 gp | Lvl 24 | +5 | 525,000 gp |
| Lvl 19 | +4 | 105,000 gp | Lvl 29 | +6 | 2,625,000 gp |

Armor: Cloth, Leather

Enhancement: AC

Property: Resist 10 radiant.

Level 24 or 29: Resist 15 radiant.

Power (Encounter): Minor Action. Until the end of your next turn, you gain concealment and no creatures can make opportunity attacks against you.

Armor of Resistance — Level 2+

Special wards in this armor provide extra resistance.

Lvl 2	+1	520 gp	Lvl 17	+4	65,000 gp
Lvl 7	+2	2,600 gp	Lvl 22	+5	325,000 gp
Lvl 12	+3	13,000 gp	Lvl 27	+6	1,625,000 gp

Armor: Any

Enhancement: AC

Property: Resist 5 to a damage type chosen from the following list at the time the armor is created: acid, cold, fire, force, lightning, necrotic, poison, psychic, thunder.

Level 12 or 17: Resist 10.

Level 22 or 27: Resist 15.

Armor of Sacrifice — Level 5+

These plain robes offer no apparent defensive value, yet they aid your allies when they suffer.

Lvl 5	+1	1,000 gp	Lvl 20	+4	125,000 gp
Lvl 10	+2	5,000 gp	Lvl 25	+5	625,000 gp
Lvl 15	+3	25,000 gp	Lvl 30	+6	3,125,000 gp

Armor: Chain, Scale, Plate

Enhancement: AC.

Power (At-Will): Minor Action. Use this power when you are adjacent to an ally who is subject to an effect that a save can end. The ally is no longer affected, and you now have the effect. You cannot make a saving throw against this effect until the end of your next turn.

Power (Daily ✦ Healing): Minor Action. Spend a healing surge. One ally within 5 squares of you regains hit points as though he or she had spent a healing surge.

Armor of Starlight — Level 13+

Bathed in the radiance of distant stars, this armor protects against light that would harm you. The stars' light also shields you from attack.

| Lvl 13 | +3 | 17,000 gp | Lvl 23 | +5 | 425,000 gp |
| Lvl 18 | +4 | 85,000 gp | Lvl 28 | +6 | 2,125,000 gp |

Armor: Cloth

Enhancement: AC

Property: Resist 10 radiant.

Level 23 or 28: Resist 15 radiant.

Power (Encounter ✦ Radiant): Minor Action. Until the end of your next turn, any enemy that hits you with an opportunity attack is blinded (save ends).

Assassinbane Armor — Level 15+

Decorated with symbols resembling stylized eyes, this armor prevents foes from getting the drop on you.

| Lvl 15 | +3 | 25,000 gp | Lvl 25 | +5 | 625,000 gp |
| Lvl 20 | +4 | 125,000 gp | Lvl 30 | +6 | 3,125,000 gp |

Armor: Any

Enhancement: AC

Property: You cannot be surprised.

Beastlord Armor — Level 8+

Made from animal skins and pelts, this armor is adorned with horns, teeth, and claws and makes any beast think twice before attacking the wearer.

Lvl 8	+2	3,400 gp	Lvl 23	+5	425,000 gp
Lvl 13	+3	17,000 gp	Lvl 28	+6	2,125,000 gp
Lvl 18	+4	85,000 gp			

Armor: Leather, Hide

Enhancement: AC

Power (Daily): Minor Action. Until the end of the encounter, beasts must make a saving throw to attack you. Once a beast has made a save, it can attack you normally.

Bestial Armor
Level 3+

Crafted from the skin, fur, and bones of cave bears, this armor gives its wearer a feral relentlessness when pursuing prey.

Lvl 3	+1	680 gp	Lvl 18	+4	85,000 gp
Lvl 8	+2	3,400 gp	Lvl 23	+5	425,000 gp
Lvl 13	+3	17,000 gp	Lvl 28	+6	2,125,000 gp

Armor: Leather, Hide

Enhancement: AC

Power (Daily): Free Action. Use this power when you hit a target after a charge. Make a melee basic attack with a +2 power bonus against the same target.

Bloodfire Armor
Level 13+

This armor sheathes its bloodied wearer in scouring flames.

Lvl 13	+3	17,000 gp	Lvl 23	+5	425,000 gp
Lvl 18	+4	85,000 gp	Lvl 28	+6	2,125,000 gp

Armor: Chain, Scale, Plate

Enhancement: AC

Property: When you are bloodied, you gain an aura of flame. Any creature that starts its turn adjacent to you takes 2 fire damage.
Level 23 or 28: 5 fire damage.

Bloodiron Armor
Level 8+

Forged from hammered iron cooled in blood, this armor protects best those who shed the most blood.

Lvl 8	+2	3,400 gp	Lvl 23	+5	425,000 gp
Lvl 13	+3	17,000 gp	Lvl 28	+6	2,125,000 gp
Lvl 18	+4	85,000 gp			

Armor: Scale, Plate

Enhancement: AC

Property: When you hit a target, you gain a +2 item bonus to AC against attacks from that target until the end of your next turn.

Bloodtheft Armor
Level 19+

The surface of this armor looks as though it is constantly covered with blood that slowly cascades down its surface.

Lvl 19	+4	105,000 gp	Lvl 29	+6	2,625,000 gp
Lvl 24	+5	525,000 gp			

Armor: Leather

Enhancement: AC

Power (Encounter ✦ Necrotic): Immediate Reaction. When you become bloodied by an attack, you gain temporary hit points equal to the armor's enhancement bonus plus your Constitution modifier, and the attacker who rendered you bloodied takes an equal amount of necrotic damage.

Bolstering Armor
Level 25+

Any leader is proud to wear this armor, for he can do nothing greater than help his allies in a time of desperation.

Lvl 25	+5	625,000 gp	Lvl 30	+6	3,125,000 gp

Armor: Chain, Scale, Plate

Enhancement: AC

Power (Daily ✦ Healing): Free Action. Use this power when you use your second wind. All allies that can see you can spend a healing surge as a free action.

Bonegrim Armor
Level 14+

Forelimb bones adorn your arms and legs, rib cages are stretched across your chest, and a skull sits atop your head like a helmet.

Lvl 14	+3	21,000 gp	Lvl 24	+5	525,000 gp
Lvl 19	+4	105,000 gp	Lvl 29	+6	2,625,000 gp

Armor: Plate

Enhancement: AC

Property: Gain a +2 item bonus to Intimidate checks and resist 5 necrotic and resist 5 poison.
Level 18: Resist 10 necrotic and resist 10 poison. You no longer require food.
Level 23: Resist 15 necrotic and resist 15 poison. You no longer require food.
Level 28: Resist 15 necrotic and resist 15 poison. You no longer require food, and you can remain awake during an extended rest.

Cursed: Removing the armor from a living creature requires a Remove Affliction ritual with a penalty to the Heal check equal to the armor's level.

Breaching Armor — Level 3+

Walls are no obstacle for you while wearing this armor.

Lvl 3	+1	680 gp	Lvl 18	+4	85,000 gp
Lvl 8	+2	3,400 gp	Lvl 23	+5	425,000 gp
Lvl 13	+3	17,000 gp	Lvl 28	+6	2,125,000 gp

Armor: Any

Enhancement: AC

Power (Daily ✦ Teleportation): Move Action. Use this power when you are adjacent to a wall to teleport to the other side of the wall. This teleport does not require line of sight and moves you no more than 3 squares (allowing you to teleport past a wall no more than 2 squares thick). If you attempt to teleport into an occupied square, you go nowhere; your move action is not spent, but the daily power is expended.

Briartwine Armor — Level 8+

The eladrin are said to be the architects of this armor, creating a form of protection that remains concealed until worn.

Lvl 8	+2	3,400 gp	Lvl 23	+5	425,000 gp
Lvl 13	+3	17,000 gp	Lvl 28	+6	2,125,000 gp
Lvl 18	+4	85,000 gp			

Armor: Chain, Scale, Plate

Enhancement: AC

Power (Daily): Minor Action. Until the end of the encounter, a creature that hits you with a melee attack takes damage equal to this armor's enhancement bonus.

Champion's Armor — Level 9+

Imbued with the spirit of a great hero of a previous age, this armor strives to ensure your own efforts are no less legendary.

Lvl 9	+2	4,200 gp	Lvl 24	+5	525,000 gp
Lvl 14	+3	21,000 gp	Lvl 29	+6	2,625,000 gp
Lvl 19	+4	105,000 gp			

Armor: Scale, Plate

Enhancement: AC

Power (Daily): Immediate Reaction. Use this power when you are hit by an attack. Gain temporary hit points equal to the damage you take until the end of your next turn.

Chaos Weave Armor — Level 14+

Woven from pure chaos, this armor features abstract patterns that seem to slowly swirl or spin.

| Lvl 14 | +3 | 21,000 gp | Lvl 24 | +5 | 525,000 gp |
| Lvl 19 | +4 | 105,000 gp | Lvl 29 | +6 | 2,625,000 gp |

Armor: Any

Enhancement: AC

Power (Daily): Immediate Interrupt. Use this power when you are hit with an attack that deals acid, cold, fire, lightning, or thunder damage. Gain resist 10 to that damage type until the end of the encounter.
Level 24 or 29: Resist 20.

Coral Armor — Level 13+

This heavy armor was first crafted by elves who sought to create amphibious patrols to safeguard the rivers and lakes bordering their land.

| Lvl 13 | +3 | 17,000 gp | Lvl 23 | +5 | 425,000 gp |
| Lvl 18 | +4 | 85,000 gp | Lvl 28 | +6 | 2,125,000 gp |

Armor: Scale, Plate

Enhancement: AC

Property: You swim at full speed in this armor and breathe water as easily as air. Attacks you make with weapons underwater take no penalties, even if they are not from the spear or crossbow groups.

Crystal Armor — Level 4+

Seemingly made of solid quartz, this armor bolsters your mental abilities when you're badly injured.

Lvl 4	+1	840 gp	Lvl 19	+4	105,000 gp
Lvl 9	+2	4,200 gp	Lvl 24	+5	525,000 gp
Lvl 14	+3	21,000 gp	Lvl 29	+6	2,625,000 gp

Armor: Scale, Plate

Enhancement: AC

Property: Gain a +2 item bonus to Will defense when bloodied.

Darkforged Armor — Level 12+

This armor not only absorbs physical force, but becomes even more durable with prolonged battering.

| Lvl 12 | +3 | 13,000 gp | Lvl 22 | +5 | 325,000 gp |
| Lvl 17 | +4 | 65,000 gp | Lvl 27 | +6 | 1,625,000 gp |

Armor: Chain, Scale, Plate

Enhancement: AC

Power (Daily): Minor Action. Gain resist 6 to all damage until the end of your next turn.
Level 17: Resist 8 to all damage.
Level 22: Resist 10 to all damage.
Level 27: Resist 12 to all damage.

Deflection Armor — Level 22+

This armor is more resilient than it appears at first glance, and many enemies have been surprised to find their attacks suddenly deflected toward an ally.

| Lvl 22 | +5 | 325,000 gp | Lvl 27 | +6 | 1,625,000 gp |

Armor: Chain, Scale, Plate

Enhancement: AC

Power (Daily): Immediate Reaction. Use this power when a melee or ranged attack misses you. The attacker rerolls the attack against a target of your choice, which must be adjacent to you.

Displacer Armor — Level 14+

When wearing this armor, you appear as though you're in many places at once.

Lvl 14	+3	21,000 gp	Lvl 24	+5	525,000 gp
Lvl 19	+4	105,000 gp	Lvl 29	+6	2,625,000 gp

Armor: Cloth, Leather, Hide
Enhancement: AC
Power (Daily ✦ Illusion): Minor Action. Any enemy making a melee or ranged attack against you must roll two d20s for the attack roll and use the lower result. This effect lasts until the end of the encounter.

Dragonscale Armor, Black — Level 18+

The sleek, black scales of this armor grant the wearer some of the power of a black dragon.

Lvl 18	+4	85,000 gp	Lvl 28	+6	2,125,000 gp
Lvl 23	+5	425,000 gp			

Armor: Scale
Enhancement: AC
Property: Resist 10 acid.
  Level 23: Resist 15 acid.
  Level 28: Resist 20 acid.
Power (Daily ✦ Acid): Free Action. Use this power when you hit a target with a melee attack. You shroud yourself in wisps of shadow that last until the end of your next turn. You gain concealment. Any enemy that hits you with a melee attack while this power is in effect takes acid damage equal to 1d6 + your Constitution modifier.
  Level 23: 2d6 + Constitution modifier.
  Level 28: 3d6 + Constitution modifier.

Dragonscale Armor, Blue — Level 19+

Arcs of lightning leap from this vibrant blue armor to strike nearby enemies.

Lvl 19	+4	105,000 gp	Lvl 29	+6	2,625,000 gp
Lvl 24	+5	525,000 gp			

Armor: Scale
Enhancement: AC
Property: Resist 10 lightning.
  Level 24: Resist 15 lightning.
  Level 29: Resist 20 lightning.
Power (Daily ✦ Lightning): Free Action. Use this power when you hit a target with a melee attack. Two creatures other than the target of the attack that are within 5 squares of you take lightning damage equal to 1d8 + your Constitution modifier.
  Level 24: 2d8 + Constitution modifier.
  Level 29: 3d8 + Constitution modifier.

Dragonscale Armor, Green — Level 19+

This green scale armor makes poison attacks you use more potent.

Lvl 19	+4	105,000 gp	Lvl 29	+6	2,625,000 gp
Lvl 24	+5	525,000 gp			

Armor: Scale
Enhancement: AC
Property: Resist 10 poison.
  Level 24: Resist 15 poison.
  Level 29: Resist 20 poison.
Power (Daily ✦ Poison): Free Action. Use this power when you hit a target with a melee attack. Close burst 2, centered on that target; targets enemies; Constitution vs. Fortitude; on a hit, the target takes 1d6 + Constitution modifier poison damage and is dazed until the start of your next turn; on a miss, the target takes half damage and is not dazed.
  Level 24: 2d6 + Constitution modifier poison damage.
  Level 29: 3d6 + Constitution modifier poison damage.

Dragonscale Armor, Red — Level 20+

When you strike a powerful blow, flames flow from the bright red scales of this armor, up your arm and weapon, and onto your foe.

Lvl 20	+4	125,000 gp	Lvl 30	+6	3,125,000 gp
Lvl 25	+5	625,000 gp			

Armor: Scale

Enhancement: AC

Property: Resist 10 fire.
 Level 25: Resist 15 fire.
 Level 30: Resist 20 fire.

Power (Daily ✦ Fire): Free Action. Use this power when you hit a target with a melee attack. It is immobilized and gains ongoing fire damage equal to 5 + your Constitution modifier (save ends both).
 Level 25: Ongoing 10 + Constitution modifier fire damage.
 Level 30: Ongoing 15 + Constitution modifier fire damage.

Dragonscale Armor, White — Level 18+

From between the white scales of this armor, a chilling mist flows from your body to your target as you strike.

Lvl 18	+4	85,000 gp	Lvl 28	+6	2,125,000 gp
Lvl 23	+5	425,000 gp			

Armor: Scale

Enhancement: AC

Property: Resist 10 cold.
 Level 23: Resist 15 cold.
 Level 28: Resist 20 cold.

Power (Daily ✦ Cold): Free Action. Use this power when you hit a target with a melee attack. The target and its adjacent allies take additional cold damage equal to 1d4 + your Constitution modifier.
 Level 23: 2d4 + Constitution modifier cold damage.
 Level 28: 3d4 + Constitution modifier cold damage.

Elukian Clay Armor — Level 13+

Sculpted from stone found in the Elemental Chaos, this armor repels even the most severe acid.

Lvl 13	+3	17,000 gp	Lvl 23	+5	425,000 gp
Lvl 18	+4	85,000 gp	Lvl 28	+6	2,125,000 gp

Armor: Chain, Scale, Plate

Enhancement: AC

Property: You automatically succeed on saving throws against ongoing acid damage.

Power (Encounter): Immediate Reaction. Use this power when you gain ongoing acid damage. The ongoing acid damage ends.

Feymind Armor — Level 14+

Motes of silvery light dance around the head of one who dares attack you.

Lvl 14	+3	21,000 gp	Lvl 24	+5	525,000 gp
Lvl 19	+4	105,000 gp	Lvl 29	+6	2,625,000 gp

Armor: Cloth, Leather

Enhancement: AC

Power (Daily): Immediate Interrupt. Use this power when an enemy targets you with a melee or ranged attack. Make a Charisma attack against the enemy's Will defense, applying the armor's enhancement bonus as an enhancement bonus to the attack roll. If you hit, the attacker is dazed (save ends).
 Level 24 or 29: The target is stunned (save ends).

Flickersight Armor — Level 12+

Your body becomes indistinct and hazy to onlookers who must now squint to see you clearly.

Lvl 12	+3	13,000 gp	Lvl 22	+5	325,000 gp
Lvl 17	+4	65,000 gp	Lvl 27	+6	1,625,000 gp

Armor: Cloth, Leather, Hide

Enhancement: AC

Property: You can treat dim light as bright light within 5 squares of you.

Power (Daily): Minor Action. Until the end of your next turn, you gain concealment against enemies farther than 5 squares away from you.
 Level 22: Concealment lasts until the end of encounter.

Fortification Armor — Level 4+

Dragonborn are no strangers to battle, and they developed this armor to deflect the deadliest enemy attacks.

Lvl 4	+1	840 gp	Lvl 19	+4	105,000 gp
Lvl 9	+2	4,200 gp	Lvl 24	+5	525,000 gp
Lvl 14	+3	21,000 gp	Lvl 29	+6	2,625,000 gp

Armor: Scale, Plate

Enhancement: AC

Property: Whenever a critical hit is scored against you, roll 1d20. On a result of 16–20, the critical hit becomes a normal hit.

Frostburn Armor — Level 14+

A fine layer of ice coats the plates of this armor, protecting you or an ally against extreme cold and heat.

Lvl 14	+3	21,000 gp	Lvl 24	+5	525,000 gp
Lvl 19	+4	105,000 gp	Lvl 29	+6	2,625,000 gp

Armor: Plate

Enhancement: AC

Property: Resist 5 cold and resist 5 fire.
 Level 24 or 29: Resist 10 cold and resist 10 fire.

Power (Encounter): Immediate Interrupt. Use this power when you or an ally within 5 squares of you is targeted by an attack. You or that ally gains resist 10 cold or resist 10 fire (your choice) until the start of your next turn.
 Level 24 or 29: Resist 20 cold or resist 20 fire.

Frozen Armor
Level 4+

Motes of frost float around this armor, yet a wearer remains warm and resistant to the cold.

Lvl 4	+1	840 gp	Lvl 19	+4	105,000 gp
Lvl 9	+2	4,200 gp	Lvl 24	+5	525,000 gp
Lvl 14	+3	21,000 gp	Lvl 29	+6	2,625,000 gp

Armor: Scale, Plate

Enhancement: AC

Property: Resist 5 cold.
  Level 14 or 19: Resist 10 cold.
  Level 24 or 29: Resist 15 cold.

Power (Daily ✦ Cold): Immediate Reaction. Use this power when you are struck by a melee attack. Deal 1d6 cold damage per plus of the armor, and the attacker is immobilized until the end of your next turn.

Giantdodger Armor
Level 13+

This armor protects against the attacks of larger creatures.

Lvl 13	+3	17,000 gp	Lvl 23	+5	425,000 gp
Lvl 18	+4	85,000 gp	Lvl 28	+6	2,125,000 gp

Armor: Leather

Enhancement: AC

Power (Encounter): Immediate Reaction. When a creature of a size category larger than you misses you with a melee attack, you can shift 2 squares.
  Level 23 or 28: Shift 4 squares.

Heartening Armor
Level 3+

Your spirits never fail while you wear this armor.

Lvl 3	+1	680 gp	Lvl 18	+4	85,000 gp
Lvl 8	+2	3,400 gp	Lvl 23	+5	425,000 gp
Lvl 13	+3	17,000 gp	Lvl 28	+6	2,125,000 gp

Armor: Scale, Plate

Enhancement: AC

Property: Gain a saving throw bonus against fear effects equal to the armor's enhancement bonus. When you use your second wind, you gain temporary hit points equal to three times the armor's enhancement bonus.

Illithid Robes
Level 15+

These robes are tight and sleek, with a crest behind the head. They partially protect you from harm if you can compel some poor fool to assist you.

Lvl 15	+3	25,000 gp	Lvl 25	+5	625,000 gp
Lvl 20	+4	125,000 gp	Lvl 30	+6	3,125,000 gp

Armor: Cloth

Enhancement: AC

Property: Resist 10 psychic.
  Level 25 or 30: Resist 15 psychic.

Power (Daily): Immediate Reaction. When you are hit by an attack, you and an ally within 2 squares of you each take half of the damage from the attack (round fractions up). The damage dealt to the ally can't be reduced by resistances or immunity.
  Level 25 or 30: Share damage with an ally within 5 squares of you.

Heartening armor

Immunizing Armor
Level 2+

This sleek, white armor gives its wearer a sense of physical purity, as if she might resist even the deadliest poisons and diseases.

Lvl 2	+1	520 gp	Lvl 17	+4	65,000 gp
Lvl 7	+2	2,600 gp	Lvl 22	+5	325,000 gp
Lvl 12	+3	13,000 gp	Lvl 27	+6	1,625,000 gp

Armor: Scale, Plate

Enhancement: AC

Property: You automatically succeed on saving throws against ongoing poison damage.

Power (Encounter): Immediate Reaction. Use this power when you gain ongoing poison damage. The ongoing poison damage ends.

Imposter's Armor
Level 6+

In the blink of an eye, this metal armor can fade into rags or robes, providing the perfect disguise for any situation.

Lvl 6	+2	1,800 gp	Lvl 21	+5	225,000 gp
Lvl 11	+3	9,000 gp	Lvl 26	+6	1,125,000 gp
Lvl 16	+4	45,000 gp			

Armor: Chain, Scale, Plate

Enhancement: AC

Power (At-Will ✦ Polymorph): Minor Action. You can transform this armor into a normal-looking set of clothes. While in clothes form, the armor does not provide an armor bonus, but neither does it impose an armor check penalty or speed reduction. You can add this armor's enhancement bonus to any Bluff check made to attempt to disguise your appearance. You can change this armor back into its true form as a minor action.

CHRIS SEAMAN

Irrefutable Armor — Level 7+

A simple suit of metal plates, this armor asserts your will as it protects your flesh.

Lvl 7	+2	2,600 gp	Lvl 22	+5	325,000 gp
Lvl 12	+3	13,000 gp	Lvl 27	+6	1,625,000 gp
Lvl 17	+4	65,000 gp			

Armor: Any

Enhancement: AC

Power (Daily): Free Action. Use this power when you miss with an attack that targets Will defense. Reroll your attack with a power bonus equal to the enhancement bonus of this armor.

Laughing Death Armor — Level 9+

The wearer of this armor scoffs at necrotic powers and can unleash a blast of withering black energy upon adversaries.

Lvl 9	+2	4,200 gp	Lvl 24	+5	525,000 gp
Lvl 14	+3	21,000 gp	Lvl 29	+6	2,625,000 gp
Lvl 19	+4	105,000 gp			

Armor: Cloth, Leather, Hide

Enhancement: AC

Property: Resist 5 necrotic.

Level 13 or 18: Resist 10 necrotic.

Level 23 or 28: Resist 15 necrotic.

Power (Encounter ✦ Necrotic): Immediate Reaction. Use this power when struck by a melee attack. The attacker takes 1d6 necrotic damage per plus of the armor and also takes a -2 penalty to Fortitude defense until the end of your next turn.

Lifegiving Armor — Level 3+

Protecting you against necrotic energy, this armor also brings you extended health when you need it.

Lvl 3	+1	680 gp	Lvl 18	+4	85,000 gp
Lvl 8	+2	3,400 gp	Lvl 23	+5	425,000 gp
Lvl 13	+3	17,000 gp	Lvl 28	+6	2,125,000 gp

Armor: Plate

Enhancement: AC

Property: Resist 5 necrotic.

Level 13 or 18: Resist 10 necrotic.

Level 23 or 28: Resist 15 necrotic.

Power (Daily ✦ Healing): Minor Action. Usable only while you are bloodied. Regain hit points equal to 20 minus the number of healing surges you have remaining.

Level 13 or 18: Regain hit points equal to 30 minus the number of healing surges you have remaining.

Level 23 or 28: Regain hit points equal to 40 minus the number of healing surges you have remaining.

Loamweave Armor — Level 9+

Made by the elves using a secret technique that involves spinning soil into fabric, these soft cloth vestments give the wearer a degree of control over earth and plants.

Lvl 9	+2	4,200 gp	Lvl 24	+5	525,000 gp
Lvl 14	+3	21,000 gp	Lvl 29	+6	2,625,000 gp
Lvl 19	+4	105,000 gp			

Armor: Cloth

Enhancement: AC

Power (Daily): Minor Action. Use this power on a target within 10 squares of you that is standing on soil or sand. Grasping arms of earth and entangling vines seize the target, and it is restrained (save ends).

Martyr's Armor — Level 2+

This crimson-tinted armor empowers its wearer to protect allies even at the expense of his or her own health.

Lvl 2	+1	520 gp	Lvl 17	+4	65,000 gp
Lvl 7	+2	2,600 gp	Lvl 22	+5	325,000 gp
Lvl 12	+3	13,000 gp	Lvl 27	+6	1,625,000 gp

Armor: Scale, Plate

Enhancement: AC

Power (At-Will): Minor Action. You take a -1 penalty to AC until the end of your next turn, and allies adjacent to you gain a +1 power bonus to AC until the end of your next turn.

Power (Daily): Immediate Interrupt. Use this power when an adjacent ally is attacked. You take a penalty to your AC equal to the enhancement bonus of this armor; your ally adds an equal power bonus to his AC. Both effects last until the end of your next turn.

Meliorating Armor — Level 3+

This dull steel armor looks extremely well-made, but also quite simple. The more you get hit, the harder the armor gets.

Lvl 3	+1	680 gp	Lvl 18	+4	85,000 gp
Lvl 8	+2	3,400 gp	Lvl 23	+5	425,000 gp
Lvl 13	+3	17,000 gp	Lvl 28	+6	2,125,000 gp

Armor: Chain, Scale, Plate

Enhancement: AC

Property: Each time you reach a milestone in a day, the enhancement bonus of this armor increases by 1. This bonus resets to the armor's normal enhancement bonus after an extended rest.

Mirrorsheen Coat — Level 9+

Magic woven into this armor makes it highly reflective and bright. It's effective against radiant energy and gaze attacks.

Lvl 9	+2	4,200 gp	Lvl 24	+5	525,000 gp
Lvl 14	+3	21,000 gp	Lvl 29	+6	2,625,000 gp
Lvl 19	+4	105,000 gp			

Armor: Cloth, Leather, Hide

Enhancement: AC

Property: Gain a +2 item bonus to all defenses against radiant and gaze attacks. An attacker that hits you with such an attack takes a -2 penalty to attack rolls until the end of its next turn.

Power (Daily): Immediate Interrupt. Use this power when you are targeted by a ranged attack. You can switch the target to another creature within 5 squares of you. The new target cannot be the attacker.

Mithral Armor — Level 4+

Mithral armor shines like polished silver. Most who use it claim it has saved them on more than one occasion.

Lvl 4	+1	840 gp	Lvl 19	+4	105,000 gp
Lvl 9	+2	4,200 gp	Lvl 24	+5	525,000 gp
Lvl 14	+3	21,000 gp	Lvl 29	+6	2,625,000 gp

Armor: Chain, Scale, Plate

Enhancement: AC

Power (Daily): Immediate Reaction. Use this power when a melee or ranged attack hits you. Take half damage.

Pelaurum Armor — Level 4+

A blessing from Pelor makes golden armor surprisingly sturdy.

Lvl 4	+1	840 gp	Lvl 19	+4	105,000 gp
Lvl 9	+2	4,200 gp	Lvl 24	+5	525,000 gp
Lvl 14	+3	21,000 gp	Lvl 29	+6	2,625,000 gp

Armor: Chain, Scale, Plate

Enhancement: AC

Property: Resist 5 fire and resist 5 radiant.
  Level 14 or 19: Resist 10 fire and resist 10 radiant.
  Level 24 or 29: Resist 15 fire and resist 15 radiant.

Prismatic Robe — Level 19+

Varied dull hues entwine across this robe, springing to vibrant life to dazzle onlookers when you're attacked.

Lvl 19	+4	105,000 gp	Lvl 29	+6	2,625,000 gp
Lvl 24	+5	525,000 gp			

Armor: Cloth

Enhancement: AC

Property: When you are hit by a melee or ranged attack, the robe's colors become a clashing array of dazzling light. The attacker takes a -2 penalty to melee and ranged attack rolls against you until the start of your next turn.

Rat Form Armor — Level 8+

Tiny, sleek skins seem to make up this coat of leather, which has tassels that look disturbingly like rodent tails. With it, you can take the stealthy shape of a rat.

Lvl 8	+2	3,400 gp	Lvl 23	+5	425,000 gp
Lvl 13	+3	17,000 gp	Lvl 28	+6	2,125,000 gp
Lvl 18	+4	85,000 gp			

Armor: Leather

Enhancement: AC

Power (Daily ✦ Polymorph): Standard Action. You and your gear assume the form of a common sewer rat. While in this form:
  • You can't attack.
  • Your gear is merged into your form and unusable.
  • You gain a +5 bonus to Stealth checks.
  • All your defenses remain the same.
You can sustain this power as a standard action on your turn and end the power to return to your normal form as a free action. You resume normal form if knocked unconscious or dropped to 0 or fewer hit points.

Reflexive Armor — Level 9+

This armor protects less dextrous wearers from the brunt of attacks that generally ignore armor.

Lvl 9	+2	4,200 gp	Lvl 24	+5	525,000 gp
Lvl 14	+3	21,000 gp	Lvl 29	+6	2,625,000 gp
Lvl 19	+4	105,000 gp			

Armor: Chain, Scale, Plate

Enhancement: AC

Power (Daily): Immediate Interrupt. Use this power when an attack targets your Reflex defense. Until the end of your next turn, you can resist attacks against Reflex with your AC instead.

Reinforcing Armor — Level 4+

This armor protects you even when you aren't cautious enough to protect yourself.

Lvl 4	+1	840 gp	Lvl 19	+4	105,000 gp
Lvl 9	+2	4,200 gp	Lvl 24	+5	525,000 gp
Lvl 14	+3	21,000 gp	Lvl 29	+6	2,625,000 gp

Armor: Scale, Plate

Enhancement: AC

Property: If you take damage from a melee attack, you gain a +1 item bonus to all defenses until the start of your next turn.

Repulsion Armor
Level 2+

Inlaid with esoteric runes, this armor can repel even though most persistent foes.

Lvl 2	+1	520 gp	Lvl 17	+4	65,000 gp
Lvl 7	+2	2,600 gp	Lvl 22	+5	325,000 gp
Lvl 12	+3	13,000 gp	Lvl 27	+6	1,625,000 gp

Armor: Cloth, Leather

Enhancement: AC

Power (Daily): Minor Action. Whenever an enemy moves into an adjacent square, you can push that enemy 1 square as an immediate reaction. This power lasts until the end of the encounter.

Righteous Armor
Level 9+

Infused with its creator's righteous conviction, this armor punishes enemies who don't fight fair.

Lvl 9	+2	4,200 gp	Lvl 24	+5	525,000 gp
Lvl 14	+3	21,000 gp	Lvl 29	+6	2,625,000 gp
Lvl 19	+4	105,000 gp			

Armor: Plate

Enhancement: AC

Property: When you are hit by an enemy with combat advantage against you, it takes radiant damage equal to the armor's enhancement bonus.

Robe of Bloodwalking
Level 17+

This cloth armor rewards you for destroying your foes.

| Lvl 17 | +4 | 65,000 gp | Lvl 27 | +6 | 1,625,000 gp |
| Lvl 22 | +5 | 325,000 gp | | | |

Armor: Cloth

Enhancement: AC

Power (Encounter ✦ Healing, Teleportation): Free Action. Use this power when you reduce a target within 10 squares of you to 0 or fewer hit points. Teleport to any square the target occupied.

Robe of Contingency
Level 4+

Stitched with thread from the Feywild, this robe is favored by many wizards for its ability to escape a bind.

Lvl 4	+1	840 gp	Lvl 19	+4	105,000 gp
Lvl 9	+2	4,200 gp	Lvl 24	+5	525,000 gp
Lvl 14	+3	21,000 gp	Lvl 29	+6	2,625,000 gp

Armor: Cloth

Enhancement: AC

Power (Daily ✦ Teleportation): Immediate Reaction. Use this power while you are bloodied and when an attack damages you. Teleport 6 squares, and you can spend a healing surge.

Robe of Defying Flames
Level 13+

Emblazoned with fiery imagery, this robe can both repel and summon flames.

| Lvl 13 | +3 | 17,000 gp | Lvl 23 | +5 | 425,000 gp |
| Lvl 18 | +4 | 85,000 gp | Lvl 28 | +6 | 2,125,000 gp |

Armor: Cloth

Enhancement: AC

Property: Resist 10 fire.

Level 23 or 28: Resist 15 fire.

Power (Daily ✦ Healing): Immediate Interrupt. Use this power when you would take fire damage. You take no fire damage, you gain a +2 power bonus to speed until the end of your next turn, and you can spend a healing surge.

Robe of Defying Frost
Level 13+

Minute ice crystals from the Elemental Chaos stud this robe, which protects against the effects of cold and imbues your attacks with an icy chill.

| Lvl 13 | +3 | 17,000 gp | Lvl 23 | +5 | 425,000 gp |
| Lvl 18 | +4 | 85,000 gp | Lvl 28 | +6 | 2,125,000 gp |

Armor: Cloth

Enhancement: AC

Property: Resist 10 cold.

Level 23 or 28: Resist 15 cold.

Power (Daily ✦ Healing): Immediate Interrupt. Use this power when you would take cold damage. You take no cold damage, you gain a +1 power bonus to AC until the end of your next turn, and you can spend a healing surge.

Robe of Defying Storms
Level 14+

Embroidered patterns on these robes resemble clouds and great, slashing bursts of lightning. You gain both protection from storms and the ability to call upon their power.

| Lvl 14 | +3 | 21,000 gp | Lvl 24 | +5 | 525,000 gp |
| Lvl 19 | +4 | 105,000 gp | Lvl 29 | +6 | 2,625,000 gp |

Armor: Cloth

Enhancement: AC

Property: Resist 10 lightning and resist 10 thunder.

Level 25 or 30: Resist 15 lightning and resist 15 thunder.

Power (Daily ✦ Healing): Immediate Interrupt. Use this power when you would take lightning or thunder damage. You take no lightning or thunder damage, you gain a +1 power bonus to attack rolls until the end of your next turn, and you can spend a healing surge.

Robe of Eyes — Level 2+

This fine silk cloth appears to be covered in swirls of color or peacock feather patterns, but in fact depicts dozens of unblinking eyes.

Lvl 2	+1	520 gp	Lvl 17	+4	65,000 gp
Lvl 7	+2	2,600 gp	Lvl 22	+5	325,000 gp
Lvl 12	+3	13,000 gp	Lvl 27	+6	1,625,000 gp

Armor: Cloth

Enhancement: AC

Property: You cannot be blinded and gain an item bonus to Perception checks equal to the armor's enhancement bonus.

Robe of Forbearance — Level 24+

This robe's plain cloth makes many enemies underestimate the defenses of the wearer.

Lvl 24	+5	525,000 gp	Lvl 29	+6	2,625,000 gp

Armor: Cloth

Enhancement: AC

Power (Daily): Immediate Reaction. Use this power when an enemy hits you. The enemy takes a penalty equal to the enhancement bonus of the armor to attack rolls against you until the end of the encounter. This effect ends if you attack it.

Robe of Quills — Level 3+

Thin spines cover this robe, making any adversary reconsider before attacking the wearer.

Lvl 3	+1	680 gp	Lvl 18	+4	85,000 gp
Lvl 8	+2	3,400 gp	Lvl 23	+5	425,000 gp
Lvl 13	+3	17,000 gp	Lvl 28	+6	2,125,000 gp

Armor: Cloth

Enhancement: AC

Power (Daily): Immediate Reaction. Use this power when an adjacent enemy makes a melee attack against you. The quills bristle, dealing 1d6 damage per plus of the armor to the enemy and ongoing damage to the enemy equal to the enhancement bonus of the armor (save ends).

Robe of Sapping — Level 17+

This robe saps the durability of an attacker's armor, making the creature no more protected than the robe's wearer.

Lvl 17	+4	65,000 gp	Lvl 27	+6	1,625,000 gp
Lvl 22	+5	325,000 gp			

Armor: Cloth

Enhancement: AC

Power (Daily): Immediate Reaction. Use this power when a melee attack hits you. The attacker takes a -2 penalty to AC (save ends), and you gain a +2 power bonus to AC while the attacker is under the effect. The target cannot make a saving throw against the effect until the end of its next turn. *Aftereffect:* The target takes a -1 penalty to AC (save ends), and you gain a +1 power bonus to AC while the target is under the effect.

Robe of Scintillation — Level 2+

Made of fine silks, this robe sheds light when you want it to, and it can also unleash a swirling melange of color that befuddles foes.

Lvl 2	+1	520 gp	Lvl 17	+4	65,000 gp
Lvl 7	+2	2,600 gp	Lvl 22	+5	325,000 gp
Lvl 12	+3	13,000 gp	Lvl 27	+6	1,625,000 gp

Armor: Cloth

Enhancement: AC

Power (At-Will ✦ Radiant): Minor Action. The robe radiates colored lights, illuminating like a torch. You can end the illumination as a free action.

Power (Daily ✦ Radiant): Standard Action. The robe shines bright with myriad colors. Make an attack: Close burst 2; Intelligence or Charisma vs. Will (add the robe's enhancement bonus as an enhancement bonus to the attack roll); on a hit, the target is dazed (save ends).

Robe of Stars — Level 13+

The dark, velvet fabric of this robe glimmers with delicate points of light that can burn brightly on command.

Lvl 13	+3	17,000 gp	Lvl 23	+5	425,000 gp
Lvl 18	+4	85,000 gp	Lvl 28	+6	2,125,000 gp

Armor: Cloth

Enhancement: AC

Power (Daily ✦ Radiant): Minor Action. Until the end of your next turn, all enemies who attack you are blinded (save ends).

Robe of the Archfiend — Level 20+

Woven from the skin of humans, devils, and demons, these grim robes draw a viewer's eyes to the dominating gaze of the wearer.

Lvl 20	+4	125,000 gp	Lvl 30	+6	3,125,000 gp
Lvl 25	+5	625,000 gp			

Armor: Cloth

Enhancement: AC

Power (Daily): Immediate Reaction. Use this power when a creature within 10 squares of you attacks you. Make an attack: Charisma vs. Will (add the robe's enhancement bonus as an enhancement bonus to the attack roll); on a hit, the target is dominated until the end of your next turn. *Sustain Minor:* Repeat the attack. On a hit, the target remains dominated. If the attack fails, you can no longer sustain this power.

Salubrious Armor — Level 4+

The shiny steel of the armor flushes red when its wearer heals, bestowing extra defense.

Lvl 4	+1	840 gp	Lvl 19	+4	105,000 gp
Lvl 9	+2	4,200 gp	Lvl 24	+5	525,000 gp
Lvl 14	+3	21,000 gp	Lvl 29	+6	2,625,000 gp

Armor: Scale, Plate
Enhancement: AC
Property: Any time you regain hit points, you gain a +1 item bonus to AC until the end of your next turn.
Level 14 or 19: +2 bonus to AC.
Level 24 or 29: +3 bonus to AC.

Screaming Armor — Level 2+

This impressive armor is covered in ornate patterns of screaming faces, enhancing your ability to shatter your foe's resolve.

Lvl 2	+1	520 gp	Lvl 17	+4	65,000 gp
Lvl 7	+2	2,600 gp	Lvl 22	+5	325,000 gp
Lvl 12	+3	13,000 gp	Lvl 27	+6	1,625,000 gp

Armor: Hide, Scale, Plate
Enhancement: AC
Property: Gain an item bonus to Intimidate checks equal to the enhancement bonus of this armor.
Power (Encounter ✦ Fear): Minor Action. An enemy within 5 squares of you a –2 penalty to attack rolls until the end of your next turn.

Serpentskin Armor — Level 3+

Made from the discarded scales of a giant snake, this armor still carries the serpent's resistance to poison.

Lvl 3	+1	680 gp	Lvl 18	+4	85,000 gp
Lvl 8	+2	3,400 gp	Lvl 23	+5	425,000 gp
Lvl 13	+3	17,000 gp	Lvl 28	+6	2,125,000 gp

Armor: Leather, Hide
Enhancement: AC
Power (Daily): Move Action. Shift 3 squares. This shift can move through enemies' spaces, though you must end your move in a legal space.

Shared Suffering Armor — Level 5+

When enemies deal ongoing damage, this armor lets you deliver ongoing damage upon them as well.

Lvl 5	+1	1,000 gp	Lvl 20	+4	125,000 gp
Lvl 10	+2	5,000 gp	Lvl 25	+5	625,000 gp
Lvl 15	+3	25,000 gp	Lvl 30	+6	3,125,000 gp

Armor: Any
Enhancement: AC
Power (Encounter): Immediate Reaction. Use this power when an attack gives you ongoing damage. The attacker gains an equal amount of untyped ongoing damage.

Shimmering Armor — Level 4+

The sheen of this armor glints brightest when you most need its magical protection.

Lvl 4	+1	840 gp	Lvl 19	+4	105,000 gp
Lvl 9	+2	4,200 gp	Lvl 24	+5	525,000 gp
Lvl 14	+3	21,000 gp	Lvl 29	+6	2,625,000 gp

Armor: Cloth
Enhancement: AC
Property: You do not provoke opportunity attacks when you make ranged or area attacks.

Shocking Armor — Level 27

Created from forges charged with lightning, this armor ripples with electricity and makes any foe rue the decision to attack you.

Lvl 27	+6	1,625,000 gp

Armor: Chain, Scale, Plate
Enhancement: AC
Power (Daily ✦ Lightning): Immediate Reaction. Use this power when an enemy misses you with a melee attack. That enemy takes lightning damage equal to your level.

RYAN BARGER

Skeletal Armor — Level 19+

Encased in bones, the wearer of this armor presents a terrible image of an undead creature, gaining similar resistances and making any undead hesitant to attack.

Lvl 19	+4	105,000 gp		Lvl 29	+6	2,625,000 gp
Lvl 24	+5	525,000 gp				

Armor: Chain, Plate, Scale

Enhancement: AC

Property: Resist 10 necrotic.
  Level 23 or 28: Resist 15 necrotic.

Power (Daily): Minor Action. Close burst 5; targets undead; the attack is this item's level + enhancement bonus vs. Will; the target cannot attack you (save ends).

Skybound Armor — Level 5+

This armor constantly flows like clouds across a gray sky and gives its wearer a feeling of weightlessness when moving.

Lvl 5	+1	1,000 gp		Lvl 20	+4	125,000 gp
Lvl 10	+2	5,000 gp		Lvl 25	+5	625,000 gp
Lvl 15	+3	25,000 gp		Lvl 30	+6	3,125,000 gp

Armor: Cloth, Leather

Enhancement: AC

Power (Encounter): Free Action. Use this power when you make an Athletics check to jump. You jump an additional number of squares equal to this armor's enhancement bonus. This jump can exceed your normal movement.

Slick Armor — Level 2+

It's hard to get a hold on you while you wear this armor.

Lvl 2	+1	520 gp		Lvl 17	+4	65,000 gp
Lvl 7	+2	2,600 gp		Lvl 22	+5	325,000 gp
Lvl 12	+3	13,000 gp		Lvl 27	+6	1,625,000 gp

Armor: Cloth, Leather, Hide

Enhancement: AC

Property: Gain a bonus to Acrobatics checks to escape actions equal to twice the armor's enhancement bonus.

Snakefang Armor — Level 8+

Bedecked in the fangs of serpents, this armor not only bestows resistance to deadly venoms but also endangers attackers.

Lvl 8	+2	3,400 gp		Lvl 23	+5	425,000 gp
Lvl 13	+3	17,000 gp		Lvl 28	+6	2,125,000 gp
Lvl 18	+4	85,000 gp				

Armor: Leather, Hide

Enhancement: AC

Property: Resist 5 poison.
  Level 18 or 23: Resist 10 poison.
  Level 28: Resist 15 poison.

Power (Daily ✦ Poison): Immediate Reaction. When you take damage from a melee attack, the attacker takes ongoing poison damage equal to this armor's poison resist value (save ends).

Solar Armor — Level 9+

This copper-plated armor seems to soak up the sun, shining with a red glow that is warm and invigorating.

Lvl 9	+2	4,200 gp		Lvl 24	+5	525,000 gp
Lvl 14	+3	21,000 gp		Lvl 29	+6	2,625,000 gp
Lvl 19	+4	105,000 gp				

Armor: Scale, Plate

Enhancement: AC

Power (At-Will ✦ Healing): Immediate Reaction. When you take radiant damage, you can spend a healing surge. You regain hit points equal to your healing surge value plus additional hit points equal to the armor's enhancement bonus.

Power (Daily ✦ Radiant): Standard Action. Enemies within a close burst 2 take radiant damage equal to twice the enhancement bonus of the armor and also take a -2 penalty to attack rolls until the end of your next turn.

JAMES ZHANG

Soulwarding Armor — Level 24+

This armor strengthens your physical and mental resolve.

Lvl 24	+5	525,000 gp	Lvl 29	+6	2,625,000 gp

Armor: Chain, Scale, or Plate

Enhancement: AC

Property: Resist 10 necrotic and resist 10 psychic.

Property: You do not lose a healing surge when an enemy's attack would cause you to do so.

Spiritlink Armor — Level 15+

This armor absorbs both light and dark energy, and it can even transform that destructive energy into healing.

Lvl 15	+3	25,000 gp	Lvl 25	+5	625,000 gp
Lvl 20	+4	125,000 gp	Lvl 30	+6	3,125,000 gp

Armor: Chain

Enhancement: AC

Property: Resist 5 necrotic and resist 5 radiant.

Level 24: Resist 10 necrotic and resist 10 radiant.

Level 29: Resist 15 necrotic and resist 15 radiant.

Power (Daily ✦ Healing): Immediate Interrupt. When an ally within 5 squares of you is hit by an attack dealing necrotic or radiant damage, the ally gains immunity to the necrotic and/or radiant damage from that attack. The ally can spend a healing surge and regain additional hit points equal to twice the armor's enhancement bonus.

Stalker's Armor — Level 18+

Shadowfell and Feywild energies blend to make this armor the ultimate hunter's apparel.

Lvl 18	+4	85,000 gp	Lvl 28	+6	2,125,000 gp
Lvl 23	+5	425,000 gp			

Armor: Leather, Hide

Enhancement: AC

Property: When you have concealment from a creature at the start of your turn, you remain concealed from that creature until the start of your next turn.

Stoneborn Armor — Level 3+

Worked from rough stone, the plates of this bulky armor enable its wearer to tap into the limitless endurance of the earth.

Lvl 3	+1	680 gp	Lvl 18	+4	85,000 gp
Lvl 8	+2	3,400 gp	Lvl 23	+5	425,000 gp
Lvl 13	+3	17,000 gp	Lvl 28	+6	2,125,000 gp

Armor: Plate

Enhancement: AC

Power (Daily): Minor Action. Gain temporary hit points equal to 10 + your Constitution modifier. They last until depleted or until you take an extended rest.

Level 8: 15 + Constitution modifier temporary hit points.

Level 13: 20 + Constitution modifier temporary hit points.

Level 18: 25 + Constitution modifier temporary hit points.

Level 23: 30 + Constitution modifier temporary hit points.

Level 28: 35 + Constitution modifier temporary hit points.

Stoneskin Robes — Level 3+

In battle, these gray robes harden your skin and grant additional resilience.

Lvl 3	+1	680 gp	Lvl 18	+4	85,000 gp
Lvl 8	+2	3,400 gp	Lvl 23	+5	425,000 gp
Lvl 13	+3	17,000 gp	Lvl 28	+6	2,125,000 gp

Armor: Cloth

Enhancement: AC

Power (Encounter): Minor Action. You gain 5 temporary hit points until the end of the encounter.

Level 13 or 18: 10 temporary hit points.

Level 23 or 28: 15 temporary hit points.

Stormlord Armor — Level 15+

With this armor, you can bend the elements to your will, harnessing the power of the storm.

Lvl 15	+3	25,000 gp	Lvl 25	+5	625,000 gp
Lvl 20	+4	125,000 gp	Lvl 30	+6	3,125,000 gp

Armor: Chain, Scale, Plate

Enhancement: AC

Property: Resist 10 lightning and resist 10 thunder.

Level 25 or 30: Resist 15 lightning and resist 15 thunder.

Power (Daily): Immediate Interrupt. Use this power when an ally within 10 squares of you takes lightning and/or thunder damage from an attack. The attack hits you instead, and you gain a +2 power bonus to attack rolls until the end of your next turn.

Summoned Armor — Level 6+

One need never worry about being caught unarmored while possessing this extraordinary armor.

Lvl 6	+2	1,800 gp	Lvl 21	+5	225,000 gp
Lvl 11	+3	9,000 gp	Lvl 26	+6	1,125,000 gp
Lvl 16	+4	45,000 gp			

Armor: Any

Enhancement: AC

Power (At-Will): Minor Action. You banish this armor to a secure extradimensional location. At any point in the future, unless you are wearing armor, you can use another minor action to recall the armor. The armor appears on you as though you had donned it normally.

Surge Armor — Level 13+

Many great heroes have survived dangerous battles thanks to the offensive and defensive benefits of this armor.

Lvl 13	+3	17,000 gp	Lvl 23	+5	425,000 gp
Lvl 18	+4	85,000 gp	Lvl 28	+6	2,125,000 gp

Armor: Any

Enhancement: AC

Power (Daily): Minor Action. Gain a +2 power bonus to all defenses. This bonus is reduced by 1 at the start of each of your turns.

Level 23 or 28: +3 power bonus.

Survivor's Armor — Level 9+

This armor fills its wearer with a sense of security while in the company of devoted allies.

Lvl 9	+2	4,200 gp	Lvl 24	+5	525,000 gp
Lvl 14	+3	21,000 gp	Lvl 29	+6	2,625,000 gp
Lvl 19	+4	105,000 gp			

Armor: Cloth, Leather, Hide

Enhancement: AC

Power (Daily): Immediate Interrupt. Use this power when hit by an attack. Choose a willing ally within 5 squares of you. That ally takes the damage instead.

Level 24 or 29: Ally within 10 squares of you.

Tactician's Armor — Level 5+

In battle, strength of mind is as important as strength of the body, and this armor ensures that you have both.

Lvl 5	+1	1,000 gp	Lvl 20	+4	125,000 gp
Lvl 10	+2	5,000 gp	Lvl 25	+5	625,000 gp
Lvl 15	+3	25,000 gp	Lvl 30	+6	3,125,000 gp

Armor: Chain, Scale, Plate

Enhancement: AC

Property: When a power or class feature calls on your Intelligence modifier to determine a value other than your attack bonus, add 1 to that value. This does not change your Intelligence modifier for any other purpose.

Thunderhead Armor — Level 9+

The metal of this armor seems to roil with various shades of purple and gray, as though it's filled with storm clouds. The wearer feels resistant to the powers of the storm.

Lvl 9	+2	4,200 gp	Lvl 24	+5	525,000 gp
Lvl 14	+3	21,000 gp	Lvl 29	+6	2,625,000 gp
Lvl 19	+4	105,000 gp			

Armor: Chain, Scale, Plate

Enhancement: AC

Power (Daily ✦ Lightning or Thunder): Immediate Reaction. When you take lightning or thunder damage, all enemies within 2 squares of you take 5 damage of the same type.

Level 19 or 24: 10 damage of the same type.

Level 29: 15 damage of the same type.

Vaporform Armor — Level 19+

While wearing this armor, no prison can hold you, no door can block your path, and no height is beyond your reach.

Lvl 19	+4	105,000 gp	Lvl 29	+6	2,625,000 gp
Lvl 24	+5	525,000 gp			

Armor: Cloth, Leather, Hide

Enhancement: AC

Power (Daily): Move Action. You become insubstantial and can fit through even the smallest spaces without squeezing. You also gain fly 6 (hover) and can only take move actions until you return to your natural form, which you can do as a free action. While in vaporous form, you take 5 damage at the start of each turn.

Versatile Armor — Level 3+

The wearer of this armor moves with more alacrity than one might expect, and can employ that speed to his or her advantage against unprepared enemies.

Lvl 3	+1	680 gp	Lvl 18	+4	85,000 gp
Lvl 8	+2	3,400 gp	Lvl 23	+5	425,000 gp
Lvl 13	+3	17,000 gp	Lvl 28	+6	2,125,000 gp

Armor: Chain, Plate

Enhancement: AC

Power (At-Will): Minor Action. You take a -1 AC penalty but ignore penalties to speed and checks caused by armor. This persists until you use a minor action to return the armor to normal.

Verve Armor — Level 4+

This armor protects your body and fortifies your spirit.

Lvl 4	+1	840 gp	Lvl 19	+4	105,000 gp
Lvl 9	+2	4,200 gp	Lvl 24	+5	525,000 gp
Lvl 14	+3	21,000 gp	Lvl 29	+6	2,625,000 gp

Armor: Scale, Plate

Enhancement: AC

Property: You gain a +2 bonus to death saving throws.

Power (Daily): No Action. Use this power when you fail a saving throw. The result of that saving throw is 20 instead.

Whiteflame armor

Veteran's Armor — Level 2+

Battered and worn, this unassuming armor helps you get the most out of your experiences.

Lvl 2	+1	520 gp	Lvl 17	+4	65,000 gp
Lvl 7	+2	2,600 gp	Lvl 22	+5	325,000 gp
Lvl 12	+3	13,000 gp	Lvl 27	+6	1,625,000 gp

Armor: Any
Enhancement: AC
Property: When you spend an action point, you gain a +1 item bonus to all attack rolls and defenses until the end of your next turn.
Power (Daily): Free Action. Spend an action point. You do not gain the normal extra action. Instead, you regain the use of one expended daily power.

Voidcrystal Armor — Level 14+

Black as a starless night, this armor destabilizes weapons it deflects.

Lvl 14	+3	21,000 gp	Lvl 24	+5	525,000 gp
Lvl 19	+4	105,000 gp	Lvl 29	+6	2,625,000 gp

Armor: Any
Enhancement: AC
Power (Daily): Immediate Reaction. Use this power when a melee attack misses your AC. The weapon used to attack you deals only half damage (save ends). If the attacker was unarmed (using a fist or claws, for example), the attacker instead takes ongoing 10 damage (save ends).
Level 24 or 29: Ongoing 15 damage.

Warsheath Armor — Level 10+

This armor ensures that its wearer is surrounded not just by protective layers, but also by eager foes

Lvl 10	+2	5,000 gp	Lvl 25	+5	625,000 gp
Lvl 15	+3	25,000 gp	Lvl 30	+6	3,125,000 gp
Lvl 20	+4	125,000 gp			

Armor: Plate
Enhancement: AC
Power (Daily): Minor Action. Enemies within a number of squares equal to this armor's enhancement bonus of you are pulled adjacent to you.

Whiteflame Armor — Level 3+

This armor absorbs light and can be converted to protect against other effects.

Lvl 3	+1	680 gp	Lvl 18	+4	85,000 gp
Lvl 8	+2	3,400 gp	Lvl 23	+5	425,000 gp
Lvl 13	+3	17,000 gp	Lvl 28	+6	2,125,000 gp

Armor: Chain, Scale, Plate
Enhancement: AC
Property: Resist 5 radiant.
Level 14 or 19: Resist 10 radiant.
Level 24 or 29: Resist 15 radiant.
Power (Daily): Minor Action. Change the type of resist this armor grants to resist fire, resist lightning, or resist thunder until the end of the encounter.

Wildleaf Armor — Level 17+

Fashioned by elves from fallen leaves, these suits of armor are favored by rangers and rogues who patrol the wilderness.

Lvl 17	+4	65,000 gp	Lvl 27	+6	1,625,000 gp
Lvl 22	+5	325,000 gp			

Armor: Cloth, Leather, Hide
Enhancement: AC
Property: You ignore difficult terrain while outdoors.

Zealot's Armor — Level 15+

This armor is surrounded by motes of light that grow in intensity as undead approach the wearer.

Lvl 15	+3	25,000 gp	Lvl 25	+5	625,000 gp
Lvl 20	+4	125,000 gp	Lvl 30	+6	3,125,000 gp

Armor: Cloth
Enhancement: AC
Property: Whenever an undead creature hits you with a melee attack, it takes radiant damage equal to the enhancement bonus of this armor.

WEAPONS

The line that separates a novice from a skilled weapon master is defined by a simple realization–that the weapon and body are one. Treat your weapon as an extension of your body, and nothing can stop you.

Weapons are perhaps the most utilitarian piece of gear that an adventurer carries. A dwarf paladin might use his +3 *righteous warhammer* to unleash holy retribution upon a lich, or a tiefling rogue might sneak up behind a pair of marut guards and quietly dispatch them with her +6 *assassin's short sword*. Each weapon represents a different tool in an adventurer's hand–and a very potent tool once magic is added.

Like enchanted armors, a magic weapon has an enhancement bonus that corresponds to the item's level. Some magic weapons are available at the lowest levels, with improved versions of the weapon available every five levels up until the highest levels. Other weapons are of such power that they are not even available until a PC has achieved epic greatness.

Weapon Properties

Many weapons have properties that provide a constant benefit. To gain the benefit of a weapon's property, you must be wielding the weapon. Unless specified otherwise, a property affects only the weapon to which it's attached. For example, a +2 *cunning dagger*, which bestows a –2 penalty to an enemy's saving throws against your weapon powers, affects only powers that are delivered using that weapon. You couldn't hold the weapon in your off-hand and gain the benefit of the property on powers delivered using a main weapon.

MAGIC WEAPONS

Lvl	Name	Price (gp)	Categories
1	Distance +1	360	Any ranged
2	Bloodclaw +1	520	Any melee
2	Defensive +1	520	Any
2	Flesh seeker +1	520	Any melee
2	Gambler's +1	520	Light Blade
2	Holy healer's +1	520	Mace, Staff
2	Mage's +1	520	Heavy Blade, Light Blade
2	Pact hammer +1	520	Hammer
2	Pact sword +1	520	Longsword
2	Parrying +1	520	Any melee
2	Pinning +1	520	Any melee
2	Prime shot +1	520	Any ranged
2	Reproachful +1	520	Any melee
2	Staggering +1	520	Axe, Flail, Hammer, Heavy Blade, Mace

MAGIC WEAPONS (CONTINUED)

Lvl	Name	Price (gp)	Categories
3	Inescapable +1	680	Any
3	Inspiring +1	680	Any
3	Luckblade +1	680	Heavy Blade, Light Blade
3	Paired +1	680	Any one-handed melee
3	Point blank +1	680	Any ranged
3	Quick +1	680	Any
3	Reckless +1	680	Any nonreach melee
3	Scalebane +1	680	Any
3	Skewering +1	680	Pick, Spear
3	Strongheart +1	680	Any melee
3	Subtle +1	680	Any melee
3	Swiftshot +1	680	Crossbow
3	Vanguard +1	680	Any melee
4	Acidic +1	840	Heavy Blade, Light Blade, Spear
4	Battlecrazed +1	840	Axe, Heavy Blade
4	Communal +1	840	Any melee
4	Deathstalker +1	840	Any
4	Lullaby +1	840	Flail, Hammer, Mace, Staff
4	Medic's +1	840	Any
4	Oathblade +1	840	Heavy Blade, Light Blade
4	Opportunistic +1	840	Any melee
4	Rending +1	840	Axe
4	Sunblade +1	840	Heavy Blade
4	Wounding +1	840	Axe, Bow, Crossbow, Heavy Blade, Light Blade, Spear
5	Poisoned +1	1,000	Bow, Crossbow, Light Blade, Pick, Spear
5	Thieving +1	1,000	Light Blade
5	Vengeful +1	1,000	Any melee
6	Distance +2	1,800	Any ranged
6	Dynamic + 2	1,800	Any melee
6	Grasping +2	1,800	Polearm, Spear
6	Sacrificial +2	1,800	Any melee
7	Bloodclaw +2	2,600	Any melee
7	Defensive +2	2,600	Any
7	Flesh seeker +2	2,600	Any melee
7	Gambler's +2	2,600	Light Blade
7	Holy healer's +2	2,600	Mace, Staff
7	Mage's +2	2,600	Heavy Blade, Light Blade
7	Pact hammer +2	2,600	Hammer
7	Pact sword +2	2,600	Longsword
7	Parrying +2	2,600	Any melee
7	Piercing +2	2,600	Spear
7	Pinning +2	2,600	Any melee
7	Prime shot +2	2,600	Any ranged
7	Reproachful +2	2,600	Any melee
7	Retribution +2	2,600	Any melee

CHAPTER 2 | *Magic Items*

Lvl	Name	Price (gp)	Categories
7	Splitting +2	2,600	Flail
7	Staggering +2	2,600	Axe, Flail, Hammer, Heavy Blade, Mace
7	Transference +2	2,600	Any
8	Adamantine +2	3,400	Any melee
8	Assassin's +2	3,400	Light Blade
8	Bronzewood +2	3,400	Any melee
8	Cloaked +2	3,400	Any
8	Cold iron +2	3,400	Any
8	Controlling +2	3,400	Polearm
8	Cunning +2	3,400	Any melee
8	Decerebrating +2	3,400	Hammer, Mace
8	Determined +2	3,400	Any thrown
8	Dread +2	3,400	Any
8	Earthbreaker +2	3,400	Axe, Flail, Hammer, Mace, Pick, Sling
8	Flanking +2	3,400	Any melee
8	Force +2	3,400	Any
8	Graceful +2	3,400	Flail, Heavy Blade, Light Blade, Spear
8	Inescapable +2	3,400	Any
8	Inspiring +2	3,400	Any
8	Luckblade +2	3,400	Heavy Blade, Light Blade
8	Mace of healing +2	3,400	Mace
8	Mauling +2	3,400	Hammer, Heavy Blade, Mace
8	Paired +2	3,400	Any one-handed melee
8	Point blank +2	3,400	Any ranged
8	Quick +2	3,400	Any
8	Reckless +2	3,400	Any nonreach melee
8	Scalebane +2	3,400	Any
8	Skewering +2	3,400	Pick, Spear
8	Stout +2	3,400	Axe, Hammer, Mace, Pick, Staff
8	Strongheart +2	3,400	Any melee
8	Subtle +2	3,400	Any melee
8	Swiftshot +2	3,400	Crossbow
8	Tigerclaw gauntlets +2	3,400	Gauntlets
8	Tyrant's +2	3,400	Any melee
8	Vanguard +2	3,400	Any melee
8	Waterbane +2	3,400	Axe, Crossbow, Light Blade, Heavy Blade, Spear
9	Acidic +2	4,200	Heavy Blade, Light Blade, Spear
9	Battlecrazed +2	4,200	Axe, Heavy Blade
9	Communal +2	4,200	Any melee
9	Crusader's +2	4,200	Hammer, Mace
9	Deathstalker +2	4,200	Any
9	Demonbane +2	4,200	Any
9	Feyslaughter +2	4,200	Any

Lvl	Name	Price (gp)	Categories
9	Lullaby +2	4,200	Flail, Hammer, Mace, Staff
9	Medic's +2	4,200	Any
9	Oathblade +2	4,200	Heavy Blade, Light Blade
9	Opportunistic +2	4,200	Any melee
9	Rending +2	4,200	Axe
9	Shapechanger's sorrow +2	4,200	Axe, Heavy Blade, Light Blade
9	Skyrender +2	4,200	Any ranged
9	Sunblade +2	4,200	Heavy Blade
9	Thoughtstealer +2	4,200	Any thrown
9	Vampiric +2	4,200	Heavy Blade, Light Blade
9	Wounding +2	4,200	Axe, Bow, Crossbow, Heavy Blade, Light Blade, Spear
10	Blackshroud +2	5,000	Axe, Heavy Blade, Light Blade
10	Footpad's friend + 2	5,000	Light blade
10	Poisoned +2	5,000	Bow, Crossbow, Light Blade, Pick, Spear
10	Righteous +2	5,000	Any melee
10	Thieving +2	5,000	Light Blade
10	Vengeful +2	5,000	Any melee
11	Battering +3	9,000	Hammer
11	Blacksmelt +3	9,000	Flail, Hammer, Mace
11	Distance +3	9,000	Any ranged
11	Dynamic + 3	9,000	Any melee
11	Grasping +3	9,000	Polearm, Spear
11	Ricochet +3	9,000	Sling
11	Sacrificial +3	9,000	Any melee
12	Blade of night +3	13,000	Light Blade
12	Bloodclaw +3	13,000	Any melee
12	Defensive +3	13,000	Any
12	Elukian clay +3	13,000	Bow, Crossbow
12	Flesh seeker +3	13,000	Any melee
12	Gambler's +3	13,000	Light Blade
12	Holy healer's +3	13,000	Mace, Staff
12	Jagged +3	13,000	Axe, Heavy Blade, Light Blade
12	Mage's +3	13,000	Heavy Blade, Light Blade
12	Pact hammer +3	13,000	Hammer
12	Pact sword +3	13,000	Longsword
12	Parrying +3	13,000	Any melee
12	Piercing +3	13,000	Spear
12	Pinning +3	13,000	Any melee
12	Prime shot +3	13,000	Any ranged
12	Reproachful +3	13,000	Any melee
12	Retribution +3	13,000	Any melee
12	Splitting +3	13,000	Flail

Lvl	Name	Price (gp)	Categories
12	Staggering +3	13,000	Axe, Flail, Hammer, Heavy Blade, Mace
12	Transference +3	13,000	Any
13	Adamantine +3	17,000	Any melee
13	Assassin's +3	17,000	Light Blade
13	Bloodiron +3	17,000	Any
13	Bloodthirsty +3	17,000	Any melee
13	Bronzewood +3	17,000	Any melee
13	Chaos weave +3	17,000	Any
13	Cloaked +3	17,000	Any
13	Cold iron +3	17,000	Any
13	Controlling +3	17,000	Polearm
13	Cunning +3	17,000	Any melee
13	Decerebrating +3	17,000	Hammer, Mace
13	Desiccating +3	17,000	Any melee
13	Determined +3	17,000	Any thrown
13	Dread +3	17,000	Any
13	Earthbreaker +3	17,000	Axe, Flail, Hammer, Mace, Pick, Sling
13	Farslayer +3	17,000	Any melee
13	Flanking +3	17,000	Any melee
13	Force +3	17,000	Any
13	Graceful +3	17,000	Flail, Heavy Blade, Light Blade, Spear
13	Inescapable +3	17,000	Any
13	Inspiring +3	17,000	Any
13	Luckblade +3	17,000	Heavy Blade, Light Blade
13	Mace of healing +3	17,000	Mace
13	Mauling +3	17,000	Hammer, Heavy Blade, Mace
13	Necrotic +3	17,000	Axe, Heavy Blade, Light Blade
13	Paired +3	17,000	Any one-handed melee
13	Paralyzing +3	17,000	Any ranged
13	Point blank +3	17,000	Any ranged
13	Predatory +3	17,000	Any
13	Quick +3	17,000	Any
13	Reckless +3	17,000	Any nonreach melee
13	Scalebane +3	17,000	Any
13	Skewering +3	17,000	Pick, Spear
13	Sniper's +3	17,000	Crossbow
13	Stout +3	17,000	Axe, Hammer, Mace, Pick, Staff
13	Strongheart +3	17,000	Any melee
13	Subtle +3	17,000	Any melee
13	Swiftshot +3	17,000	Crossbow
13	Thunderbolt +3	17,000	Any ranged
13	Thundergod +3	17,000	Any melee
13	Tigerclaw gauntlets +3	17,000	Gauntlets
13	Tyrant's +3	17,000	Any melee

Lvl	Name	Price (gp)	Categories
13	Vanguard +3	17,000	Any melee
13	Waterbane +3	17,000	Axe, Crossbow, Light Blade, Heavy Blade, Spear
13	Withering +3	17,000	Any melee
14	Acidic +3	21,000	Heavy Blade, Light Blade, Spear
14	Battlecrazed +3	21,000	Axe, Heavy Blade
14	Battlemaster's +3	21,000	Any
14	Bilethorn +3	21,000	Any melee
14	Communal +3	21,000	Any melee
14	Crusader's +3	21,000	Hammer, Mace
14	Deathstalker +3	21,000	Any
14	Demonbane +3	21,000	Any
14	Feyslaughter +3	21,000	Any
14	Forbidding +3	21,000	Any
14	Healing +3	21,000	Any ranged
14	Lullaby +3	21,000	Flail, Hammer, Mace, Staff
14	Medic's +3	21,000	Any
14	Mindiron +3	21,000	Bow, Crossbow
14	Oathblade +3	21,000	Heavy Blade, Light Blade
14	Opportunistic +3	21,000	Any melee
14	Rending +3	21,000	Axe
14	Shapechanger's sorrow +3	21,000	Axe, Heavy Blade, Light Blade
14	Skyrender +3	21,000	Any ranged
14	Stormbolt +3	21,000	Spear
14	Sunblade +3	21,000	Heavy Blade
14	Thoughtstealer +3	21,000	Any thrown
14	Transposing +3	21,000	Any
14	Vampiric +3	21,000	Heavy Blade, Light Blade
14	Voidcrystal +3	21,000	Any melee
14	Wounding +3	21,000	Axe, Bow, Crossbow, Heavy Blade, Light Blade, Spear
15	Blackshroud +3	25,000	Axe, Heavy Blade, Light Blade
15	Footpad's friend +3	25,000	Light blade
15	Poisoned +3	25,000	Bow, Crossbow, Light Blade, Pick, Spear
15	Radiant +3	25,000	Any
15	Righteous +3	25,000	Any melee
15	Thieving +3	25,000	Light Blade
15	Vengeful +3	25,000	Any melee
16	Battering +4	45,000	Hammer
16	Blacksmelt +4	45,000	Flail, Hammer, Mace
16	Distance +4	45,000	Any ranged
16	Dynamic +4	45,000	Any melee
16	Forceful +4	45,000	Bow
16	Grasping +4	45,000	Polearm, Spear

Lvl	Name	Price (gp)	Categories
16	Ricochet +4	45,000	Sling
16	Sacrificial +4	45,000	Any melee
17	Avandra's whisper +4	65,000	Light Blade
17	Blade of night +4	65,000	Light Blade
17	Bloodclaw +4	65,000	Any melee
17	Defensive +4	65,000	Any
17	Elukian clay +4	65,000	Bow, Crossbow
17	Flesh seeker +4	65,000	Any melee
17	Gambler's +4	65,000	Light Blade
17	Holy healer's +4	65,000	Mace, Staff
17	Jagged +4	65,000	Axe, Heavy Blade, Light Blade
17	Mage's +4	65,000	Heavy Blade, Light Blade
17	Pact hammer +4	65,000	Hammer
17	Pact sword +4	65,000	Longsword
17	Parrying +4	65,000	Any melee
17	Piercing +4	65,000	Spear
17	Pinning +4	65,000	Any melee
17	Prime shot +4	65,000	Any ranged
17	Reproachful +4	65,000	Any melee
17	Retribution +4	65,000	Any melee
17	Splitting +4	65,000	Flail
17	Staggering +4	65,000	Axe, Flail, Hammer, Heavy Blade, Mace
17	Transference +4	65,000	Any
18	Adamantine +4	85,000	Any melee
18	Assassin's +4	85,000	Light Blade
18	Bloodiron +4	85,000	Any
18	Bloodthirsty +4	85,000	Any melee
18	Bronzewood +4	85,000	Any melee
18	Chaos weave +4	85,000	Any
18	Cloaked +4	85,000	Any
18	Cold iron +4	85,000	Any
18	Controlling +4	85,000	Polearm
18	Cunning +4	85,000	Any melee
18	Decerebrating +4	85,000	Hammer, Mace
18	Desiccating +4	85,000	Any melee
18	Determined +4	85,000	Any thrown
18	Dread +4	85,000	Any
18	Earthbreaker +4	85,000	Axe, Flail, Hammer, Mace, Pick, Sling
18	Farslayer +4	85,000	Any melee
18	Flanking +4	85,000	Any melee
18	Force +4	85,000	Any
18	Graceful +4	85,000	Flail, Heavy Blade, Light Blade, Spear
18	Impaling +4	85,000	Any ranged
18	Inescapable +4	85,000	Any
18	Inspiring +4	85,000	Any
18	Luckblade +4	85,000	Heavy Blade, Light Blade
18	Mace of healing +4	85,000	Mace

Lvl	Name	Price (gp)	Categories
18	Mauling +4	85,000	Hammer, Heavy, Blade, Mace
18	Necrotic +4	85,000	Axe, Heavy Blade, Light Blade
18	Paired +4	85,000	Any one-handed melee
18	Paralyzing +4	85,000	Any ranged
18	Point blank +4	85,000	Any ranged
18	Predatory +4	85,000	Any
18	Quick +4	85,000	Any
18	Reckless +4	85,000	Any nonreach melee
18	Scalebane +4	85,000	Any
18	Skewering +4	85,000	Pick, Spear
18	Sniper's +4	85,000	Crossbow
18	Stout +4	85,000	Axe, Hammer, Mace, Pick, Staff
18	Strongheart +4	85,000	Any melee
18	Subtle +4	85,000	Any melee
18	Swiftshot +4	85,000	Crossbow
18	Thunderbolt +4	85,000	Any ranged
18	Thundergod +4	85,000	Any melee
18	Tigerclaw gauntlets +4	85,000	Gauntlets
18	Tyrant's +4	85,000	Any melee
18	Vanguard +4	85,000	Any melee
18	Waterbane +4	85,000	Axe, Crossbow, Light Blade, Heavy Blade, Spear
18	Withering +4	85,000	Any melee
19	Acidic +4	105,000	Heavy Blade, Light Blade, Spear
19	Battlecrazed +4	105,000	Axe, Heavy Blade
19	Battlemaster's +4	105,000	Any
19	Bilethorn +4	105,000	Any melee
19	Communal +4	105,000	Any melee
19	Crusader's +4	105,000	Hammer, Mace
19	Deathstalker +4	105,000	Any
19	Demonbane +4	105,000	Any
19	Feyslaughter +4	105,000	Any
19	Forbidding +4	105,000	Any
19	Healing +4	105,000	Any ranged
19	Lullaby +4	105,000	Flail, Hammer, Mace, Staff
19	Medic's +4	105,000	Any
19	Mindiron +4	105,000	Bow, Crossbow
19	Moradin's +4	105,000	Hammer
19	Oathblade +4	105,000	Heavy Blade, Light Blade
19	Opportunistic +4	105,000	Any melee
19	Blade of Bahamut +4	105,000	Heavy Blade
19	Rending +4	105,000	Axe
19	Shapechanger's sorrow +4	105,000	Axe, Heavy Blade, Light Blade
19	Skyrender +4	105,000	Any ranged
19	Stormbolt +4	105,000	Spear
19	Sunblade +4	105,000	Heavy Blade

Lvl	Name	Price (gp)	Categories
19	Tenacious +4	105,000	Any
19	Thoughtstealer +4	105,000	Any thrown
19	Transposing +4	105,000	Any
19	Vampiric +4	105,000	Heavy Blade, Light Blade
19	Voidcrystal +4	105,000	Any melee
19	Wounding +4	105,000	Axe, Bow, Crossbow, Heavy Blade, Light Blade, Spear
20	Blackshroud +4	125,000	Axe, Heavy Blade, Light Blade
20	Footpad's friend + 4	125,000	Light blade
20	Jarring +4	125,000	Flail, Hammer, Mace
20	Lucklender +4	125,000	Any
20	Poisoned +4	125,000	Bow, Crossbow, Light Blade, Pick, Spear
20	Radiant +4	125,000	Any
20	Righteous +4	125,000	Any melee
20	Thieving +4	125,000	Light Blade
20	Vengeful +4	125,000	Any melee
21	Battering +5	225,000	Hammer
21	Blacksmelt +5	225,000	Flail, Hammer, Mace
21	Distance +5	225,000	Any ranged
21	Dynamic + 5	225,000	Any melee
21	Forceful +5	225,000	Bow
21	Grasping +5	225,000	Polearm, Spear
21	Ricochet +5	225,000	Sling
21	Sacrificial +5	225,000	Any melee
22	Avandra's whisper +5	325,000	Light Blade
22	Blade of night +5	325,000	Light Blade
22	Bloodclaw +5	325,000	Any melee
22	Defensive +5	325,000	Any
22	Elukian clay +5	325,000	Bow, Crossbow
22	Flesh seeker +5	325,000	Any melee
22	Gambler's +5	325,000	Light Blade
22	Holy healer's +5	325,000	Mace, Staff
22	Jagged +5	325,000	Axe, Heavy Blade, Light Blade
22	Mage's +5	325,000	Heavy Blade, Light Blade
22	Pact hammer +5	325,000	Hammer
22	Pact sword +5	325,000	Longsword
22	Parrying +5	325,000	Any melee
22	Piercing +5	325,000	Spear
22	Pinning +5	325,000	Any melee
22	Prime shot +5	325,000	Any ranged
22	Reproachful +5	325,000	Any melee
22	Retribution +5	325,000	Any melee
22	Shadow spike +5	325,000	Light Blade
22	Splitting +5	325,000	Flail

Lvl	Name	Price (gp)	Categories
22	Staggering +5	325,000	Axe, Flail, Hammer, Heavy Blade, Mace
22	Transference +5	325,000	Any
23	Adamantine +5	425,000	Any melee
23	Assassin's +5	425,000	Light Blade
23	Bloodiron +5	425,000	Any
23	Bloodthirsty +5	425,000	Any melee
23	Bronzewood +5	425,000	Any melee
23	Chaos weave +5	425,000	Any
23	Cloaked +5	425,000	Any
23	Cold iron +5	425,000	Any
23	Controlling +5	425,000	Polearm
23	Cunning +5	425,000	Any melee
23	Decerebrating +5	425,000	Hammer, Mace
23	Desiccating +5	425,000	Any melee
23	Determined +5	425,000	Any thrown
23	Dread +5	425,000	Any
23	Earthbreaker +5	425,000	Axe, Flail, Hammer, Mace, Pick, Sling
23	Farslayer +5	425,000	Any melee
23	Flanking +5	425,000	Any melee
23	Force +5	425,000	Any
23	Graceful +5	425,000	Flail, Heavy Blade, Light Blade, Spear
23	Impaling +5	425,000	Any ranged
23	Inescapable +5	425,000	Any
23	Inspiring +5	425,000	Any
23	Luckblade +5	425,000	Heavy Blade, Light Blade
23	Mace of healing +5	425,000	Mace
23	Mauling +5	425,000	Hammer, Heavy Blade, Mace
23	Necrotic +5	425,000	Axe, Heavy Blade, Light Blade
23	Paired +5	425,000	Any one-handed melee
23	Paralyzing +5	425,000	Any ranged
23	Point blank +5	425,000	Any ranged
23	Predatory +5	425,000	Any
23	Quick +5	425,000	Any
23	Reckless +5	425,000	Any nonreach melee
23	Scalebane +5	425,000	Any
23	Skewering +5	425,000	Pick, Spear
23	Sniper's +5	425,000	Crossbow
23	Stout +5	425,000	Axe, Hammer, Mace, Pick, Staff
23	Strongheart +5	425,000	Any melee
23	Subtle +5	425,000	Any melee
23	Swiftshot +5	425,000	Crossbow
23	Thunderbolt +5	425,000	Any ranged
23	Thundergod +5	425,000	Any melee
23	Tigerclaw gauntlets +5	425,000	Gauntlets
23	Tyrant's +5	425,000	Any melee

Lvl	Name	Price (gp)	Categories
23	Vanguard +5	425,000	Any melee
23	Waterbane +5	425,000	Axe, Crossbow, Light Blade, Heavy Blade, Spear
23	Withering +5	425,000	Any melee
24	Acidic +5	525,000	Heavy Blade, Light Blade, Spear
24	Battlecrazed +5	525,000	Axe, Heavy Blade
24	Battlemaster's +5	525,000	Any
24	Bilethorn +5	525,000	Any melee
24	Communal +5	525,000	Any melee
24	Crusader's +5	525,000	Hammer, Mace
24	Deathstalker +5	525,000	Any
24	Demonbane +5	525,000	Any
24	Feyslaughter +5	525,000	Any
24	Forbidding +5	525,000	Any
24	Healing +5	525,000	Any ranged
24	Lullaby +5	525,000	Flail, Hammer, Mace, Staff
24	Medic's +5	525,000	Any
24	Mindiron +5	525,000	Bow, Crossbow
24	Moradin's +5	525,000	Hammer
24	Oathblade +5	525,000	Heavy Blade, Light Blade
24	Opportunistic +5	525,000	Any melee
24	Blade of Bahamut +5	525,000	Heavy Blade
24	Rending +5	525,000	Axe
24	Shapechanger's sorrow +5	525,000	Axe, Heavy Blade, Light Blade
24	Skyrender +5	525,000	Any ranged
24	Stormbolt +5	525,000	Spear
24	Sunblade +5	525,000	Heavy Blade
24	Tenacious +5	525,000	Any
24	Thoughtstealer +5	525,000	Any thrown
24	Transposing +5	525,000	Any
24	Vampiric +5	525,000	Heavy Blade, Light Blade
24	Voidcrystal +5	525,000	Any melee
24	Wounding +5	525,000	Axe, Bow, Crossbow, Heavy Blade, Light Blade, Spear
25	Blackshroud +5	625,000	Axe, Heavy Blade, Light Blade
25	Brilliant energy +5	625,000	Any
25	Footpad's friend +5	625,000	Light blade
25	Ghost chain +5	625,000	Any ranged
25	Jarring +5	625,000	Flail, Hammer, Mace
25	Legendary +5	625,000	Any
25	Lucklender +5	625,000	Any
25	Overreaching +5	625,000	Polearm
25	Poisoned +5	625,000	Bow, Crossbow, Light Blade, Pick, Spear
25	Radiant +5	625,000	Any
25	Righteous +5	625,000	Any melee
25	Thieving +5	625,000	Light Blade
25	Trespasser's bane +5	625,000	Any
25	Vengeful +5	625,000	Any melee
26	Battering +6	1,125,000	Hammer
26	Blacksmelt +6	1,125,000	Flail, Hammer, Mace
26	Distance +6	1,125,000	Any ranged
26	Dynamic +6	1,125,000	Any melee
26	Forceful +6	1,125,000	Bow
26	Grasping +6	1,125,000	Polearm, Spear
26	Ricochet +6	1,125,000	Sling
26	Sacrificial +6	1,125,000	Any melee
27	Avandra's whisper +6	1,625,000	Light Blade
27	Blade of night +6	1,625,000	Light Blade
27	Bloodclaw +6	1,625,000	Any melee
27	Defensive +6	1,625,000	Any
27	Elukian clay +6	1,625,000	Bow, Crossbow
27	Flesh seeker +6	1,625,000	Any melee
27	Gambler's +6	1,625,000	Light Blade
27	Holy healer's +6	1,625,000	Mace, Staff
27	Jagged +6	1,625,000	Axe, Heavy Blade, Light Blade
27	Mage's +6	1,625,000	Heavy Blade, Light Blade
27	Pact hammer +6	1,625,000	Hammer
27	Pact sword +6	1,625,000	Longsword
27	Parrying +6	1,625,000	Any melee
27	Piercing +6	1,625,000	Spear
27	Pinning +6	1,625,000	Any melee
27	Prime shot +6	1,625,000	Any ranged
27	Reproachful +6	1,625,000	Any melee
27	Retribution +6	1,625,000	Any melee
27	Shadow spike +6	1,625,000	Light Blade
27	Splitting +6	1,625,000	Flail
27	Staggering +6	1,625,000	Axe, Flail, Hammer, Heavy Blade, Mace
27	Transference +6	1,625,000	Any
28	Adamantine +6	2,125,000	Any melee
28	Assassin's +6	2,125,000	Light Blade
28	Bloodiron +6	2,125,000	Any
28	Bloodthirsty +6	2,125,000	Any melee
28	Bronzewood +6	2,125,000	Any melee
28	Chaos weave +6	2,125,000	Any
28	Cloaked +6	2,125,000	Any
28	Cold iron +6	2,125,000	Any
28	Controlling +6	2,125,000	Polearm
28	Cunning +6	2,125,000	Any melee
28	Decerebrating +6	2,125,000	Hammer, Mace
28	Desiccating +6	2,125,000	Any melee
28	Determined +6	2,125,000	Any thrown
28	Dread +6	2,125,000	Any
28	Earthbreaker +6	2,125,000	Axe, Flail, Hammer, Mace, Pick, Sling

Lvl	Name	Price (gp)	Categories
28	Farslayer +6	2,125,000	Any melee
28	Flanking +6	2,125,000	Any melee
28	Force +6	2,125,000	Any
28	Graceful +6	2,125,000	Flail, Heavy Blade, Light Blade, Spear
28	Impaling +6	2,125,000	Any ranged
28	Inescapable +6	2,125,000	Any
28	Inspiring +6	2,125,000	Any
28	Luckblade +6	2,125,000	Heavy Blade, Light Blade
28	Mace of healing +6	2,125,000	Mace
28	Mauling +6	2,125,000	Hammer, Heavy Blade, Mace
28	Necrotic +6	2,125,000	Axe, Heavy Blade, Light Blade
28	Paired +6	2,125,000	Any one-handed melee
28	Paralyzing +6	2,125,000	Any ranged
28	Point blank +6	2,125,000	Any ranged
28	Predatory +6	2,125,000	Any
28	Quick +6	2,125,000	Any
28	Reckless +6	2,125,000	Any nonreach melee
28	Scalebane +6	2,125,000	Any
28	Skewering +6	2,125,000	Pick, Spear
28	Sniper's +6	2,125,000	Crossbow
28	Stout +6	2,125,000	Axe, Hammer, Mace, Pick, Staff
28	Strongheart +6	2,125,000	Any melee
28	Subtle +6	2,125,000	Any melee
28	Swiftshot +6	2,125,000	Crossbow
28	Thunderbolt +6	2,125,000	Any ranged
28	Thundergod +6	2,125,000	Any melee
28	Tigerclaw gauntlets +6	2,125,000	Gauntlets
28	Tyrant's +6	2,125,000	Any melee
28	Vanguard +6	2,125,000	Any melee
28	Waterbane +6	2,125,000	Axe, Crossbow, Light Blade, Heavy Blade, Spear
28	Withering +6	2,125,000	Any melee
29	Acidic +6	2,625,000	Heavy Blade, Light Blade, Spear
29	Battlecrazed +6	2,625,000	Axe, Heavy Blade
29	Battlemaster's +6	2,625,000	Any
29	Bilethorn +6	2,625,000	Any melee
29	Communal +6	2,625,000	Any melee
29	Crusader's +6	2,625,000	Hammer, Mace
29	Deathstalker +6	2,625,000	Any
29	Demonbane +6	2,625,000	Any
29	Feyslaughter +6	2,625,000	Any
29	Forbidding +6	2,625,000	Any
29	Healing +6	2,625,000	Any ranged
29	Lullaby +6	2,625,000	Flail, Hammer, Mace, Staff
29	Medic's +6	2,625,000	Any
29	Mindiron +6	2,625,000	Bow, Crossbow

Lvl	Name	Price (gp)	Categories
29	Moradin's +6	2,625,000	Hammer
29	Oathblade +6	2,625,000	Heavy Blade, Light Blade
29	Opportunistic +6	2,625,000	Any melee
29	Blade of Bahamut +6	2,625,000	Heavy Blade
29	Rending +6	2,625,000	Axe
29	Shapechanger's sorrow +6	2,625,000	Axe, Heavy Blade, Light Blade
29	Skyrender +6	2,625,000	Any ranged
29	Stormbolt +6	2,625,000	Spear
29	Sunblade +6	2,625,000	Heavy Blade
29	Tenacious +6	2,625,000	Any
29	Thoughtstealer +6	2,625,000	Any thrown
29	Transposing +6	2,625,000	Any
29	Vampiric +6	2,625,000	Heavy Blade, Light Blade
29	Voidcrystal +6	2,625,000	Any melee
29	Wounding +6	2,625,000	Axe, Bow, Crossbow, Heavy Blade, Light Blade, Spear
30	Blackshroud +6	3,125,000	Axe, Heavy Blade, Light Blade
30	Brilliant energy +6	3,125,000	Any
30	Footpad's friend + 6	3,125,000	Light blade
30	Ghost chain +6	3,125,000	Any ranged
30	Jarring +6	3,125,000	Flail, Hammer, Mace
30	Legendary +6	3,125,000	Any
30	Lucklender +6	3,125,000	Any
30	Overreaching +6	3,125,000	Polearm
30	Poisoned +6	3,125,000	Bow, Crossbow, Light Blade, Pick, Spear
30	Radiant +6	3,125,000	Any
30	Righteous +6	3,125,000	Any melee
30	Thieving +6	3,125,000	Light Blade
30	Trespasser's bane +6	3,125,000	Any
30	Vengeful +6	3,125,000	Any melee

Acidic Weapon — Level 4+

A stream of acid lashes out from this melee weapon, burning a target who might otherwise be out of reach.

Lvl 4	+1	840 gp	Lvl 19	+4	105,000 gp
Lvl 9	+2	4,200 gp	Lvl 24	+5	525,000 gp
Lvl 14	+3	21,000 gp	Lvl 29	+6	2,625,000 gp

Weapon: Heavy Blade, Light Blade, Spear

Enhancement: Attack rolls and damage rolls

Critical: +1d6 acid damage per plus

Power (Encounter ✦ Acid): Standard Action. Make a melee basic attack with the weapon against a target within 5 squares of you. All damage dealt by this basic attack is acid damage.

Power (Daily ✦ Acid): Free Action. Use this power when you hit with the weapon. Deal ongoing 5 acid damage (save ends).

Level 14 or 19: Ongoing 10 acid damage.

Level 24 or 29: Ongoing 15 acid damage.

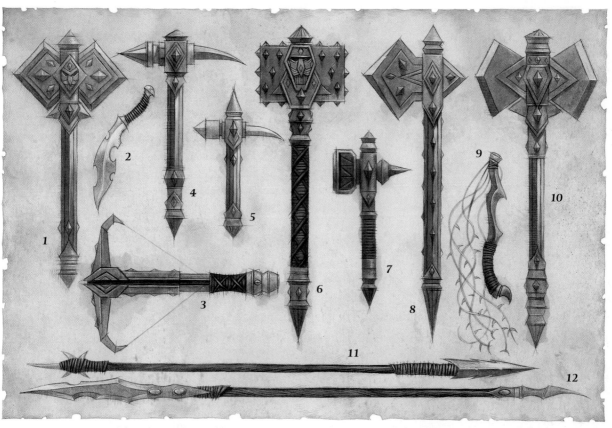

1. Waraxe; 2. Kukri; 3. Superior crossbow; 4. Heavy war pick; 5. Light war pick; 6. Mordenkrad; 7. Craghammer; 8. Urgrosh; 9. Scourge; 10. Execution axe; 11. Tratnyr; 12. Greatspear

Adamantine Weapon — Level 8+

This glossy black weapon pierces the toughest shells.

Lvl 8	+2	3,400 gp	Lvl 23	+5	425,000 gp
Lvl 13	+3	17,000 gp	Lvl 28	+6	2,125,000 gp
Lvl 18	+4	85,000 gp			

Weapon: Any melee

Enhancement: Attack rolls and damage rolls

Critical: +1d10 damage per plus

Property: Untyped damage done with this weapon ignores a number of points of resistance equal to twice the weapon's enhancement bonus.

Assassin's Weapon — Level 8+

A favored weapon of rogues and assassins, this plain-looking blade contains the power to afflict victims with a deadly poison.

Lvl 8	+2	3,400 gp	Lvl 23	+5	425,000 gp
Lvl 13	+3	17,000 gp	Lvl 28	+6	2,125,000 gp
Lvl 18	+4	85,000 gp			

Weapon: Light Blade

Enhancement: Attack rolls and damage rolls

Critical: Ongoing 5 poison damage (save ends)

Level 13: Ongoing 7 poison damage (save ends)

Level 18: Ongoing 10 poison damage (save ends)

Level 23: Ongoing 12 poison damage (save ends)

Level 28: Ongoing 15 poison damage (save ends)

Power (Daily ✦ Poison): Free Action. Use this power when you hit with this weapon. The target takes ongoing 5 poison damage and is slowed (save ends both).

Level 13 or 18: Ongoing 10 poison damage.

Level 23 or 28: Ongoing 15 poison damage.

Avandra's Whisper — Level 17+

Followers of Avandra use these blades to channel her powers of luck.

Lvl 17	+4	65,000 gp	Lvl 27	+6	1,625,000 gp
Lvl 22	+5	325,000 gp			

Weapon: Light Blade

Enhancement: Attack rolls and damage rolls

Critical: +1d6 damage per plus

Property: If you worship Avandra, you can use this weapon as a holy symbol. It adds its enhancement bonus (but not its proficiency bonus) to attack rolls and damage rolls when used in this manner. If you do not worship Avandra, you do not benefit from this weapon's property and cannot use this weapon's power.

Power (Daily): Free Action. Reroll one attack roll or damage roll made with this weapon. You must use the result of the second roll.

Battering Weapon — Level 11+

This hammer rumbles with seismic power.

Lvl 11	+3	9,000 gp	Lvl 21	+5	225,000 gp
Lvl 16	+4	45,000 gp	Lvl 26	+6	1,125,000 gp

Weapon: Hammer

Enhancement: Attack rolls and damage rolls

Critical: None

Power (Daily): Standard Action. Make a melee basic attack with this weapon against all enemies within a close blast 3.

Battering weapon

Battlecrazed Weapon Level 4+

The weapon seeks blood where it can be found, whether among the enemy or from its wielder.

Lvl 4	+1	840 gp	Lvl 19	+4	105,000 gp
Lvl 9	+2	4,200 gp	Lvl 24	+5	525,000 gp
Lvl 14	+3	21,000 gp	Lvl 29	+6	2,625,000 gp

Weapon: Axe, Heavy Blade

Enhancement: Attack rolls and damage rolls

Critical: +1d6 per plus

Property: While you are bloodied, you deal +1d6 damage when you hit with this weapon.

Level 14 or 19: +2d6 damage while bloodied.

Level 24 or 29: +3d6 damage while bloodied.

Power (Daily): Minor Action. Deal damage to yourself equal to half your level, ignoring any resistances. You are considered bloodied for all purposes (including beneficial effects, such as Dragonborn Fury and this weapon's property) until the end of your next turn.

Battlemaster's Weapon Level 14+

This weapon lets you reuse exhausted powers.

Lvl 14	+3	21,000 gp	Lvl 24	+5	525,000 gp
Lvl 19	+4	105,000 gp	Lvl 29	+6	2,625,000 gp

Weapon: Any

Enhancement: Attack rolls and damage rolls

Critical: +1d6 damage per plus

Power (Daily): Minor Action. You regain the use of one encounter power.

Bilethorn Weapon Level 14+

Poison covers the sleek surface of this weapon.

Lvl 14	+3	21,000 gp	Lvl 24	+5	525,000 gp
Lvl 19	+4	105,000 gp	Lvl 29	+6	2,625,000 gp

Weapon: Any melee

Enhancement: Attack rolls and damage rolls

Critical: +1d6 poison damage per plus

Power (Daily ✦ Poison): Free Action. Use this power when you hit with a melee basic attack. At the start of your next turn, your target takes the damage again, but all of the damage is poison.

Blackshroud Weapon Level 10+

Whenever this weapon snuffs out the life force of an enemy, it grants a boon in return.

Lvl 10	+2	5,000 gp	Lvl 25	+5	625,000 gp
Lvl 15	+3	25,000 gp	Lvl 30	+6	3,125,000 gp
Lvl 20	+4	125,000 gp			

Weapon: Axe, Heavy Blade, Light Blade

Enhancement: Attack rolls and damage rolls

Critical: Gain 1d8 temporary hit points per plus.

Property: Whenever an attack with this weapon reduces a target to 0 hit points or fewer, you gain concealment until the end of your next turn.

Blacksmelt Weapon Level 11+

This weapon can break through virtually any material.

Lvl 11	+3	9,000 gp	Lvl 21	+5	225,000 gp
Lvl 16	+4	45,000 gp	Lvl 26	+6	1,125,000 gp

Weapon: Flail, Hammer, Mace

Enhancement: Attack rolls and damage rolls

Critical: None

Power (Daily): Minor Action. Your attacks with this weapon deal extra damage equal to the weapon's enhancement bonus until the end of your next turn.

Blade of Bahamut Level 19+

Emblazoned with the holy symbol of Bahamut, this platinum blade empowers the wielder to unleash divine retribution upon enemies while bolstering his or her allies.

Lvl 19	+4	105,000 gp	Lvl 29	+6	2,625,000 gp
Lvl 24	+5	525,000 gp			

Weapon: Heavy Blade

Enhancement: Attack rolls and damage rolls

Critical: +1d10 damage per plus

Property: If you worship Bahamut, you can use this weapon as a holy symbol. It adds its enhancement bonus (but not its proficiency bonus) to attack rolls and damage rolls when used in this manner. If you do not worship Bahamut, you do not benefit from this weapon's property and cannot use this weapon's power.

Power (Daily ✦ Force): Standard Action. Close blast 5; targets enemies; Charisma vs. Reflex (apply a bonus to the attack roll equal to the weapon's enhancement bonus); 2d8 + Charisma modifier force damage. Allies in the blast take no damage and regain hit points equal to your Wisdom modifier + your Charisma modifier.

Level 29: 3d8 + Charisma modifier force damage.

Blade of Night — Level 12+

When the wielder of this blade strikes at an enemy's vulnerable spot, he magically blinds the target as well.

Lvl 12	+3	13,000 gp	Lvl 22	+5	325,000 gp
Lvl 17	+4	65,000 gp	Lvl 27	+6	1,625,000 gp

Weapon: Light Blade

Enhancement: Attack rolls and damage rolls

Critical: The target is blinded until the end of your next turn.

Power (Daily ✦ Zone): Minor Action. Use this power to create a zone in a close burst 2. The zone blocks line of sight and lasts until the end of your next turn.

Bloodclaw Weapon — Level 2+

The hilt of this weapon digs into its wielder's hand, drawing blood while inflicting a more grievous wound upon an enemy.

Lvl 2	+1	520 gp	Lvl 17	+4	65,000 gp
Lvl 7	+2	2,600 gp	Lvl 22	+5	325,000 gp
Lvl 12	+3	13,000 gp	Lvl 27	+6	1,625,000 gp

Weapon: Any melee

Enhancement: Attack rolls and damage rolls

Critical: +1d6 damage per plus

Power (At-Will): Free Action. Use this power before making a melee attack on your turn. You take damage up to a maximum of the weapon's enhancement bonus (a +3 weapon deals up to 3 damage to its wielder). This damage cannot be reduced or prevented in any way. If you hit, increase the damage your target takes by double the amount of damage you took, triple if you are wielding the weapon in two hands.

Bloodiron Weapon — Level 13+

Forged from iron tainted with the ichor of devils, this weapon is cruel.

Lvl 13	+3	17,000 gp	Lvl 23	+5	425,000 gp
Lvl 18	+4	85,000 gp	Lvl 28	+6	2,125,000 gp

Weapon: Any

Enhancement: Attack rolls and damage rolls

Critical: +1d10 damage per plus

Property: When you deal extra critical hit damage with this weapon, deal the extra critical hit damage to the target again at the start of your next turn.

Bloodthirsty Weapon — Level 13+

This weapon drinks the blood of its victims.

Lvl 13	+3	17,000 gp	Lvl 23	+5	425,000 gp
Lvl 18	+4	85,000 gp	Lvl 28	+6	2,125,000 gp

Weapon: Any melee

Enhancement: Attack rolls and damage rolls

Critical: +1d10 damage per plus

Property: Gain a +1 item bonus to attack rolls against bloodied targets, and add an item bonus equal to the enhancement bonus of this weapon to damage rolls against bloodied targets.

Brilliant Energy Weapon — Level 25+

Infused with light, this weapon passes through armor and into flesh.

Lvl 25	+5	625,000 gp	Lvl 30	+6	3,125,000 gp

Weapon: Any

Enhancement: Attack rolls and damage rolls

Critical: +1d10 radiant damage per plus

Property: This weapon gives off bright light in a 5-square radius unless covered and sheathed.

Power (At-Will ✦ Radiant): Free Action. All damage dealt by this weapon is radiant damage. Another free action returns the damage to normal.

Power (Encounter ✦ Radiant): Free Action. Use this power when making an attack that targets AC. The attack targets Reflex defense instead. All damage from the attack is radiant damage.

Bronzewood Weapon — Level 8+

Creatures of the Shadowfell react poorly to this hard, red-brown wood.

Lvl 8	+2	3,400 gp	Lvl 23	+5	425,000 gp
Lvl 13	+3	17,000 gp	Lvl 28	+6	2,125,000 gp
Lvl 18	+4	85,000 gp			

Weapon: Any melee

Enhancement: Attack rolls and damage rolls

Critical: +1d6 damage per plus, or +1d10 damage per plus against shadow creatures.

Power (Daily): Free Action. Use this power when you hit with the weapon. The target is outlined by a golden nimbus and does not gain the benefit of concealment or cover (save ends). The target benefits from total concealment or superior cover as normal. If the target is a creature that has the shadow origin, then it also takes a -2 penalty to attack rolls (ends on same save as above).

Chaos Weave Weapon — Level 13+

Forged from the quintessence of the Elemental Chaos, this weapon pierces demons' defenses.

Lvl 13	+3	17,000 gp	Lvl 23	+5	425,000 gp
Lvl 18	+4	85,000 gp	Lvl 28	+6	2,125,000 gp

Weapon: Any

Enhancement: Attack rolls and damage rolls

Critical: +1d6 damage per plus, or +1d12 damage per plus against a creature that has variable resistance.

Property: Attacks with this weapon ignore an amount of variable resistance equal to twice the weapon's enhancement bonus.

Cloaked Weapon — Level 8+

This naturally invisible weapon becomes visible when it hits.

Lvl 8	+2	3,400 gp	Lvl 23	+5	425,000 gp
Lvl 13	+3	17,000 gp	Lvl 28	+6	2,125,000 gp
Lvl 18	+4	85,000 gp			

Weapon: Any

Enhancement: Attack rolls and damage rolls

Critical: +1d6 damage per plus

Property: This weapon is invisible to everyone but the creature possessing it. As the wielder of the weapon, you gain combat advantage with melee attacks made using the weapon until you successfully hit, at which point the weapon becomes visible to everyone.

A cloaked weapon turns invisible again after being sheathed for a short rest (5 minutes).

Cold Iron Weapon — Level 8+

Denizens of the Feywild loathe this weapon forged from the coldest, darkest iron.

Lvl 8	+2	3,400 gp	Lvl 23	+5	425,000 gp
Lvl 13	+3	17,000 gp	Lvl 28	+6	2,125,000 gp
Lvl 18	+4	85,000 gp			

Weapon: Any

Enhancement: Attack rolls and damage rolls

Critical: +1d6 damage per plus, or +1d10 damage per plus against fey creatures

Power (Daily): Free Action. Use this power when you hit with the weapon. The target is immobilized (save ends). If the target is a creature that has the fey origin, it also takes 1d10 damage.

Level 13 or 18: 2d10 damage.
Level 23 or 28: 3d10 damage.

Communal Weapon — Level 4+

Combat can bring some people together, and you can lend aid to your allies with this weapon.

Lvl 4	+1	840 gp	Lvl 19	+4	105,000 gp
Lvl 9	+2	4,200 gp	Lvl 24	+5	525,000 gp
Lvl 14	+3	21,000 gp	Lvl 29	+6	2,625,000 gp

Weapon: Any melee

Enhancement: Attack rolls and damage rolls

Critical: +1d6 damage per plus

Power (At-Will): Free Action. Use this power after an ally within 5 squares of you makes a d20 roll. Add a +1 power bonus to the result. You can do this a number of times in a day equal to the enhancement bonus of the weapon.

Controlling Weapon — Level 8+

Waves of force radiate from this polearm when it hits its target, forcing the creature to move.

Lvl 8	+2	3,400 gp	Lvl 23	+5	425,000 gp
Lvl 13	+3	17,000 gp	Lvl 28	+6	2,125,000 gp
Lvl 18	+4	85,000 gp			

Weapon: Polearm

Enhancement: Attack rolls and damage rolls

Critical: +1d6 damage per plus

Property: When you pull or push a target with this weapon, increase the effect by 1 square.

Power (Encounter): Free Action. Use this power when you would pull or push a target with this weapon. You slide the target the same distance instead.

Crusader's Weapon — Level 9+

Those who hunt undead favor this weapon for its ability to strike at the creatures' vulnerabilities.

Lvl 9	+2	4,200 gp	Lvl 24	+5	525,000 gp
Lvl 14	+3	21,000 gp	Lvl 29	+3	2,625,000 gp
Lvl 19	+4	105,000 gp			

Weapon: Hammer, Mace

Enhancement: Attack rolls and damage rolls

Critical: +1d6 per plus, or +1d10 damage per plus against undead creatures.

Property: Half the damage dealt with this weapon is radiant damage.

Property: You can use this weapon as a holy symbol. It adds its enhancement bonus to attack rolls and damage rolls when used in this manner.

Power (Daily): Standard Action. Gain one additional use of Channel Divinity for this encounter.

JASON A. ENGLE

Cunning Weapon · Level 8+

Finely crafted and ornately etched, this weapon makes its target succumb more easily to adverse conditions.

Lvl 8	+2	3,400 gp	Lvl 23	+5	425,000 gp
Lvl 13	+3	17,000 gp	Lvl 28	+6	2,125,000 gp
Lvl 18	+4	85,000 gp			

Weapon: Any melee

Enhancement: Attack rolls and damage rolls

Critical: +1d8 damage per plus

Property: Against any effect delivered with this weapon that a save can end, the target takes a -2 penalty to saving throws.
Level 18 or 23: -3 penalty to saving throws.
Level 28: -4 penalty to saving throws.

Deathstalker Weapon · Level 4+

This weapon leaves a wound that is black and withered, which continues to plague an enemy long after the attack was made.

Lvl 4	+1	840 gp	Lvl 19	+4	105,000 gp
Lvl 9	+2	4,200 gp	Lvl 24	+5	525,000 gp
Lvl 14	+3	21,000 gp	Lvl 29	+6	2,625,000 gp

Weapon: Any

Enhancement: Attack rolls and damage rolls

Critical: +1d6 necrotic damage per plus

Power (Daily ✦ Necrotic): Free Action. Use this power when you hit with the weapon. The target takes ongoing 5 necrotic damage (save ends). Saves made to end this effect take a -2 penalty.
Level 12 or 17: Ongoing 10 necrotic.
Level 22 or 27: Ongoing 15 necrotic.

Decerebrating Weapon · Level 8+

This weapon shatters the mind and batters the senses.

Lvl 8	+2	3,400 gp	Lvl 23	+5	425,000 gp
Lvl 13	+3	17,000 gp	Lvl 28	+6	2,125,000 gp
Lvl 18	+4	85,000 gp			

Weapon: Hammer, Mace

Enhancement: Attack rolls and damage rolls

Critical: +1d6 damage per plus, and the target takes a -2 penalty to Will defense until the end of your next turn.

Power (Daily): Free Action. Use this power when you hit with the weapon. Your target takes a -2 penalty to Will defense until the end of your next turn.

Defensive Weapon · Level 2+

This weapon glows blue when its wielder takes a second wind or goes on total defense.

Lvl 2	+1	520 gp	Lvl 17	+4	65,000 gp
Lvl 7	+2	2,600 gp	Lvl 22	+5	325,000 gp
Lvl 12	+3	13,000 gp	Lvl 27	+6	1,625,000 gp

Weapon: Any

Enhancement: Attack rolls and damage rolls

Critical: +1d6 damage per plus

Property: When you take the total defense or second wind action, add the enhancement bonus of this weapon as an item bonus to all of your defenses until the start of your next turn.

Demonbane Weapon · Level 9+

This weapon glimmers with white flecks of energy from the Astral Sea that are anathema to demons.

Lvl 9	+2	4,200 gp	Lvl 24	+5	525,000 gp
Lvl 14	+3	21,000 gp	Lvl 29	+3	2,625,000 gp
Lvl 19	+4	105,000 gp			

Weapon: Any

Enhancement: Attack rolls and damage rolls

Critical: +1d8 damage per plus, or +1d10 damage per plus against demons.

Property: You regain resist equal to the enhancement bonus of the weapon to damage dealt by demons.

Power (Daily): Free Action. Use this power when you attack a demon with this weapon. Gain a +5 power bonus to the attack roll and ignore any resist value the demon has.

Desiccating Weapon · Level 13+

This weapon weakens the body of an enemy with each new strike.

Lvl 13	+3	17,000 gp	Lvl 23	+5	425,000 gp
Lvl 18	+4	85,000 gp	Lvl 28	+6	2,125,000 gp

Weapon: Any melee

Enhancement: Attack rolls and damage rolls

Critical: +1d6 damage per plus

Property: Each time you hit with this weapon, your target takes a cumulative -1 penalty to its Fortitude defense (save ends). One saving throw ends the entire penalty, though the target can receive the penalty again with future attacks.

Determined Weapon · Level 8+

When you throw this weapon, it continues to attack your foe before returning to you.

Lvl 8	+2	3,400 gp	Lvl 23	+5	425,000 gp
Lvl 13	+3	17,000 gp	Lvl 28	+6	2,125,000 gp
Lvl 18	+4	85,000 gp			

Weapon: Any thrown

Enhancement: Attack rolls and damage rolls

Critical: +1d6 damage per plus

Property: Increase this item's normal range and long range by your Strength modifier or your Dexterity modifier.

Power (Daily): Free Action. Use this power after you miss with a ranged attack using this weapon. This weapon does not return to you this turn. At the start of the target's next turn, make a ranged basic attack with this weapon against that target. After this attack, the weapon returns to you.

Distance Weapon
Level 1+

This weapon flashes brightly as it hurtles forth, moving with enough force to carry it much farther than normal.

Lvl 1	+1	360 gp	Lvl 16	+4	45,000 gp
Lvl 6	+2	1,800 gp	Lvl 21	+5	225,000 gp
Lvl 11	+3	9,000 gp	Lvl 26	+6	1,125,000 gp

Weapon: Any ranged

Enhancement: Attack rolls and damage rolls

Critical: None

Property: Increase the weapon's normal range by 5 squares and the long range by 10 squares.

Dread Weapon
Level 8+

Those who suffer a telling blow from this weapon fill with despair, losing all hope.

Lvl 8	+2	3,400 gp	Lvl 23	+5	425,000 gp
Lvl 13	+3	17,000 gp	Lvl 28	+6	2,125,000 gp
Lvl 18	+4	85,000 gp			

Weapon: Any

Enhancement: Attack rolls and damage rolls

Critical: +1d6 damage per plus, and the target takes the weapon's enhancement bonus as a penalty to defenses and checks until the end of your next turn.

Power (Daily ✦ Fear): Free Action. Use this power when you hit with this weapon. The target takes the weapon's enhancement bonus as a penalty to defenses and checks until the end of your next turn.

Dynamic Weapon
Level 6+

This weapon transforms into any other melee weapon that its wielder desires.

Lvl 6	+2	1,800 gp	Lvl 21	+5	225,000 gp
Lvl 11	+3	9,000 gp	Lvl 26	+6	1,125,000 gp
Lvl 16	+4	45,000 gp			

Weapon: Any melee

Enhancement: Attack rolls and damage rolls

Critical: +1d6 damage per plus

Power (Encounter ✦ Polymorph): Minor Action. Change the weapon into a different weapon from any melee category (simple, military, or superior). This effect lasts until the end of the encounter, or until you end it as a minor action.

Earthbreaker Weapon
Level 8+

Creatures of the earth suffer most at the strike of this weapon.

Lvl 8	+2	3,400 gp	Lvl 23	+5	425,000 gp
Lvl 13	+3	17,000 gp	Lvl 28	+6	2,125,000 gp
Lvl 18	+4	85,000 gp			

Weapon: Axe, Flail, Hammer, Mace, Pick, Sling

Enhancement: Attack rolls and damage rolls

Critical: +1d6 damage per plus, and a target that has the earth or plant keyword is also dazed until the end of your next turn.

Power (Daily): Free Action. Use this power when you hit with the weapon. The target is restrained (save ends). If the target has the earth or plant keyword, it takes a -5 penalty to the saving throw.

Elukian Clay Weapon
Level 12+

This stone bow has surprising flexibility.

| Lvl 12 | +3 | 13,000 gp | Lvl 22 | +5 | 325,000 gp |
| Lvl 17 | +4 | 65,000 gp | Lvl 27 | +6 | 1,625,000 gp |

Weapon: Bow, Crossbow

Enhancement: Attack rolls and damage rolls

Critical: +1d6 damage per plus

Property: You can draw this weapon as part of the same action used to attack with this weapon.

Power (Daily): Free Action. Use this power when you miss with an attack using this weapon. Reroll the attack with a +2 power bonus. You must take the result of the reroll.

Farslayer Weapon
Level 13+

As you swing this weapon through the air, wounds magically appear on enemies beyond your normal reach.

| Lvl 13 | +3 | 17,000 gp | Lvl 23 | +5 | 425,000 gp |
| Lvl 18 | +4 | 85,000 gp | Lvl 28 | +6 | 2,125,000 gp |

Weapon: Any melee

Enhancement: Attack rolls and damage rolls

Critical: +1d6 damage per plus

Power (At-Will): Standard Action. Make a melee basic attack with this weapon against a target up to 5 squares away from you.

Feyslaughter Weapon
Level 9+

A bane of fey and teleporting creatures, this blackened weapon is favored by many hunters.

Lvl 9	+2	4,200 gp	Lvl 24	+5	525,000 gp
Lvl 14	+3	21,000 gp	Lvl 29	+3	2,625,000 gp
Lvl 19	+4	105,000 gp			

Weapon: Any

Enhancement: Attack rolls and damage rolls

Critical: +1d6 damage per plus, or +1d10 damage per plus against fey creatures.

Property: When you hit a creature with this weapon, that creature cannot telepot until the end of your next turn.

Flanking Weapon
Level 8+

Your enemies are loath to take their eyes off your weapon in battle, allowing you and your allies to catch them off guard more easily.

Lvl 8	+2	3,400 gp	Lvl 23	+5	425,000 gp
Lvl 13	+3	17,000 gp	Lvl 28	+6	2,125,000 gp
Lvl 18	+4	85,000 gp			

Weapon: Any melee

Enhancement: Attack rolls and damage rolls

Critical: +1d6 damage per plus, or +1d8 damage when you are flanking an opponent.

Power (Daily): Minor Action. You are considered to be flanking an enemy anytime both you and an ally are adjacent to that enemy. This power lasts until the end of your next turn.

1. Feyslaughter weapon; 2. Flesh seeker

Forbidding Weapon
Level 14+

A creature you strike with this weapon cannot teleport.

Lvl 14	+3	21,000 gp	Lvl 24	+5	525,000 gp
Lvl 19	+4	105,000 gp	Lvl 29	+6	2,625,000 gp

Weapon: Any

Enhancement: Attack rolls and damage rolls

Critical: +1d6 damage per plus

Power (Daily): Immediate Reaction. Use this power when a creature teleports into a space adjacent to you. The creature takes 1[W] damage and cannot teleport (save ends).

Force Weapon
Level 8+

The business end of this weapon shimmers. With a single attack, the wielder can trap an enemy with bands of force.

Lvl 8	+2	3,400 gp	Lvl 23	+5	425,000 gp
Lvl 13	+3	17,000 gp	Lvl 28	+6	2,125,000 gp
Lvl 18	+4	85,000 gp			

Weapon: Any

Enhancement: Attack rolls and damage rolls

Critical: +1d6 force damage per plus

Power (At-Will ✦ Force): Free Action. All damage dealt by this weapon is force damage. Another free action returns the damage to normal.

Power (Daily ✦ Force): Free Action. Use this power when you hit with the weapon. The target is slided 1 square and restrained until the end of your next turn.

Forceful Weapon
Level 16+

The extreme curve of this bow makes every shot hit with the force of a charging bull.

Lvl 16	+4	45,000 gp	Lvl 26	+6	1,125,000 gp
Lvl 21	+5	225,000 gp			

Weapon: Bow

Enhancement: Attack rolls and damage rolls

Critical: None

Property: Any arrow fired by this weapon also pushes the target 1 square when it hits.

Gambler's Weapon
Level 2+

Favored by scoundrels and rogues, this unpredictable blade is not for the faint of heart.

Lvl 2	+1	520 gp	Lvl 17	+4	65,000 gp
Lvl 7	+2	2,600 gp	Lvl 22	+5	325,000 gp
Lvl 12	+3	13,000 gp	Lvl 27	+6	1,625,000 gp

Weapon: Light Blade

Enhancement: Attack rolls and damage rolls

Critical: +1d6 damage per plus, and you can shift 1 square.

Power (Encounter): Free Action. Use this power before you make an attack roll. Roll 1d6 and subtract 3; the result is a power bonus or a penalty to your attack roll.

Flesh Seeker
Level 2+

Thinner than most weapons of its type, this weapon slips between armored plates and even magic defenses.

Lvl 2	+1	520 gp	Lvl 17	+4	65,000 gp
Lvl 7	+2	2,600 gp	Lvl 22	+5	325,000 gp
Lvl 12	+3	13,000 gp	Lvl 27	+6	1,625,000 gp

Weapon: Any melee

Enhancement: Attack rolls and damage

Critical: +1d6 damage per plus

Power (Encounter): Free Action. Use when you hit an enemy with this weapon. You gain a +1 power bonus on your next attack against that target with this weapon.

Footpad's Friend
Level 10+

When you catch an enemy unaware, this blade is as sharp as your smile.

Lvl 10	+2	5,000 gp	Lvl 25	+5	625,000 gp
Lvl 15	+3	25,000 gp	Lvl 30	+6	3,125,000 gp
Lvl 20	+4	125,000 gp			

Weapon: Light Blade

Enhancement: Attack rolls and damage rolls

Critical: +1d6 damage per plus

Property: When you hit with this weapon and deal extra damage from your Sneak Attack class feature, add your Charisma modifier to the damage roll.

Ghost Chain Weapon — Level 25+

Ghostly chains bind creatures you strike with this weapon and pull them toward you.

Lvl 25	+5	625,000 gp	Lvl 30	+6	3,125,000 gp

Weapon: Any ranged

Enhancement: Attack rolls and damage rolls

Critical: +1d6 damage per plus

Power (Encounter): Free Action. Use this power when you hit with this weapon. Pull the target a number of squares equal to the enhancement bonus of the weapon.

Graceful Weapon — Level 8+

Light and razor-sharp, this weapon responds to even your most intricate movements.

Lvl 8	+2	3,400 gp	Lvl 23	+5	425,000 gp
Lvl 13	+3	17,000 gp	Lvl 28	+6	2,125,000 gp
Lvl 18	+4	85,000 gp			

Weapon: Flail, Heavy Blade, Light Blade, Spear

Enhancement: Attack rolls and damage rolls

Critical: + Dexterity modifier damage per plus

Power (Daily): Immediate Reaction. Use this power when an enemy within your reach makes a melee attack against you. Make a melee basic attack against that enemy.

Grasping Weapon — Level 6+

This malleable weapon not only strikes at enemies but also grasps and holds them in place.

Lvl 6	+2	1,800 gp	Lvl 21	+5	225,000 gp
Lvl 11	+3	9,000 gp	Lvl 26	+6	1,125,000 gp
Lvl 16	+4	45,000 gp			

Weapon: Polearm, Spear

Enhancement: Attack rolls and damage rolls

Critical: None

Property: You can use this weapon to grab targets, adding the weapon's enhancement bonus to your grab attack. You can still use this weapon to attack a target you've grabbed with it.

Power (Encounter): Free Action. Use this power when you hit with the weapon. Pull the target into an unoccupied space adjacent to you. The target is grabbed (until escape).

Healing Weapon — Level 14+

This bow is strung with what looks like healer's stitch thread, and the wielder can send a arrow of glowing white energy at an ally to heal him or her.

Lvl 14	+3	21,000 gp	Lvl 24	+5	525,000 gp
Lvl 19	+4	105,000 gp	Lvl 29	+6	2,625,000 gp

Weapon: Any ranged

Enhancement: Attack rolls and damage rolls

Critical: +1d6 damage per plus

Power (Daily ✦ Healing): Standard Action. One creature within 20 squares of you and in your line of sight can regain hit points as if it had spent a healing surge.

Holy Healer's Weapon — Level 2+

Healers who wield this weapon relish combat and enjoy healing their allies while attacking their enemies.

Lvl 2	+1	520 gp	Lvl 17	+4	65,000 gp
Lvl 7	+2	2,600 gp	Lvl 22	+5	325,000 gp
Lvl 12	+3	13,000 gp	Lvl 27	+6	1,625,000 gp

Weapon: Mace, Staff

Enhancement: Attack rolls and damage rolls

Critical: +1d6 damage per plus

Property: Add this weapon's enhancement bonus to the amount healed by your *healing word*.

Power (Daily ✦ Healing): Minor Action. An ally within 5 squares of you can spend a healing surge to regain hit points equal to 5 + your Wisdom modifier.

Level 7: Regain 10 + Wisdom modifier hit points.
Level 12: Regain 15 + Wisdom modifier hit points.
Level 17: Regain 20 + Wisdom modifier hit points.
Level 22: Regain 25 + Wisdom modifier hit points.
Level 27: Regain 30 + Wisdom modifier hit points.

Impaling Weapon — Level 18+

This weapon can fire clear through one creature's body and penetrate another creature behind it.

Lvl 18	+4	85,000 gp	Lvl 28	+6	2,125,000 gp
Lvl 23	+5	425,000 gp			

Weapon: Any ranged

Enhancement: Attack rolls and damage rolls

Critical: +1d8 damage per plus

Property: Once per round, when an attack with this weapon reduces a target to 0 hit points or fewer, you can make a ranged basic attack against another creature adjacent to the target of the first attack.

Inescapable Weapon — Level 3+

This weapon grows increasingly eager to strike those you have trouble hitting.

Lvl 3	+1	680 gp	Lvl 18	+4	85,000 gp
Lvl 8	+2	3,400 gp	Lvl 23	+5	425,000 gp
Lvl 13	+3	17,000 gp	Lvl 28	+6	2,125,000 gp

Weapon: Any

Enhancement: Attack rolls and damage rolls

Critical: +1d6 damage per plus

Property: Each time you miss a target with this weapon, you gain a cumulative +1 bonus (up to the weapon's enhancement bonus) to your next attack roll with this weapon against the same target. The bonus ends if you attack a different target or when you hit.

Inspiring Weapon — Level 3+

Leaders use this weapon to rally allies around them for a powerful attack.

Lvl 3	+1	680 gp	Lvl 18	+4	85,000 gp
Lvl 8	+2	3,400 gp	Lvl 23	+5	425,000 gp
Lvl 13	+3	17,000 gp	Lvl 28	+6	2,125,000 gp

Weapon: Any

Enhancement: Attack rolls and damage rolls

Critical: +1d6 damage per plus

Power (Daily): Minor Action. Allies adjacent to you gain a power bonus to damage rolls equal to the enhancement bonus of the weapon until the end of your next turn.

Jagged Weapon — Level 12+

This weapon is pitted, scarred, and unadorned, but it deals grievous wounds.

Lvl 12	+3	13,000 gp	Lvl 22	+5	325,000 gp
Lvl 17	+4	65,000 gp	Lvl 27	+6	1,625,000 gp

Weapon: Axe, Heavy Blade, Light Blade

Enhancement: Attack rolls and damage rolls

Critical: Ongoing 10 damage

   Level 22 and 27: Ongoing 20 damage

Property: This weapon scores critical hits on a 19 or 20.

Jarring Weapon — Level 20+

This weapon smashes through your enemy's defenses, leaving them rattled from the severe blow of the attack.

Lvl 20	+4	125,000 gp	Lvl 30	+6	3,125,000 gp
Lvl 25	+5	625,000 gp			

Weapon: Flail, Hammer, Mace

Enhancement: Attack rolls and damage rolls

Critical: +1d6 damage per plus

Power (Daily): Free Action. Use this power when you hit with a melee attack. Your target is weakened and dazed (save ends both).

Legendary Weapon — Level 25+

Legends are made when heroes do incredible things, and this weapon gives them a few more opportunities.

Lvl 25	+5	625,000 gp	Lvl 30	+6	3,125,000 gp

Weapon: Any

Enhancement: Attack rolls and damage rolls

Critical: +1d6 damage per plus

Power (Daily): Free Action. Use this power when you score a critical hit. Take a standard action.

Luckblade — Level 3+

Luck favors the bold—and the wielder of this blade.

Lvl 3	+1	680 gp	Lvl 18	+4	85,000 gp
Lvl 8	+2	3,400 gp	Lvl 23	+5	425,000 gp
Lvl 13	+3	17,000 gp	Lvl 28	+6	2,125,000 gp

Weapon: Heavy Blade, Light Blade

Enhancement: Attack rolls and damage rolls

Critical: +1d8 damage per plus

Power (Daily): Free Action. Reroll an attack roll you just made. Use the second result even if it's lower.

Lucklender — Level 20+

This weapon can turn bad luck into good fortune.

Lvl 20	+4	125,000 gp	Lvl 30	+6	3,125,000 gp
Lvl 25	+5	625,000 gp			

Weapon: Any

Enhancement: Attack rolls and damage rolls

Critical: +1d6 damage per plus

Property: When you roll a 1 on an attack roll during combat or when a critical hit is scored on you, this weapon gains a charge. There is no limit on the number of charges, but the weapon resets to 2 charges after an extended rest.

Power (At-Will): Free Action. Spend a number of charges up to the weapon's enhancement bonus to gain a power bonus to your next attack roll with this weapon equal to the number of expended charges.

Lullaby Weapon
Level 4+

With a swing of this weapon, your enemy becomes lethargic, moving slower until finally collapsing into a snoring heap.

Lvl 4	+1	840 gp	Lvl 19	+4	105,000 gp
Lvl 9	+2	4,200 gp	Lvl 24	+5	525,000 gp
Lvl 14	+3	21,000 gp	Lvl 29	+6	2,625,000 gp

Weapon: Flail, Hammer, Mace, Staff

Enhancement: Attack rolls and damage rolls

Critical: +1d6 damage per plus

Power (Daily ✦ Sleep): Free Action. Use this power when you hit with the weapon. Make a secondary attack against the target's Will defense, with an attack bonus equal to the level of this weapon plus its enhancement bonus. If this attack hits, the target is slowed (save ends). If the target fails its first saving throw against this power, it becomes unconscious (save ends).

Mace of Healing
Level 8+

When you bolster your allies, this weapon increases the potency of your healing.

Lvl 8	+2	3,400 gp	Lvl 23	+5	425,000 gp
Lvl 13	+3	17,000 gp	Lvl 28	+6	2,125,000 gp
Lvl 18	+4	85,000 gp			

Weapon: Mace

Enhancement: Attack rolls and damage rolls

Critical: +1d6 damage per plus

Property: When you use a power that restores hit points to an ally, add an item bonus equal to this weapon's enhancement bonus to the amount restored.

Mage's Weapon
Level 2+

Some spellcasters choose this blade for its ability to convert a spell's power into accuracy in melee.

Lvl 2	+1	520 gp	Lvl 17	+4	65,000 gp
Lvl 7	+2	2,600 gp	Lvl 22	+5	325,000 gp
Lvl 12	+3	13,000 gp	Lvl 27	+6	1,625,000 gp

Weapon: Heavy Blade, Light Blade

Enhancement: Attack rolls and damage rolls

Critical: +1d6 damage per plus

Property: Anyone proficient with simple weapons or the dagger is proficient with this weapon.

Power (Encounter): Minor Action. You can expend an arcane encounter power to regain the use of a martial encounter power you know of up to the same level.

Mauling Weapon
Level 8+

This weapon excels at smashing down barriers, knocking over foes, and breaking open containers.

Lvl 8	+2	3,400 gp	Lvl 23	+5	425,000 gp
Lvl 13	+3	17,000 gp	Lvl 28	+6	2,125,000 gp
Lvl 18	+4	85,000 gp			

Weapon: Hammer, Heavy Blade, Mace

Enhancement: Attack rolls and damage rolls

Critical: +1d6 damage per plus, or +1d12 damage per plus against constructs and objects.

Power (Daily): Free Action. Use this power when you hit with the weapon. Until the end of your next turn, when the target moves on its turn with a mode of movement other than teleportation, you determine the first square the creature moves to. In addition, if the creature has the construct keyword it takes 1d10 damage.
Level 13 or 18: 2d10 damage.
Level 23 or 28: 3d10 damage.

Medic's Weapon
Level 4+

A divine warrior of any kind can use this weapon to bring victory in the name of his deity.

Lvl 4	+1	840 gp	Lvl 19	+4	105,000 gp
Lvl 9	+2	4,200 gp	Lvl 24	+5	525,000 gp
Lvl 14	+3	21,000 gp	Lvl 29	+6	2,625,000 gp

Weapon: Any

Enhancement: Attack rolls and damage rolls

Critical: +1d6 radiant damage per plus

Property: When you use a Channel Divinity power during combat, an ally within 10 squares of you regains an amount of hit points equal to your Charisma modifier plus this weapon's enhancement bonus.

Power (Daily): Standard Action. Gain one additional use of Channel Divinity for this encounter.

Mindiron Weapon
Level 14+

This metal weapon projects arrows or bolts partially into the realm of the mind.

Lvl 14	+3	21,000 gp	Lvl 24	+5	525,000 gp
Lvl 19	+4	105,000 gp	Lvl 29	+6	2,625,000 gp

Weapon: Bow, Crossbow

Enhancement: Attack rolls and damage rolls

Critical: +1d6 psychic damage per plus

Power (At-Will ✦ Psychic): Free Action. Half the damage dealt by this weapon becomes psychic. Another free action returns the damage to normal.

Power (Encounter ✦ Psychic): Free Action. Use this power when you attack a creature with this weapon. That attack targets a creature's Will defense and deals psychic damage. Typed damage from the attack gains the psychic type as well as the original type.

Moradin's Weapon — Level 19+

This hammer carries the weight of the earth and gives a follower of Moradin the concussive power to knock down his or her enemies.

Lvl 19	+4	105,000 gp	Lvl 29	+6	2,625,000 gp
Lvl 24	+5	525,000 gp			

Weapon: Hammer

Enhancement: Attack rolls and damage rolls

Critical: +1d12 damage per plus

Property: If you worship Moradin, you can use this weapon as a holy symbol. It adds its enhancement bonus (but not its proficiency bonus) to attack rolls and damage rolls when used in this manner. If you do not worship Moradin, you do not benefit from this weapon's property and cannot activate this weapon's power.

Power (Daily): Free Action. Use this power when you hit with the weapon. Make a secondary attack: Area burst 2 centered on the creature you hit; targets enemies only; Strength or Constitution vs. Fortitude (apply a bonus to the attack roll equal to the weapon's enhancement bonus); on a hit, the target takes 2d6 + Constitution modifier damage and is knocked prone. This secondary attack does not provoke opportunity attacks.
Level 29: 3d6 + Constitution modifier damage.

Necrotic Weapon — Level 13+

The wounds inflicted by this weapon also drain an enemy's vitality.

Lvl 13	+3	17,000 gp	Lvl 23	+5	425,000 gp
Lvl 18	+4	85,000 gp	Lvl 28	+6	2,125,000 gp

Weapon: Axe, Heavy Blade, Light Blade

Enhancement: Attack rolls and damage rolls

Critical: +1d8 necrotic damage per plus

Power (At-Will ✦ Necrotic): Free Action. Half the damage you deal with this weapon is necrotic damage. Another free action returns the damage to normal.

Power (Daily ✦ Necrotic): Free Action. Use this power when you hit with this weapon. Your target gains vulnerable 10 necrotic until the end of your next turn.
Level 23 or 28: Vulnerable 15 necrotic.

Oathblade — Level 4+

This fine steel weapon strikes deadly blows against the foe you swear to vanquish.

Lvl 4	+1	840 gp	Lvl 19	+4	105,000 gp
Lvl 9	+2	4,200 gp	Lvl 24	+5	525,000 gp
Lvl 14	+3	21,000 gp	Lvl 29	+6	2,625,000 gp

Weapon: Heavy Blade, Light Blade

Enhancement: Attack rolls and damage rolls

Critical: +1d6 per plus, or +1d10 damage per plus against a target marked by you.

Power (Daily): Minor Action. Your next attack against a creature marked by you deals an extra 1d6 damage per plus.

1. Necrotic weapon; 2. Moradin's weapon

Opportunistic Weapon — Level 4+

An enemy quickly regrets turning its back to the wielder of this weapon.

Lvl 4	+1	840 gp	Lvl 19	+4	105,000 gp
Lvl 9	+2	4,200 gp	Lvl 24	+5	525,000 gp
Lvl 14	+3	21,000 gp	Lvl 29	+6	2,625,000 gp

Weapon: Any melee

Enhancement: Attack rolls and damage rolls

Critical: +1d6 damage per plus, or +1d12 damage per plus with opportunity attacks.

Power (Daily): Immediate Reaction. Use this power when an enemy provokes an opportunity attack. Make an additional opportunity attack against the provoking creature.

Overreaching Weapon — Level 25+

This polearm extends as you strike at distant enemies, putting them within your range.

Lvl 25	+5	625,000 gp	Lvl 30	+6	3,125,000 gp

Weapon: Polearm

Enhancement: Attack rolls and damage rolls

Critical: +1d6 damage per plus

Property: With this weapon, you can attack targets that are 3 squares away from you as well as nearer targets. You can still make opportunity attacks only against adjacent targets.

WAYNE ENGLAND

Pact Hammer — Level 2+

This dark steel hammer is the prized possession of any dwarven warlock who wishes to wield weapon and magic with equal effectiveness.

Lvl 2	+1	520 gp	Lvl 17	+4	65,000 gp
Lvl 7	+2	2,600 gp	Lvl 22	+5	325,000 gp
Lvl 12	+3	13,000 gp	Lvl 27	+6	1,625,000 gp

Weapon: Hammer

Enhancement: Attack rolls and damage rolls

Critical: +1d6 damage per plus

Property: If you are a dwarf, this hammer functions as a warlock implement for you (but do not apply the weapon's proficiency bonus to attack rolls for warlock powers).

Property: When you hit a target affected by your Warlock's Curse with this weapon, you deal your extra curse damage against that target.

Pact Sword — Level 2+

Eladrin warlocks favor these sinister longswords for their ability to combine weapon and magic and for the power to control an enemy's position.

Lvl 2	+1	520 gp	Lvl 17	+4	65,000 gp
Lvl 7	+2	2,600 gp	Lvl 22	+5	325,000 gp
Lvl 12	+3	13,000 gp	Lvl 27	+6	1,625,000 gp

Weapon: Longsword

Enhancement: Attack rolls and damage rolls

Critical: +1d6 damage per plus

Property: If you are an eladrin, this longsword functions as a warlock implement for you (but do not apply the weapon's proficiency bonus to attack rolls for warlock powers).

Power (Daily ✦ Teleportation): Free Action. Use this power when you hit a target affected by your Warlock's Curse with this weapon. Teleport the target a number of squares equal to 1 + this weapon's enhancement bonus.

Paired Weapon — Level 3+

One weapon suddenly becomes two with startling speed.

Lvl 3	+1	680 gp	Lvl 18	+4	85,000 gp
Lvl 8	+2	3,400 gp	Lvl 23	+5	425,000 gp
Lvl 13	+3	17,000 gp	Lvl 28	+6	2,125,000 gp

Weapon: Any one-handed melee

Enhancement: Attack rolls and damage rolls

Critical: +1d6 damage per plus

Power (At-Will): Minor Action. Split the weapon into two identical weapons, one in your primary hand and one in your off-hand. You can spend another minor action to recombine the weapons into one. If you have the Quick Draw feat, you can split or recombine the weapon as a free action.

Paralyzing Weapon — Level 13+

This crossbow is enameled with stylized images of poisonous snakes. The bolts it fires drip with toxic venom.

Lvl 13	+3	17,000 gp	Lvl 23	+5	425,000 gp
Lvl 18	+4	85,000 gp	Lvl 28	+6	2,125,000 gp

Weapon: Any ranged

Enhancement: Attack rolls and damage rolls

Critical: +1d6 damage per plus

Power (Daily ✦ Poison): Free Action. Use this power when you hit with this weapon. The target is immobilized and weakened until the end of your next turn.

Parrying Weapon — Level 2+

A wielder of this weapon never truly lowers his or her defenses.

Lvl 2	+1	520 gp	Lvl 17	+4	65,000 gp
Lvl 7	+2	2,600 gp	Lvl 22	+5	325,000 gp
Lvl 12	+3	13,000 gp	Lvl 27	+6	1,625,000 gp

Weapon: Any melee

Enhancement: Attack rolls and damage rolls

Critical: +1d6 damage per plus

Power (Daily): Immediate Reaction. Use this power when an enemy makes a melee attack against you. Make a melee basic attack against that enemy, with a power bonus on your attack roll equal to this weapon's enhancement bonus; if your result exceeds that of the attack roll against you, the enemy's attack misses. The melee basic attack you make to block your enemy's attack has no other effect and does not deal damage.

Piercing Weapon — Level 7+

This point of this spear extends, digs deep into an enemy's flesh, and leaves a weeping wound.

Lvl 7	+2	2,600 gp	Lvl 22	+5	325,000 gp
Lvl 12	+3	13,000 gp	Lvl 27	+6	1,625,000 gp
Lvl 17	+4	65,000 gp			

Weapon: Spear

Enhancement: Attack rolls and damage rolls

Critical: +1d6 damage per plus

Power (Daily): Free Action. Use this power when you hit a target with this weapon. The target takes ongoing damage equal to your Dexterity modifier + this weapon's enhancement bonus (save ends).

Pinning Weapon — Level 2+

You use this weapon to root your enemy to the spot.

Lvl 2	+1	520 gp	Lvl 17	+4	65,000 gp
Lvl 7	+2	2,600 gp	Lvl 22	+5	325,000 gp
Lvl 12	+3	13,000 gp	Lvl 27	+6	1,625,000 gp

Weapon: Any melee

Enhancement: Attack rolls and damage rolls

Critical: +1d6 damage per plus

Power (Daily): Free Action. Use this power when you hit an enemy with this weapon. That enemy is immobilized until you are no longer adjacent to it.

Point Blank Weapon
Level 3+

The wielder of this weapon need not fear wading into melee.

Lvl 3	+1	680 gp	Lvl 18	+4	85,000 gp
Lvl 8	+2	3,400 gp	Lvl 23	+5	425,000 gp
Lvl 13	+3	17,000 gp	Lvl 28	+6	2,125,000 gp

Weapon: Any ranged

Enhancement: Attack rolls and damage rolls

Critical: +1d6 damage per plus

Property: Gain a +2 item bonus to AC against opportunity attacks provoked by making a ranged attack with this weapon.

Power (Encounter): Free Action. Use this power when you make a ranged attack with this weapon; the attack does not provoke opportunity attacks.

Poisoned Weapon
Level 5+

This weapon leaves a debilitating poison that saps an enemy's vitality and strength.

Lvl 5	+1	1,000 gp	Lvl 20	+4	125,000 gp
Lvl 10	+2	5,000 gp	Lvl 25	+5	625,000 gp
Lvl 15	+3	25,000 gp	Lvl 30	+6	3,125,000 gp

Weapon: Bow, Crossbow, Light Blade, Pick, Spear

Enhancement: Attack rolls and damage rolls

Critical: +1d6 poison damage per plus

Power (Daily ✦ Poison): Free Action. Use this power when you hit with the weapon. The target takes ongoing 5 poison damage and is weakened (save ends both).
Level 15 or 20: Ongoing 10 poison damage and weakened (save ends both).
Level 25 or 30: Ongoing 15 poison damage and weakened (save ends both).

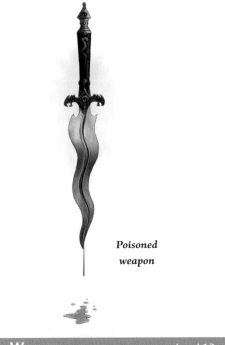

Poisoned weapon

Predatory Weapon
Level 13+

This weapon silently urges its wielder to hunt new prey even before finishing off his or her present foe.

Lvl 13	+3	17,000 gp	Lvl 23	+5	425,000 gp
Lvl 18	+4	85,000 gp	Lvl 28	+6	2,125,000 gp

Weapon: Any

Enhancement: Attack rolls and damage rolls

Critical: +1d6 damage per plus, or +1d12 damage per plus if you have marked the target

Power (Encounter): Free Action. Use this power when you hit with the weapon. Mark a target within 5 squares of you. This mark lasts until the end of your next turn.

Prime Shot Weapon   Level 2+

This weapon demands a wily and cunning wielder who darts from cover to cover while sniping at enemies.

Lvl 2	+1	520 gp	Lvl 17	+4	65,000 gp
Lvl 7	+2	2,600 gp	Lvl 22	+5	325,000 gp
Lvl 12	+3	13,000 gp	Lvl 27	+6	1,625,000 gp

Weapon: Any ranged

Enhancement: Attack rolls and damage rolls

Critical: +1d6 damage per plus

Property: You deal +1 damage if no ally is closer to the target than you are.
Level 12 or 17: +2 damage.
Level 22 or 27: +3 damage.

Quick Weapon   Level 3+

You can use this weapon to attack with preternatural speed.

Lvl 3	+1	680 gp	Lvl 18	+4	85,000 gp
Lvl 8	+2	3,400 gp	Lvl 23	+5	425,000 gp
Lvl 13	+3	17,000 gp	Lvl 28	+6	2,125,000 gp

Weapon: Any

Enhancement: Attack rolls and damage rolls

Critical: +1d6 damage per plus

Power (Daily): Free Action. Use this power when you hit a target with this weapon. Make a basic attack with this weapon against a target of your choice.

Radiant Weapon   Level 15+

This weapon burns with glowing, radiant energy.

Lvl 15	+3	25,000 gp	Lvl 25	+5	625,000 gp
Lvl 20	+4	125,000 gp	Lvl 30	+6	3,125,000 gp

Weapon: Any

Enhancement: Attack rolls and damage rolls

Critical: +1d6 radiant damage per plus

Property: When this weapon is used to deal radiant damage, add its enhancement bonus as an item bonus to damage rolls.

Power (At-Will ✦ Radiant): Free Action. All damage dealt by this weapon is radiant damage. Another free action returns the damage to normal.

Reckless Weapon   Level 3+

Some fighters favor force over accuracy—this weapon is for them.

Lvl 3	+1	680 gp	Lvl 18	+4	85,000 gp
Lvl 8	+2	3,400 gp	Lvl 23	+5	425,000 gp
Lvl 13	+3	17,000 gp	Lvl 28	+6	2,125,000 gp

Weapon: Any melee except reach weapons

Enhancement: Attack rolls and damage rolls

Critical: +1d8 damage per plus

Power (At-Will): Free Action. Use this power before making a melee attack against an adjacent target. You gain a power bonus to that attack's damage roll equal to twice this weapon's enhancement bonus. You take a -2 penalty to AC until the end of your next turn.

Rending Weapon   Level 4+

When this axe scores a devastating strike, you can continue your assault.

Lvl 4	+1	840 gp	Lvl 19	+4	105,000 gp
Lvl 9	+2	4,200 gp	Lvl 24	+5	525,000 gp
Lvl 14	+3	21,000 gp	Lvl 29	+6	2,625,000 gp

Weapon: Axe

Enhancement: Attack rolls and damage rolls

Critical: +1d6 damage per plus, and make a melee basic attack with this weapon against the same target.

Reproachful Weapon   Level 2+

A strike from this weapon renders your enemy less able to respond.

Lvl 2	+1	520 gp	Lvl 17	+4	65,000 gp
Lvl 7	+2	2,600 gp	Lvl 22	+5	325,000 gp
Lvl 12	+3	13,000 gp	Lvl 27	+6	1,625,000 gp

Weapon: Any melee

Enhancement: Attack rolls and damage rolls

Critical: +1d6 damage per plus

Power (Daily): Free Action. Use this power when you hit with the weapon. Your target takes a -2 penalty to its attack rolls (save ends).

Retribution Weapon   Level 7+

This blade bestows power to those who seek vengeance against an adversary.

Lvl 7	+2	2,600 gp	Lvl 22	+5	325,000 gp
Lvl 12	+3	13,000 gp	Lvl 27	+6	1,625,000 gp
Lvl 17	+4	65,000 gp			

Weapon: Any melee

Enhancement: Attack rolls and damage rolls

Critical: +1d6 damage per plus

Property: Whenever an enemy scores a critical hit against you, your next attack with this weapon against that enemy deals +1d6 damage per plus of this weapon. The effect ends at the end of your next turn.

Ricochet Weapon   Level 11+

When you fire a stone from this sling, it bounces off the target to hit another.

Lvl 11	+3	9,000 gp	Lvl 21	+5	225,000 gp
Lvl 16	+4	45,000 gp	Lvl 26	+6	1,125,000 gp

Weapon: Sling

Enhancement: Attack rolls and damage rolls

Critical: None

Power (Daily): Free Action. Use this power when you make a ranged attack with this weapon. After that attack is resolved, make a ranged basic attack with this weapon against a second target within 2 squares of the first target (treating the first target's space as the origin of the attack for purposes of determining cover).

Righteous Weapon
Level 10+

Crafted with faith and wrath, this weapon is a scourge of evil.

Lvl 10	+2	5,000 gp	Lvl 25	+5	625,000 gp
Lvl 15	+3	25,000 gp	Lvl 30	+6	3,125,000 gp
Lvl 20	+4	125,000 gp			

Weapon: Any melee

Enhancement: Attack rolls and damage rolls

Critical: +1d6 damage per plus, or +1d8 damage per plus against evil creatures

Power (Daily): Free Action. Use this power when you hit with the weapon. The target is dazed until the end of your next turn. If the target is evil or chaotic evil, the target is instead dazed (save ends).

Sacrificial Weapon
Level 6+

The true severity of this weapon comes at a cost to the wielder's own vitality.

Lvl 6	+2	1,800 gp	Lvl 21	+5	225,000 gp
Lvl 11	+3	9,000 gp	Lvl 26	+6	1,125,000 gp
Lvl 16	+4	45,000 gp			

Weapon: Any melee

Enhancement: Attack rolls and damage rolls

Critical: +1d6 damage per plus

Power (Daily): Free Action. Use this power when you hit with the weapon. Spend a healing surge, and instead of regaining hit points, you cause the target to become weakened until the end of your next turn.

Scalebane Weapon
Level 3+

Reptilian creatures have good cause to fear this weapon.

Lvl 3	+1	680 gp	Lvl 18	+4	85,000 gp
Lvl 8	+2	3,400 gp	Lvl 23	+5	425,000 gp
Lvl 13	+3	17,000 gp	Lvl 28	+6	2,125,000 gp

Weapon: Any

Enhancement: Attack rolls and damage rolls

Critical: +1d6 damage per plus, or +1d12 damage per plus against reptiles.

Power (Daily): Free Action. Use this power when you hit with the weapon. The attack deals an extra 1d4 damage. If the target has the reptile keyword, it deals an extra 1d20 damage instead.

Level 13 or 18: An extra 2d4 damage or an extra 2d12 damage if the target has the reptile keyword.

Level 23 or 28: An extra 3d4 damage and an extra 3d12 damage if the target has the reptile keyword.

Shadow Spike
Level 22+

The wielder of this weapon moves like a shadow, silent and invisible until striking, and then only to disappear again.

Lvl 22	+5	325,000 gp	Lvl 27	+6	1,625,000 gp

Weapon: Light Blade

Enhancement: Attack rolls and damage rolls

Critical: +1d6 damage per plus

Power (Daily ✦ Illusion): Free Action. Use this power when you use this weapon to hit a target granting you combat advantage. You are invisible until the end of your next turn.

Shapechanger's Sorrow
Level 9+

This weapon traps a shapechanging creature in its present form.

Lvl 9	+2	4,200 gp	Lvl 24	+5	525,000 gp
Lvl 14	+3	21,000 gp	Lvl 29	+3	2,625,000 gp
Lvl 19	+4	105,000 gp			

Weapon: Axe, Heavy Blade, Light Blade

Enhancement: Attack rolls and damage rolls

Critical: +1d6 per plus, or +1d12 damage per plus against creatures not in their natural form.

Property: You gain a +1 bonus to all defenses against creatures not in their natural form.

Power (Daily): Free Action. Use this power when you hit with the weapon. The target reverts to its natural form and cannot use powers that have the polymorph keyword (save ends).

1. Shapechanger's Sorrow; 2. Rending weapon

Skewering Weapon
Level 3+

This weapon leaves behind an ephemeral shard that holds your foe in place.

Lvl 3	+1	680 gp	Lvl 18	+4	85,000 gp
Lvl 8	+2	3,400 gp	Lvl 23	+5	425,000 gp
Lvl 13	+3	17,000 gp	Lvl 28	+6	2,125,000 gp

Weapon: Pick, Spear

Enhancement: Attack rolls and damage rolls

Critical: +1d6 damage per plus

Power (Daily): Free Action. Use this power when you hit a target with this weapon. The target is immobilized (save ends).

Skyrender Weapon — Level 9+

Air roils along the path of your ammunition, hindering or disabling a flying creature's ability to stay aloft.

Lvl 9	+2	4,200 gp	Lvl 24	+5	525,000 gp
Lvl 14	+3	21,000 gp	Lvl 29	+3	2,625,000 gp
Lvl 19	+4	105,000 gp			

Weapon: Any ranged

Enhancement: Attack rolls and damage rolls

Critical: +1d6 damage per plus, or +1d12 damage against a flying target.

Property: When you hit a flying target with this weapon, halve the target's fly speed until the end of your next turn.

Power (Daily): Free Action. Use this power when you hit an airborne target using this weapon. The target falls 10 squares. If it hits the ground, it is prone but takes no damage from the fall.

Sniper's Weapon — Level 13+

A bolt fired from this crossbow flies along a perfect path, ignoring all outside forces.

Lvl 13	+3	17,000 gp	Lvl 23	+5	425,000 gp
Lvl 18	+4	85,000 gp	Lvl 28	+6	2,125,000 gp

Weapon: Crossbow

Enhancement: Attack rolls and damage rolls

Critical: +1d8 damage per plus

Property: Attacks with this weapon do not take the -2 penalty for long range.

Power (Daily): Minor Action. The next attack roll you make with this weapon during this turn gains a power bonus equal to your Wisdom modifier.

Splitting Weapon — Level 7+

This weapon breaks apart when you attack with it, hitting multiple enemies and then reforming.

Lvl 7	+2	2,600 gp	Lvl 22	+5	325,000 gp
Lvl 12	+3	13,000 gp	Lvl 27	+6	1,625,000 gp
Lvl 17	+4	65,000 gp			

Weapon: Flail

Enhancement: Attack rolls and damage rolls

Critical: +1d6 damage per plus

Power (Daily): Free Action. Use this power when you hit with the weapon. An enemy adjacent to the attack's target takes damage equal to your Dexterity modifier + the weapon's enhancement bonus.

Staggering Weapon — Level 2+

When you hit with this weapon, you send your foes lurching headlong whichever way you wish.

Lvl 2	+1	520 gp	Lvl 17	+4	65,000 gp
Lvl 7	+2	2,600 gp	Lvl 22	+5	325,000 gp
Lvl 12	+3	13,000 gp	Lvl 27	+6	1,625,000 gp

Weapon: Axe, Flail, Hammer, Heavy Blade, Mace

Enhancement: Attack rolls and damage rolls

Critical: +1d6 damage per plus, and the target is knocked prone.

Property: When you use a power with the weapon keyword that slides a target, you can add this weapon's enhancement bonus to the number of squares the target slides.

Power (Daily): Free Action. Use this power when you hit with the weapon. Slide the target a number of squares equal to the weapon's enhancement bonus.

Stormbolt Weapon — Level 14+

This weapon pulses with elemental energy, and wielding it is like holding the power and fury of a thunderstorm in your hand.

Lvl 14	+3	21,000 gp	Lvl 24	+5	525,000 gp
Lvl 19	+4	105,000 gp	Lvl 29	+6	2,625,000 gp

Weapon: Hammer, Spear

Enhancement: Attack rolls and damage rolls

Critical: +1d6 lightning damage per plus

Power (Daily ✦ Lightning): Standard Action. The weapon discharges a bolt of lightning. Make an attack: Ranged 10; Strength or Constitution vs. Reflex (apply a bonus to the attack roll equal to the weapon's enhancement bonus); on a hit, the target takes 2[W] + Strength modifier lightning damage, and the bolt deals lightning damage equal to the weapon's enhancement bonus to all creatures adjacent to the target.

Level 24 or 29: 3[W] + Strength modifier lightning damage to the target, and lightning damage equal to twice the weapon's enhancement bonus to all enemies adjacent to the target.

Stout Weapon — Level 8+

This weapon looks for cracks in an enemy's fortitude instead of chinks in his armor.

Lvl 8	+2	3,400 gp	Lvl 23	+5	425,000 gp
Lvl 13	+3	17,000 gp	Lvl 28	+6	2,125,000 gp
Lvl 18	+4	85,000 gp			

Weapon: Axe, Hammer, Mace, Pick, Staff

Enhancement: Attack rolls and damage rolls

Critical: + Constitution modifier damage per plus

Power (Daily): Free Action. Use this power when you make an attack against AC with this weapon. This attack targets Fortitude defense instead.

Stormbolt weapon

Strongheart Weapon — Level 3+

You can overcome bodily weakness when you attack with this weapon.

Lvl 3	+1	680 gp	Lvl 18	+4	85,000 gp
Lvl 8	+2	3,400 gp	Lvl 23	+5	425,000 gp
Lvl 13	+3	17,000 gp	Lvl 28	+6	2,125,000 gp

Weapon: Any melee

Enhancement: Attack rolls and damage rolls

Critical: +1d8 damage per plus

Power (Encounter): Minor Action. Until the end of your next turn, you do not deal half damage while weakened.

Subtle Weapon — Level 3+

Plain and simple, this weapon works best when you already have an edge on your foe.

Lvl 3	+1	680 gp	Lvl 18	+4	85,000 gp
Lvl 8	+2	3,400 gp	Lvl 23	+5	425,000 gp
Lvl 13	+3	17,000 gp	Lvl 28	+6	2,125,000 gp

Weapon: Any melee

Enhancement: Attack rolls and damage rolls

Critical: +1d6 damage per plus

Property: Deal extra damage equal to this weapon's enhancement bonus when attacking with combat advantage.

Sunblade — Level 4+

This heavy golden sword attacks with the power and intensity of the sun, burning nearby enemies.

Lvl 4	+1	840 gp	Lvl 19	+4	105,000 gp
Lvl 9	+2	4,200 gp	Lvl 24	+5	525,000 gp
Lvl 14	+3	21,000 gp	Lvl 29	+6	2,625,000 gp

Weapon: Heavy Blade

Enhancement: Attack rolls and damage rolls

Critical: +1d6 damage per plus

Property: This weapon can shed bright or dim light up to 20 squares. You control the brightness and range of the light.

Power (At-Will ✦ Radiant): Free Action. All damage dealt by this weapon is radiant damage. Another free action returns the damage to normal.

Power (Daily ✦ Radiant): Standard Action. You cause motes of light to burst out and attach to your enemies. Make an attack: Close burst 1; targets enemies; Strength vs. Reflex (apply a bonus to the attack roll equal to the weapon's enhancement bonus); on a hit, the target takes 1d8 radiant damage.
Level 14 or 19: 2d8 radiant damage.
Level 24 or 29: Close burst 2; 3d8 radiant damage.

Swiftshot Weapon — Level 3+

This weapon reloads and fires faster than any other crossbow.

Lvl 3	+1	680 gp	Lvl 18	+4	85,000 gp
Lvl 8	+2	3,400 gp	Lvl 23	+5	425,000 gp
Lvl 13	+3	17,000 gp	Lvl 28	+6	2,125,000 gp

Weapon: Crossbow

Enhancement: Attack rolls and damage rolls

Critical: +1d6 damage per plus

Property: Loading this crossbow is a free action.

Power (Encounter): Minor Action. Make a ranged basic attack with this weapon.

Tenacious Weapon — Level 19+

A wielder of this weapon favors dependability over luck.

| Lvl 19 | +4 | 105,000 gp | Lvl 29 | +6 | 2,625,000 gp |
| Lvl 24 | +5 | 525,000 gp | | | |

Weapon: Any

Enhancement: Attack rolls and damage rolls

Critical: +1d6 damage per plus

Power (Encounter): Free Action. Use this power before you make an attack roll with this weapon. Roll twice and take the better of the two results.

Thieving Weapon — Level 5+

This weapon adds insult to injury by stealing away its victim's possessions.

Lvl 5	+1	1,000 gp	Lvl 20	+4	125,000 gp
Lvl 10	+2	5,000 gp	Lvl 25	+5	625,000 gp
Lvl 15	+3	25,000 gp	Lvl 30	+6	3,125,000 gp

Weapon: Light Blade

Enhancement: Attack rolls and damage rolls

Critical: +1d6 damage per plus

Power (Daily): Free Action. Use this power when you hit with the weapon. Make a Thievery check to pick the target's pockets, ignoring the -10 penalty for using the skill in battle. In addition, you gain a power bonus equal to the weapon's enhancement bonus to the check.

Thoughtstealer Weapon — Level 9+

With this weapon, you not only break through an enemy's physical defenses but its mental defenses as well.

Lvl 9	+2	4,200 gp	Lvl 24	+5	525,000 gp
Lvl 14	+3	21,000 gp	Lvl 29	+6	2,625,000 gp
Lvl 19	+4	105,000 gp			

Weapon: Any thrown

Enhancement: Attack rolls and damage rolls

Critical: +1d6 psychic damage per plus

Power (Daily): Free Action. Use this power when you hit with the weapon. Make a secondary attack against the target's Will defense. The attack bonus is equal to the level of this weapon plus its enhancement bonus. If the attack hits, you learn the answer to a question that the subject knows the answer to and which can be answered by a "yes" or "no." If the subject doesn't know the answer, the power fails.
Level 14 or 19: Learn answers to two yes/no questions.
Level 24 or 29: Learn answers to three yes/no questions.

Thunderbolt Weapon — Level 13+

This weapon imbues its ammunition with electricity and can create a bolt that jumps from one target to another.

| Lvl 13 | +3 | 17,000 gp | Lvl 23 | +5 | 425,000 gp |
| Lvl 18 | +4 | 85,000 gp | Lvl 28 | +6 | 2,125,000 gp |

Weapon: Any ranged

Enhancement: Attack rolls and damage rolls

Critical: +1d6 lightning damage per plus

Power (At-Will ✦ Lightning): Free Action. All damage dealt by this weapon is lightning damage. Another free action returns the damage to normal.

Power (Daily ✦ Lightning): Free Action. Use this power after you make a ranged attack with this weapon. Whether the attack hits or misses, make a ranged basic attack with this weapon against a second target within 10 squares and line of effect of the first target. All of the damage from this secondary attack is lightning damage.

Thundergod Weapon — Level 13+

A loud crash of thunder erupts from this weapon when you charge and strike an enemy.

| Lvl 13 | +3 | 17,000 gp | Lvl 23 | +5 | 425,000 gp |
| Lvl 18 | +4 | 85,000 gp | Lvl 28 | +6 | 2,125,000 gp |

Weapon: Any melee

Enhancement: Attack rolls and damage rolls

Critical: +1d6 thunder damage per plus, or +1d12 thunder damage per plus on a charge

Property: Your melee attacks deal +1d6 thunder damage when you charge.
Level 23 or 28: +2d6 thunder damage on a charge.

Tigerclaw Gauntlets — Level 8+

These gauntlets, which imbue you with the power of a pouncing tiger, have a sharp talon extending outward from each.

Lvl 8	+2	3,400 gp	Lvl 23	+5	425,000 gp
Lvl 13	+3	17,000 gp	Lvl 28	+6	2,125,000 gp
Lvl 18	+4	85,000 gp			

Weapon: Spiked gauntlets

Enhancement: Attack rolls and damage rolls

Critical: +1d6 damage per plus

Property: Gain a +2 item bonus to your speed when charging.

Power (Encounter): Standard Action. Make a charge attack. At the end of your charge, make two melee basic attack rolls against one target using this weapon. If you hit with both, deal an extra 1d6 damage.
Level 13 and 18: +2d6 damage.
Level 23 and 28: +3d6 damage.

JAMES ZHANG

Transference Weapon
Level 7+

With this weapon, your enemies need take heed of what afflictions they place on you, lest they suffer them as well.

Lvl 7	+2	2,600 gp		Lvl 22	+5	325,000 gp
Lvl 12	+3	13,000 gp		Lvl 27	+6	1,625,000 gp
Lvl 17	+4	65,000 gp				

Weapon: Any

Enhancement: Attack rolls and damage rolls

Critical: +1d6 damage per plus

Power (Daily): Free Action. Use this power when you hit with the weapon. Transfer a condition or ongoing damage effect that is affecting you to the target you hit. The condition or ongoing damage continues to run its course as normal on the target.

Transposing Weapon
Level 14+

Thanks to this weapon, you and the target of your attack switch places.

Lvl 14	+3	21,000 gp		Lvl 24	+5	525,000 gp
Lvl 19	+4	105,000 gp		Lvl 29	+6	2,625,000 gp

Weapon: Any

Enhancement: Attack rolls and damage rolls

Critical: +1d6 damage per plus

Power (Encounter ✦ Teleportation): Free Action. Use this power when you hit a target with the weapon. You and the target switch locations.

Trespasser's Bane Weapon
Level 25+

No enemy can elude this weapon's wielder without risk.

Lvl 25	+5	625,000 gp		Lvl 30	+6	3,125,000 gp

Weapon: Any melee

Enhancement: Attack rolls and damage rolls

Critical: +1d6 damage per plus

Power (Encounter): Immediate Interrupt. Use this power when an enemy moves out of a square within your reach. Make a melee basic attack against that enemy. If the attack hits, the target is slowed until the end of its next turn.

Tyrant's Weapon
Level 8+

This harsh-looking weapon lets you capitalize on your enemies' vulnerabilities.

Lvl 8	+2	3,400 gp		Lvl 23	+5	425,000 gp
Lvl 13	+3	17,000 gp		Lvl 28	+6	2,125,000 gp
Lvl 18	+4	85,000 gp				

Weapon: Any melee

Enhancement: Attack rolls and damage rolls

Critical: +1d6 damage per plus, and the target is knocked prone.

Power (Daily): Minor Action. Until the end of your next turn, your attacks with this weapon deal an extra 1d6 damage per plus to a target that is blinded, prone, restrained, or helpless.

Vampiric Weapon
Level 9+

This blade saps life from its opponent, bestowing you with the creature's lost vitality.

Lvl 9	+2	4,200 gp		Lvl 24	+5	525,000 gp
Lvl 14	+3	21,000 gp		Lvl 29	+6	2,625,000 gp
Lvl 19	+4	105,000 gp				

Weapon: Heavy Blade, Light Blade

Enhancement: Attack rolls and damage rolls

Critical: +1d4 damage per plus, and you regain hit points equal to the damage dealt by this weapon's critical property.

Property: All damage dealt by this weapon is necrotic damage.

Power (Daily ✦ Healing, Necrotic): Free Action. Use this power when you make a successful attack with the weapon. That attack deals an extra 1d8 necrotic damage, and you regain an equal amount of hit points.
Level 14 or 19: +2d8 necrotic damage and regain the same amount of hit points.
Level 24 or 29: +3d8 necrotic damage and regain the same amount of hit points.

Vanguard Weapon
Level 3+

Favored by soldiers of the frontline, this weapon makes any charge formidable.

Lvl 3	+1	680 gp		Lvl 18	+4	85,000 gp
Lvl 8	+2	3,400 gp		Lvl 23	+5	425,000 gp
Lvl 13	+3	17,000 gp		Lvl 28	+6	2,125,000 gp

Weapon: Any melee

Enhancement: Attack rolls and damage rolls

Critical: +1d8 damage per plus

Property: Deal +1d8 damage on any successful charge.

Power (Daily): Minor Action. Use this power when you make a charge attack. If you hit with your charge attack, all allies within 10 squares of you gain a +1 bonus to attack rolls and gain your Charisma bonus as a bonus to damage rolls until the start of your next turn.

Vengeful Weapon
Level 5+

When an ally's life is on the line, the wielder of this weapon becomes a deadly adversary.

Lvl 5	+1	1,000 gp		Lvl 20	+4	125,000 gp
Lvl 10	+2	5,000 gp		Lvl 25	+5	625,000 gp
Lvl 15	+3	25,000 gp		Lvl 30	+6	3,125,000 gp

Weapon: Any melee

Enhancement: Attack rolls and damage rolls

Critical: +1d6 damage per plus

Power (Encounter): Free Action. Use this power when an attack hits a bloodied ally within 10 squares of you. Gain a +2 power bonus to attack rolls and +1d10 on damage rolls against the attacker until the end of your next turn.
Level 15 or 20: +2d10 damage.
Level 25 or 30: +3d10 damage.

Waterbane Weapon
Level 8+

Creatures of stream and sea have reason to tremble before this weapon.

Lvl 8	+2	3,400 gp	Lvl 23	+5	425,000 gp
Lvl 13	+3	17,000 gp	Lvl 28	+6	2,125,000 gp
Lvl 18	+4	85,000 gp			

Weapon: Axe, Crossbow, Heavy Blade, Light Blade, Spear

Enhancement: Attack rolls and damage rolls

Critical: +1d6 damage per plus, or +1d10 damage per plus against creatures that have the aquatic or water keyword.

Property: You take no attack penalty when using this weapon underwater.

Power (Daily): Minor Action. Your next attack with this weapon gains a +2 power bonus to the attack roll if you are underwater, or a +5 power bonus to the attack roll against a creature that has the water or the aquatic keyword.

Withering Weapon
Level 13+

Each blow with this weapon weakens armor and resolve.

Lvl 13	+3	17,000 gp	Lvl 23	+5	425,000 gp
Lvl 18	+4	85,000 gp	Lvl 28	+6	2,125,000 gp

Weapon: Any melee

Enhancement: Attack rolls and damage rolls

Critical: +1d6 damage per plus

Property: Each time you hit with this weapon in melee, your target takes a cumulative -1 penalty to AC. The target can make a saving throw to end the entire penalty, but it can receive the penalty again with future attacks.

Wounding Weapon
Level 4+

This weapon tears through an enemy's flesh, creating wounds that bleed profusely.

Lvl 4	+1	840 gp	Lvl 19	+4	105,000 gp
Lvl 9	+2	4,200 gp	Lvl 24	+5	525,000 gp
Lvl 14	+3	21,000 gp	Lvl 29	+6	2,625,000 gp

Weapon: Axe, Bow, Crossbow, Heavy Blade, Light Blade, Spear

Enhancement: Attack rolls and damage rolls

Critical: +1d6 damage per plus

Property: When an attack with this weapon deals untyped ongoing damage, the target of the attack takes a penalty to the saving throw equal to this weapon's enhancement bonus.

Power (Daily): Free Action. Use this power when you hit with the weapon. The target also takes ongoing 5 damage (save ends).

Level 14 or 19: Ongoing 10 damage (save ends).

Level 24 or 29: Ongoing 15 damage (save ends).

Voidcrystal Weapon
Level 14+

This black crystal weapon can briefly banish a creature to a dark, secluded location.

Lvl 14	+3	21,000 gp	Lvl 24	+5	525,000 gp
Lvl 19	+4	105,000 gp	Lvl 29	+6	2,625,000 gp

Weapon: Any melee

Enhancement: Attack rolls and damage rolls

Critical: +1d6 damage per plus

Power (Daily ✦ Teleportation): Free Action. Use this power when you hit a creature with this weapon. The target disappears from the world until the start of your next turn, at which point the target reappears in an unoccupied space of your choice within 3 squares of you.

Waterbane weapon

HOLY SYMBOLS

Channeled through this holy symbol, my faith is a weapon to fear.

Holy symbols come in a variety of shapes and designs, and champions of the gods use them as implements in battle. In the hand of clerics and paladins, they are as much weapons as swords are to fighters.

Sometimes a holy symbol is keyed to a specific deity and can be used only by worshipers of that deity. If the gods in your game world are different from the ones featured in the *Player's Handbook*, feel free to tweak the names and prerequisites of these holy symbols to serve the needs of your home campaign.

HOLY SYMBOLS

Lvl	Name	Price (gp)
2	Symbol of divinity +1	520
2	Symbol of good fortune +1	520
2	Symbol of reproach +1	520
2	Symbol of resilience +1	520
3	Symbol of confrontation +1	680
3	Symbol of divine reach +1	680
4	Symbol of astral might +1	840
4	Symbol of mortality +1	840
4	Symbol of vengeance +1	840
5	Symbol of dire fate +1	1,000
7	Symbol of divinity +2	2,600
7	Symbol of freedom +2	2,600
7	Symbol of good fortune +2	2,600
7	Symbol of perseverance +2	2,600
7	Symbol of reproach +2	2,600
7	Symbol of resilience +2	2,600
7	Symbol of shielding +2	2,600
8	Black feather of the Raven Queen +2	3,400
8	Cog of Erathis +2	3,400

HOLY SYMBOLS (CONTINUED)

Lvl	Name	Price (gp)
8	Dragonscale of Bahamut +2	3,400
8	Eye of Ioun +2	3,400
8	Fist of Kord +2	3,400
8	Mask of Melora +2	3,400
8	Moon disk of Sehanine +2	3,400
8	Moradin's indestructible anvil +2	3,400
8	Star of Corellon +2	3,400
8	Stone of Avandra +2	3,400
8	Sun disk of Pelor +2	3,400
8	Symbol of confrontation +2	3,400
8	Symbol of divine reach +2	3,400
9	Symbol of astral might +2	4,200
9	Symbol of mortality +2	4,200
9	Symbol of penitence +2	4,200
9	Symbol of vengeance +2	4,200
10	Symbol of dire fate +2	5,000
12	Symbol of divinity +3	13,000
12	Symbol of freedom +3	13,000
12	Symbol of good fortune +3	13,000
12	Symbol of lifebonding +3	13,000
12	Symbol of perseverance +3	13,000
12	Symbol of reproach +3	13,000
12	Symbol of resilience +3	13,000
12	Symbol of shielding +3	13,000
13	Black feather of the Raven Queen +3	17,000
13	Cog of Erathis +3	17,000
13	Dragonscale of Bahamut +3	17,000
13	Eye of Ioun +3	17,000
13	Fist of Kord +3	17,000
13	Mask of Melora +3	17,000
13	Moon disk of Sehanine +3	17,000
13	Moradin's indestructible anvil +3	17,000
13	Star of Corellon +3	17,000
13	Stone of Avandra +3	17,000
13	Sun disk of Pelor +3	17,000
13	Symbol of confrontation +3	17,000

WILLIAM O'CONNOR

Lvl	Name	Price (gp)
13	Symbol of divine reach +3	17,000
14	Symbol of astral might +3	21,000
14	Symbol of censure +3	21,000
14	Symbol of mortality +3	21,000
14	Symbol of penitence +3	21,000
14	Symbol of vengeance +3	21,000
15	Symbol of brilliance +3	25,000
15	Symbol of dire fate +3	25,000
15	Symbol of renewal +3	25,000
15	Symbol of the warpriest +3	25,000
17	Symbol of dedication +4	65,000
17	Symbol of divinity +4	65,000
17	Symbol of freedom +4	65,000
17	Symbol of good fortune +4	65,000
17	Symbol of lifebonding +4	65,000
17	Symbol of perseverance +4	65,000
17	Symbol of reproach +4	65,000
17	Symbol of resilience +4	65,000
17	Symbol of shielding +4	65,000
17	Symbol of sustenance +4	65,000
18	Black feather of the Raven Queen +4	85,000
18	Cog of Erathis +4	85,000
18	Dragonscale of Bahamut +4	85,000
18	Eye of Ioun +4	85,000
18	Fist of Kord +4	85,000
18	Mask of Melora +4	85,000
18	Moon disk of Sehanine +4	85,000
18	Moradin's indestructible anvil +4	85,000
18	Star of Corellon +4	85,000
18	Stone of Avandra +4	85,000
18	Sun disk of Pelor +4	85,000
18	Symbol of confrontation +4	85,000
18	Symbol of divine reach +4	85,000
18	Symbol of sacrifice +4	85,000
19	Symbol of astral might +4	105,000
19	Symbol of censure +4	105,000
19	Symbol of mortality +4	105,000
19	Symbol of penitence +4	105,000
19	Symbol of vengeance +4	105,000
20	Symbol of brilliance +4	125,000
20	Symbol of dire fate +4	125,000
20	Symbol of renewal +4	125,000
20	Symbol of the warpriest +4	125,000
22	Symbol of dedication +5	325,000
22	Symbol of divinity +5	325,000
22	Symbol of freedom +5	325,000
22	Symbol of good fortune +5	325,000
22	Symbol of lifebonding +5	325,000
22	Symbol of perseverance +5	325,000
22	Symbol of reproach +5	325,000
22	Symbol of resilience +5	325,000
22	Symbol of shielding +5	325,000
22	Symbol of sustenance +5	325,000
23	Black feather of the Raven Queen +5	425,000
23	Cog of Erathis +5	425,000

Lvl	Name	Price (gp)
23	Dragonscale of Bahamut +5	425,000
23	Eye of Ioun +5	425,000
23	Fist of Kord +5	425,000
23	Mask of Melora +5	425,000
23	Moon disk of Sehanine +5	425,000
23	Moradin's indestructible anvil +5	425,000
23	Star of Corellon +5	425,000
23	Stone of Avandra +5	425,000
23	Sun disk of Pelor +5	425,000
23	Symbol of confrontation +5	425,000
23	Symbol of divine reach +5	425,000
23	Symbol of sacrifice +5	425,000
24	Symbol of astral might +5	525,000
24	Symbol of censure +5	525,000
24	Symbol of mortality +5	525,000
24	Symbol of penitence +5	525,000
24	Symbol of vengeance +5	525,000
25	Symbol of brilliance +5	625,000
25	Symbol of damnation +5	625,000
25	Symbol of dire fate +5	625,000
25	Symbol of radiant vengeance +5	625,000
25	Symbol of renewal +5	625,000
25	Symbol of the warpriest +5	625,000
27	Symbol of dedication +6	1,625,000
27	Symbol of divinity +6	1,625,000
27	Symbol of freedom +6	1,625,000
27	Symbol of good fortune +6	1,625,000
27	Symbol of lifebonding +6	1,625,000
27	Symbol of perseverance +6	1,625,000
27	Symbol of reproach +6	1,625,000
27	Symbol of resilience +6	1,625,000
27	Symbol of shielding +6	1,625,000
27	Symbol of sustenance +6	1,625,000
28	Black feather of the Raven Queen +6	2,125,000
28	Cog of Erathis +6	2,125,000
28	Dragonscale of Bahamut +6	2,125,000
28	Eye of Ioun +6	2,125,000
28	Fist of Kord +6	2,125,000
28	Mask of Melora +6	2,125,000
28	Moon disk of Sehanine +6	2,125,000
28	Moradin's indestructible anvil +6	2,125,000
28	Star of Corellon +6	2,125,000
28	Stone of Avandra +6	2,125,000
28	Sun disk of Pelor +6	2,125,000
28	Symbol of confrontation +6	2,125,000
28	Symbol of divine reach +6	2,125,000
28	Symbol of sacrifice +6	2,125,000
29	Symbol of astral might +6	2,625,000
29	Symbol of censure +6	2,625,000
29	Symbol of mortality +6	2,625,000
29	Symbol of penitence +6	2,625,000
29	Symbol of vengeance +6	2,625,000
30	Symbol of brilliance +6	3,125,000
30	Symbol of damnation +6	3,125,000
30	Symbol of dire fate +6	3,125,000

HOLY SYMBOLS (CONTINUED)

Lvl	Name	Price (gp)
30	Symbol of radiant vengeance +6	3,125,000
30	Symbol of renewal +6	3,125,000
30	Symbol of revivification +6	3,125,000
30	Symbol of the warpriest +6	3,125,000

Black Feather of the Raven Queen — Level 8+

This onyx feather transforms the life force of a slain enemy into cold energy that can be unleashed upon another adversary.

Lvl 8	+2	3,400 gp	Lvl 23	+5	425,000 gp
Lvl 13	+3	17,000 gp	Lvl 28	+6	2,125,000 gp
Lvl 18	+4	85,000 gp			

Implement (Holy Symbol)

Prerequisite: To use this symbol, you must worship the Raven Queen.

Enhancement: Attack rolls and damage rolls

Critical: +1d6 cold damage per plus

Power (Daily ✦ Cold): Free Action. Use this power when you reduce a target to 0 hit points or fewer with an attack using this holy symbol. One creature within 5 squares of the target takes cold damage equal to your Charisma modifier and is immobilized (save ends).

Cog of Erathis — Level 8+

This holy symbol allows you to momentarily harness the will of Erathis to propel an ally to act with alacrity.

Lvl 8	+2	3,400 gp	Lvl 23	+5	425,000 gp
Lvl 13	+3	17,000 gp	Lvl 28	+6	2,125,000 gp
Lvl 18	+4	85,000 gp			

Implement (Holy Symbol)

Prerequisite: To use this symbol, you must worship Erathis.

Enhancement: Attack rolls and damage rolls

Critical: +1d6 damage per plus

Power (Daily): Free Action. Use this power when you hit with an attack using this holy symbol. An ally within 10 squares of you takes his next turn as soon as your turn ends. Move his place in the initiative order to directly after your own.

Dragonscale of Bahamut — Level 8+

Emblazoned with the image of the Platinum Dragon, this dragon scale-shaped symbol bestows protection on nearby allies.

Lvl 8	+2	3,400 gp	Lvl 23	+5	425,000 gp
Lvl 13	+3	17,000 gp	Lvl 28	+6	2,125,000 gp
Lvl 18	+4	85,000 gp			

Implement (Holy Symbol)

Prerequisite: To use this symbol, you must worship Bahamut.

Enhancement: Attack rolls and damage rolls

Critical: +1d8 damage per plus

Power (Daily): Free Action. Use this power when you hit with an attack using this holy symbol. Each ally within 2 squares of you gains a +1 power bonus to all defenses until the end of your next turn.

1. *Fist of Kord;* 2. *Star of Corellon;* 3. *Sun disk of Pelor;* 4. *Black feather of the Raven Queen;* 5. *Cog of Erathis;* 6. *Moradin's indestructible Anvil*

LEE MOYER

Eye of Ioun
Level 8+

A holy symbol shaped like an eye, this icon of Ioun allows you to tap into the power of prophecy to avoid future danger.

Lvl 8	+2	3,400 gp	Lvl 23	+5	425,000 gp
Lvl 13	+3	17,000 gp	Lvl 28	+6	2,125,000 gp
Lvl 18	+4	85,000 gp			

Implement (Holy Symbol)

Prerequisite: To use this symbol, you must worship Ioun.

Enhancement: Attack rolls and damage rolls

Critical: +1d6 damage per plus

Power (Daily): Free Action. Use this power when you hit with an attack using this holy symbol. At any one time until the end of the encounter, you can force the target you hit to reroll an attack roll made against you. It must use the new result.

Fist of Kord
Level 8+

Kord favors those who show strength, so when you succeed on an attack with this fist-shaped symbol, your next attack strikes harder.

Lvl 8	+2	3,400 gp	Lvl 23	+5	425,000 gp
Lvl 13	+3	17,000 gp	Lvl 28	+6	2,125,000 gp
Lvl 18	+4	85,000 gp			

Implement (Holy Symbol)

Prerequisite: To use this symbol, you must worship Kord.

Enhancement: Attack rolls and damage rolls

Critical: +1d8 lightning damage per plus

Property: When you hit with an attack delivered by this implement, you gain a bonus to damage rolls with melee weapon attacks equal to the holy symbol's enhancement bonus until the end of your next turn. (This bonus stacks with any enhancement bonus of the weapon delivering the attack.)

Mask of Melora
Level 8+

Shaped as a leaf or seashell, this symbol channels your faith to bolster your conviction against unnatural creatures.

Lvl 8	+2	3,400 gp	Lvl 23	+5	425,000 gp
Lvl 13	+3	17,000 gp	Lvl 28	+6	2,125,000 gp
Lvl 18	+4	85,000 gp			

Implement (Holy Symbol)

Prerequisite: To use this symbol, you must worship Melora.

Enhancement: Attack rolls and damage rolls

Critical: +1d6 damage per plus, or +1d10 damage per plus against aberrant creatures.

Power (Daily): Free Action. Use this power when you hit an aberrant creature with an attack using this holy symbol. You gain a +1 power bonus to attack rolls against aberrant creatures until the end of the encounter.

Moon Disk of Sehanine
Level 8+

This symbol allows its user to lower a darkening veil over an enemy, temporarily confounding the creature.

Lvl 8	+2	3,400 gp	Lvl 23	+5	425,000 gp
Lvl 13	+3	17,000 gp	Lvl 28	+6	2,125,000 gp
Lvl 18	+4	85,000 gp			

Implement (Holy Symbol)

Prerequisite: To use this symbol, you must worship Sehanine.

Enhancement: Attack rolls and damage rolls

Critical: +1d6 damage per plus

Power (Daily): Free Action. Use this power when you hit with an attack using this holy symbol. The target takes a –5 penalty to the first attack roll it makes before the start of your next turn.

Moradin's Indestructible Anvil
Level 8+

This anvil-shaped holy symbol allows one to bestow the durability of Moradin's crafts upon a recipient.

Lvl 8	+2	3,400 gp	Lvl 23	+5	425,000 gp
Lvl 13	+3	17,000 gp	Lvl 28	+6	2,125,000 gp
Lvl 18	+4	85,000 gp			

Implement (Holy Symbol)

Prerequisite: To use this symbol, you must worship Moradin.

Enhancement: Attack rolls and damage rolls

Critical: +1d6 damage per plus

Power (Daily): Free Action. Use this power when you hit with an attack using this holy symbol. One ally within 5 squares of you gains resist 5 to all damage until the start of your next turn.
Level 18 or 23: Resist 10 to all damage.
Level 28: Resist 15 to all damage.

Star of Corellon
Level 8+

This star-shaped pendant flashes with an inner light when you unleash arcane or divine energy.

Lvl 8	+2	3,400 gp	Lvl 23	+5	425,000 gp
Lvl 13	+3	17,000 gp	Lvl 28	+6	2,125,000 gp
Lvl 18	+4	85,000 gp			

Implement (Holy Symbol)

Prerequisite: To use this symbol, you must worship Corellon.

Enhancement: Attack rolls and damage rolls

Critical: +1d6 damage per plus

Property: You can use this holy symbol as an implement for any arcane power.

Power (Daily): Free Action. Use this power when you hit with an attack using this holy symbol. Gain an additional use of your *healing word* power or your Channel Divinity class feature for this encounter.

Stone of Avandra — Level 8+

Breathing a quick prayer to Avandra, your faith is channeled through this stone to turn the fates in your favor.

Lvl 8	+2	3,400 gp	Lvl 23	+5	425,000 gp
Lvl 13	+3	17,000 gp	Lvl 28	+6	2,125,000 gp
Lvl 18	+4	85,000 gp			

Implement (Holy Symbol)

Prerequisite: To use this symbol, you must worship Avandra.

Enhancement: Attack rolls and damage rolls

Critical: +1d6 damage per plus

Power (Daily): Free Action. Reroll an attack roll you made using this holy symbol and use the new result.

Sun Disk of Pelor — Level 8+

This holy symbol flashes with light as your faith unleashes radiant energy that sears your enemies.

Lvl 8	+2	3,400 gp	Lvl 23	+5	425,000 gp
Lvl 13	+3	17,000 gp	Lvl 28	+6	2,125,000 gp
Lvl 18	+4	85,000 gp			

Implement (Holy Symbol)

Prerequisite: To use this symbol, you must worship Pelor.

Enhancement: Attack rolls and damage rolls

Critical: +1d10 radiant damage per plus

Power (At-Will ✦ Radiant): Free Action. All damage dealt by powers using this holy symbol is radiant damage. Another free action returns the damage to normal.

Symbol of Astral Might — Level 4+

This symbol is a potent tool against creatures from the Elemental Chaos.

Lvl 4	+1	840 gp	Lvl 19	+4	105,000 gp
Lvl 9	+2	4,200 gp	Lvl 24	+5	525,000 gp
Lvl 14	+3	21,000 gp	Lvl 29	+6	2,625,000 gp

Implement (Holy Symbol)

Enhancement: Attack rolls and damage rolls

Critical: +1d6 damage per plus, or +1d10 damage per plus against elemental creatures.

Power (Daily): Free Action. Use this power when you hit with an attack using this holy symbol. Deal +1d10 damage to each elemental creature hit by the attack.
Level 14 or 19: +2d10 damage against elemental creatures.
Level 24 or 29: +3d10 damage against elemental creatures.

Symbol of Brilliance — Level 15+

This holy symbol shines with the fiery spirit of your devotion, infusing the intensity of your beliefs into blinding power.

| Lvl 15 | +3 | 25,000 gp | Lvl 25 | +5 | 625,000 gp |
| Lvl 20 | +4 | 125,000 gp | Lvl 30 | +6 | 3,125,000 gp |

Implement (Holy Symbol)

Enhancement: Attack rolls and damage rolls

Critical: +1d6 radiant damage per plus, and the target is blinded until the start of your next turn.

Power (Daily): Free Action. Use this power when you hit with an attack using this holy symbol. The target is blinded until the start of your next turn.

Symbol of Censure — Level 14+

Your faith transforms this mundane-looking holy symbol into a mesmerizing beacon that distracts your enemy.

| Lvl 14 | +3 | 21,000 gp | Lvl 24 | +5 | 525,000 gp |
| Lvl 19 | +4 | 105,000 gp | Lvl 29 | +6 | 2,625,000 gp |

Implement (Holy Symbol)

Enhancement: Attack rolls and damage rolls

Critical: +1d6 damage per plus, and the target is dazed until the start of your next turn.

Power (Daily): Free Action. Use this power when you hit with an attack using this holy symbol. The target is dazed until the start of your next turn.

Symbol of brilliance

Symbol of Confrontation — Level 3+

This holy symbol enhances the power of your divine challenge.

Lvl 3	+1	680 gp	Lvl 18	+4	85,000 gp
Lvl 8	+2	3,400 gp	Lvl 23	+5	425,000 gp
Lvl 13	+3	17,000 gp	Lvl 28	+6	2,125,000 gp

Implement (Holy Symbol)

Enhancement: Attack rolls and damage rolls

Critical: +1d6 damage per plus, or +1d10 damage per plus against enemies currently marked by you.

Power (Daily): Free Action. Use this power when you hit with an attack using this holy symbol. Your divine challenge remains in effect on its current target until the end of your next turn, even if it would normally end.

Symbol of Damnation — Level 25+

Your pious hatred for an enemy is enhanced by this holy symbol.

| Lvl 25 | +5 | 625,000 gp | Lvl 30 | +6 | 3,125,000 gp |

Implement (Holy Symbol)

Enhancement: Attack rolls and damage rolls

Critical: +1d8 damage per plus, and the target gains vulnerable 5 to all attacks until the start of your next turn.

Power (Daily): Free Action. Use this power when you hit with an attack using this holy symbol. The target gains vulnerable 5 to all attacks until the start of your next turn.

Symbol of Dedication — Level 17+

When you smite foes that you have marked as an enemy of your god, this holy symbol gives you divine protection against that enemy.

| Lvl 17 | +4 | 65,000 gp | Lvl 27 | +6 | 1,625,000 gp |
| Lvl 22 | +5 | 325,000 gp |

Implement (Holy Symbol)

Enhancement: Attack rolls and damage rolls

Critical: +1d6 damage per plus, or +1d10 damage per plus against enemies currently marked by you.

Power (Daily): Free Action. Use this power when you hit a target currently marked by you with an attack delivered by this symbol. Gain a +2 power bonus to all defenses until the end of your next turn.

Symbol of Dire Fate — Level 5+

This symbol glimmers with divine light as you press your advantage against an enemy.

Lvl 5	+1	1,000 gp	Lvl 20	+4	125,000 gp
Lvl 10	+2	5,000 gp	Lvl 25	+5	625,000 gp
Lvl 15	+3	25,000 gp	Lvl 30	+6	3,125,000 gp

Implement (Holy Symbol)

Enhancement: Attack rolls and damage rolls

Critical: +1d6 damage per plus, or +1d12 damage per plus against enemies currently marked by you.

Property: When you use this holy symbol to attack a target currently marked by you, you gain a +1 bonus to the attack roll.

Symbol of Divine Reach — Level 3+

This symbol lets you extend the reach of your retribution against enemies of your deity.

Lvl 3	+1	680 gp	Lvl 18	+4	85,000 gp
Lvl 8	+2	3,400 gp	Lvl 23	+5	425,000 gp
Lvl 13	+3	17,000 gp	Lvl 28	+6	2,125,000 gp

Implement (Holy Symbol)

Enhancement: Attack rolls and damage rolls

Critical: +1d6 damage per plus, or +1d10 damage per plus with ranged and area attacks.

Property: When using this holy symbol to deliver a ranged or area prayer, add the symbol's enhancement bonus to the range. For example, a +3 *symbol of divine reach* would increase "area burst 5 within 10 squares" to "area burst 5 within 13 squares."

Symbol of Divinity — Level 2+

This holy symbol gathers the power of your divine attacks, allowing you to rechannel that might.

Lvl 2	+1	520 gp	Lvl 17	+4	65,000 gp
Lvl 7	+2	2,600 gp	Lvl 22	+5	325,000 gp
Lvl 12	+3	13,000 gp	Lvl 27	+6	1,625,000 gp

Implement (Holy Symbol)

Enhancement: Attack rolls and damage rolls

Critical: +1d6 damage per plus

Power (Daily): Free Action. Use this power when you hit with an attack using this holy symbol. Gain one additional use of Channel Divinity for this encounter.

Symbol of Freedom — Level 7+

This symbol allows you or one of your allies to shrug off certain debilitating conditions.

Lvl 7	+2	2,600 gp	Lvl 22	+5	325,000 gp
Lvl 12	+3	13,000 gp	Lvl 27	+6	1,625,000 gp
Lvl 17	+4	65,000 gp

Implement (Holy Symbol)

Enhancement: Attack rolls and damage rolls

Critical: +1d6 damage per plus

Power (Daily): Free Action. Use this power when you hit with an attack using this holy symbol. You or any one ally within 10 squares of you can roll a saving throw against the any effect that includes the dominated, immobilized, restrained, or slowed condition. Add the symbol's enhancement bonus as a power bonus to the save.

Symbol of Good Fortune — Level 2+

Divine fortune favors you, bolstering your ability to strike accurately at your enemies.

Lvl 2	+1	520 gp	Lvl 17	+4	65,000 gp
Lvl 7	+2	2,600 gp	Lvl 22	+5	325,000 gp
Lvl 12	+3	13,000 gp	Lvl 27	+6	1,625,000 gp

Implement (Holy Symbol)

Enhancement: Attack rolls and damage rolls

Critical: +1d6 damage per plus

Power (Daily): Free Action. Use this power when you hit with an attack using this holy symbol. Gain a +2 power bonus to the next attack roll you make before the end of your next turn.

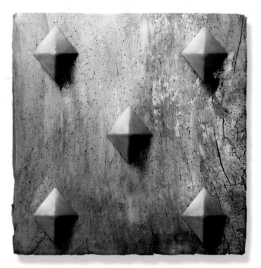
Symbol of good fortune

Symbol of Penitence — Level 9+

This symbol ensures that light continues to sear your enemy even after your initial attack.

Lvl 9	+2	4,200 gp	Lvl 24	+5	525,000 gp
Lvl 14	+3	21,000 gp	Lvl 29	+3	2,625,000 gp
Lvl 19	+4	105,000 gp			

Implement (Holy Symbol)

Enhancement: Attack rolls and damage rolls

Critical: +1d6 radiant damage per plus

Power (Daily ✦ Radiant): Free Action. Use this power when you hit with a radiant attack delivered by this holy symbol. The target takes 5 radiant damage when it uses a standard action to attack (save ends).
Level 19 or 24: 10 radiant damage.
Level 29: 15 radiant damage.

Symbol of Perseverance — Level 7+

This symbol glows with an inner light, preserving a fragment of your life force to bestow when you or an ally needs it most.

Lvl 7	+2	2,600 gp	Lvl 22	+5	325,000 gp
Lvl 12	+3	13,000 gp	Lvl 27	+6	1,625,000 gp
Lvl 17	+4	65,000 gp			

Implement (Holy Symbol)

Enhancement: Attack rolls and damage rolls

Critical: +1d6 damage per plus

Power (Daily ✦ Healing): Free Action. Use this power when you hit with an attack delivered by this holy symbol. A dying ally within 20 squares of you regains hit points as if he had spent a healing surge; add the symbol's enhancement bonus to the hit points regained.

Symbol of Radiant Vengeance — Level 25+

As you assail an enemy with attacks, this symbol causes your strikes to burn with radiant energy.

Lvl 25	+5	625,000 gp	Lvl 30	+6	3,125,000 gp

Implement (Holy Symbol)

Enhancement: Attack rolls and damage rolls

Critical: +1d6 radiant damage per plus, or +1d10 radiant damage per plus if the target attacked an ally of yours since the end of your last turn.

Property: If your attack with this holy symbol hits an enemy that attacked an ally of yours since the end of your last turn, you deal an extra 1d10 radiant damage to that enemy.

Symbol of Renewal — Level 15+

You channel your conviction through this symbol and grant yourself or a nearby ally remarkable regenerative powers.

Lvl 15	+3	25,000 gp	Lvl 25	+5	625,000 gp
Lvl 20	+4	125,000 gp	Lvl 30	+6	3,125,000 gp

Implement (Holy Symbol)

Enhancement: Attack rolls and damage rolls

Critical: +1d6 damage per plus

Power (Daily ✦ Healing): Free Action. Use this power when you reduce a target to 0 or fewer hit points with an attack delivered by this holy symbol. You or one ally within 5 squares of you gains regeneration 5 for the rest of encounter.
Level 25 or 30: Regeneration 10.

Symbol of Lifebonding — Level 12+

This symbol diverts some the energy devoted to your attack into healing for a nearby ally.

Lvl 12	+3	13,000 gp	Lvl 22	+5	325,000 gp
Lvl 17	+4	65,000 gp	Lvl 27	+6	1,625,000 gp

Implement (Holy Symbol)

Enhancement: Attack rolls and damage rolls

Critical: +1d6 damage per plus

Power (Daily ✦ Healing): Free Action. Use this power when you hit with an attack using this holy symbol. The attack deals only half the normal damage. You or an ally within 10 squares of you regains hit points equal to the reduced amount of damage dealt.

Symbol of Mortality — Level 4+

This symbol is a potent tool against undead and immortals.

Lvl 4	+1	840 gp	Lvl 19	+4	105,000 gp
Lvl 9	+2	4,200 gp	Lvl 24	+5	525,000 gp
Lvl 14	+3	21,000 gp	Lvl 29	+6	2,625,000 gp

Implement (Holy Symbol)

Enhancement: Attack rolls and damage rolls

Critical: +1d6 damage per plus, or +1d10 damage per plus against undead or immortal creatures.

Power (Daily): Minor Action. Your next attack with this holy symbol deals an extra 1d4 damage. If the creature has the immortal origin or the undead keyword, the creature takes an extra 1d8 damage instead.
Level 14 or 19: An extra 2d4 damage or an extra 2d8 damage if the target has the immortal origin or undead keyword.
Level 24 or 29: An extra 2d4 damage or an extra 2d8 damage if the target has the immortal origin or undead keyword.

Symbol of Reproach — Level 2+

This symbol delivers a debilitating attack that saps your enemy's vitality and impairs its ability to persevere.

Lvl 2	+1	520 gp	Lvl 17	+4	65,000 gp
Lvl 7	+2	2,600 gp	Lvl 22	+5	325,000 gp
Lvl 12	+3	13,000 gp	Lvl 27	+6	1,625,000 gp

Implement (Holy Symbol)

Enhancement: Attack rolls and damage rolls

Critical: +1d6 damage per plus

Power (Daily): Free Action. Use this power when you hit a target with an attack delivered by this holy symbol. Until the end of your next turn, that target takes a -2 penalty to saving throws and can't regain hit points by any means.

Symbol of Resilience — Level 2+

This symbol bolsters confidence and allows allies to shrug off even the deadliest effects.

Lvl 2	+1	520 gp	Lvl 17	+4	65,000 gp
Lvl 7	+2	2,600 gp	Lvl 22	+5	325,000 gp
Lvl 12	+3	13,000 gp	Lvl 27	+6	1,625,000 gp

Implement (Holy Symbol)

Enhancement: Attack rolls and damage rolls

Critical: +1d6 damage per plus

Power (Daily): Free Action. Use this power when you hit with an attack delivered by this symbol. You or an ally within 10 squares of you can roll a saving throw against one effect that a save can end; add the symbol's enhancement bonus as a power bonus to that saving throw.

Symbol of Revivification — Level 30

This symbol holds the power to revive a dead or dying ally.

Lvl 30	+6	3,125,000 gp

Implement (Holy Symbol)

Enhancement: Attack rolls and damage rolls

Critical: +1d6 damage per plus

Power (Daily ✦ Healing): Free Action. Use this power when you hit with an attack using this holy symbol. Spend two healing surges, do not regain any hit points, and choose a dying or dead ally within 10 squares of you. That ally is returned to life at his bloodied hit point total. This power does not revive an ally who's been dead for longer than 1 day.

Symbol of Sacrifice — Level 18+

When you attack with this symbol, you can choose to sacrifice some of your vitality to aid a nearby comrade.

Lvl 18	+4	85,000 gp	Lvl 28	+6	2,125,000 gp
Lvl 23	+5	425,000 gp			

Implement (Holy Symbol)

Enhancement: Attack rolls and damage rolls

Critical: +1d6 damage per plus

Property: Each time you hit with an attack using this holy symbol, you can choose to lose hit points up to the symbol's enhancement bonus. If you do, an ally within 5 squares of you can make a saving throw against one effect that a save can end, with a bonus to the roll equal to the number of hit points you lost.

Symbol of shielding

Symbol of Shielding — Level 7+

Your holy symbol glows as you conjure a nimbus of protection.

Lvl 7	+2	2,600 gp	Lvl 22	+5	325,000 gp
Lvl 12	+3	13,000 gp	Lvl 27	+6	1,625,000 gp
Lvl 17	+4	65,000 gp			

Implement (Holy Symbol)

Enhancement: Attack rolls and damage rolls

Critical: +1d6 damage per plus

Power (Daily): Free Action. Use this power when you hit with an attack using this holy symbol. You or one ally within 2 squares of you gains a +2 power bonus to AC and Reflex defense until the end of your next turn.

Symbol of Sustenance — Level 17+

This symbol is infused with a fragment of your consciousness that allows you to turn your attention elsewhere in battle while maintaining other powers.

Lvl 17	+4	65,000 gp	Lvl 27	+6	1,625,000 gp
Lvl 22	+5	325,000 gp			

Implement (Holy Symbol)

Enhancement: Attack rolls and damage rolls

Critical: +1d6 damage per plus

Power (Daily): Minor Action. One of your powers that has an effect that will end this turn instead lasts until the end of your next turn.

Symbol of the Warpriest — Level 15+

This symbol lets you turn your advantage in battle into a bolstering effect for your allies.

Lvl 15	+3	25,000 gp	Lvl 25	+5	625,000 gp
Lvl 20	+4	125,000 gp	Lvl 30	+6	3,125,000 gp

Implement (Holy Symbol)

Enhancement: Attack rolls and damage rolls

Critical: +1d6 damage per plus

Property: Each time you hit with an attack using this holy symbol, one conscious ally within 5 squares of you regains hit points equal to the symbol's enhancement bonus.

Symbol of Vengeance — Level 4+

This symbol allows you to exact your wrath upon enemies, returning their attacks with devastation.

Lvl 4	+1	840 gp	Lvl 19	+4	105,000 gp
Lvl 9	+2	4,200 gp	Lvl 24	+5	525,000 gp
Lvl 14	+3	21,000 gp	Lvl 29	+6	2,625,000 gp

Implement (Holy Symbol)

Enhancement: Attack rolls and damage rolls

Critical: +1d6 damage per plus

Power (Daily): Free Action. Use this power when you hit with an attack using this holy symbol. If the target of your attack dealt damage to you or an ally since the end of your last turn, you deal an extra 1d8 damage.

If the target of your attack reduced you or an ally to 0 or fewer hit points since the end of your last turn, you instead deal an extra 2d8 damage.

Level 14 or 19: +2d8 or +4d8 damage.

Level 24 or 29: +3d8 or +6d8 damage.

ORBS

The orb held many secrets and great power, yet in those unfathomable depths, one could find madness.

These arcane implements come in a variety of materials and shades, yet all share one defining feature—their spherical shape. Their powers, however, are diverse. An orb might strike terror into the target, or it might overcome the target with a fit of insanity. On the other hand, an orb might enhance the effectiveness of a wielder's psychic powers or allow him or her to see a place that is otherwise beyond sight.

ORBS

Lvl	Name	Price (gp)
2	Orb of debilitating languor +1	520
3	Orb of far seeing +1	680
3	Orb of insurmountable force +1	680
3	Orb of judicious conjuration +1	680
3	Orb of sweet sanctuary +1	680
3	Orb of unlucky exchanges +1	680
4	Orb of fickle fate +1	840
4	Orb of harmonic agony +1	840
6	Orb of impenetrable escape +2	1,800
6	Orb of mental dominion +2	1,800
7	Orb of debilitating languor +2	2,600
7	Orb of spatial contortion +2	2,600
8	Orb of crystalline terror +2	3,400
8	Orb of far seeing +2	3,400
8	Orb of inescapable consequences +2	3,400
8	Orb of insurmountable force +2	3,400
8	Orb of judicious conjuration +2	3,400
8	Orb of sweet sanctuary +2	3,400
8	Orb of unlucky exchanges +2	3,400
9	Orb of fickle fate +2	4,200
9	Orb of harmonic agony +2	4,200

ORBS (CONTINUED)

Lvl	Name	Price (gp)
11	Orb of impenetrable escape +3	9,000
11	Orb of mental dominion +3	9,000
12	Orb of augmented stasis +3	13,000
12	Orb of debilitating languor +3	13,000
12	Orb of spatial contortion +3	13,000
12	Orb of sudden insanity +3	13,000
13	Orb of crystalline terror +3	17,000
13	Orb of far seeing +3	17,000
13	Orb of indefatigable concentration +3	17,000
13	Orb of inescapable consequences +3	17,000
13	Orb of insurmountable force +3	17,000
13	Orb of judicious conjuration +3	17,000
13	Orb of karmic resonance +3	17,000
13	Orb of sweet sanctuary +3	17,000
13	Orb of unlucky exchanges +3	17,000
14	Orb of crimson commitment +3	21,000
14	Orb of draconic majesty +3	21,000
14	Orb of fickle fate +3	21,000
14	Orb of harmonic agony +3	21,000
15	Orb of mighty retort +3	25,000
15	Orb of weakness intensified +3	25,000
16	Orb of impenetrable escape +4	45,000
16	Orb of mental dominion +4	45,000
17	Orb of augmented stasis +4	65,000
17	Orb of debilitating languor +4	65,000
17	Orb of revenant magic +4	65,000
17	Orb of spatial contortion +4	65,000
17	Orb of sudden insanity +4	65,000
18	Orb of crystalline terror +4	85,000
18	Orb of far seeing +4	85,000
18	Orb of indefatigable concentration +4	85,000
18	Orb of inescapable consequences +4	85,000
18	Orb of insurmountable force +4	85,000
18	Orb of judicious conjuration +4	85,000
18	Orb of karmic resonance +4	85,000
18	Orb of unintended solitude +4	85,000
18	Orb of sweet sanctuary +4	85,000
18	Orb of unlucky exchanges +4	85,000
19	Orb of coercive dementia +4	105,000
19	Orb of crimson commitment +4	105,000
19	Orb of draconic majesty +4	105,000
19	Orb of fickle fate +4	105,000
19	Orb of harmonic agony +4	105,000
20	Orb of mighty retort +4	125,000
20	Orb of weakness intensified +4	125,000
21	Orb of impenetrable escape +5	225,000
21	Orb of mental dominion +5	225,000
22	Orb of augmented stasis +5	325,000
22	Orb of debilitating languor +5	325,000
22	Orb of revenant magic +5	325,000
22	Orb of spatial contortion +5	325,000
22	Orb of sudden insanity +5	325,000
23	Orb of unintended solitude +5	425,000
23	Orb of far seeing +5	425,000
23	Orb of indefatigable concentration +5	425,000

ORBS (CONTINUED)

Lvl	Name	Price (gp)
23	Orb of inescapable consequences +5	425,000
23	Orb of insurmountable force +5	425,000
23	Orb of judicious conjuration +5	425,000
23	Orb of karmic resonance +5	425,000
23	Orb of sweet sanctuary +5	425,000
23	Orb of the usurper +5	425,000
23	Orb of unintended solitude +5	425,000
23	Orb of crystalline terror +5	425,000
23	Orb of unlucky exchanges +5	425,000
24	Orb of arcane generosity +5	525,000
24	Orb of coercive dementia +5	525,000
24	Orb of crimson commitment +5	525,000
24	Orb of draconic majesty +5	525,000
24	Orb of fickle fate +5	525,000
24	Orb of harmonic agony +5	525,000
25	Orb of mighty retort +5	625,000
25	Orb of weakness intensified +5	625,000
26	Orb of mental dominion +6	1,125,000
27	Orb of augmented stasis +6	1,625,000
27	Orb of debilitating languor +6	1,625,000
27	Orb of revenant magic +6	1,625,000
27	Orb of spatial contortion +6	1,625,000
27	Orb of sudden insanity +6	1,625,000
28	Orb of crystalline terror +6	2,125,000
28	Orb of far seeing +6	2,125,000
28	Orb of impenetrable escape +6	2,125,000
28	Orb of indefatigable concentration +6	2,125,000
28	Orb of inescapable consequences +6	2,125,000
28	Orb of insurmountable force +6	2,125,000
28	Orb of judicious conjuration +6	2,125,000
28	Orb of karmic resonance +6	2,125,000
28	Orb of sweet sanctuary +6	2,125,000
28	Orb of the usurper +6	2,125,000
28	Orb of unintended solitude +6	2,125,000
28	Orb of unlucky exchanges +6	2,125,000
29	Orb of arcane generosity +6	2,625,000
29	Orb of coercive dementia +6	2,625,000
29	Orb of crimson commitment +6	2,625,000
29	Orb of draconic majesty +6	2,625,000
29	Orb of fickle fate +6	2,625,000
29	Orb of harmonic agony +6	2,625,000
30	Orb of mighty retort +6	3,125,000
30	Orb of weakness intensified +6	3,125,000

Orb of Arcane Generosity — Level 24+

Not all wizards are selfish, power hungry curmudgeons. This orb best serves those gifted with a more generous spirit.

Lvl 24	+5	525,000 gp	Lvl 29	+6	2,625,000 gp

Implement (Orb)

Enhancement: Attack rolls and damage rolls

Critical: +1d8 damage per plus

Power (Daily ✦ Healing): Free Action. Use this power when you use an arcane utility power. All allies within 5 squares of you can spend a healing surge and regain an additional 3d6 hit points.

Orb of Augmented Stasis — Level 12+

When you use this orb to hold a foe in place, that foe also suffers a mental block that limits his actions.

Lvl 12	+3	13,000 gp	Lvl 22	+5	325,000 gp
Lvl 17	+4	65,000 gp	Lvl 27	+6	1,625,000 gp

Implement (Orb)

Enhancement: Attack rolls and damage rolls

Critical: +1d6 damage per plus

Power (Daily): Free Action. Use this power when your attack with this implement immobilizes a target. As long as it is immobilized, the target is also dazed.

Orb of Coercive Dementia — Level 19+

With the use of this orb, a spellcaster sends his enemy spiraling into confusion, depriving the creature of its most powerful attack.

Lvl 19	+4	105,000 gp	Lvl 29	+6	2,625,000 gp
Lvl 24	+5	525,000 gp			

Implement (Orb)

Enhancement: Attack rolls and damage rolls

Critical: +1d8 damage per plus

Power (Daily): Standard Action. Make an attack: Ranged 5; Intelligence vs. Will (add the orb's enhancement bonus to the attack roll); on a hit, the target loses one of its unexpended powers for the rest of the encounter. The lost power is the one with the slowest recharge (daily is slower than encounter, encounter is slower than recharge 6, and so on). If multiple powers qualify as having the slowest recharge, randomly determine which one is lost. If the target has no unexpended powers that are not at-will, you regain the use of this power.

Orb of Crimson Commitment — Level 14+

This orb glows a bright red when in use, bestowing power and luck to your attack.

Lvl 14	+3	21,000 gp	Lvl 24	+5	525,000 gp
Lvl 19	+4	105,000 gp	Lvl 29	+6	2,625,000 gp

Implement (Orb)

Enhancement: Attack rolls and damage rolls

Critical: +1d6 damage per plus, or +1d12 damage per plus while you are bloodied.

Power (Daily): Free Action. Use this power when an attack with this orb misses. Spend a healing surge to reroll the attack, adding a +5 power bonus to the attack roll. You do not regain hit points by spending the healing surge.

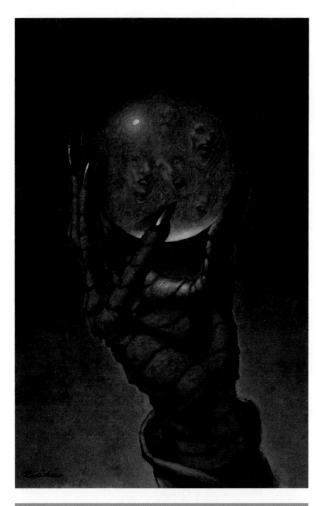

Orb of Draconic Majesty — Level 14+

A winged, draconic shape dances in the orb, lending you the fearsome seeming of a dragon when you wish.

| Lvl 14 | +3 | 21,000 gp | Lvl 24 | +5 | 525,000 gp |
| Lvl 19 | +4 | 105,000 gp | Lvl 29 | +6 | 2,625,000 gp |

Implement (Orb)

Enhancement: Attack rolls and damage rolls

Critical: +1d6 damage per plus

Power (Daily ✦ Fear): Free Action. Use this power when your close or area attack with this implement drops a target to 0 or fewer hit points. Any other targets hit by the same attack are dazed until the end of your next turn.

Orb of Far Seeing — Level 3+

You capture the image of your enemy in this translucent sphere, leaving him no place to hide.

Lvl 3	+1	680 gp	Lvl 18	+4	85,000 gp
Lvl 8	+2	3,400 gp	Lvl 23	+5	425,000 gp
Lvl 13	+3	17,000 gp	Lvl 28	+6	2,125,000 gp

Implement (Orb)

Enhancement: Attack rolls and damage rolls

Critical: +1d6 damage per plus

Power (Encounter): Minor Action. Choose a target within 10 squares of you. Until the end of the encounter, this target is considered half as far away for the purpose of ranged attacks made with this orb.

Power (Daily): Free Action. Use this power when you make a ranged attack with this implement on the target affected by this orb's encounter power. The attack does not require line of sight or line of effect and takes no penalty for concealment or cover.

Orb of Fickle Fate — Level 4+

Light and shadow swirl inside this globe when you bestow the implement's boon upon an ally and its curse upon an enemy.

Lvl 4	+1	840 gp	Lvl 19	+4	105,000 gp
Lvl 9	+2	4,200 gp	Lvl 24	+5	525,000 gp
Lvl 14	+3	21,000 gp	Lvl 29	+6	2,625,000 gp

Implement (Orb)

Enhancement: Attack rolls and damage rolls

Critical: +1d6 damage per plus

Power (Daily): Minor Action. A target within 10 squares of you takes a -2 penalty to saving throws and you or an ally within 10 squares of you gains a +2 power bonus to saving throws (target's save ends both).
Level 14 or 19: -4 penalty/+4 bonus.
Level 24 or 29: -6 penalty/+6 bonus.

Orb of Crystalline Terror — Level 8+

The screaming faces of past victims roil within this dread orb, striking fear into your enemy's heart.

Lvl 8	+2	3,400 gp	Lvl 23	+5	425,000 gp
Lvl 13	+3	17,000 gp	Lvl 28	+6	2,125,000 gp
Lvl 18	+4	85,000 gp			

Implement (Orb)

Enhancement: Attack rolls and damage rolls

Critical: +1d6 damage per plus, or +1d8 damage per plus if the attack has the fear keyword.

Power (Daily ✦ Fear): Free Action. Use this power when an attack with this orb hits the target's Will defense. The target takes a -2 penalty to all defenses (save ends).

Orb of Debilitating Languor — Level 2+

This shadowy orb leaves your enemy enfeebled.

Lvl 2	+1	520 gp	Lvl 17	+4	65,000 gp
Lvl 7	+2	2,600 gp	Lvl 22	+5	325,000 gp
Lvl 12	+3	13,000 gp	Lvl 27	+6	1,625,000 gp

Implement (Orb)

Enhancement: Attack rolls and damage rolls

Critical: +1d6 damage per plus

Power (Daily): Free Action. Use this power when an attack with this orb hits the target's Fortitude defense. The target is slowed (save ends).

Orb of Harmonic Agony · Level 4+

When tapped, this orb rings with a clear bass tone, combining with your thunder attacks to rattle an enemy's senses.

Lvl 4	+1	840 gp	Lvl 19	+4	105,000 gp
Lvl 9	+2	4,200 gp	Lvl 24	+5	525,000 gp
Lvl 14	+3	21,000 gp	Lvl 29	+6	2,625,000 gp

Implement (Orb)

Enhancement: Attack rolls and damage rolls

Critical: +1d6 thunder damage per plus

Power (Daily ✦ Thunder): Free Action. Use this power when you hit with a power that has the thunder keyword. The target is deafened for the rest of the encounter and takes ongoing thunder 5 damage (save ends).
Level 14 or 19: Ongoing 10 thunder.
Level 24 or 29: Ongoing 15 thunder.

Orb of Impenetrable Escape · Level 6+

This murky orb reflects the visage of your enemy suffering from an ongoing barrage of conditions and afflictions.

Lvl 6	+2	1,800 gp	Lvl 21	+5	225,000 gp
Lvl 11	+3	9,000 gp	Lvl 26	+6	1,125,000 gp
Lvl 16	+4	45,000 gp			

Implement (Orb)

Enhancement: Attack rolls and damage rolls

Critical: +1d6 damage per plus

Power (Daily): Free Action. Use this power when a creature makes a save against one of your powers. It rerolls its saving throw and must take the new result.

Orb of Indefatigable Concentration · Level 13+

The wielder of this crystalline orb can temporarily transfers a fraction of his consciousness into it, allowing him to focus his attention elsewhere.

| Lvl 13 | +3 | 17,000 gp | Lvl 23 | +5 | 425,000 gp |
| Lvl 18 | +4 | 85,000 gp | Lvl 28 | +6 | 2,125,000 gp |

Implement (Orb)

Enhancement: Attack rolls and damage rolls

Critical: +1d6 damage per plus

Power (Daily): Free Action. When you use an arcane power that can be sustained by minor actions, you can sustain the power without spending minor actions to do so for a number of turns equal to the orb's enhancement bonus. You can continue to sustain the power normally after the orb stops.

Orb of Inescapable Consequences · Level 8+

With this orb in hand, your powers can have their intended effects even if your accuracy is lacking.

Lvl 8	+2	3,400 gp	Lvl 23	+5	425,000 gp
Lvl 13	+3	17,000 gp	Lvl 28	+6	2,125,000 gp
Lvl 18	+4	85,000 gp			

Implement (Orb)

Enhancement: Attack rolls and damage rolls

Critical: +1d6 damage per plus

Power (Daily): Free Action. Use this power when an attack with this orb misses its target. The target is affected by any conditions or effects of the attack as if the attack had hit.

Orb of Insurmountable Force · Level 3+

The repulsive force emanating from this orb makes it hard to grasp.

Lvl 3	+1	680 gp	Lvl 18	+4	85,000 gp
Lvl 8	+2	3,400 gp	Lvl 23	+5	425,000 gp
Lvl 13	+3	17,000 gp	Lvl 28	+6	2,125,000 gp

Implement (Orb)

Enhancement: Attack rolls and damage rolls

Critical: +1d6 force damage per plus

Power (Encounter): Free Action. Use this power when you use an arcane attack power with this orb. If the attack is successful, you can push the target a number of squares equal to the enhancement bonus of the orb.

Orb of Judicious Conjuration · Level 3+

This orb ensures the longevity of your conjuration spells and also allows you to sustain effects more easily.

Lvl 3	+1	680 gp	Lvl 18	+4	85,000 gp
Lvl 8	+2	3,400 gp	Lvl 23	+5	425,000 gp
Lvl 13	+3	17,000 gp	Lvl 28	+6	2,125,000 gp

Implement (Orb)

Enhancement: Attack rolls and damage rolls

Critical: +1d6 damage per plus

Property: Add the enhancement bonus of this implement to your Will defense when *dispel magic* is used against one of your conjuration powers.

Power (Encounter): Free Action. Use this power on your turn to sustain a power that would otherwise require a minor action to do so.

Orb of Karmic Resonance · Level 13+

With this orb, you steal good luck from enemies and send them ill fortune.

Lvl 13	+3	17,000 gp	Lvl 23	+5	425,000 gp
Lvl 18	+4	85,000 gp	Lvl 28	+6	2,125,000 gp

Implement (Orb)

Enhancement: Attack rolls and damage rolls

Critical: +1d6 damage per plus

Power (Daily): Free Action. Use this power when an enemy succeeds on a saving throw. Choose one of the following effects:

✦ End an effect or condition currently affecting you or one ally within 5 squares of you.

✦ The enemy's saving throw fails instead of succeeding. Regardless of your choice, your next saving throw made in this encounter also fails.

Orb of Mental Dominion · Level 6+

A spellcaster channeling his mind through this orb gains mental prowess over foes, forcing them to relive the effects of a spell.

Lvl 6	+2	1,800 gp	Lvl 21	+5	225,000 gp
Lvl 11	+3	9,000 gp	Lvl 26	+6	1,125,000 gp
Lvl 16	+4	45,000 gp			

Implement (Orb)

Enhancement: Attack rolls and damage rolls

Critical: +1d6 psychic damage per plus

Power (Daily): Free Action. Use this power when an attack with this orb succeeds against the target's Will defense. When the target makes a saving throw against an effect from that attack, the target must roll twice and take the lower result.

Orb of Mighty Retort · Level 15+

Your enemies suffer dire consequences for daring to attack you while you wield this orb.

Lvl 15	+3	25,000 gp	Lvl 25	+5	625,000 gp
Lvl 20	+4	125,000 gp	Lvl 30	+6	3,125,000 gp

Implement (Orb)

Enhancement: Attack rolls and damage rolls

Critical: +1d6 damage per plus

Power (Daily): Immediate Reaction. Use this power when you take damage from an attack. You can use an at-will or encounter attack power, as long as the attack includes your attacker as a target. If you use an encounter power, you're dazed until the end of your next turn.

Orb of Revenant Magic · Level 17+

To the wielder of this orb, failure is not a concern.

Lvl 17	+4	65,000 gp	Lvl 27	+6	1,625,000 gp
Lvl 22	+5	325,000 gp			

Implement (Orb)

Enhancement: Attack rolls and damage rolls

Critical: +1d8 damage per plus

Power (Daily): Free Action. Use this power when you hit no targets with a power that has an effect on a miss. That effect does not take place. Instead, you regain use of the power that missed.

Orb of Spatial Contortion · Level 7+

The crystal shell of this orb refracts your spell energy, scattering it in different directions.

Lvl 7	+2	2,600 gp	Lvl 22	+5	325,000 gp
Lvl 12	+3	13,000 gp	Lvl 27	+6	1,625,000 gp
Lvl 17	+4	65,000 gp			

Implement (Orb)

Enhancement: Attack rolls and damage rolls

Critical: +1d6 damage per plus

Power (Daily): Free Action. Use this power when you use a close blast power. It becomes a close burst of a size 2 smaller than the blast (for example, a close blast 5 becomes a close burst 3).

Orb of Sudden Insanity
Level 12+

This orb holds a grip on your enemy's sanity, forcing him to act in uncharacteristic ways.

Lvl 12	+3	13,000 gp	Lvl 22	+5	325,000 gp
Lvl 17	+4	65,000 gp	Lvl 27	+6	1,625,000 gp

Implement (Orb)

Enhancement: Attack rolls and damage rolls

Critical: +1d6 psychic damage per plus

Power (Daily): Free Action. Use this power when you deal psychic damage with this orb. The target makes a melee basic attack against an adjacent creature of your choice as a free action.

Orb of Sweet Sanctuary
Level 3+

The silvery sheen of this orb grows to surround you at your will, warding off danger.

Lvl 3	+1	680 gp	Lvl 18	+4	85,000 gp
Lvl 8	+2	3,400 gp	Lvl 23	+5	425,000 gp
Lvl 13	+3	17,000 gp	Lvl 28	+6	2,125,000 gp

Implement (Orb)

Enhancement: Attack rolls and damage rolls

Critical: +1d6 damage per plus

Power (Daily): Standard Action. Add 5 + the enhancement bonus of the orb to your defenses until the end of your next turn.

Orb of the Usurper
Level 23+

Thanks to this orb, what at first was an attack on a foe's mind becomes a crushing grip upon the foe's freedom of will.

Lvl 23	+5	425,000 gp	Lvl 28	+6	2,125,000 gp

Implement (Orb)

Enhancement: Attack rolls and damage rolls

Critical: +1d10 psychic damage per plus

Power (Daily ✦ Charm): Free Action. Use this power when you score a critical hit with an attack with this implement that targets Will defense. You do not deal extra damage for the critical hit; instead, you dominate the target until the end of your next turn.

Orb of Ultimate Imposition
Level 3+

The will of this orb's wielder imposes great force on an enemy, crippling his power.

Lvl 3	+1	680 gp	Lvl 18	+4	85,000 gp
Lvl 8	+2	3,400 gp	Lvl 23	+5	425,000 gp
Lvl 13	+3	17,000 gp	Lvl 28	+6	2,125,000 gp

Implement (Orb)

Enhancement: Attack rolls and damage rolls

Critical: +1d6 damage per plus

Power (Daily): Free Action. Use this power when you use your orb of imposition class feature. Increase the penalty bestowed on your target by an amount equal to the enhancement bonus of this orb.

Orb of Unintended Solitude
Level 18+

Gazing into this dark sphere hints at the nature of the mysterious location into which its victims are cast.

Lvl 18	+4	85,000 gp	Lvl 28	+6	2,125,000 gp
Lvl 23	+5	425,000 gp			

Implement (Orb)

Enhancement: Attack rolls and damage rolls

Critical: +1d8 damage per plus

Power (Daily ✦ Teleportation): Free Action. Use this power when you affect a target with a pull, push, slide, or teleport effect. Instead of being pulled, pushed, slid, or teleported, it is cast into an empty realm of nothingness. At the end of the target's next turn, it reappears in the space it left or, if that space is not vacant, in the nearest unoccupied space.

Orb of Unlucky Exchanges
Level 3+

This orb offers relief to an ally and unleashes terrible retribution upon an enemy.

Lvl 3	+1	680 gp	Lvl 18	+4	85,000 gp
Lvl 8	+2	3,400 gp	Lvl 23	+5	425,000 gp
Lvl 13	+3	17,000 gp	Lvl 28	+6	2,125,000 gp

Implement (Orb)

Enhancement: Attack rolls and damage rolls

Critical: +1d6 damage per plus

Power (Daily): Free Action. Use this power when you hit a target with an attack with this implement. One effect affecting you or an ally within 5 squares of you ends. The target gains that effect with the same duration.

Orb of Weakness Intensified   Level 15+

Swirling with purple energy, this orb laces a spell with a crippling effect that debilitates your foe.

Lvl 15	+3	25,000 gp	Lvl 25	+5	625,000 gp
Lvl 20	+4	125,000 gp	Lvl 30	+6	3,125,000 gp

Implement (Orb)

Enhancement: Attack rolls and damage rolls

Critical: +1d8 damage per plus

Power (Daily): Free Action. Use this power when you hit a target with this orb. The target is weakened (save ends).

RODS

Forged of strange eldritch energies, rods deliver unto their enemies curses that bite into the soul.

Rods are commonly associated with warlocks, and several of the rods described herein are especially potent in the hands of a warlock.

Some rods vary in powers according to the warlock pact with which they're associated. Although a warlock need not choose a rod that aligns with his or her pact, the power such a rod bestows can be of great benefit and ongoing advantage to the wielder.

RODS

Lvl	Name	Price (gp)
2	Quickcurse rod +1	520
2	Rod of cursed honor +1	520
3	Rod of blasting +1	680
3	Rod of malign conveyance +1	680
3	Vicious rod +1	680
4	Bloodcurse rod +1	840
4	Rod of the dragonborn +1	840
4	Rod of the shadow walker +1	840
6	Mercurial rod +2	1,800
7	Quickcurse rod +2	2,600
7	Rod of cursed honor +2	2,600
7	Rod of feythorns +2	2,600
8	Rod of blasting +2	3,400
8	Rod of malign conveyance +2	3,400
8	Rod of the Feywild +2	3,400
8	Rod of the hidden star +2	3,400
8	Rod of the infernal +2	3,400
8	Vicious rod +2	3,400
9	Bloodcurse rod +2	4,200
9	Lifesapper rod +2	4,200
9	Rod of brutality +2	4,200
9	Rod of the dragonborn +2	4,200
9	Rod of the shadow walker +2	4,200
10	Rod of mindbending +2	5,000
10	Rod of starlight +2	5,000
11	Mercurial rod +3	9,000
12	Quickcurse rod +3	13,000
12	Rod of cursed honor +3	13,000
12	Rod of feythorns +3	13,000

2

RODS (CONTINUED)

Lvl	Name	Price (gp)
12	Rod of the churning inferno +3	13,000
13	Rod of blasting +3	17,000
13	Rod of malign conveyance +3	17,000
13	Rod of the Feywild +3	17,000
13	Rod of the hidden star +3	17,000
13	Rod of the infernal +3	17,000
13	Vicious rod +3	17,000
14	Adamantine rod +3	21,000
14	Bloodcurse rod +3	21,000
14	Bloodiron rod +3	21,000
14	Lifesapper rod +3	21,000
14	Rod of brutality +3	21,000
14	Rod of the dragonborn +3	21,000
14	Rod of the shadow walker +3	21,000
14	Rod of the sorrowsworn +3	21,000
15	Rod of mindbending +3	25,000
15	Rod of starlight +3	25,000
15	Rod of vulnerability +3	25,000
16	Mercurial rod +4	45,000
17	Quickcurse rod +4	65,000
17	Rod of cursed honor +4	65,000
17	Rod of feythorns +4	65,000
17	Rod of the bloodthorn +4	65,000
17	Rod of the churning inferno +4	65,000
18	Feyrod +4	85,000
18	Hellrod +4	85,000
18	Rod of blasting +4	85,000
18	Rod of malign conveyance +4	85,000
18	Rod of the Feywild +4	85,000
18	Rod of the hidden star +4	85,000
18	Rod of the infernal +4	85,000
18	Star rod +4	85,000
18	Vicious rod +4	85,000
19	Adamantine rod +4	105,000
19	Bloodcurse rod +4	105,000
19	Bloodiron rod +4	105,000
19	Lifesapper rod +4	105,000
19	Rod of brutality +4	105,000
19	Rod of the dragonborn +4	105,000
19	Rod of the shadow walker +4	105,000
19	Rod of the sorrowsworn +4	105,000
20	Rod of mindbending +4	125,000
20	Rod of starlight +4	125,000
20	Rod of vulnerability +4	125,000
21	Mercurial rod +5	225,000
22	Quickcurse rod +5	325,000
22	Rod of cursed honor +5	325,000
22	Rod of feythorns +5	325,000
22	Rod of the bloodthorn +5	325,000
22	Rod of the churning inferno +5	325,000
22	Rod of the star spawn +5	325,000
23	Feyrod +5	425,000
23	Hellrod +5	425,000
23	Rod of blasting +5	425,000
23	Rod of malign conveyance +5	425,000

RODS (CONTINUED)

Lvl	Name	Price (gp)
23	Rod of the Feywild +5	425,000
23	Rod of the hidden star +5	425,000
23	Rod of the infernal +5	425,000
23	Star rod +5	425,000
23	Vicious rod +5	425,000
24	Adamantine rod +5	525,000
24	Bloodcurse rod +5	525,000
24	Bloodiron rod +5	525,000
24	Lifesapper rod +5	525,000
24	Rod of brutality +5	525,000
24	Rod of the dragonborn +5	525,000
24	Rod of the shadow walker +5	525,000
24	Rod of the sorrowsworn +5	525,000
25	Rod of mindbending +5	625,000
25	Rod of starlight +5	625,000
25	Rod of vulnerability +5	625,000
26	Mercurial rod +6	1,125,000
27	Quickcurse rod +6	1,625,000
27	Rod of cursed honor +6	1,625,000
27	Rod of feythorns +6	1,625,000
27	Rod of the bloodthorn +6	1,625,000
27	Rod of the churning inferno +6	1,625,000
27	Rod of the star spawn +6	1,625,000
28	Feyrod +6	2,125,000
28	Hellrod +6	2,125,000
28	Rod of blasting +6	2,125,000
28	Rod of malign conveyance +6	2,125,000
28	Rod of the Feywild +6	2,125,000
28	Rod of the hidden star +6	2,125,000
28	Rod of the infernal +6	2,125,000
28	Star rod +6	2,125,000
28	Vicious rod +6	2,125,000
29	Adamantine rod +6	2,625,000
29	Bloodcurse rod +6	2,625,000
29	Bloodiron rod +6	2,625,000
29	Lifesapper rod +6	2,625,000
29	Rod of brutality +6	2,625,000
29	Rod of the dragonborn +6	2,625,000
29	Rod of the shadow walker +6	2,625,000
29	Rod of the sorrowsworn +6	2,625,000
30	Rod of mindbending +6	3,125,000
30	Rod of starlight +6	3,125,000
30	Rod of vulnerability +6	3,125,000

Adamantine Rod · Level 14+

Collected from meteor rock lodged within the world's crust, this metal makes rods that shine with a piercing light.

Lvl			Lvl		
Lvl 14	+3	21,000 gp	Lvl 24	+5	525,000 gp
Lvl 19	+4	105,000 gp	Lvl 29	+6	2,625,000 gp

Implement (Rod)

Enhancement: Attack rolls and damage rolls

Critical: +1d10 radiant damage per plus

Property: Radiant damage dealt by this rod ignores a number of points of radiant resist equal to twice the implement's enhancement bonus.

Bloodcurse Rod · Level 4+

This rod empowers its wielder to use his pact boon more often.

Lvl			Lvl		
Lvl 4	+1	840 gp	Lvl 19	+4	105,000 gp
Lvl 9	+2	4,200 gp	Lvl 24	+5	525,000 gp
Lvl 14	+3	21,000 gp	Lvl 29	+6	2,625,000 gp

Implement (Rod)

Enhancement: Attack rolls and damage rolls

Critical: +1d6 damage per plus

Property: Your pact boon triggers when an attack you make with this rod makes a target affected by your Warlock's Curse bloodied. (It still triggers when you reduce a target to 0 or fewer hit points.)

Bloodiron Rod · Level 14+

Channel your fury at being wounded through this potent device.

Lvl			Lvl		
Lvl 14	+3	21,000 gp	Lvl 24	+5	525,000 gp
Lvl 19	+4	105,000 gp	Lvl 29	+6	2,625,000 gp

Implement (Rod)

Enhancement: Attack rolls and damage rolls

Critical: +1d6 damage per plus

Power (Daily): Immediate Reaction. Use this power when you take damage. Make a ranged basic attack that uses this implement against the source of the damage. If the attack hits, gain 10 temporary hit points.
Level 24 or 29: 15 temporary hit points.

Feyrod · Level 18+

The capricious arcane power of the fey can be channeled into this rod, allowing you to temporarily gain the benefits of the fey pact.

Lvl			Lvl		
Lvl 18	+4	85,000 gp	Lvl 28	+6	2,125,000 gp
Lvl 23	+5	425,000 gp			

Implement (Rod)

Enhancement: Attack rolls and damage rolls

Critical: +1d6 psychic damage per plus

Power (Daily): Minor Action. Until the end of the encounter, when you use a warlock power that has an additional effect if you have the fey pact, you gain the benefit even if you don't have the fey pact.

Hellrod · Level 18+

This rod draws upon infernal power, granting you the benefits of a warlock trained in manipulating such forces.

Lvl			Lvl		
Lvl 18	+4	85,000 gp	Lvl 28	+6	2,125,000 gp
Lvl 23	+5	425,000 gp			

Implement (Rod)

Enhancement: Attack rolls and damage rolls

Critical: +1d6 fire damage per plus

Power (Daily): Minor Action. Until the end of the encounter, when you use a warlock power that has an additional effect if you have the infernal pact, you gain the benefit even if you don't have the infernal pact.

Lifesapper Rod — Level 9+

This rod lets you drain the life from your enemies and transfer it to your allies or yourself.

Lvl 9	+2	4,200 gp	Lvl 24	+5	525,000 gp
Lvl 14	+3	21,000 gp	Lvl 29	+3	2,625,000 gp
Lvl 19	+4	105,000 gp			

Implement (Rod)

Enhancement: Attack rolls and damage rolls

Critical: +1d6 damage per plus

Power (Daily): Free Action. Use this power when you place a Warlock's Curse on a target. The target gains ongoing 3 damage (save ends). Each time the enemy takes ongoing damage from this power, you or one ally within 5 squares of you regains that amount of hit points.
Level 14: Ongoing 5 damage.
Level 19: Ongoing 8 damage.
Level 24: Ongoing 10 damage.
Level 29: Ongoing 15 damage.

Mercurial Rod — Level 6+

You can forgo your curse to make one attack more potent when you use this rod.

Lvl 6	+2	1,800 gp	Lvl 21	+5	225,000 gp
Lvl 11	+3	9,000 gp	Lvl 26	+6	1,125,000 gp
Lvl 16	+4	45,000 gp			

Implement (Rod)

Enhancement: Attack rolls and damage rolls

Critical: None

Power (Daily): Free Action. Use this power when you deal your Warlock's Curse damage. Deal an additional two dice of damage, but after the attack, the target is no longer cursed by you. You can curse the target again normally. If this attack drops the target to 0 or fewer hit points, your pact boon triggers normally.

Quickcurse Rod — Level 2+

With this rod, you can curse any creature you can see, and more quickly than usual.

Lvl 2	+1	520 gp	Lvl 17	+4	65,000 gp
Lvl 7	+2	2,600 gp	Lvl 22	+5	325,000 gp
Lvl 12	+3	13,000 gp	Lvl 27	+6	1,625,000 gp

Implement (Rod)

Enhancement: Attack rolls and damage rolls

Critical: +1d6 damage per plus

Power (Encounter): Free Action. Place a Warlock's Curse on any target in sight.

Rod of Blasting — Level 3+

This graven rod allows you to target multiple foes with your eldritch blast.

Lvl 3	+1	680 gp	Lvl 18	+4	85,000 gp
Lvl 8	+2	3,400 gp	Lvl 23	+5	425,000 gp
Lvl 13	+3	17,000 gp	Lvl 28	+6	2,125,000 gp

Implement (Rod)

Enhancement: Attack rolls and damage rolls

Critical: +1d6 damage per plus

Power (Daily): Free Action. Use this power when you use *eldritch blast* with this implement. Target one or two creatures with the attack.
Level 18, 23, or 28: Target one, two, or three creatures.

1. Bloodcurse rod; 2. Lifesapper rod

Rod of Brutality — Level 9+

This glass rod brutally punishes those you curse.

Lvl 9	+2	4,200 gp	Lvl 24	+5	525,000 gp
Lvl 14	+3	21,000 gp	Lvl 29	+3	2,625,000 gp
Lvl 19	+4	105,000 gp			

Implement (Rod)

Enhancement: Attack rolls and damage rolls

Critical: +1d6 damage per plus, or +1d8 damage per plus against targets affected by your Warlock's Curse

Property: Reroll all 1s rolled on the extra damage granted by your Warlock's Curse.
Level 19 or 24: Reroll 1s and 2s.
Level 29: Reroll 1s, 2s, and 3s.

Rod of Cursed Honor — Level 2+

You can channel the power of your curse when you use this rod, increasing your defenses.

Lvl 2	+1	520 gp	Lvl 17	+4	65,000 gp
Lvl 7	+2	2,600 gp	Lvl 22	+5	325,000 gp
Lvl 12	+3	13,000 gp	Lvl 27	+6	1,625,000 gp

Implement (Rod)

Enhancement: Attack rolls and damage rolls

Critical: +1d6 damage per plus

Property: Whenever you place a Warlock's Curse on a target, you gain a +1 power bonus to your Fortitude, Reflex, and Will defenses until the end of your next turn.

Rod of Feythorns — Level 7+

Formed of a stalk and strange root bulb, this rod seems to weep steaming toxic liquid in battle. It magically poisons even those foes normally immune.

Lvl 7	+2	2,600 gp	Lvl 22	+5	325,000 gp
Lvl 12	+3	13,000 gp	Lvl 27	+6	1,625,000 gp
Lvl 17	+4	65,000 gp			

Implement (Rod)

Enhancement: Attack rolls and damage rolls

Critical: +1d8 poison damage per plus

Property: When you place a Warlock's Curse upon a target, that target loses resist poison (save ends).
Level 18 or 23: Vulnerable 10 poison.
Level 28: Vulnerable 15 poison.

Rod of Malign Conveyance — Level 3+

A smoky crystal caps this rod, which allows you to use your personal teleportation powers as weapons.

Lvl 3	+1	680 gp	Lvl 18	+4	85,000 gp
Lvl 8	+2	3,400 gp	Lvl 23	+5	425,000 gp
Lvl 13	+3	17,000 gp	Lvl 28	+6	2,125,000 gp

Implement (Rod)

Enhancement: Attack rolls and damage rolls

Critical: +1d6 damage per plus, and teleport the target a number of squares equal to the rod's enhancement bonus

Power (Daily ✦ Teleportation): Move Action. Teleport yourself, an ally within 5 squares of you, and an enemy within 5 squares of you each a number of squares equal to the rod's enhancement bonus.

Rod of Mindbending — Level 10+

Your enemies may have weak minds, but this implement softens them even more.

Lvl 10	+2	5,000 gp	Lvl 25	+5	625,000 gp
Lvl 15	+3	25,000 gp	Lvl 30	+6	3,125,000 gp
Lvl 20	+4	125,000 gp			

Implement (Rod)

Enhancement: Attack rolls and damage rolls

Critical: +1d6 psychic damage per plus

Property: When you place your Warlock's Curse on a target, it gains vulnerability to psychic damage equal to the rod's enhancement bonus until the end of your next turn.

Rod of Starlight — Level 10+

This rod makes targets you curse feel the full force of the radiance you cull from distant stars.

Lvl 10	+2	5,000 gp	Lvl 25	+5	625,000 gp
Lvl 15	+3	25,000 gp	Lvl 30	+6	3,125,000 gp
Lvl 20	+4	125,000 gp			

Implement (Rod)

Enhancement: Attack rolls and damage rolls

Critical: +1d6 radiant damage per plus

Property: When you place your Warlock's Curse on a target, it gains vulnerability to radiant damage equal to the rod's enhancement bonus until the end of your next turn.

Rod of the Bloodthorn — Level 17+

This rod thirsts for the blood of its prey and master alike.

Lvl 17	+4	65,000 gp	Lvl 27	+6	1,625,000 gp
Lvl 22	+5	325,000 gp			

Implement (Rod)

Enhancement: Attack rolls and damage rolls

Critical: +1d8 damage per plus, or +1d10 damage per plus if you or the target is bloodied.

Property: Gain a +1 bonus to attack rolls with the rod if you or the target is bloodied. These bonuses stack with each other.

Power (Daily ✦ Healing): Free Action. Use this power when you score a critical hit with this rod. Drain one healing surge from the target and add it to your total. If you are already at your maximum number of healing surges, you instead regain hit points equal to your healing surge value.

Rod of the Churning Inferno — Level 12+

Flames you create with this rod burn longer and spread to more foes.

Lvl 12	+3	13,000 gp	Lvl 22	+5	325,000 gp
Lvl 17	+4	65,000 gp	Lvl 27	+6	1,625,000 gp

Implement (Rod)

Enhancement: Attack rolls and damage rolls

Critical: +1d6 fire damage per plus

Power (Daily ✦ Fire): Free Action. Use this power when you deal fire damage with an arcane attack power that uses this rod. The target also takes ongoing 5 fire damage (save ends). When the target takes this ongoing damage, creatures adjacent to it take an equal amount of fire damage.
Level 17 or 22: Ongoing 10 fire damage (save ends)
Level 27: Ongoing 15 fire damage (save ends)

1. *Rod of the sorrowsworn;*
2 *Rod of the churning inferno*

Rod of the Dragonborn — Level 4+

A fierce dragon head tops this scaly scepter.

Lvl 4	+1	840 gp	Lvl 19	+4	105,000 gp
Lvl 9	+2	4,200 gp	Lvl 24	+5	525,000 gp
Lvl 14	+3	21,000 gp	Lvl 29	+6	2,625,000 gp

Implement (Rod)

Enhancement: Attack rolls and damage rolls

Critical: +1d6 damage per plus

Property: When you use a power with this implement, the damage you deal with the power is of the same damage type as the damage dealt by your *dragon breath*.

Power (Daily): Free Action. Use this power when you hit a target affected by your Warlock's Curse with an arcane power using this implement. Until the end of your next turn, when you attack with your *dragon breath*, you force the affected creature to exhale your attack in a direction you choose. Treat the affected creature as the origin square of the blast; the attack also targets the affected creature.

Rod of the Feywild — Level 8+

Formed from exotic woods of the Feywild, this rod enhances the wielder's ability to teleport using the fey pact.

Lvl 8	+2	3,400 gp	Lvl 23	+5	425,000 gp
Lvl 13	+3	17,000 gp	Lvl 28	+6	2,125,000 gp
Lvl 18	+4	85,000 gp			

Implement (Rod)

Enhancement: Attack rolls and damage rolls

Critical: +1d6 damage per plus, or +1d10 damage per plus with powers of the fey pact.

Property: When you trigger your fey pact boon, you can teleport an additional number of squares equal to the rod's enhancement bonus.

Power (Encounter ✦ Teleportation): Move Action. Teleport a number of squares equal to 3 + the enhancement bonus of the rod.

Rod of the Hidden Star — Level 8+

Formed of iridescent stone drawn from the Far Realm, this rod enhances the boon from the star pact, increasing your own powers and aiding allies as well.

Lvl 8	+2	3,400 gp	Lvl 23	+5	425,000 gp
Lvl 13	+3	17,000 gp	Lvl 28	+6	2,125,000 gp
Lvl 18	+4	85,000 gp			

Implement (Rod)

Enhancement: Attack rolls and damage rolls

Critical: +1d6 damage per plus, or +1d8 damage per plus with powers of the star pact.

Power (Daily): Free Action. Use this power when your star pact boon triggers. All allies within a number of squares equal to the enhancement bonus of this rod gain a +1 bonus on any one d20 roll until the end of your next turn.

Power (Daily): Free Action. Use this power when your star pact boon triggers. Add the enhancement bonus of this rod to the bonus your pact gives you.

Rod of the Infernal — Level 8+

This rod enhances one's ability to draw life from enemies using the infernal pact.

Lvl 8	+2	3,400 gp	Lvl 23	+5	425,000 gp
Lvl 13	+3	17,000 gp	Lvl 28	+6	2,125,000 gp
Lvl 18	+4	85,000 gp			

Implement (Rod)

Enhancement: Attack rolls and damage rolls

Critical: +1d6 damage per plus, or +1d10 damage per plus with powers of the infernal pact.

Property: When you trigger your infernal pact boon, you can add the enhancement bonus of the rod to the number of temporary hit points gained.

Power (Encounter): Minor Action. Gain temporary hit points equal to your level + your Intelligence modifier.

Rod of the Shadow Walker — Level 4+

With this gloom-shrouded rod in hand, the shadows that coalesce around you seem deeper to those you've cursed.

Lvl 4	+1	840 gp	Lvl 19	+4	105,000 gp
Lvl 9	+2	4,200 gp	Lvl 24	+5	525,000 gp
Lvl 14	+3	21,000 gp	Lvl 29	+6	2,625,000 gp

Implement (Rod)

Enhancement: Attack rolls and damage rolls

Critical: +1d6 damage per plus

Property: Whenever you place a Warlock's Curse on a target, you gain concealment from the target until the end of your next turn.

Rod of the Sorrowsworn — Level 14+

This rod allows the wielder's curse to consume an enemy with sorrow and misery.

Lvl 14	+3	21,000 gp	Lvl 24	+5	525,000 gp
Lvl 19	+4	105,000 gp	Lvl 29	+6	2,625,000 gp

Implement (Rod)

Enhancement: Attack rolls and damage rolls

Critical: +1d8 damage per plus

Power (Daily): Free Action. Use this power when you place a Warlock's Curse on a target. The target is overcome with sorrow and takes a -2 penalty to attack rolls (save ends).

Rod of the Star Spawn — Level 22+

This crooked rod allows the wielder to draw upon the power of an insane entity known as the Star Spawn. The rod draws sustenance from your most devastating attacks.

Lvl 22	+5	325,000 gp	Lvl 27	+6	1,625,000 gp

Implement (Rod)

Enhancement: Attack rolls and damage rolls

Critical: +1d8 damage per plus, and you can spend a healing surge.

Property: Attacks with this rod score critical hits on a natural roll of 19 or 20.

Rod of Vulnerability Level 15+

This rod adapts to the weaknesses of those you curse.

| Lvl 15 | +3 | 25,000 gp | Lvl 25 | +5 | 625,000 gp |
| Lvl 20 | +4 | 125,000 gp | Lvl 30 | +6 | 3,125,000 gp |

Implement (Rod)

Enhancement: Attack rolls and damage rolls

Critical: +1d6 damage per plus, or +1d8 damage per plus
against a cursed target.

Power (Daily): Free Action. Use this power when you use
Warlock's Curse on a target. Until the end of your next
turn, the target gains vulnerable 10 to all of your attacks.
Level 25 or 30: Vulnerable 15.

Star Rod Level 18+

*Made from metal refined from meteorites, this dark rod glim-
mers with pinpoints of light. It allows the wielder to temporarily
gain access to the powers associated with the star pact.*

| Lvl 18 | +4 | 85,000 gp | Lvl 28 | +6 | 2,125,000 gp |
| Lvl 23 | +5 | 425,000 gp | | | |

Implement (Rod)

Enhancement: Attack rolls and damage rolls

Critical: +1d6 radiant damage per plus

Power (Daily): Minor Action. Until the end of the
encounter, when you use a warlock power that has an
additional effect if you have the star pact, you gain the
benefit even if you don't have the star pact.

Vicious Rod Level 3+

This rod enhances the deadliness of your curse.

Lvl 3	+1	680 gp	Lvl 18	+4	85,000 gp
Lvl 8	+2	3,400 gp	Lvl 23	+5	425,000 gp
Lvl 13	+3	17,000 gp	Lvl 28	+6	2,125,000 gp

Implement (Rod)

Enhancement: Attack rolls and damage rolls

Critical: +1d10 damage per plus

Property: When you deal your Warlock's Curse damage
with this rod, you roll d8s instead of d6s.

STAFFS

*A staff is more than an implement—more than a physical
support. it is a friend to lean on, and an ally from which to
gain protection.*

Favored by more conservative wizards, staffs usually
offer protection to their wielders. However, a few
staffs also lend powerful arcane aid in combat.

STAFFS

Lvl	Name	Price (gp)
2	Defensive staff +1	520
2	Mnemonic staff +1	520
2	Staff of missile master +1	520
2	Utility staff +1	520
3	Earthroot staff +1	680
3	Force staff +1	680
3	Staff of ruin +1	680
3	Staff of spectral hands +1	680
3	Staff of ultimate defense +1	680
4	Feyswarm staff +1	840
4	Staff of light +1	840
4	Staff of unparalleled vision +1	840
5	Architect's staff +1	1,000
7	Defensive staff +2	2,600
7	Mnemonic staff +2	2,600
7	Staff of missile master +2	2,600
7	Staff of the serpent +2	2,600
7	Utility staff +2	2,600
8	Earthroot staff +2	3,400
8	Force staff +2	3,400
8	Staff of ruin +2	3,400
8	Staff of spectral hands +2	3,400
8	Staff of ultimate defense +2	3,400
9	Feyswarm staff +2	4,200
9	Staff of elemental prowess +2	4,200
9	Staff of light +2	4,200
9	Staff of unparalleled vision +2	4,200
10	Architect's staff +2	5,000
10	Staff of acid and flame +2	5,000
10	Staff of gathering +2	5,000
12	Defensive staff +3	13,000
12	Mnemonic staff +3	13,000

Lvl	Name	Price (gp)
12	Staff of missile master +3	13,000
12	Staff of searing death +3	13,000
12	Staff of the serpent +3	13,000
12	Utility staff +3	13,000
13	Earthroot staff +3	17,000
13	Force staff +3	17,000
13	Reliable staff +3	17,000
13	Staff of ruin +3	17,000
13	Staff of spectral hands +3	17,000
13	Staff of ultimate defense +3	17,000
14	Feyswarm staff +3	21,000
14	Quickening staff +3	21,000
14	Staff of elemental prowess +3	21,000
14	Staff of light +3	21,000
14	Staff of transposition +3	21,000
14	Staff of unparalleled vision +3	21,000
15	Architect's staff +3	25,000
15	Staff of acid and flame +3	25,000
15	Staff of gathering +3	25,000
15	Striking staff +3	25,000
17	Defensive staff +4	65,000
17	Mnemonic staff +4	65,000
17	Staff of missile master +4	65,000
17	Staff of searing death +4	65,000
17	Staff of the serpent +4	65,000
17	Utility staff +4	65,000
18	Earthroot staff +4	85,000
18	Force staff +4	85,000
18	Reliable staff +4	85,000
18	Staff of corrosion +4	85,000
18	Staff of ruin +4	85,000
18	Staff of spectral hands +4	85,000
18	Staff of ultimate defense +4	85,000
19	Feyswarm staff +4	105,000
19	Quickening staff +4	105,000
19	Staff of elemental prowess +4	105,000
19	Staff of light +4	105,000
19	Staff of transposition +4	105,000
19	Staff of unparalleled vision +4	105,000
20	Architect's staff +4	125,000
20	Staff of acid and flame +4	125,000
20	Staff of gathering +4	125,000
20	Striking staff +4	125,000
22	Defensive staff +5	325,000
22	Mnemonic staff +5	325,000
22	Staff of missile master +5	325,000
22	Staff of searing death +5	325,000
22	Staff of the iron tower +5	325,000
22	Staff of the serpent +5	325,000
22	Utility staff +5	325,000
23	Earthroot staff +5	425,000
23	Force staff +5	425,000
23	Reliable staff +5	425,000
23	Staff of corrosion +5	425,000
23	Staff of ruin +5	425,000

STAFFS

Lvl	Name	Price (gp)
23	Staff of spectral hands +5	425,000
23	Staff of ultimate defense +5	425,000
24	Feyswarm staff +5	525,000
24	Quickening staff +5	525,000
24	Staff of light +5	525,000
24	Staff of elemental prowess +5	525,000
24	Staff of transposition +5	525,000
24	Staff of unparalleled vision +5	525,000
25	Architect's staff +5	625,000
25	Destiny staff +5	625,000
25	Staff of acid and flame +5	625,000
25	Staff of gathering +5	625,000
25	Striking staff +5	625,000
27	Defensive staff +6	1,625,000
27	Mnemonic staff +6	1,625,000
27	Staff of missile master +6	1,625,000
27	Staff of searing death +6	1,625,000
27	Staff of the iron tower +6	1,625,000
27	Staff of the serpent +6	1,625,000
27	Utility staff +6	1,625,000
28	Earthroot staff +6	2,125,000
28	Force staff +6	2,125,000
28	Reliable staff +6	2,125,000
28	Staff of corrosion +6	2,125,000
28	Staff of ruin +6	2,125,000
28	Staff of spectral hands +6	2,125,000
28	Staff of ultimate defense +6	2,125,000
29	Feyswarm staff +6	2,625,000
29	Quickening staff +6	2,625,000
29	Staff of elemental prowess +6	2,625,000
29	Staff of light +6	2,625,000
29	Staff of transposition +6	2,625,000
29	Staff of unparalleled vision +6	2,625,000
30	Architect's staff +6	3,125,000
30	Destiny staff +6	3,125,000
30	Staff of acid and flame +6	3,125,000
30	Staff of gathering +6	3,125,000
30	Striking staff +6	3,125,000

Architect's Staff — Level 5+

Stylized architectural and elemental motifs adorn this staff, which helps you control spells that create barriers or change terrain.

Lvl 5	+1	1,000 gp	Lvl 20	+4	125,000 gp
Lvl 10	+2	5,000 gp	Lvl 25	+5	625,000 gp
Lvl 15	+3	25,000 gp	Lvl 30	+6	3,125,000 gp

Implement (Staff)

Enhancement: Attack rolls and damage rolls

Critical: +1d6 damage per plus

Property: Add squares equal to the enhancement bonus of this staff to the area of a zone or a wall cast with this staff.

Power (Daily): Standard Action. Reshape one existing wall effect that you cast. At least one square of the wall must remain stationary.

Defensive Staff — Level 2+

This staff increases your resistance to all types of attacks.

Lvl 2	+1	520 gp	Lvl 17	+4	65,000 gp
Lvl 7	+2	2,600 gp	Lvl 22	+5	325,000 gp
Lvl 12	+3	13,000 gp	Lvl 27	+6	1,625,000 gp

Implement (Staff)

Enhancement: Attack rolls and damage rolls

Critical: +1d8 damage per plus

Property: Gain a +1 item bonus to your Fortitude, Reflex, and Will defenses. If you have the Staff of Defense class feature, you also gain a +1 item bonus to your AC.

Destiny Staff — Level 25+

A black raven's head with diamond eyes tops this mighty staff. It bolsters your fate, increasing your odds of survival and allowing you to act when others aren't quick enough.

| Lvl 25 | +5 | 625,000 gp | Lvl 30 | +6 | 3,125,000 gp |

Implement (Staff)

Enhancement: Attack rolls and damage rolls

Critical: +1d8 damage per plus

Property: When one of your attacks cast through this staff reduces a target to 0 hit points, you can spend a healing surge.

Power (Daily): Free Action. Use this power when one of your attacks reduces a target to 0 hit points. Take a standard action.

Earthroot Staff — Level 3+

This staff is as light as wood, but it seems to be made of earth and stone with a fine crystal atop it. It can bind your enemies to the earth and protect you against the same.

Lvl 3	+1	680 gp	Lvl 18	+4	85,000 gp
Lvl 8	+2	3,400 gp	Lvl 23	+5	425,000 gp
Lvl 13	+3	17,000 gp	Lvl 28	+6	2,125,000 gp

Implement (Staff)

Enhancement: Attack rolls and damage rolls

Critical: The target is restrained until the end of your next turn.

Property: Against your attacks that impose immobilized, petrified, restrained, or slowed conditions, enemies take a saving throw penalty equal to this staff's enhancement bonus.

Force Staff — Level 3+

Use this staff to knock down your enemies and drag them across the ground.

Lvl 3	+1	680 gp	Lvl 18	+4	85,000 gp
Lvl 8	+2	3,400 gp	Lvl 23	+5	425,000 gp
Lvl 13	+3	17,000 gp	Lvl 28	+6	2,125,000 gp

Implement (Staff)

Enhancement: Attack rolls and damage rolls

Critical: +1d6 force damage per plus, and the target is knocked prone.

Power (Daily ✦ Force): Free Action. Use this power when you hit with a power that has the force keyword. You can slide the target a number of squares equal to this staff's enhancement bonus.

Feyswarm Staff — Level 4+

This staff seems to have burrowing insects moving under its surface. When used to attack, it can unleash these magical pests on your enemies.

Lvl 4	+1	840 gp	Lvl 19	+4	105,000 gp
Lvl 9	+2	4,200 gp	Lvl 24	+5	525,000 gp
Lvl 14	+3	21,000 gp	Lvl 29	+6	2,625,000 gp

Implement (Staff)

Enhancement: Attack rolls and damage rolls

Critical: The target is dazed by stinging magical insects until the end of your next turn.

Power (Daily): Free Action. Use this power when an attack made with this implement hits. Magical stinging insects daze the target until the end of your next turn.

Mnemonic Staff — Level 2+

The glyphs carved into this staff suggest its ability to recall mundane and magical secrets.

Lvl 2	+1	520 gp	Lvl 17	+4	65,000 gp
Lvl 7	+2	2,600 gp	Lvl 22	+5	325,000 gp
Lvl 12	+3	13,000 gp	Lvl 27	+6	1,625,000 gp

Implement (Staff)

Enhancement: Attack rolls and damage rolls

Critical: +1d6 damage per plus

Property: Gain a +2 item bonus to any monster knowledge skill check.

Power (Daily): Minor Action. Swap a power you've prepared for another power in your spellbook of equal or lower level. Each power must also be of equal or lower level than the level of the staff.

Quickening Staff — Level 14+

The witches of the White Spire were known for their ability to combine different forms of magic using staffs like this one.

| Lvl 14 | +3 | 21,000 gp | Lvl 24 | +5 | 525,000 gp |
| Lvl 19 | +4 | 105,000 gp | Lvl 29 | +6 | 2,625,000 gp |

Implement (Staff)

Enhancement: Attack rolls and damage rolls

Critical: +1d6 damage per plus

Power (Daily): Free Action. Use this power when you hit with a daily power. You can use an at-will power.

Reliable Staff — Level 13+

No power is wasted with this sturdy oak staff in your hands.

| Lvl 13 | +3 | 17,000 gp | Lvl 23 | +5 | 425,000 gp |
| Lvl 18 | +4 | 85,000 gp | Lvl 28 | +6 | 2,125,000 gp |

Implement (Staff)

Enhancement: Attack rolls and damage rolls

Critical: +1d6 damage per plus

Power (Daily): Free Action. Use this power after you hit no target with an encounter attack power cast through this implement. That power is not expended.

Staff of Acid and Flame — Level 10+

This metal staff looks scorched and acid-scored, and it grants the wielder the power to sear enemies with acid and flame.

Lvl 10	+2	5,000 gp	Lvl 25	+5	625,000 gp
Lvl 15	+3	25,000 gp	Lvl 30	+6	3,125,000 gp
Lvl 20	+4	125,000 gp			

Implement (Staff)

Enhancement: Attack rolls and damage rolls

Critical: +1d6 acid and fire damage per plus

Power (At-Will ✦ Acid): Free Action. All fire damage dealt using this staff as an implement is acid damage. Another free action returns the damage to normal.

Power (At-Will ✦ Fire): Free Action. All acid damage dealt using this staff as an implement is fire damage. Another free action returns the damage to normal.

Staff of Corrosion — Level 18+

Inlaid with fragments of jade, this staff devours an enemy's flesh with biting acid.

| Lvl 18 | +4 | 85,000 gp | Lvl 28 | +6 | 2,125,000 gp |
| Lvl 23 | +5 | 425,000 gp | | | |

Implement (Staff)

Enhancement: Attack rolls and damage rolls

Critical: +1d8 acid damage per plus

Property: Any melee attack made with this staff deals +1d6 acid damage.

Power (Daily): Free Action. Use this power when an attack with this staff with the acid keyword misses. Roll again and use the second result.

HOWARD LYON

Staff of Elemental Prowess — Level 9+

This staff grants mastery over—and protection from—the harsh elements.

Lvl 9	+2	4,200 gp	Lvl 24	+5	525,000 gp
Lvl 14	+3	21,000 gp	Lvl 29	+6	2,625,000 gp
Lvl 19	+4	105,000 gp			

Implement (Staff)

Enhancement: Attack rolls and damage rolls

Critical: +1d6 damage of the same type as the attack per plus

Property: Gain a +1 item bonus to damage rolls when you deal acid, cold, fire, or lightning damage with this implement.
Level 14 or 19: +2 item bonus to damage rolls.
Level 24 or 29: +3 item bonus to damage rolls.

Power (Daily): Immediate Interrupt. Use this power when you are attacked by a power with the fire, cold, acid, or lightning keyword. Choose one of those damage types. You and all allies within 2 squares of you gain resist 10 against that damage type until the end of your next turn.
Level 19 or 24: You and allies within 5 squares of you gain resist 15 against the chosen damage type.
Level 29: You and allies within 10 squares of you gain resist 20 against the chosen damage type.

Staff of Gathering — Level 10+

The sphere of smoked glass topping this staff transforms into a ball of raw energy when the wielder is struck by spells.

Lvl 10	+2	5,000 gp	Lvl 25	+5	625,000 gp
Lvl 15	+3	25,000 gp	Lvl 30	+6	3,125,000 gp
Lvl 20	+4	125,000 gp			

Implement (Staff)

Enhancement: Attack rolls and damage rolls

Critical: +1d6 damage per plus

Power (Daily): Immediate Interrupt. Use this power when you take damage from an attack with the fire, force, lightning, necrotic, or radiant keyword. You take half damage from the attack. You gain a +2 power bonus to attack rolls and +10 power bonus to damage rolls with your next attack that has the arcane and implement keywords.

Staff of Light — Level 4+

Clerics and paladins are not the only ones with radiant powers that sear undead.

Lvl 4	+1	840 gp	Lvl 19	+4	105,000 gp
Lvl 9	+2	4,200 gp	Lvl 24	+5	525,000 gp
Lvl 14	+3	21,000 gp	Lvl 29	+6	2,625,000 gp

Implement (Staff)

Enhancement: Attack rolls and damage rolls

Critical: +1d6 radiant damage per plus

Power (Daily ✦ Radiant): Free Action. Use this power while the wizard's *light* power is on this staff. Until the *light* spell ends, undead creatures within the radius of the light at the start of their turn take radiant damage equal to the staff's enhancement bonus.

Staff of Missile Mastery — Level 2+

This dark wooden staff empowers a wizard's most basic attack.

Lvl 2	+1	520 gp	Lvl 17	+4	65,000 gp
Lvl 7	+2	2,600 gp	Lvl 22	+5	325,000 gp
Lvl 12	+3	13,000 gp	Lvl 27	+6	1,625,000 gp

Implement (Staff)

Enhancement: Attack rolls and damage rolls

Critical: +1d6 damage per plus, or +1d8 damage per plus when using *magic missile.*

Property: When you cast *magic missile* with this implement, you gain a +1 item bonus to attack rolls and an item bonus to damage rolls equal to the staff's enhancement bonus.

Power (Daily): Free Action. Use this power when you cast *magic missile*. Target one or two creatures with the attack. No target can be more than 5 squares from any other target.

Level 17, 22, or 27: Target one, two, or three creatures with the attack.

Staff of Ruin — Level 3+

This gnarled, jagged staff fits the hand of any wizard seeking to devastate her opponent.

Lvl 3	+1	680 gp	Lvl 18	+4	85,000 gp
Lvl 8	+2	3,400 gp	Lvl 23	+5	425,000 gp
Lvl 13	+3	17,000 gp	Lvl 28	+6	2,125,000 gp

Implement (Staff)

Enhancement: Attack rolls and damage rolls

Critical: +1d10 damage per plus

Property: In addition to the normal enhancement bonus, add the staff's enhancement bonus to damage rolls as an item bonus.

Staff of Searing Death — Level 12+

This staff causes your fiery attacks to burn even hotter.

Lvl 12	+3	13,000 gp	Lvl 22	+5	325,000 gp
Lvl 17	+4	65,000 gp	Lvl 27	+6	1,625,000 gp

Implement (Staff)

Enhancement: Attack rolls and damage rolls

Critical: +1d6 damage per plus, or +1d8 fire damage per plus if the attack has the fire keyword.

Power (Daily ✦ Fire): Free Action. Use this power when an attack with this staff hits and deals ongoing fire damage. Increase the ongoing damage by 5.

Level 22 or 27: Increase the ongoing damage by 10.

Staff of the Iron Tower — Level 22+

This iron staff provides a bastion for your mind and the minds of your allies.

Lvl 22	+5	325,000 gp	Lvl 27	+6	1,625,000 gp

Implement (Staff)

Enhancement: Attack rolls and damage rolls

Critical: +1d6 psychic damage per plus

Power (Daily): Free Action. Use this power when you use a power that has the psychic keyword with this staff. You and all allies within 5 squares of you can each make a saving throw against one effect that has the charm, fear, illusion, or sleep keyword that a save can end.

1. Staff of searing death; 2. Staff of unparalled vision

Staff of the Serpent — Level 7+

Shaped like a rigid cobra, this bronze staff enables you to wield poison as a deadly weapon.

Lvl 7	+2	2,600 gp	Lvl 22	+5	325,000 gp
Lvl 12	+3	13,000 gp	Lvl 27	+6	1,625,000 gp
Lvl 17	+4	65,000 gp			

Implement (Staff)

Enhancement: Attack rolls and damage rolls

Critical: +1d8 poison damage per plus

Property: Any melee attack made with this staff deals +1d6 poison damage.

Power (Daily ✦ Poison): Free Action. Use this power when you deal poison damage with a power cast through this implement. The target takes ongoing poison damage equal to the enhancement bonus of the staff (save ends). If the power already deals ongoing poison damage, add the enhancement bonus of the staff as an item bonus to that damage each round.

WAYNE ENGLAND

Staff of Spectral Hands — Level 3+

The true power of this staff lies in its clever utility.

Lvl 3	+1	680 gp	Lvl 18	+4	85,000 gp
Lvl 8	+2	3,400 gp	Lvl 23	+5	425,000 gp
Lvl 13	+3	17,000 gp	Lvl 28	+6	2,125,000 gp

Implement (Staff)

Enhancement: Attack rolls and damage rolls

Critical: +1d6 damage per plus

Property: When you use the *mage hand* power, you can conjure a number of hands equal to your Wisdom modifier (minimum 1, maximum of 1 + the staff's enhancement bonus). You can sustain all of the hands each round with a single minor action.

Staff of Transposition — Level 14+

A wizard armed with this staff needn't fear catching his allies within range of his most destructive spells.

| Lvl 14 | +3 | 21,000 gp | Lvl 24 | +5 | 525,000 gp |
| Lvl 19 | +4 | 105,000 gp | Lvl 29 | +6 | 2,625,000 gp |

Implement (Staff)

Enhancement: Attack rolls and damage rolls

Critical: +1d6 damage per plus

Power (Daily ✦ Teleportation): Free Action. Use this power when you use a close or area power. Any allies in the area of effect, rather than being affected by the power, are teleported to the nearest unaffected square of your choice.

Staff of Ultimate Defense — Level 3+

This sturdy wooden staff may not be the favored implement of war wizards, yet many find the safety it offers desirable.

Lvl 3	+1	680 gp	Lvl 18	+4	85,000 gp
Lvl 8	+2	3,400 gp	Lvl 23	+5	425,000 gp
Lvl 13	+3	17,000 gp	Lvl 28	+6	2,125,000 gp

Implement (Staff)

Enhancement: Attack rolls and damage rolls

Critical: +1d6 damage per plus

Property: When you use the staff of defense form of the Arcane Implement Mastery class feature, increase the bonus to defense by an amount equal to the enhancement bonus of this staff.

Staff of Unparalleled Vision — Level 4+

Wizards who keep to the outskirts of a battlefield favor this glass-topped staff.

Lvl 4	+1	840 gp	Lvl 19	+4	105,000 gp
Lvl 9	+2	4,200 gp	Lvl 24	+5	525,000 gp
Lvl 14	+3	21,000 gp	Lvl 29	+6	2,625,000 gp

Implement (Staff)

Enhancement: Attack rolls and damage rolls

Critical: +1d6 damage per plus

Property: When you use a ranged or area arcane power, add the enhancement bonus of this staff to the power's range. For example, a +3 *staff of unparalleled vision* would increase "area burst 5 within 10 squares" to "area burst 5 within 13 squares."

Striking Staff — Level 15+

This steel staff is favored by wizards who enjoy fighting in the thick of a battle.

| Lvl 15 | +3 | 25,000 gp | Lvl 25 | +5 | 625,000 gp |
| Lvl 20 | +4 | 125,000 gp | Lvl 30 | +6 | 3,125,000 gp |

Implement (Staff)

Enhancement: Attack rolls and damage rolls

Critical: +1d8 damage per plus, or +1d10 damage per plus when used as a melee weapon.

Property: You can make a melee basic attack with this staff. This is an Intelligence attack against AC and applies the staff's enhancement bonus to the attack rolls and damage rolls.

Utility Staff — Level 2+

A boon to practical spellcasters, this staff increases the range of one's utility spells.

Lvl 2	+1	520 gp	Lvl 17	+4	65,000 gp
Lvl 7	+2	2,600 gp	Lvl 22	+5	325,000 gp
Lvl 12	+3	13,000 gp	Lvl 27	+6	1,625,000 gp

Implement (Staff)

Enhancement: Attack rolls and damage rolls

Critical: +1d6 damage per plus

Property: Increase the range of your arcane utility powers by a number of squares equal to this staff's enhancement bonus.

WANDS

In the hands of a spellcaster, a wand turns even the simplest spells into a deadly arsenal.

Some wands contain inherent power that allows their wielders to unleash terrific blasts of energy. Other wands transform at-will powers into much deadlier attacks.

WANDS

Lvl	Name	Price (gp)
3	Flame wand +1	680
3	Force wand +1	680
3	Hellfire wand +1	680
3	Master's wand of cloud of daggers +1	680
3	Master's wand of dire radiance +1	680
3	Master's wand of eldritch blast +1	680
3	Master's wand of eyebite +1	680
3	Master's wand of hellish rebuke +1	680
3	Master's wand of magic missile +1	680
3	Master's wand of ray of frost +1	680
3	Master's wand of scorching burst +1	680
3	Master's wand of thunderwave +1	680
3	Thunder wand +1	680
3	Wand of cold +1	680
3	Wand of psychic ravaging +1	680
3	Wand of radiance +1	680
3	Wand of swarming force +1	680

Lvl	Name	Price (gp)
8	Flame wand +2	3,400
8	Force wand +2	3,400
8	Hellfire wand +2	3,400
8	Master's wand of cloud of daggers +2	3,400
8	Master's wand of dire radiance +2	3,400
8	Master's wand of eldritch blast +2	3,400
8	Master's wand of eyebite +2	3,400
8	Master's wand of hellish rebuke +2	3,400
8	Master's wand of magic missile +2	3,400
8	Master's wand of ray of frost +2	3,400
8	Master's wand of scorching burst +2	3,400
8	Master's wand of thunderwave +2	3,400
8	Thunder wand +2	3,400
8	Wand of cold +2	3,400
8	Wand of psychic ravaging +2	3,400
8	Wand of radiance +2	3,400
8	Wand of swarming force +2	3,400
10	Precise wand of color spray +2	5,000
13	Flame wand +3	17,000
13	Force wand +3	17,000
13	Hellfire wand +3	17,000
13	Master's wand of cloud of daggers +3	17,000
13	Master's wand of dire radiance +3	17,000
13	Master's wand of eldritch blast +3	17,000
13	Master's wand of eyebite +3	17,000
13	Master's wand of hellish rebuke +3	17,000
13	Master's wand of magic missile +3	17,000
13	Master's wand of ray of frost +3	17,000
13	Master's wand of scorching burst +3	17,000
13	Master's wand of thunderwave +3	17,000
13	Thunder wand +3	17,000
13	Wand of cold +3	17,000
13	Wand of psychic ravaging +3	17,000
13	Wand of radiance +3	17,000
13	Wand of swarming force +3	17,000
14	Assured wand of frostburn +3	21,000
14	Assured wand of howl of doom +3	21,000
15	Precise wand of color spray +3	25,000
15	Wand of erupting flame +3	25,000
18	Flame wand +4	85,000
18	Force wand +4	85,000
18	Hellfire wand +4	85,000
18	Master's wand of cloud of daggers +4	85,000
18	Master's wand of dire radiance +4	85,000
18	Master's wand of eldritch blast +4	85,000
18	Master's wand of eyebite +4	85,000
18	Master's wand of hellish rebuke +4	85,000
18	Master's wand of magic missile +4	85,000
18	Master's wand of ray of frost +4	85,000
18	Master's wand of scorching burst +4	85,000
18	Master's wand of thunderwave +4	85,000
18	Thunder wand +4	85,000
18	Wand of cold +4	85,000
18	Wand of psychic ravaging +4	85,000
18	Wand of radiance +4	85,000

Lvl	Name	Price (gp)
18	Wand of swarming force +4	85,000
19	Assured wand of frostburn +4	105,000
19	Assured wand of howl of doom +4	105,000
20	Precise wand of color spray +4	125,000
20	Wand of erupting flame +4	125,000
23	Flame wand +5	425,000
23	Force wand +5	425,000
23	Hellfire wand +5	425,000
23	Master's wand of cloud of daggers +5	425,000
23	Master's wand of dire radiance +5	425,000
23	Master's wand of eldritch blast +5	425,000
23	Master's wand of eyebite +5	425,000
23	Master's wand of hellish rebuke +5	425,000
23	Master's wand of magic missile +5	425,000
23	Master's wand of ray of frost +5	425,000
23	Master's wand of scorching burst +5	425,000
23	Master's wand of thunderwave +5	425,000
23	Thunder wand +5	425,000
23	Wand of cold +5	425,000
23	Wand of psychic ravaging +5	425,000
23	Wand of radiance +5	425,000
23	Wand of swarming force +5	425,000
24	Assured wand of frostburn +5	525,000
24	Assured wand of howl of doom +5	525,000
25	Precise wand of color spray +5	625,000
25	Wand of erupting flame +5	625,000
28	Flame wand +6	2,125,000
28	Force wand +6	2,125,000
28	Hellfire wand +6	2,125,000
28	Master's wand of cloud of daggers +6	2,125,000
28	Master's wand of dire radiance +6	2,125,000
28	Master's wand of eldritch blast +6	2,125,000
28	Master's wand of eyebite +6	2,125,000
28	Master's wand of hellish rebuke +6	2,125,000
28	Master's wand of magic missile +6	2,125,000
28	Master's wand of ray of frost +6	2,125,000
28	Master's wand of scorching burst +6	2,125,000
28	Master's wand of thunderwave +6	2,125,000
28	Thunder wand +6	2,125,000
28	Wand of cold +6	2,125,000
28	Wand of psychic ravaging +6	2,125,000
28	Wand of radiance +6	2,125,000
28	Wand of swarming force +6	2,125,000
29	Assured wand of frostburn +6	2,625,000
29	Assured wand of howl of doom +6	2,625,000
30	Precise wand of color spray +6	3,125,000
30	Wand of erupting flame +6	3,125,000

Assured Wand of Frostburn — Level 14+

Your ability to use the frostburn power exceeds the normal boundaries of chance, allowing you an extra measure of confidence.

| Lvl 14 | +3 | 21,000 gp | Lvl 24 | +5 | 525,000 gp |
| Lvl 19 | +4 | 105,000 gp | Lvl 29 | +6 | 2,625,000 gp |

Implement (**Wand**)

Enhancement: Attack rolls and damage rolls

Critical: +1d6 damage per plus

Property: The first time in an encounter you attack with the *frostburn* power using this implement and your natural roll is equal to or lower than the enhancement bonus of this wand, you can reroll the attack.

Power (Daily ✦ Arcane, Cold, Fire, Implement): Standard Action. As the wizard's *frostburn* power (*PH* 164).

Assured Wand of Howl of Doom — Level 14+

When using the howl of doom power, your knowledge reaches beyond probability and you can manipulate a small fraction of luck and destiny.

| Lvl 14 | +3 | 21,000 gp | Lvl 24 | +5 | 525,000 gp |
| Lvl 19 | +4 | 105,000 gp | Lvl 29 | +6 | 2,625,000 gp |

Implement (**Wand**)

Enhancement: Attack rolls and damage rolls

Critical: +1d6 damage per plus

Property: The first time in an encounter you attack with *howl of doom* with this implement and your natural roll is equal to or lower than the enhancement bonus of this wand, you can reroll the attack.

Power (Daily ✦ Arcane, Fear, Implement, Thunder): Standard Action. As the warlock's *howl of doom* power (*PH* 135).

Flame Wand — Level 3+

Small flames become conflagrations when channeled through this wand.

Lvl 3	+1	680 gp	Lvl 18	+4	85,000 gp
Lvl 8	+2	3,400 gp	Lvl 23	+5	425,000 gp
Lvl 13	+3	17,000 gp	Lvl 28	+6	2,125,000 gp

Implement (**Wand**)

Enhancement: Attack rolls and damage rolls

Critical: +1d8 fire damage per plus

Property: Gain a +1 item bonus to damage rolls when you use this wand to attack with a power that has the fire and implement keywords.
Level 13 or 18: +2 item bonus.
Level 23 or 28: +3 item bonus.

Power (Encounter ✦ Arcane, Fire, Implement): Standard Action. As the wizard's *scorching burst* power (*PH* 159).

Force Wand — Level 3+

With this wand, your force powers pack a bigger punch.

Lvl 3	+1	680 gp	Lvl 18	+4	85,000 gp
Lvl 8	+2	3,400 gp	Lvl 23	+5	425,000 gp
Lvl 13	+3	17,000 gp	Lvl 28	+6	2,125,000 gp

Implement (**Wand**)

Enhancement: Attack rolls and damage rolls

Critical: +1d8 force damage per plus

Property: Gain a +1 item bonus to damage rolls when you use this wand to attack with a power that has the force keyword.
Level 13 or 18: +2 item bonus.
Level 23 or 28: +3 item bonus.

Power (Encounter ✦ Arcane, Force, Implement): Standard Action. As the wizard's *magic missile* power (*PH* 159).

Hellfire Wand — Level 3+

Your fires burn with the fury of the Nine Hells when wielding this wand.

Lvl 3	+1	680 gp	Lvl 18	+4	85,000 gp
Lvl 8	+2	3,400 gp	Lvl 23	+5	425,000 gp
Lvl 13	+3	17,000 gp	Lvl 28	+6	2,125,000 gp

Implement (**Wand**)

Enhancement: Attack rolls and damage rolls

Critical: +1d8 fire damage per plus

Property: Gain a +1 item bonus to damage rolls when you use this wand to attack with a power that has the fire and implement keywords.
Level 13 or 18: +2 item bonus.
Level 23 or 28: +3 item bonus.

Power (Encounter ✦ Arcane, Force, Implement): Standard Action. As the warlock's *hellish rebuke* power (*PH* 132).

Master's Wand of Cloud of Daggers — Level 3+

Your cloud of daggers strikes with deadly accuracy.

Lvl 3	+1	680 gp	Lvl 18	+4	85,000 gp
Lvl 8	+2	3,400 gp	Lvl 23	+5	425,000 gp
Lvl 13	+3	17,000 gp	Lvl 28	+6	2,125,000 gp

Implement (**Wand**)

Enhancement: Attack rolls and damage rolls

Critical: +1d8 damage per plus

Property: When a creature moves into a *cloud of daggers* you create with this wand, it takes twice your Wisdom modifier in damage (minimum 2) instead of damage equal to your Wisdom modifier.

Power (Encounter ✦ Arcane, Force, Implement): Standard Action. As the wizard's *cloud of daggers* power (*PH* 159).

Master's Wand of Dire Radiance — Level 3+

Your dire radiance presses against foes with an invisible force.

Lvl 3	+1	680 gp	Lvl 18	+4	85,000 gp
Lvl 8	+2	3,400 gp	Lvl 23	+5	425,000 gp
Lvl 13	+3	17,000 gp	Lvl 28	+6	2,125,000 gp

Implement (Wand)

Enhancement: Attack rolls and damage rolls

Critical: +1d8 damage per plus

Property: Each square a target affected by your *dire radiance* moves toward you costs 1 extra square of movement.

Power (Encounter ✦ Arcane, Fear, Implement, Radiant): Standard Action. As the warlock's *dire radiance* power (*PH* 131).

Master's Wand of Eldritch Blast — Level 3+

Your eldritch blast viciously scours your enemies.

Lvl 3	+1	680 gp	Lvl 18	+4	85,000 gp
Lvl 8	+2	3,400 gp	Lvl 23	+5	425,000 gp
Lvl 13	+3	17,000 gp	Lvl 28	+6	2,125,000 gp

Implement (Wand)

Enhancement: Attack rolls and damage rolls

Critical: +1d8 damage per plus

Property: Gain a +1 item bonus to damage rolls when you use this wand to attack with *eldritch blast*.
Level 13 or 18: +2 item bonus.
Level 23 or 28: +3 item bonus.

Power (Encounter ✦ Arcane, Implement): Standard Action. As the warlock's *eldritch blast* power (*PH* 132).

Master's Wand of Eyebite — Level 3+

Your eyebite spell occludes you just a moment longer than normal.

Lvl 3	+1	680 gp	Lvl 18	+4	85,000 gp
Lvl 8	+2	3,400 gp	Lvl 23	+5	425,000 gp
Lvl 13	+3	17,000 gp	Lvl 28	+6	2,125,000 gp

Implement (Wand)

Enhancement: Attack rolls and damage rolls

Critical: +1d8 damage per plus

Property: When you hit a target with *eyebite* using this wand, you gain combat advantage against the target on your first attack next turn.

Power (Encounter ✦ Arcane, Charm, Implement, Psychic): Standard Action. As the warlock's *eyebite* power (*PH* 132).

Master's Wand of Hellish Rebuke — Level 3+

Your hellish rebuke consumes your attacker and its nearby allies.

Lvl 3	+1	680 gp	Lvl 18	+4	85,000 gp
Lvl 8	+2	3,400 gp	Lvl 23	+5	425,000 gp
Lvl 13	+3	17,000 gp	Lvl 28	+6	2,125,000 gp

Implement (Wand)

Enhancement: Attack rolls and damage rolls

Critical: +1d8 damage per plus

Property: When *hellish rebuke* causes a target to take damage from attacking you, all of its adjacent allies take damage equal to half that amount.

Power (Encounter ✦ Arcane, Fire, Implement): Standard Action. As the warlock's *hellish rebuke* power (*PH* 132).

Master's Wand of Magic Missile — Level 3+

Your magic missiles impact a foe with the force of a bull rush.

Lvl 3	+1	680 gp	Lvl 18	+4	85,000 gp
Lvl 8	+2	3,400 gp	Lvl 23	+5	425,000 gp
Lvl 13	+3	17,000 gp	Lvl 28	+6	2,125,000 gp

Implement (Wand)

Enhancement: Attack rolls and damage rolls

Critical: +1d8 damage per plus

Property: Any target you hit with the *magic missile* power is pushed 1 square.

Power (Encounter ✦ Arcane, Force, Implement): Standard Action. As the wizard's *magic missile* power (*PH* 159).

Master's Wand of Ray of Frost — Level 3+

Your ray of frost accurately strikes a target hiding among its allies.

Lvl 3	+1	680 gp	Lvl 18	+4	85,000 gp
Lvl 8	+2	3,400 gp	Lvl 23	+5	425,000 gp
Lvl 13	+3	17,000 gp	Lvl 28	+6	2,125,000 gp

Implement (Wand)

Enhancement: Attack rolls and damage rolls

Critical: +1d8 damage per plus

Property: You ignore cover from enemies when you cast *ray of frost*.

Power (Encounter ✦ Arcane, Cold, Implement): Standard Action. As the wizard's *ray of frost* power (*PH* 159).

Master's Wand of Scorching Burst — Level 3+

Your scorching burst burns devastatingly hot at its core.

Lvl 3	+1	680 gp	Lvl 18	+4	85,000 gp
Lvl 8	+2	3,400 gp	Lvl 23	+5	425,000 gp
Lvl 13	+3	17,000 gp	Lvl 28	+6	2,125,000 gp

Implement (Wand)

Enhancement: Attack rolls and damage rolls

Critical: +1d8 damage per plus

Property: You deal an additional 1d6 fire damage to a creature occupying the origin square of your *scorching burst* power.

Power (Encounter ✦ Arcane, Fire, Implement): Standard Action. As the wizard's *scorching burst* power (*PH* 159).

Master's Wand of Thunderwave — Level 3+

This wand grants the ability to reshape your thunderwave power.

Lvl 3	+1	680 gp	Lvl 18	+4	85,000 gp
Lvl 8	+2	3,400 gp	Lvl 23	+5	425,000 gp
Lvl 13	+3	17,000 gp	Lvl 28	+6	2,125,000 gp

Implement (Wand)

Enhancement: Attack rolls and damage rolls

Critical: +1d8 damage per plus

Property: When you use the *thunderwave* power, you can make it a close burst 1.

Power (Encounter ✦ Arcane, Implement, Thunder): Standard Action. As the wizard's *thunderwave* power (*PH* 161).

Wand of Cold   Level 3+

Frost covers the tip of this wand, threatening to unleash its icy chill.

Lvl 3	+1	680 gp	Lvl 18	+4	85,000 gp
Lvl 8	+2	3,400 gp	Lvl 23	+5	425,000 gp
Lvl 13	+3	17,000 gp	Lvl 28	+6	2,125,000 gp

Implement (Wand)

Enhancement: Attack rolls and damage rolls

Critical: +1d8 cold damage per plus

Property: Gain a +1 item bonus to damage rolls when you use this wand to attack with a power that has the cold and implement keywords.

> *Level 13 or 18:* +2 item bonus.

> *Level 23 or 28:* +3 item bonus.

Power (Encounter ✦ Arcane, Cold, Implement): Standard Action. As the wizard's *ray of frost* power (*PH* 159).

Wand of Erupting Flame   Level 15+

Your mastery over flame increases the more you fight.

Lvl 15	+3	25,000 gp	Lvl 25	+5	625,000 gp
Lvl 20	+4	125,000 gp	Lvl 30	+6	3,125,000 gp

Implement (Wand)

Enhancement: Attack rolls and damage rolls

Critical: +1d6 fire damage per plus

Power (Daily ✦ Arcane, Fire, Implement): Standard Action. As the wizard's *scorching burst* power (*PH* 159). If you have reached at least one milestone, you can instead use the wizard's *burning hands* power (*PH* 159). If you have reached at least two milestones, you can instead use the wizard's *burning hands* power (*PH* 159), and you can exclude one ally in the blast from the attack.

Wand of Psychic Ravaging   Level 3+

With this wand in hand, your psychic attacks tear through your enemies' minds.

Lvl 3	+1	680 gp	Lvl 18	+4	85,000 gp
Lvl 8	+2	3,400 gp	Lvl 23	+5	425,000 gp
Lvl 13	+3	17,000 gp	Lvl 28	+6	2,125,000 gp

Implement (Wand)

Enhancement: Attack rolls and damage rolls

Critical: +1d8 psychic damage per plus

Property: Gain a +1 item bonus to damage rolls when you use this wand to attack with a power that has the implement and psychic keywords.

> *Level 13 or 18:* +2 item bonus.

> *Level 23 or 28:* +3 item bonus.

Power (Encounter ✦ Arcane, Charm, Implement, Psychic): Standard Action. As the warlock's *eyebite* power (*PH* 132).

Thunder wand

Precise Wand of Color Spray   Level 10+

Wielding this wand, you display deadly accuracy with color spray.

Lvl 10	+2	5,000 gp	Lvl 25	+5	625,000 gp
Lvl 15	+3	25,000 gp	Lvl 30	+6	3,125,000 gp
Lvl 20	+4	125,000 gp			

Implement (Wand)

Enhancement: Attack rolls and damage rolls

Critical: +1d6 damage per plus

Property: Gain a +1 item bonus to *color spray* attack rolls made using this implement.

Power (Daily ✦ Arcane, Implement, Radiant): Standard Action. As the wizard's *color spray* power (*PH* 161). If your first attack roll with the power hits, you score a critical hit.

Thunder Wand   Level 3+

This sturdy wand enhances the destructive might of your thunder attacks.

Lvl 3	+1	680 gp	Lvl 18	+4	85,000 gp
Lvl 8	+2	3,400 gp	Lvl 23	+5	425,000 gp
Lvl 13	+3	17,000 gp	Lvl 28	+6	2,125,000 gp

Implement (Wand)

Enhancement: Attack rolls and damage rolls

Critical: +1d8 thunder damage per plus

Property: Gain a +1 item bonus to damage rolls when you use this wand to attack with a power that has the implement and thunder keywords.

> *Level 13 or 18:* +2 item bonus.

> *Level 23 or 28:* +3 item bonus.

Power (Encounter ✦ Arcane, Implement, Thunder): Standard Action. As the wizard's *thunderwave* power (*PH* 159).

Wand of radiance

Wand of Swarming Force — Level 3+

The invisible forces you wield through this wand strike with deadly power.

Lvl 3	+1	680 gp	Lvl 18	+4	85,000 gp
Lvl 8	+2	3,400 gp	Lvl 23	+5	425,000 gp
Lvl 13	+3	17,000 gp	Lvl 28	+6	2,125,000 gp

Implement (Wand)

Enhancement: Attack rolls and damage rolls

Critical: +1d8 force damage per plus

Property: Gain a +1 item bonus to damage rolls when you use this wand to attack with a power that has the force and implement keywords.

Level 13 or 18: +2 item bonus.

Level 23 or 28: +3 item bonus.

Power (Encounter ✦ Arcane, Force, Implement): Standard Action. As the wizard's *cloud of daggers* power (PH 159).

ARMS SLOT ITEMS

From the shield, you gain strength. From the bracers, you gain deadliness.

A variety of items might find their way onto an adventurer's arms, but primary among these are shields and bracers.

A set of qualities that pertains to a magic shield can usually be applied to either a light shield or a heavy shield; exceptions are noted. A shield's magical properties are usually defensive; however, some shields allow their wearers to unleash vicious attacks or to gain unusual magical powers.

Bracers, in contrast, provide offensive powers and benefits. A set of bracers on the arms of a ranger or rogue might allow that character to unleash a barrage of attacks or deliver a particularly deadly strike. If a spellcaster can't use a shield, bracers provide an excellent alternative.

ARMS SLOT ITEMS

Lvl	Name	Price (gp)
1	Floating shield	360
2	Bloodguard shield	520
2	Bracers of respite	520
2	Darkleaf shield	520
2	Jousting shield	520
2	Razor shield	520
2	Shield of the guardian	520
3	Flame bracers	680
4	Battleforged shield	840
4	Bloodthirst bracers	840
4	Counterstrike guards	840
4	Feyleaf vambraces	840
4	Mountain shield	840
4	Shield of eyes	840
5	Breach bracers	1,000

Wand of Radiance — Level 3+

A pinpoint of light dances on the tip of this wand.

Lvl 3	+1	680 gp	Lvl 18	+4	85,000 gp
Lvl 8	+2	3,400 gp	Lvl 23	+5	425,000 gp
Lvl 13	+3	17,000 gp	Lvl 28	+6	2,125,000 gp

Implement (Wand)

Enhancement: Attack rolls and damage rolls

Critical: +1d8 radiant damage per plus

Property: Gain a +1 item bonus to damage rolls when you use this wand to attack with a power that has the implement and radiant keywords.

Level 13 or 18: +2 item bonus.

Level 23 or 28: +3 item bonus.

Power (Encounter ✦ Arcane, Fear, Implement, Radiant): Standard Action. As the warlock's *dire radiance* power (PH 131).

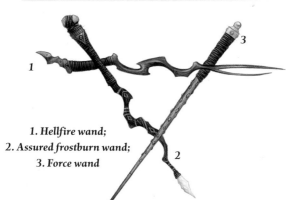

1. Hellfire wand;
2. Assured frostburn wand;
3. Force wand

Lvl	Name	Price (gp)
5	Cold iron shield	1,000
5	Couters of second chances	1,000
5	Direbeast shield	1,000
5	Quickhit bracers	1,000
5	Shimmerlight shield	1,000
6	Bracers of archery	1,800
6	Bracers of mental might	1,800
6	Bracers of tactical blows	1,800
6	Cold iron bracers	1,800
6	Flamedrinker shield	1,800
6	Iron armbands of power	1,800
6	Throwing shield	1,800
7	Pelaurum shield	2,600
7	Razor bracers	2,600
7	Skull bracers	2,600
7	Trauma bracers	2,600
8	Bracers of bold maneuvering	3,400
8	Bracers of rejuvenation	3,400
8	Manticore shield	3,400
8	Mindiron vambraces	3,400
8	Mithral shield	3,400
8	Storm shield	3,400
8	Wyrmguard shield	3,400
9	Angelsteel shield	4,200
9	Bloodshored shield	4,200
9	Bloodsoaked shield	4,200
9	Diamond bracers	4,200
9	Recoil shield	4,200
9	Shadowflow shield	4,200
10	Bloodsoaked bracers	5,000
10	Healer's shield	5,000
11	Bracers of infinite blades	9,000
11	Warlock's bracers	9,000
12	Bloodguard shield	13,000
12	Bracers of respite	13,000
12	Darkleaf shield	13,000
12	Jousting shield	13,000
12	Razor shield	13,000
12	Ricochet shield	13,000
12	Shield of the guardian	13,000
12	Tauran shield	13,000
13	Bracers of wound closure	17,000
13	Flame bracers	17,000
13	Stonewall shield	17,000
14	Battleforged shield	21,000
14	Bloodthirst bracers	21,000
14	Bracers of iron arcana	21,000
14	Counterstrike guards	21,000
14	Flaring shield	21,000
14	Hypnotic shield	21,000
14	Mountain shield	21,000
14	Spellshield	21,000
15	Breach bracers	25,000
15	Cold iron shield	25,000
15	Couters of second chances	25,000

Lvl	Name	Price (gp)
15	Direbeast shield	25,000
15	Quickhit bracers	25,000
15	Rapidstrike bracers	25,000
15	Shimmerlight shield	25,000
16	Bracers of archery	45,000
16	Bracers of infinite blades	45,000
16	Bracers of tactical blows	45,000
16	Cold iron bracers	45,000
16	Flamedrinker shield	45,000
16	Iron armbands of power	45,000
16	Throwing shield	45,000
17	Pelaurum shield	65,000
17	Razor bracers	65,000
17	Shield of blocking	65,000
17	Skull bracers	65,000
18	Bracers of bold maneuvering	85,000
18	Manticore shield	85,000
18	Mindiron vambraces	85,000
18	Mithral shield	85,000
18	Storm shield	85,000
18	Wyrmguard shield	85,000
19	Angelsteel shield	105,000
19	Bloodshored shield	105,000
19	Bloodsoaked shield	105,000
19	Diamond bracers	105,000
19	Shadowflow shield	105,000
19	Trollhide bracers	105,000
20	Bloodsoaked bracers	125,000
20	Healer's shield	125,000
22	Bloodguard shield	325,000
22	Bracers of respite	325,000
22	Darkleaf shield	325,000
22	Jousting shield	325,000
22	Razor shield	325,000
22	Shield of the guardian	325,000
23	Flame bracers	425,000
23	Stonewall shield	425,000
24	Battleforged shield	525,000
24	Bloodthirst bracers	525,000
25	Breach bracers	625,000
25	Cold iron shield	625,000
25	Couters of second chances	625,000
25	Direbeast shield	625,000
25	Quickhit bracers	625,000
25	Shimmerlight shield	625,000
26	Bracers of archery	1,125,000
26	Bracers of tactical blows	1,125,000
26	Cold iron bracers	1,125,000
26	Flamedrinker shield	1,125,000
26	Iron armbands of power	1,125,000
26	Throwing shield	1,125,000
27	Pelaurum shield	1,625,000
27	Razor bracers	1,625,000
27	Reflective shield	1,625,000
27	Shield of blocking	1,625,000

Lvl	Name	Price (gp)
27	Skull bracers	1,625,000
27	Trauma bracers	1,625,000
28	Manticore shield	2,125,000
28	Mindiron vambraces	2,125,000
28	Mithral shield	2,125,000
28	Storm shield	2,125,000
29	Angelsteel shield	2,625,000
29	Bloodshored shield	2,625,000
29	Bloodsoaked shield	2,625,000
29	Diamond bracers	2,625,000
29	Trollhide bracers	2,625,000
30	Bloodsoaked bracers	3,125,000
30	Healer's shield	3,125,000

Angelsteel Shield — Level 9+

This fine, steel shield flickers with light that flows out at times to help defend your allies.

Lvl 9	4,200 gp	Lvl 29	2,625,000 gp
Lvl 19	105,000 gp		

Item Slot: Arms
Shield: Any

Power (Daily): Immediate Reaction. Use this power when an ally adjacent to you is hit by an attack. That ally gains a +1 power bonus to the defense that the attack targeted until the end of the encounter.
Level 19: +2 power bonus.
Level 29: +3 power bonus.

Battleforged Shield — Level 4+

Covered in Dwarven and Draconic runes, this shield aids badly wounded allies.

Lvl 4	840 gp	Lvl 24	525,000 gp
Lvl 14	21,000 gp		

Item Slot: Arms
Shield: Heavy

Power (Daily ✦ Healing): Free Action. Use this power when an ally adjacent to you regains hit points. That ally regains additional hit points as though it had spent a healing surge.
Level 14: 2d8 hit points.
Level 24: 3d8 hit points.

Bloodguard Shield — Level 2+

As your foe's weapon strikes deep, this bronze shield flares red and covers you in a protective aura.

Lvl 2	520 gp	Lvl 22	325,000 gp
Lvl 12	13,000 gp		

Item Slot: Arms
Shield: Any

Power (Daily): Immediate Interrupt. Use this power when a critical hit is scored against you. Gain resist 5 to all damage until the end of your next turn.
Level 12: Resist 10 to all damage.
Level 22: Resist 15 to all damage.

Bloodshored Shield — Level 9+

This strong, steel shield protects the bloodied.

Lvl 9	4,200 gp	Lvl 29	2,625,000 gp
Lvl 19	105,000 gp		

Item Slot: Arms
Shield: Any

Power (Daily): Minor Action. Until the end of your next turn, you or an adjacent ally gains resist 5 to all damage. This power affects bloodied targets only.
Level 19: Resist 10 to all damage.
Level 29: Resist 15 to all damage.

Bloodsoaked Bracers — Level 10+

Your spilled blood causes these studded leather bracers to tremble with power.

Lvl 10	5,000 gp	Lvl 30	3,125,000 gp
Lvl 20	125,000 gp		

Item Slot: Arms

Power (Daily): Minor Action. Use this power while you are bloodied. Gain a +5 power bonus to melee damage rolls until the end of the encounter or until you are no longer bloodied, whichever comes first.
Level 20: +10 power bonus.
Level 30: +15 power bonus.

Bloodsoaked Shield — Level 9+

A sheen of wet blood coats this wooden shield, protecting you when you are seriously injured.

Lvl 9	4,200 gp	Lvl 29	2,625,000 gp
Lvl 19	105,000 gp		

Item Slot: Arms
Shield: Any

Power (Daily): Minor Action. Use this power while you are bloodied. Gain resist 2 to all damage until the end of the encounter, or until you are no longer bloodied, whichever comes first.
Level 19: Resist 5 to all damage.
Level 29: Resist 8 to all damage.

Bloodthirst Bracers — Level 4+

The crystals set in these golden bracers help you deal wounds that continue to impair your foe even after the initial strike.

Lvl 4	840 gp	Lvl 24	525,000 gp
Lvl 14	21,000 gp		

Item Slot: Arms

Power (Daily): Free Action. Use this power when you hit an enemy with a melee attack. In addition to the normal damage from that attack, the target takes ongoing damage equal to 2 + your Charisma modifier (save ends).
Level 14: Ongoing damage equal to 5 + your Charisma modifier (save ends).
Level 24: Ongoing damage equal to 10 + your Charisma modifier (save ends).

Bracers of Archery — Level 6+

These leather armbands enhance your potency with bows and crossbows.

Lvl 6	1,800 gp	Lvl 26	1,125,000 gp
Lvl 16	45,000 gp		

Item Slot: Arms

Property: Gain a +2 item bonus to damage rolls when attacking with a bow or crossbow.

Level 16: +4 item bonus.

Level 26: +6 item bonus.

Power (Daily): Minor Action. Ignore cover on your next attack this turn when using a bow or crossbow.

Bracers of Bold Maneuvering — Level 8+

These slick cuffs help maintain your defensive guard as you move around wary foes.

Lvl 8	3,400 gp	Lvl 18	85,000 gp

Item Slot: Arms

Power (Encounter): Minor Action. Gain a +4 power bonus to AC against opportunity attacks until the end of your next turn.

Level 18: While this power is in effect, you can make one opportunity attack made against you miss. This must be done before you know whether the attack succeeds.

Bracers of Infinite Blades — Level 11+

With these metal guards, you have an arsenal at your disposal at all times.

Lvl 11	9,000 gp	Lvl 16	45,000 gp

Item Slot: Arms

Property: You can draw a +2 *dagger* from these bracers as though drawing it from a sheath. A drawn dagger disappears at the end of your turn. These bracers can also be crafted to supply other light thrown weapons, such as shuriken.

Level 16: +4 *dagger.*

Bracers of Iron Arcana — Level 14

Favored by spellcasters, these iron bracers are covered in esoteric runes that help deflect physical attacks.

Item Slot: Arms   21,000 gp

Power (Daily): Minor Action. Gain an item bonus to AC equal to your Intelligence, Wisdom, or Charisma modifier until the end of your next turn.

Bracers of Mental Might — Level 6

The adage, "mind over matter," truly applies when you wear these bracers.

Item Slot: Arms   1,800 gp

Power (Encounter): Free Action. Use this power when making a Strength attack, Strength check, or Strength-based skill check. Use your Intelligence, Wisdom, or Charisma modifier in place of your Strength modifier to determine the result of the roll.

Bracers of Rejuvenation — Level 8

These wrist guards pulse with red light when you pause to catch your breath, increasing your defenses until you rejoin the battle.

Item Slot: Arms   3,400 gp

Power (Healing Surge): Minor Action. Gain a +1 item bonus to all rolls, defenses, and saving throws until the end of your next turn.

Bracers of Respite — Level 2+

Commonly worn by combat medics, these white linen arm guards spread healing benefits.

Lvl 2	520 gp	Lvl 22	325,000 gp
Lvl 12	13,000 gp		

Item Slot: Arms

Power (Daily ✦ Healing): Free Action. Use this power when an ally adjacent to you regains hit points. You or one other ally adjacent to you regains 1d8 hit points.

Level 12: Regains 2d8 hit points.

Level 22: Regains 4d8 hit points.

DARRELL RICHE

Bracers of Tactical Blows   Level 6+

When your foes let down their guard, these dragonscale bracers make them regret it.

Lvl 6	1,800 gp	Lvl 26	1,125,000 gp
Lvl 16	45,000 gp		

Item Slot: Arms

Property: When you hit with an opportunity attack, deal an extra 1d6 damage.

Level 16: 2d6 damage.

Level 26: 3d6 damage.

Bracers of Wound Closure   Level 13

These copper bracers create a luminescent field that eliminates impairing wounds.

Item Slot: Arms   17,000 gp

Power (Daily): Immediate Reaction. Use this power when you are hit by an attack that deals ongoing damage of any type. The ongoing damage effect ends.

Breach Bracers   Level 5+

These spiked arm guards render enemies more vulnerable to your attacks.

Lvl 5	1,000 gp	Lvl 25	625,000 gp
Lvl 15	25,000 gp		

Item Slot: Arms

Power (Daily): Free Action. Use this power when you hit with a melee attack. The target of the attack gains vulnerable 5 against the next attack that hits it before the end of your next turn.

Level 15: Vulnerable 10.

Level 25: Vulnerable 15.

Cold Iron Bracers   Level 6+

The creatures of the Feywild recoil at the touch of these iron bracers.

Lvl 6	1,800 gp	Lvl 26	1,125,000 gp
Lvl 16	45,000 gp		

Item Slot: Arms

Property: Gain a +1 item bonus to AC and Reflex defense against fey creatures' attacks.

Level 16: +2 item bonus.

Level 26: +3 item bonus.

Cold Iron Shield   Level 5+

Using this heavy iron shield, you can protect an ally's mind as well as his body.

Lvl 5	1,000 gp	Lvl 25	625,000 gp
Lvl 15	25,000 gp		

Item Slot: Arms

Shield: Heavy

Power (Daily): Immediate Interrupt. Use when an attack against Will defense would hit an ally adjacent to you. That ally gains a +4 power bonus to Will defense against that attack.

Level 15: That ally gains a +4 power bonus to Will defense until the end of your next turn.

Level 25: All allies adjacent to you gain a +4 power bonus to Will defense until the end of your next turn.

Counterstrike Guards   Level 4+

A set of twin forearm shields small enough not to hinder you, these guards improve your strikes against off-balance foes.

Lvl 4	840 gp	Lvl 14	21,000 gp

Item Slot: Arms

Power (Daily): Immediate Reaction. Use this power when a melee attack misses you. You make a melee basic attack against the attacker.

Level 14: This power becomes an encounter power.

Couters of Second Chances   Level 5+

As you swing past your opponent, these armored elbow guards sparkle with energy, bringing your weapon back in line.

Lvl 5	1,000 gp	Lvl 25	625,000 gp
Lvl 15	25,000 gp		

Item Slot: Arms

Power (Daily): Free Action. Use this power when you miss with a melee attack. Reroll the attack, and use the second result, even if it's lower.

Level 15 or 25: Gain a +2 bonus to the rerolled attack roll.

Level 25: If your rerolled attack misses, make a melee basic attack against the target.

Darkleaf Shield   Level 2+

Shadowfell gravetrees provide the tightly woven branches and black leaves that form this shield.

Lvl 2	520 gp	Lvl 22	325,000 gp
Lvl 12	13,000 gp		

Item Slot: Arms

Shield: Light

Property: Gain a +1 item bonus to AC during the surprise round and the first nonsurprise round of each encounter.

Level 12: +2 item bonus.

Level 22: +3 item bonus.

Diamond Bracers   Level 9+

These clear crystal vambraces of interlocking plates can protect you from virtually anything, for a time.

Lvl 9	4,200 gp	Lvl 29	2,625,000 gp
Lvl 19	105,000 gp		

Item Slot: Arms

Power (Daily): Minor Action. Until the end of the encounter, gain resist 10 against a damage type from which you were dealt damage since the end of your last turn.

Level 19: Resist 15 against that damage type.

Level 29: Resist 20 against that damage type.

Direbeast Shield — Level 5+

Covered in bear hides and marked with a wolf's head, this shield lends the stamina of wild beasts to your allies.

Lvl 5	1,000 gp	Lvl 25	625,000 gp
Lvl 15	25,000 gp		

Item Slot: Arms
Shield: Any

Power (Daily): Immediate Interrupt. Use this power when an attack against Fortitude defense hits an ally adjacent to you. That ally gains a +4 power bonus to Fortitude defense against that attack.
Level 15: That ally gains +4 power bonus to Fortitude defense until the end of your next turn.
Level 25: All allies adjacent to you gain +4 power bonus to Fortitude defense until the end of your next turn.

Feyleaf Vambraces — Level 4

A bright blue glow erupts from these tough bark guards, and the world shifts around you.

Item Slot: Arms   840 gp

Power (Daily ✦ Teleportation): Free Action. Use this power when you attack an adjacent target, but before you roll. Teleport to the nearest square from which you and an ally flank the target.

Flame Bracers — Level 3+

Flickering flames dance across your arm guards, darting to cover your weapon on crucial attacks.

Lvl 3	680 gp	Lvl 23	425,000 gp
Lvl 13	17,000 gp		

Item Slot: Arms

Property: When you score a critical hit with a melee attack, deal an extra 1d6 fire damage.
Level 13: 1d10 fire damage.
Level 23: 2d6 fire damage.

Power (Daily): Minor Action. Your next successful weapon attack before the end of your next round deals an extra 1d6 fire damage.
Level 13: 2d6 fire damage.
Level 23: 3d6 fire damage.

Flamedrinker Shield — Level 6+

This shield swirls with gold and ruby hues as it absorbs the jet of flame meant to burn your flesh.

Lvl 6	1,800 gp	Lvl 26	1,125,000 gp
Lvl 16	45,000 gp		

Item Slot: Arms
Shield: Any

Property: Gain resist 5 fire.
Level 16: Resist 10 fire.
Level 26: Resist 15 fire.

Power (Daily): Immediate Interrupt. Use this power when an ally adjacent to you would take fire damage. Grant that ally resist 10 fire until the end of your next turn.
Level 16: Resist 20 fire.
Level 26: Resist 30 fire.

Flaring Shield — Level 14

An opponent's poorly aimed attack is met with a blinding flash of light.

Item Slot: Arms   21,000 gp
Shield: Any

Power (Daily): Immediate Reaction. Use this power when a melee attack misses you. The attacker is blinded until the end of your next turn.

Floating Shield — Level 1

Enameled with images of ocean waves, this shield eases your way in water.

Item Slot: Arms   360 gp
Shield: Any

Property: You do not sink beneath the surface of any liquid (unless you choose to do so). Also, gain a +3 item bonus to Athletics checks to swim, and to Endurance checks to swim for an hour or more. Also, you can swim at your speed on the surface of the water (but not underwater).

Healer's Shield — Level 10+

This shield shores healing powers as well as blocks enemy blows.

Lvl 10	5,000 gp	Lvl 30	3,125,000 gp
Lvl 20	125,000 gp		

Item Slot: Arms
Shield: Any

Power (Daily ✦ Healing): Free Action. Use this power when you or an ally within line of sight regains hit points. You or the ally regains hit points equal to the maximum possible result of the healing effect and also regains hit points equal to your Wisdom or Charisma modifier, whichever is higher.
Level 20: Double your ability modifier when determining the additional healing granted by this item.
Level 30: This power becomes an encounter power.

Hypnotic Shield — Level 14

The spiral pattern on this round shield mesmerizes unwary foes.

Item Slot: Arms   21,000 gp
Shield: Any

Power (Daily): Immediate Reaction. Use this power when a melee attack misses you. The attacker is dazed (save ends). This effect also ends if you are not adjacent to the attacker at the end of your turn, or if the attacker can no longer see you.

Iron Armbands of Power — Level 6+

These plate armbands enhance the damage you dole out.

Lvl 6	1,800 gp	Lvl 26	1,125,000 gp
Lvl 16	45,000 gp		

Item Slot: Arms

Property: Gain a +2 item bonus to melee damage rolls.
Level 16: +4 item bonus.
Level 26: +6 item bonus.

Jousting Shield — Level 2+

This grooved and angled shield acts as a bulwark against all attempts to alter a charger's course.

Lvl 2	520 gp	Lvl 22	325,000 gp
Lvl 12	13,000 gp		

Item Slot: Arms

Shield: Any

Property: Gain resist 5 against opportunity attacks you provoke from charging. After charging, you cannot be pulled, pushed, or slided until the end of your next turn.
Level 12: Resist 10 to all damage.
Level 22: Resist 15 to all damage.

Manticore Shield — Level 8+

Emblazoned with the emblem of a snarling manticore, this shield releases a volley of needles at your command.

Lvl 8	3,400 gp	Lvl 28	2,125,000 gp
Lvl 18	85,000 gp		

Item Slot: Arms

Shield: Any

Power (Daily): Standard Action. Make an attack: Area burst 1 within 10 squares; Dexterity + 2 vs. AC; on a hit, the target takes 1d8 + Strength modifier damage.
Level 18: Strength + 4 vs. AC; 2d8 + Dexterity modifier damage.
Level 28: Strength + 6 vs. AC; 3d10 + Dexterity modifier damage.

Mindiron Vambraces — Level 8+

These smooth crystal bracers are shot through with purple veins that pulse when you attack.

Lvl 8	3,400 gp	Lvl 28	2,125,000 gp
Lvl 18	85,000 gp		

Item Slot: Arms

Power (Daily): Free Action. Use this power when you hit with a melee attack. Make a secondary attack against the target: +11 vs. Will; on a hit, the target is dazed until the end of your next turn.
Level 18: +21 vs. Will; the target is stunned until the end of your next turn.
Level 28: +31 vs. Will; the target is dominated until the end of your next turn.

Mithral Shield — Level 8+

Light reflects brightly from this highly polished, silvery shield.

Lvl 8	3,400 gp	Lvl 28	2,125,000 gp
Lvl 18	85,000 gp		

Item Slot: Arms

Shield: Any

Property: When you are hit by an attack with the radiant keyword, the attacker takes 2 radiant damage.
Level 18: 5 radiant damage.
Level 28: 10 radiant damage.

Mountain Shield — Level 4+

Inlaid with Dwarven runes and images of mountains, this shield keeps your allies from being pulled into dangerous situations.

Lvl 4	840 gp	Lvl 14	21,000 gp

Item Slot: Arms

Shield: Heavy

Power (Encounter): Minor Action. Allies adjacent to you cannot be pushed, pulled, or slid until the end of your next turn.
Level 14: Allies within 2 squares of you.

Pelaurum Shield — Level 7+

With this sparkling copper shield, the intense energy of an errant blast fuels your power when you next strike.

Lvl 7	2,600 gp	Lvl 27	1,625,000 gp
Lvl 17	65,000 gp		

Item Slot: Arms

Shield: Any

Property: When an attack that has the fire or radiant keyword misses you, your next successful melee attack before the end of your next turn deals an extra 2 radiant damage.
Level 17: 5 radiant damage.
Level 27: 10 radiant damage.

Quickhit Bracers — Level 5+

Favored by rangers and other two-weapon warriors, these arm guards grant the speed to strike harder and more quickly.

Lvl 5	1,000 gp	Lvl 25	625,000 gp
Lvl 15	25,000 gp		

Item Slot: Arms

Property: When using a power, if you hit one creature with both your main weapon and your off-hand weapon, deal an extra 1d6 damage to that creature.
Level 15: 2d6 damage.
Level 25: 3d6 damage.

Power (Daily): Minor Action. Use this power when you hit with both your main weapon and your off-hand weapon using one power. Make a melee basic attack with your off-hand weapon.

Rapidstrike Bracers — Level 15

Wearing these bracers, even your most basic attacks can quickly become dangerous.

Item Slot: Arms   25,000 gp

Property: Gain a +2 item bonus to initiative.

Power (Encounter): Free Action. Use this power when you would make a basic attack. Attack using a 1st-level, single-target, at-will attack power instead of a basic attack. This attack does not provoke an opportunity attack even if it ordinarily would.

Razor Bracers — Level 7+

These steel arm plates are lined with sharp edges that make grappling enemies pay dearly.

| Lvl 7 | 2,600 gp | Lvl 27 | 1,625,000 gp |
| Lvl 17 | 65,000 gp | | |

Item Slot: Arms
Property: Gain a +2 item bonus to checks to escape a
grab. When a creature successfully grabs you, it takes
1d10 damage.
Level 17: 2d10 damage.
Level 27: 3d10 damage.

Razor Shield — Level 2+

Ringed in blades, this round shield is as much a weapon as an item of defense.

| Lvl 2 | 520 gp | Lvl 22 | 325,000 gp |
| Lvl 12 | 13,000 gp | | |

Item Slot: Arms
Shield: Any

Power (Daily): Immediate Reaction. Use this power when
a melee attack hits you. The attacker takes 1d8 + Constitution modifier damage.
Level 12: 2d8 + Constitution modifier damage.
Level 22: This power becomes an encounter power.

Recoil Shield — Level 9

This unassuming shield takes on surprising heft when you want to knock a foe flat.

Item Slot: Arms   4,200 gp
Shield: Any

Power (Encounter): Immediate Reaction. Use this
power when a melee attack hits you. The attacker is
knocked prone.

Reflective Shield — Level 27

A nasty surprise awaits those who make attacks against you while you wear this mirrorlike shield.

Item Slot: Arms   1,625,000 gp
Shield: Any

Power (Daily): Immediate Reaction. Use this power when
an attack against your AC or Reflex defense misses. The
source of the attack makes a new attack roll against its
own appropriate defense. If the attack roll succeeds,
it hits the attacker (apply damage and effect where
appropriate).

Ricochet Shield — Level 12

The strange, seemingly arbitrary angles of this shield take on a sinister purpose when you redirect a foe's ranged attack.

Item Slot: Arms   13,000 gp
Shield: Any

Power (Daily): Immediate Reaction. Use this power when
a ranged attack against AC misses you. The source of the
attack repeats the attack roll against a different target of
your choice within 10 squares of you. If the attack roll
succeeds, it hits that target (apply damage and effect
where appropriate).

Shadowflow Shield — Level 9+

This inky, black shield conceals nearby allies.

| Lvl 9 | 4,200 gp | Lvl 29 | 2,625,000 gp |
| Lvl 19 | 105,000 gp | | |

Item Slot: Arms
Shield: Any

Power (Encounter): Minor Action. One ally adjacent to you
gains concealment until the start of your next turn.
Level 19: All allies adjacent to you gain concealment until
the start of your next turn.

Shield of Blocking — Level 17+

The best offense is sometimes a powerful defense.

| Lvl 17 | 65,000 gp | Lvl 27 | 1,625,000 gp |

Item Slot: Arms
Shield: Any

Power (Daily): Minor Action. Gain resist 5 to all damage
from melee attacks until the end of the encounter.
Level 27: Resist 10 to all damage from melee attacks.

Shield of Eyes
Level 4

This multifaceted shield keeps you aware of lurking threats.

Item Slot: Arms   840 gp

Shield: Any

Property: Gain an item bonus equal to your shield bonus to AC against opportunity attacks.

Power (Daily): Minor Action. You do not grant combat advantage when flanked by an enemy until the end of your next turn.

Shield of the Guardian
Level 2+

This oaken shield can guard an ally as well as protect you.

Lvl 2	520 gp	Lvl 22	325,000 gp
Lvl 12	13,000 gp		

Item Slot: Arms

Shield: Any

Power (Daily): Minor Action. One ally adjacent to you gains a +1 power bonus to AC until the end of the encounter.

Level 12: +2 power bonus to AC.

Level 22: +3 power bonus to AC.

Shimmerlight Shield
Level 5+

The thin but seemingly impervious layer of enchanted cloth stretched over the surface of this shield warns against danger.

Lvl 5	1,000 gp	Lvl 25	625,000 gp
Lvl 15	25,000 gp		

Item Slot: Arms

Shield: Any

Power (Daily): Immediate Interrupt. Use this power when an ally adjacent to you would be hit by an attack against Reflex defense. That ally gains a +4 power bonus to Reflex defense against the attack.

Level 15: That ally gains a +4 power bonus to Reflex defense until the end of your next turn.

Level 25: All allies adjacent to you gain a +4 power bonus to Reflex defense until the end of your next turn.

Skull Bracers
Level 7+

These heavy bracers are each mounted with a long dragonlike skull.

Lvl 7	2,600 gp	Lvl 27	1,625,000 gp
Lvl 17	65,000 gp		

Item Slot: Arms

Power (Daily): Minor Action. The next successful attack you make before the end of your next turn deals an extra 1d10 damage.

Level 17: 2d10 damage.

Level 27: 3d10 damage.

Spellshield
Level 14

This rune-inlaid shield can shelter an ally from a wide-ranging attack.

Item Slot: Arms   21,000 gp

Shield: Any

Power (Daily): Immediate Interrupt. Use when a close or area attack targets you. One square adjacent to you within the attack's area is unaffected by the attack.

Stonewall Shield
Level 13+

Favored by dwarves, this shield can create a temporary barrier much like a wall.

Lvl 13	17,000 gp	Lvl 23	425,000 gp

Item Slot: Arms

Shield: Any

Power (Daily ✦ Conjuration): Standard Action. You create a wall of stone (wall 3 within 5 squares) that occupies contiguous squares and remains for 1 hour. You cannot create stone in an occupied square. The wall can be up to 3 squares long and up to 2 squares high. One square of wall can be destroyed by attacking it (AC 5, Fortitude 10, Reflex 5, hp 40). A DC 35 Strength check can destroy the wall in one square.

Level 23: Wall 5 within 10 squares; up to 5 squares long and up to 2 squares high; the wall in one square has 80 hit points.

Storm Shield — Level 8+

Shifting clouds play across the surface of this shield as it protects you from stormlike effects and then unleashes them on your foes.

| Lvl 8 | 3,400 gp | Lvl 28 | 2,125,000 gp |
| Lvl 18 | 85,000 gp | | |

Item Slot: Arms
Shield: Any
Property: Gain resist 5 lightning and resist 5 thunder.
  Level 18: Resist 10 lightning and resist 10 thunder.
  Level 28: Resist 10 lightning and resist 10 thunder.
Power (Daily ✦ Lightning, Thunder): Immediate Reaction. Use this power when you are hit by a melee attack. Deal 2d6 lightning and thunder damage to the attacker. (The attacker must have resistance or immunity to both damage types to reduce or ignore this damage.)
  Level 18: 4d6 lightning and thunder damage.
  Level 28: 6d6 lightning and thunder damage.

Tauran Shield — Level 12

This horn-edged shield helps you charge your foes with bull-like force.

Item Slot: Arms   13,000 gp
Shield: Any
Property: Gain a +4 item bonus to any bull rush attempt, and push the target one additional square.

Throwing Shield — Level 6+

When tossed, this throwing shield packs a hefty punch.

| Lvl 6 | 1,800 gp | Lvl 26 | 1,125,000 gp |
| Lvl 16 | 45,000 gp | | |

Item Slot: Arms
Shield: Any
Power (At-Will): Standard Action. Make an attack: Ranged 10; Strength + 2 vs. AC; on a hit, the target takes 1d8 + Strength modifier damage. The shield automatically returns to your grip after the attack.
  Level 16: Strength + 4 vs. AC; 2d8 + Strength modifier damage.
  Level 26: Strength + 6 vs. AC; 3d8 + Strength modifier damage.
Power (Daily): Free Action. Use this power after you hit a target with this shield's ranged attack. The target is pushed 1 square.
  Level 16: The target is pushed 1 square and knocked prone.
  Level 26: The target is pushed 1 square, knocked prone, and dazed until the end of its next turn.

Trauma Bracers — Level 7+

When you land a serious blow while wearing these jagged arm guards, the wounds you inflict resist healing for a time.

| Lvl 7 | 2,600 gp | Lvl 27 | 1,625,000 gp |

Item Slot: Arms
Power (Daily): Free Action. Use this power when you score a critical hit. The target can't regain hit points (save ends).
  Level 27: This power becomes an encounter power.

Trollhide Bracers — Level 19+

These ugly green wrist guards become indispensable when you are wounded.

| Lvl 19 | 105,000 gp | Lvl 29 | 2,625,000 gp |

Item Slot: Arms
Power (Daily ✦ Healing): Minor Action. Gain regeneration 5 until the end of the encounter or until you are lowered to 0 hit points or fewer. If you take acid or fire damage, the regeneration is supressed until the end of your next turn.
  Level 29: Regeneration 10.

Warlock's Bracers — Level 11

These dark leather cuffs, etched with symbols and runes, protect you against those you've cursed.

Item Slot: Arms   9,000 gp
Property: Gain a +1 item bonus to all defenses against attacks by creatures affected by your Warlock's Curse.

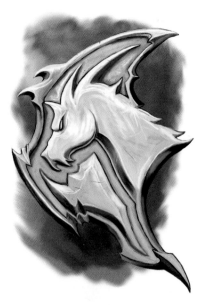

COMPANION SLOT ITEMS

Lvl	Name	Price (gp)
4	Friend's gift	840
5	Companion's defender	1,000
6	Sigil of companionship	1,800
8	Recalling harness	3,400
10	Guardian's collar	5,000
12	Transposition harness	13,000
14	Friend's gift	21,000
15	Companion's defender	25,000
16	Sigil of companionship	45,000
18	Recalling harness	85,000
22	Transposition harness	325,000
24	Friend's gift	525,000
25	Companion's defender	625,000
26	Sigil of companionship	1,125,000
28	Recalling harness	2,125,000

Wyrmguard Shield — Level 8+

This platinum-inlaid shield has the power to make serious blows much less deadly.

Lvl 8	3,400 gp	Lvl 18	85,000 gp

Item Slot: Arms

Shield: Any

Power (Daily): Immediate Interrupt. Use this power when a critical hit would be scored against you. The attack becomes a normal hit.

Level 18: Use this power when a critical hit would be scored against you or an adjacent ally.

COMPANION SLOT ITEMS

The beastmaster ranger build in the *Martial Power* supplement has a beast companion, and future classes and builds will also feature such companions.

Although the items in this section are tied to beast companions, all can be repurposed for other kinds of companions using the Transfer Enchantment ritual (see Appendix 1).

COMPANION AND MOUNT SLOT ITEMS

Characters sometimes have trained beasts that fight alongside them, serving either as companions, mounts, or both. As your character advances in level and acquires treasure, you may want to give some thought to equipping your companion or mount with some magic gear of its own.

A creature serving as your companion or mount has a single magic item slot that you can activate using your own actions (and not the creature's). A companion that doubles as a mount can use a mount item in place of a companion item, or vice versa.

Companion's Defender — Level 5+

This belt is constructed from woven bones and enhances a companion's defensive ability while adjacent to you.

Lvl 5	1,000 gp	Lvl 25	625,000 gp
Lvl 15	25,000 gp		

Item Slot: Companion

Property: While adjacent to you, your companion gains a +1 item bonus to all defenses.

Level 15: +2 item bonus.

Level 25: +3 item bonus.

Friend's Gift — Level 4+

Your companion wears this crimson badge on its chest as a sign of friendship.

Lvl 4	840 gp	Lvl 24	525,000 gp
Lvl 14	21,000 gp		

Item Slot: Companion

Property: Your companion regains an extra 5 hit points when it spends a healing surge or when you spend a healing surge to allow it to regain hit points.

Level 14: Extra 10 hit points.

Level 24: Extra 15 hit points.

Guardian's Collar — Level 10

The three small gemstones set in this collar resemble eyes and help your companion perceive its surroundings.

Item Slot: Companion   5,000 gp

Property: Your companion gains a +3 item bonus to Perception checks. If your companion is not surprised, you are not surprised.

DAVID GRIFFITH

Recalling Harness   Level 8+

Leather straps sewn with silver thread call your companion to
you when you are in need.

| Lvl 8 | 3,400 gp | Lvl 28 | 2,125,000 gp |
| Lvl 18 | 85,000 gp | | |

Item Slot: Companion

Power (Encounter): Immediate Interrupt. Use this power
   when an attack bloodies you or drops you to 0 hit points
   or fewer. Pull your companion 10 squares.
   Level 18: Your companion teleports 10 squares into an
   unoccupied square adjacent to you. This power gains the
   teleportation keyword.
   Level 28: Your companion teleports any number of
   squares into an unoccupied square adjacent to you. You
   need not have line of sight to your companion to use this
   power. This power gains the teleportation keyword.

Sigil of Companionship   Level 6+

This medal, which can be strapped to a leg or hung around a
neck, signifies the depth of experience you and your companion
have working together.

| Lvl 6 | 1,800 gp | Lvl 26 | 1,125,000 gp |
| Lvl 16 | 45,000 gp | | |

Item Slot: Companion

Property: When you flank an enemy with your companion,
   you and your companion gain a +1 item bonus to damage
   rolls against that enemy.
   Level 16: +3 item bonus.
   Level 26: +5 item bonus.

Transposition Harness   Level 12+

This silken harness fits tightly around your companion and
allows the creature to swap places with you.

| Lvl 12 | 13,000 gp | Lvl 22 | 325,000 gp |

Item Slot: Companion

Power (Daily ✦ Teleportation): Move Action. You and
   your companion swap places if you are within 10 squares
   of each other.
   Level 22: You and your companion swap places if you are
   within 20 squares of each other.

MOUNT SLOT ITEMS

Some mount slot items affect both mount and rider.
For mounts that can carry more than one creature,
the rider is the character in control of the mount.

The magic items described in this section are
designed for horses, but they can be modified to
suit almost any kind of mount. A PC who replaces
a mount might also take advantage of the Transfer
Enchantment ritual (see Appendix 1) to repurpose
an item. Magic items for mounts do not have esca-
lating enhancement bonuses like magic items for
characters do.

MOUNT SLOT ITEMS

Lvl	Name	Price (gp)
1	Impenetrable barding	360
2	Mirrored comparison	520
3	Horseshoes of speed	680
3	Saddle of strength	680
4	Ghost bridle	840
5	Bridle of rapid action	1,000
6	Martyr's saddle	1,800
8	Steadfast saddle	3,400
9	Zephyr horseshoes	4,200
11	Impenetrable barding	9,000
18	Skystrider horseshoes	85,000
15	Saddle of the nightmare	25,000
15	Saddle of the shark	25,000
21	Impenetrable barding	225,000

Bridle of Rapid Action   Level 5

This fine leather bridle lets you and your mount react more
quickly to danger.

Item Slot: Mount   1,000 gp

Power (Encounter): No Action. Use this power at the
   beginning of an encounter before you roll initiative. The
   mount you are riding rolls an initiative check using your
   initiative modifier. If its check is higher than your check,
   you can use the mount's result in place of your own.

Ghost Bridle   Level 4

This bridle gives a mount a phantasmal appearance and the
ability to slip through solid objects.

Item Slot: Mount   840 gp

Property: The mount gains resist 10 necrotic.

Power (Daily): Minor Action. You and your mount gain
   phasing until the end of your next turn.

Horseshoes of Speed   Level 3

These thin steel horseshoes grant a mount increased speed.

Item Slot: Mount   680 gp

Property: The mount's speed increases by 1 square for all
   movement modes.

Impenetrable Barding   Level 1+

Through this barding, your heroism imparts a protective aura
upon your mount that protects it.

| Lvl 1 | 360 gp | Lvl 21 | 225,000 gp |
| Lvl 11 | 9,000 gp | | |

Item Slot: Mount (apply to barding)

Property: While it is ridden, the mount gains resistance to
   all damage equal to its rider's level, maximum 10.
   Level 11: Maximum 20.
   Level 21: Maximum 30.

Martyr's Saddle — Level 6

Those who seek to protect their mounts at any cost favor this saddle.

Item Slot: Mount   1,800 gp
Property: The mount gains a +1 item bonus to all defenses.
Power (At-Will): Immediate Interrupt. Use this power when an attack would damage the mount you are riding. The mount takes half damage from the attack and you take the remainder. Nothing can reduce or prevent the damage that a rider takes in this way.

Mirrored Caparison — Level 2

This coat contains rows of faceted crystals that protect against wide-ranging attacks.

Item Slot: Mount   520 gp
Property: The mount gains a +1 item bonus to Fortitude, Reflex, and Will defenses.
Power (At-Will): Immediate Interrupt. Use this power when an area attack would target the mount you are riding. The mount is not targeted by the attack.

Saddle of Strength — Level 3

This dyed leather saddle is inset with brass and allows a mount to carry the heaviest loads.

Item Slot: Mount   680 gp
Property: The mount's carrying capacity increases by 50 percent in all categories. For example, a riding horse wearing this saddle would have a new normal load of 356 pounds, a new heavy load of 712 pounds, and a new maximum drag load of 1,781 pounds.

Saddle of the Nightmare — Level 15

This black, twisted leather bridle lets you take advantage of your mount's ability to teleport.

Item Slot: Mount   25,000 gp
Property: When a mount teleports, the rider on the mount can remain mounted and teleport along with the mount even if the mount's movement doesn't normally allow it.

Saddle of the Shark — Level 15

This saddle allows you and your mount to swim and breathe underwater.

Item Slot: Mount   25,000 gp
Property: Your mount gains the ability to breathe water as easily as it breathes air and gains a swim speed equal to its land speed. While mounted, you have the ability to breathe water as you would air, and you speak normally while underwater.

Skystrider Horseshoes — Level 18

A mount wearing these horseshoes can take to the air.

Item Slot: Mount   85,000 gp
Property: The mount gains a fly speed equal to its land speed.

Steadfast Saddle — Level 8

This saddle keeps you mounted when faced with effects that might normally knock you off your mount.

Item Slot: Mount   3,400 gp
Power (Encounter): Immediate Interrupt. Use this power when the mount you are riding would be pulled, pushed, or slid. The mount is not pulled, pushed, or slid.

Zephyr Horseshoes — Level 9

These black iron horseshoes allow a mount to race across all kinds of terrain.

Item Slot: Mount   4,200 gp
Property: The mount ignores the effect of difficult terrain and can cross liquid surfaces as if they were solid ground. Any adverse effect of that terrain, such as the damage from acid or magma, still affects the mount normally.

FEET SLOT ITEMS

With the right footwear, no cliff cannot be climbed and no river cannot be crossed. The sky really is the limit.

Magical footwear provides utility benefits related to movement, whether providing a new form of movement, an improvement to speed, or the power to skillfully evade an enemy's threatened area. Footwear is most frequently helpful in combat, but it might also offer a benefit outside of combat as well, allowing a character to easily scale a wall, pass through a guarded area unseen, or teleport across an entire continent.

FEET SLOT ITEMS

Lvl	Name	Price (gp)
2	Boots of adept charging	520
2	Feyleaf sandals	520
2	Jester shoes	520
3	Boots of stealth	680
4	Wildrunners	840
5	Surefoot boots	1,000
6	Boots of equilibrium	1,800
6	Boots of free movement	1,800
6	Goblin stompers	1,800
6	Sandals of precise stepping	1,800
7	Boots of the fencing master	2,600
7	Rushing cleats	2,600
8	Boots of quickness	3,400
8	Cat tabi	3,400
8	Quickling boots	3,400
8	Steadfast boots	3,400
9	Boots of eagerness	4,200
9	Boots of furious speed	4,200
9	Boots of many tricks	4,200
10	Boots of sand and sea	5,000
10	Branchrunners	5,000
10	Wallwalkers	5,000
11	Assassin's slippers	9,000
11	Boots of dancing	9,000
11	Tumbler's shoes	9,000
12	Assault boots	13,000
12	Butterfly sandals	13,000
12	Dragonborn greaves	13,000
12	Dwarven boots	13,000
12	Feystep lacings	13,000
12	Thornwalker slippers	13,000
13	Boots of stealth	17,000
13	Boots of swimming	17,000
14	Earthstriders	21,000
14	Fireburst boots	21,000
14	Oceanstrider boots	21,000
15	Flanker's boots	25,000
15	Floorfighter straps	25,000
16	Boots of withdrawal	45,000
16	Sandals of precise stepping	45,000
17	Earthreaver stompers	65,000
18	Boots of quickness	85,000
18	Cat tabi	85,000
18	Defiant boots	85,000
18	Dimensional stride boots	85,000
18	Dwarfstride boots	85,000
18	Phantom chaussures	85,000
18	Sandals of arcane transposition	85,000
18	Shadowsteppers	85,000
19	Anklets of opportunity	105,000
21	Lightstep slippers	225,000
21	Skygliders	225,000
22	Boots of speed	325,000
23	Boots of stealth	425,000
24	Backtrack bindings	525,000

FEET SLOT ITEMS (CONTINUED)

Lvl	Name	Price (gp)
24	Zephyr boots	525,000
25	Airstriders	625,000
25	Sandals of Avandra	625,000
26	Sandals of precise stepping	1,125,000
27	Earthreaver stompers	1,625,000
28	Boots of quickness	2,125,000
28	Boots of teleportation	2,125,000
28	Cat tabi	2,125,000

Airstriders — Level 25

These light coverings lift your feet and your spirit.

Item Slot: Feet   625,000 gp

Property: You take no damage from a fall and always land on your feet. You have a fly speed equal to your speed +2, but you must end each turn on a solid surface or you fall.

Power (Encounter): Free Action. Use this power when you would fall. You do no fall until the end of your next turn.

Anklets of Opportunity — Level 19

When your foe is distracted by an ally, these glittering anklets quicken your step.

Item Slot: Feet   105,000 gp

Property: Gain a +1 bonus to Reflex defense.

Power (Encounter): Minor Action. Use this power while you are flanking a target. Shift 1 square.

Assassin's Slippers — Level 11

You are able to press your advantage from several angles while wearing these black chamois slippers.

Item Slot: Feet   9,000 gp

Power (Encounter): Minor Action. Until the start of your next turn, you flank a target adjacent to you if any square adjacent to you is opposite an ally.

Assault Boots — Level 12

These mail boots trip up a foe when you strike a grievous blow.

Item Slot: Feet   13,000 gp

Property: When you score a critical hit with a melee weapon, your target is knocked prone.

Backtrack Bindings — Level 24

This airy footwear carries you out of whatever trouble you've gotten yourself into.

Item Slot: Feet   525,000 gp

Property: Gain a +2 bonus to Reflex defense.

Power (Encounter ✦ Teleportation): Free Action. Use this power during your turn and note the square you are currently in. At the end of your turn, teleport back to that square if it is within 10 squares of you.

Boots of Adept Charging   Level 2

Rushing in is less dangerous in these studded leather boots.

Item Slot: Feet   520 gp
Property: After charging, you can shift 1 square before your turn ends.

Boots of Dancing   Level 11

These ornate boots send you spinning and leaping out of danger.

Item Slot: Feet   9,000 gp
Property: Gain a +1 bonus to Reflex defense.
Property: You do not grant combat advantage while you are dazed.
Power (Daily): Minor Action. Gain a +5 power bonus to Acrobatics and Athletics checks until the end of your next turn.

Boots of Eagerness   Level 9

Your feet feel peppy in these handsome brocade boots.

Item Slot: Feet   4,200 gp
Power (Encounter): Free Action. Use this power during your turn to take an additional move action.

Boots of Equilibrium   Level 6

The tough mesh sole of these supple buckskin boots grips even the most slippery surfaces.

Item Slot: Feet   1,800 gp
Property: You move normally on slippery surfaces, such as grease or ice.

Boots of Free Movement   Level 6

You deftly avoid entanglement in these well-crafted boots.

Item Slot: Feet   1,800 gp
Property: Gain a +2 item bonus to saving throws against effects that apply the slowed, immobilized, or restrained condition.
Power (Encounter): Minor Action. Make a saving throw against a slow, immobilize, or restrain effect that a save can end.

Boots of Furious Speed   Level 9

When you are injured, these boots turn crimson and vibrate slightly.

Item Slot: Feet   4,200 gp
Property: Gain a +2 item bonus to speed while bloodied.
Power (Daily): Immediate Reaction. Use this power when you become bloodied. Shift a number of squares equal to half your speed.

Boots of Many Tracks   Level 9

These rugged boots conceal your steps.

Item Slot: Feet   4,200 gp
Property: The DC of any Perception check to find your tracks is increased by 10. Even if your tracks are found, identifying them takes a Nature check against the same DC. If the Nature check fails, the tracks seem to be of some animal (chosen by you at the time you made the tracks).

Boots of Quickness   Level 8+

This supple leather footwear keeps you out of harm's way.

Lvl 8   3,400 gp   Lvl 28   2,125,000 gp
Lvl 18   85,000 gp
Item Slot: Feet
Property: Gain a +1 bonus to Reflex defense.
  Level 18: +2 bonus to Reflex defense.
  Level 28: +3 bonus to Reflex defense.

Boots of Sand and Sea   Level 10

These wax-coated coverings help you glide over the earth when you are lightly encumbered, and might save you when the current runs deep.

Item Slot: Feet   5,000 gp
Property: Gain a +1 item bonus to speed while wearing light armor or no armor.
Power (Encounter): Free Action. Gain a +5 power bonus to an Athletics check to swim.

Boots of Speed   Level 22

These durable boots are designed to take you farther, faster.

Item Slot: Feet   325,000 gp
Property: Gain a +2 item bonus to speed.
Power (Daily): Minor Action. Take a move action.

Boots of Stealth   Level 3+

The soft leather soles and down lining of these supple boots quiet your footsteps.

Lvl 3   680 gp   Lvl 23   425,000 gp
Lvl 13   17,000 gp
Item Slot: Feet
Property: Gain a +2 item bonus to Stealth checks.
  Level 13: +4 item bonus.
  Level 23: +6 item bonus.

Boots of Swimming

Level 13

A fin runs down the back of these fishscale boots.

Item Slot: Feet   17,000 gp

Property: Gain a swim speed equal to your speed. You take no penalties to attack rolls while swimming or underwater.

Power (Daily): Minor Action. Breathe normally underwater until the end of the encounter.

Boots of Teleportation

Level 28

Wearing these elegant boots, you never need to raise your feet to move.

Item Slot: Feet   2,125,000 gp

Power (At-Will ✦ Teleportation): Move Action. Teleport a number of squares equal to your speed.

Boots of the Fencing Master

Level 7

Your swift step befuddles your foes.

Item Slot: Feet   2,600 gp

Property: When you shift, gain a +1 item bonus to AC and Reflex defense until the end of your next turn.

Power (Encounter): Minor Action. Shift 2 squares.

Boots of Withdrawal

Level 16

This footwear allows you to live to fight another day.

Item Slot: Feet   45,000 gp

Property: If you are bloodied and make no attacks on your turn, gain a +4 item bonus to speed, AC, and Reflex defense until the end of your next turn.

Branchrunners

Level 10

You move unhindered through the undergrowth in these supple foot wraps of treated oak leaves.

Item Slot: Feet   5,000 gp

Property: Ignore difficult terrain in forests and jungles. Also, gain a +4 item bonus to Acrobatics checks to balance or reduce damage from a fall, and to Athletics checks to climb and jump while in trees.

Power (Encounter): Move Action. Balance and climb at your speed until the end of your turn. You don't grant combat advantage while doing so.

Butterfly Sandals

Level 12

These comfortable leather sandals make you more adept while airborne.

Item Slot: Feet   13,000 gp

Property: Increase the flight speed of your flight powers and racial traits by 2.

Cat Tabi

Level 8+

This silky black footgear gives you catlike reflexes when jumping or falling.

| Lvl 8 | 3,400 gp | Lvl 28 | 2,125,000 gp |
| Lvl 18 | 85,000 gp | | |

Item Slot: Feet

Property: Gain a +3 item bonus to Athletics checks to jump. You take half damage from a fall and always land on your feet.

Level 18: +5 item bonus.

Level 28: +7 item bonus.

Power (Daily): Free Action. Use this power when you fall 10 feet or more. You take no damage from the fall and are not knocked prone.

Dwarfstride Boots — Level 18

In these boots, nothing gets in your way.

Item Slot: Feet   85,000 gp

Property: Gain a +4 item bonus to all skill checks required by special terrain (normally Athletics or Acrobatics).

Property: When an effect forces you to move—through a pull, a push, or a slide—you can move 1 square less than the effect specifies. This property stacks with the Stand Your Ground dwarf racial trait.

Dwarven Boots — Level 12

These iron boots keep you steady in the face of forceful assaults.

Item Slot: Feet   13,000 gp

Power (Daily): Immediate Interrupt. Use this power when an attack would knock you prone or pull, push, slide, or immobilize you. The attacker rerolls the attack, using the second result even if it's lower.

Earthreaver Stompers — Level 17+

These heavy, steel-soled boots allow you to sense vibrations as well as give you a powerful stomp.

| Lvl 17 | 65,000 gp | Lvl 27 | 1,625,000 gp |

Item Slot: Feet

Property: You gain tremorsense 1 square.
Level 27: Tremorsense 3 squares.

Power (Daily): Standard Action. You stomp your foot and make an attack: Close burst 2; Strength + 4 vs. Reflex; on a hit, the target is knocked prone.
Level 27: Strength + 6 vs. Reflex.

Defiant Boots — Level 18

These sturdy iron boots grip the ground when you are moved against your will.

Item Slot: Feet   85,000 gp

Property: When you are pulled, pushed, or slid, reduce the distance you are moved by 2.

Power (Daily): Free Action. Use this power when you are subject to a pull, push, or slide effect. Instead, shift a number of squares equal to the number of squares you would have been pulled, pushed, or slid.

Dimensional Stride Boots — Level 18

You step through a thin rift in space and reappear instantly in another location nearby.

Item Slot: Feet   85,000 gp

Property: Gain a +1 bonus to Reflex defense.

Power (Encounter ✦ Teleportation): Move Action. Teleport 2 squares. If you are at maximum hit points, you instead teleport a number of squares equal to your speed.

Dragonborn Greaves — Level 12

Made of thick hide covered in scales, these ornate boots tap into your pain and rage.

Item Slot: Feet   13,000 gp

Property: While you are bloodied, gain a +2 item bonus to speed and a +1 item bonus to AC and Reflex defense.

Earthstriders — Level 14

You instantly move through the earth using these blunt-toed shoes.

Item Slot: Feet   21,000 gp

Power (Daily ✦ Teleportation): Move Action. Teleport 5 squares as long as a path along the ground exists to your destination. This power does not allow you to cross open air (including pits or chasms).

Feyleaf Sandals — Level 2

This delicate footgear incorporates Feywild leaves into its design.

Item Slot: Feet   520 gp

Power (Daily ✦ Teleportation): When you fall, instead teleport safely to the nearest horizontal surface within 5 squares that can support your weight, take no falling damage, and land on your feet.

Feystep Lacings — Level 12

Cords spun from enchanted fey wool teleport you out of—or into—harm's way.

Item Slot: Feet   13,000 gp

Property: Gain a +1 bonus to Reflex defense.

Power (At-Will, 5 Charges/Day ✦ Teleportation): Move Action. Spend a number of charges to teleport that number of squares.

Fireburst Boots — Level 14

Fire fuels these scorched iron boots.

Item Slot: Feet   21,000 gp

Power (Daily ✦ Arcane, Fire, Teleportation): Move Action. Teleport 6 squares. All creatures within 1 square of you before you teleport take 2d8 fire damage.

Flanker's Boots — Level 15

With a mere thought, you use these rabbitskin boots to move into an advantageous position.

Item Slot: Feet   25,000 gp

Property: Gain +2 item bonus to Athletics checks.

Power (Daily ✦ Teleportation): Move Action. Teleport to any square adjacent to an adjacent creature.

Floorfighter Straps — Level 15

Scuffed and worn, these rawhide bands keep you dangerous even when on the ground.

Item Slot: Feet   25,000 gp

Property: While you are prone, you do not grant combat advantage and you can shift. When you stand up, you can shift 1 square as part of the same action.

Goblin Stompers — Level 6

These cured hide boots shift you safely away from an inaccurate attacker.

Item Slot: Feet   1,800 gp

Power (Encounter): Immediate Reaction. Use this power when a melee attack misses you. Shift 1 square.

Jester Shoes — Level 2

These colorful, pointed shoes help you stand out—but not stand up—in a crowd.

Item Slot: Feet   520 gp

Power (Encounter): Immediate Interrupt. Use this power when you are pushed, pulled, or slid. Reduce the distance you are pulled, pushed, or slided by 1 square and fall prone.

Lightstep Slippers — Level 21

These doeskin coverings cushion your step.

Item Slot: Feet   225,000 gp

Property: Gain a +5 item bonus to Stealth checks. Also, you do not activate traps or hazards triggered by stepping into a particular square, nor can you be detected by tremorsense.

Oceanstrider Boots — Level 14

Water is no obstacle for you in these thigh-high oilskin boots.

Item Slot: Feet   21,000 gp

Property: Gain a +1 item bonus to speed. You can move across and stand on horizontal liquid surfaces as though they were solid ground. You still take damage from hazardous liquid surfaces upon which you stand (such as acid and magma).

Phantom Chaussures — Level 18

With your lower legs bound in gossamer silk, you become ephemeral, and sometimes invisible.

Item Slot: Feet   85,000 gp

Property: if you move at least 3 squares on your turn, gain concealment until the end of your next turn.

Power (Daily ✦ Illusion): Free Action. Use this power when you have moved at least 6 squares on your turn. You become invisible until the end of your next turn.

Quickling Boots — Level 8

Your feet step more lively in this silver-stitched footgear.

Item Slot: Feet   3,400 gp

Property: Gain a +2 item bonus to Acrobatics and Athletics checks.

Power (Encounter): Move Action. Move up to your speed + 1. Gain a +2 item bonus to AC against opportunity attacks during this movement.

Skygliders

Rushing Cleats
Level 7

These rawhide boot straps are fitted with spikes.

Item Slot: Feet   2,600 gp

Property: Gain a +2 item bonus to bull rush attacks, and increase the push or slide effect of any close or melee attack you perform by 1 square.

Sandals of Arcane Transposition
Level 18

Using an arcane power can teleport you in these rune-etched, open-toed shoes.

Item Slot: Feet   85,000 gp

Power (Daily ✦ Teleportation): Free Action. Use this power after you make an arcane area or close attack. Teleport to any unoccupied square within the area of effect.

Sandals of Avandra
Level 25

These airy, corded foot coverings allow you to move past even the largest and most dangerous enemies.

Item Slot: Feet   625,000 gp

Property: Gain a +2 item bonus to speed.

Power (At-Will): Move Action. Shift a number of squares equal to half your speed.

Power (Encounter): Minor Action. Until the end of your next turn, your movement does not provoke opportunity attacks.

Sandals of Precise Stepping
Level 6+

Your steps become softer and more precise in this soft leather and cloth mesh footgear.

| Lvl 6 | 1,800 gp | Lvl 26 | 1,125,000 gp |
| Lvl 16 | 45,000 gp | | |

Item Slot: Feet

Property: Gain a +2 item bonus to Acrobatics, Athletics, and Stealth checks.
　Level 16: +3 item bonus.
　Level 26: +4 item bonus.

Shadowsteppers
Level 18

You disappear into the shadows in these matte black fur slippers.

Item Slot: Feet   85,000 gp

Power (Daily): Move Action. Teleport 5 squares and gain insubstantial until the end of your next turn. If you use this power in an area of bright light, you take 5 damage (which ignores insubstantial).

Skygliders
Level 21

This footwear allows you to walk across chasms, climb to ledges, and descend from precipices.

Item Slot: Feet   225,000 gp

Property: If you begin your turn standing on a horizontal surface, you can move through the air as if it were normal terrain. Moving upward requires 2 squares of movement for each square traveled; moving downward costs 1 square of movement for every 2 squares traveled. If you are not on a horizontal surface sufficient to bear your weight at the end of your turn, you fall to the nearest such surface, taking damage accordingly.

Power (Daily): Minor Action. Move through the air as if it were normal terrain until the end of the encounter. Glide down safely to the nearest horizontal surface that can bear your weight at that time.

Steadfast Boots
Level 8

Rough iron studs nailed to these boots buttress your defenses.

Item Slot: Feet   3,400 gp

Power (Encounter): Minor Action. As long as you stay in the same space that you began the current turn, gain a +2 power bonus to AC and all defenses until the beginning of your next turn. If you move or are moved from your starting square at any time through any means, you lose these bonuses.

Surefoot Boots
Level 5

Attached snugly by rows of shiny buckles, these boots help keep your footing.

Item Slot: Feet   1,000 gp

Property: Gain a +2 item bonus to Acrobatics checks.

Power (Daily): Free Action. Use this power when you are knocked prone. You stand up.

Thornwalker Slippers
Level 12

These padded foot coverings allow you to pass cleanly through cluttered or grasping terrain.

Item Slot: Feet   13,000 gp

Power (Encounter): Until the end of your next turn, you can move through difficult terrain. You also move normally and safely through natural environmental hazards that affect movement, such as quicksand, dense foliage, or deep snow.

ED COX

Tumbler's Shoes
Level 11

Though worn, these well-built shoes allow you to move with a cat's grace through even precarious terrain.

Item Slot: Feet   9,000 gp

Property: You can take 10 on Acrobatics and Athletics checks, even if threats or distractions would normally prevent you from doing so.

Wallwalkers
Level 10

These supple spidersilk boots give you the mobility of an arachnid, if only for a brief time.

Item Slot: Feet   5,000 gp

Property: If you begin your turn standing on a horizontal surface, you can walk on walls as if they were horizontal surfaces. If you are not on a horizontal surface sufficient to bear your weight at the end of your move, you fall to the ground, taking damage accordingly.

Power (Daily): Minor Action. Walk on walls as if they were horizontal surfaces until the end of the encounter.

Wildrunners
Level 4

Crafted from the skins of wild plains animals, these boots lend you extraordinary speed.

Item Slot: Feet   840 gp

Property: When you run, move your speed + 4 instead of speed + 2.

Power (Daily): Free Action. Use this power when you run. Enemies do not gain combat advantage against you.

Zephyr Boots
Level 24

You catch the wind and fly like bird with these light boots.

Item Slot: Feet   525,000 gp

Property: Gain a fly speed equal to your speed while wearing light armor or no armor.

HANDS SLOT ITEMS

Hands are our most capable tools. Without them, we are no better than the beasts.

Wielders of weapons and spells alike find use for gloves and gauntlets. Handwear provides powerful attack and damage bonuses, and many items also augment Strength- and Dexterity-based skills. A few hand items also augment the range of attacks, adding to the distance a wearer can fire his or her attack, or improving accuracy.

HANDS SLOT ITEMS

Lvl	Name	Price (gp)
2	Wrestler's gloves	520
4	Climbing claws	840
4	Flaying gloves	2,600
4	Hedge wizard's gloves	840
5	Cat paws	1,000
5	Gloves of agility	1,000
5	Parry gauntlets	1,000
6	Breaching gauntlets	1,800
6	Burning gauntlets	1,800
6	Caustic gauntlets	1,800
6	Knifethrower's gauntlets	1,800
6	Luckbender gloves	1,800
7	Frost gauntlets	2,600
7	Lancing gloves	2,600
8	Gloves of eldritch admixture	3,400
8	Gloves of the bounty hunter	3,400
8	Holy gauntlets	3,400
9	Gloves of storing	4,200
9	Green thumbs	4,200
9	Spell anchors	4,200
9	Sure shot gloves	4,200
10	Antipathy gloves	5,000
10	Dwarven throwers	5,000
10	Gauntlets of brilliance	5,000
10	Storm gauntlets	5,000
10	Strikebacks	5,000
11	Gauntlets of blinding strikes	9,000
11	Longshot gloves	9,000
12	Gloves of the healer	13,000
13	Giant gloves	17,000
13	Gloves of missile deflection	17,000
14	Flaying gloves	21,000
14	Gloves of dimensional repulsion	21,000
14	Gloves of transference	21,000
15	Antipathy gloves	25,000
15	Cat paws	25,000
16	Breaching gauntlets	45,000
16	Burning gauntlets	45,000
16	Caustic gauntlets	45,000
16	Gloves of accuracy	45,000

Lvl	Name	Price (gp)
16	Luckbender gloves	45,000
16	Vampiric gauntlets	45,000
16	Venom gloves	45,000
17	Frost gauntlets	65,000
18	Gloves of eldritch admixture	85,000
18	Greatreach gauntlets	85,000
18	Holy gauntlets	85,000
19	Lightning reflex gloves	105,000
20	Antipathy gloves	125,000
20	Storm gauntlets	125,000
21	Gloves of camaraderie	225,000
21	Longshot gloves	225,000
22	Gloves of the healer	325,000
24	Flaying gloves	225,000
25	Cat paws	625,000
26	Breaching gauntlets	1,125,000
26	Burning gauntlets	1,125,000
26	Caustic gauntlets	1,125,000
26	Venom gloves	1,125,000
27	Frost gauntlets	1,625,000
28	Gloves of eldritch admixture	2,125,000
28	Holy gauntlets	2,125,000
30	Antipathy gloves	3,125,000
30	Storm gauntlets	3,125,000

Antipathy Gloves — Level 10

Use these gloves to keep your enemies at bay.

Item Slot: Hands   5,000 gp

Property: An enemy must spend 1 extra square of movement to enter a square adjacent to you. An enemy that is pulled, pushed, or slid moves through those squares as normal.

Power (Daily): Standard Action. Make an attack: Ranged 10; +13 vs. Reflex; on a hit, the target is restrained (save ends).

Breaching Gauntlets — Level 6+

These thick leather gauntlets allow your attacks to bypass even the best resistances.

Lvl 6	1,800 gp	Lvl 26	1,125,000 gp
Lvl 16	45,000 gp		

Item Slot: Hands

Property: Reduce the value of any resistance an enemy has against your attacks by 1.

Level 16: Reduce resistance by 2.

Level 26: Reduce resistance by 5.

Power (Daily): Free Action. Use this power when you hit with a weapon attack, but before you deal damage. Reduce the value of any resistance the target has against your attack by 5 (save ends).

Level 16: Reduce resistance by 10.

Level 26: Reduce resistance by 15.

Burning Gauntlets — Level 6+

Made of iron and constantly trailing wisps of smoke, these plated gloves incite your inner pyromaniac.

Lvl 6	1,800 gp	Lvl 26	1,125,000 gp
Lvl 16	45,000 gp		

Item Slot: Hands

Power (Daily ✦ Fire): Free Action. Use this power when you make an attack with the fire keyword. The first target hit by that attack, if any, also takes ongoing 5 fire damage (save ends). Also, you deal an extra 1 fire damage on successful attacks with the fire keyword until the end of the encounter.

If you've reached at least one milestone today before using this power, instead deal an extra 2 fire damage on successful attacks with the fire keyword until the end of the encounter.

Level 16: Ongoing 10 fire damage, extra 3 fire damage (4 after milestone).

Level 26: Ongoing 15 fire damage, extra 5 fire damage (6 after milestone).

Cat Paws — Level 5+

Furry on the outside, silky on the inside, these gloves sprout claws that make climbing easier.

Lvl 5	1,000 gp	Lvl 25	625,000 gp
Lvl 15	25,000 gp		

Item Slot: Hands

Property: Gain a +2 item bonus to Athletics checks to climb.

Level 15: +4 item bonus.

Level 25: +6 item bonus.

Power (Daily): Free Action. Climb at normal speed and double any climbing movement granted to you by powers until the end of the encounter.

Caustic Gauntlets — Level 6+

These rough leather coverings drip with acid as you attack.

| Lvl 6 | 1,800 gp | Lvl 26 | 1,125,000 gp |
| Lvl 16 | 45,000 gp | | |

Item Slot: Hands

Power (Daily ✦ Acid): Free Action. Use this power when you make a ranged attack. Change the damage type dealt by that attack to acid. Hit or miss, creatures adjacent to the target of the attack take 1d6 acid damage. Also, you deal an extra 1 acid damage on successful ranged attacks until the end of the encounter.

If you've reached at least one milestone today, instead deal an extra 2 acid damage on successful ranged attacks with the acid keyword until the end of the encounter.

Level 16: 2d6 acid damage, extra 3 acid damage (4 after milestone).

Level 26: 3d6 acid damage, extra 5 acid damage (6 after milestone).

Climbing Claws — Level 4

Sharp claws magically unfold from the palms of these padded leather gloves.

Item Slot: Hands   840 gp

Property: Gain a +1 item bonus to Athletics checks to climb. Each of these gloves can also be used as a one-handed, off-hand, simple, light blade that applies a +2 proficiency bonus to attack rolls and deals 1d4 damage. The wearer gains proficiency with this weapon.

Dwarven Throwers — Level 10

These stout iron gauntlets turn any weapon into a ranged weapon.

Item Slot: Hands 5,000 gp

Property: Gain a +2 item bonus to thrown weapon damage rolls.

Power (Encounter): Standard Action. Make a ranged basic attack with your melee weapon, using your Strength modifier on the attack roll and damage roll, as if the weapon had the heavy thrown weapon property. Your weapon automatically returns to your grip after the ranged attack.

Flaying Gloves — Level 4+

These tight-fitting gloves allow you to deal bleeding wounds with a light blade.

| Lvl 4 | 840 gp | Lvl 24 | 525,000 gp |
| Lvl 14 | 21,000 gp | | |

Item Slot: Hands

Power (Daily): Free Action. Use this power when you hit with a light blade melee attack and have combat advantage against the target. That attack deals an extra ongoing 5 damage (save ends). If the attack already deals ongoing damage of any type, this item's power has no effect.

Level 14: Ongoing 10 damage (save ends).

Level 24: Ongoing 15 damage (save ends).

Frost Gauntlets — Level 7+

When you pick up your weapon, the ice crystal patterns etched into these gauntlets flare, coating the weapon in a thin sheet of frost.

| Lvl 7 | 2,600 gp | Lvl 27 | 1,625,000 gp |
| Lvl 17 | 65,000 gp | | |

Item Slot: Hands

Power (Daily ✦ Cold): Free Action. Use this power when you make a melee attack. Change the damage type dealt by that attack to cold. On a hit, the target is also slowed until the end of your next turn. Also, you deal an extra 1 cold damage on successful melee attacks until the end of the encounter.

If you've reached at least one milestone today, instead gain an extra 2 cold damage on successful melee attacks until the end of the encounter.

Level 17: Target is slowed (save ends), extra 3 cold damage (4 after milestone).

Level 27: Target is immobilized (save ends), extra 5 cold damage (6 after milestone).

Gauntlets of Blinding Strikes — Level 11

These sleek gauntlets speed your strikes for a limited time.

Item Slot: Hands 9,000 gp

Power (Daily): Standard Action. Make two melee basic attacks, each with a −2 penalty to the attack roll.

Gauntlets of Brilliance — Level 10

With a thought, you cause these gold-burnished gauntlets to illuminate.

Item Slot: Hands 5,000 gp

Power (At-Will): Minor Action. As the wizard's *light* power (PH 158), but cast on the gauntlets.

Power (Daily): Free Action. Use this power after you hit with a weapon attack. The attack deals an extra 10 radiant damage.

Giant Gloves — Level 13

Though they make your hands appear larger, these thick leather wraps fit comfortably and give you an impressive grip.

Item Slot: Hands 17,000 gp

Property: Gain a +3 item bonus to grab attack rolls.

Power (Encounter): Standard Action. While you have a creature of your size category or smaller grabbed, you can end the grab by throwing the creature, causing it to slide 6 squares. You can throw the creature at a target provided the thrown creature ends its forced movement in a space adjacent to the target. In this case, make an attack against the target: Dexterity + 4 vs. Reflex; on a hit, the thrown creature and the target each take 2d8 + Strength modifier damage and are knocked prone.

Gloves of Accuracy — Level 16

While wearing these fingerless deerskin gloves, your shots bypass obstacles.

Item Slot: Hands 45,000 gp

Power (At-Will): Minor Action. Your ranged attacks ignore concealment and cover (but not total concealment or superior cover) until the end of your turn.

Gloves of Agility — Level 5

As you strap on these tight-fitting, fingerless gloves, your digits tingle with magic.

Item Slot: Hands 1,000 gp

Property: Gain a +1 item bonus to Acrobatics, Stealth, and Dexterity checks (but not Dexterity attacks).

Gloves of Camaraderie — Level 21

These cashmere gloves draw an ailing ally's condition onto you.

Item Slot: Hands 225,000 gp

Power (Encounter): Immediate Reaction. Use this power when an ally within 10 squares of you gains a condition or harmful effect. You gain that condition or effect, and the ally loses it. The condition or effect lasts for the duration specified in the description of the power that caused it.

Gloves of Dimensional Repulsion — Level 14

Strange, eldritch glyphs swirl on these fine brocade coverings.

Item Slot: Hands 21,000 gp

Property: When you use a teleport power on a target other than yourself, you can increase the distance the target is teleported by 2 squares.

Power (Daily ✦ Teleportation): Standard Action. Make an attack against an adjacent target: Charisma + 4 vs. Fortitude; on a hit, the target is teleported 10 squares to an unoccupied space of your choosing.

Gloves of Eldritch Admixture — Level 8+

You funnel the energy granted by your pact through these gloves, amplifying your power.

| Lvl 8 | 3,400 gp | Lvl 28 | 2,125,000 gp |
| Lvl 18 | 85,000 gp | | |

Item Slot: Hands

Prerequisite: Warlock

Property: When you deal extra damage as a result of your Warlock's Curse, you can choose that damage to be acid, cold, or fire (or leave it untyped).

Power (At-Will, 5 Charges/Day ✦ Acid, Cold, or Fire): Free Action. The next attack you make this turn deals extra damage depending on how many charges you spend: 1 charge, 1d6 damage; 2 charges, 2d6 damage; 5 charges, 3d6 damage. This extra damage can be acid, cold, or fire damage.
Level 18: 1 charge, 1d8 damage; 2 charges, 2d8 damage; 3 charges, 3d8 damage.
Level 28: 1 charge, 1d10 damage; 2 charges, 2d10 damage; 5 charges, 3d10 damage.

Gloves of Missile Deflection — Level 13

Made of muslin covered with small shield-shaped buttons, these gloves help turn away projectiles.

Item Slot: Hands 17,000 gp

Property: Gain a +1 item bonus to AC against ranged weapon attacks.

Power (Daily): Immediate Interrupt. Use this power when you are hit by a ranged weapon attack. Gain resist 15 against that attack

Gloves of Storing — Level 9

Though these ornate chamois gloves fit snuggly, your fingertips always seem just short of touching something within them.

Item Slot: Hands 4,200 gp

Property: As a minor action, you can store one unattended item in one of the gloves. Each glove can hold one item, and each item must weigh no more than 10 pounds. As a minor action, you can cause an item stored within one glove to materialize in your hand. Weapons so produced are ready to wield, but items that require an additional action to equip (such as shields) must still be readied. Items have no weight while within the gloves.

Gloves of the Bounty Hunter — Level 8

These hide garments are weighted along the knuckles.

Item Slot: Hands 3,400 gp

Property: When your attack causes a target to be reduced to 0 hit points or below, and you choose to knock out rather than kill it, the target is restored to 1 hit point after an extended rest (normally this occurs after a short rest).

Gloves of storing

Greatreach Gauntlets — Level 18

These gauntlets are fitted with extendable steel rods that are braced to your forearms.

Item Slot: Hands 85,000 gp

Power (At-Will): Minor Action. Until the end of your next turn, increase the reach of your melee attacks by 1 square but take a -2 penalty to attack rolls.

Green Thumbs — Level 9

These bright green, wooden thimbles fit snugly over naked skin or mundane hand coverings.

Item Slot: Hands 4,200 gp

Power (Daily ✦ Conjuration): Standard Action. You create a wall 8 within 10 squares filled with thorny vines. It can be up to 4 squares high. A creature that attempts to move through the wall must succeed on a DC 20 Strength check or become restrained within the wall (escape DC 20 ends). The wall lasts until the end of your next turn. Sustain minor.

Hedge Wizard's Gloves — Level 4

With a wave of these patched gloves, you can perform magic tricks.

Item Slot: Hands 840 gp

Power (At-Will ✦ Arcane, Conjuration): Standard Action. As the wizard's *mage hand* power (PH 158).

Power (At-Will ✦ Arcane): Standard Action. As the wizard's *prestidigitation* power (PH 159).

Holy Gauntlets — Level 8+

Highly polished and marked with holy sigils, these gauntlets help to bring cleansing light to the darkness.

Lvl 8	3,400 gp	Lvl 28	2,125,000 gp
Lvl 18	85,000 gp		

Item Slot: Hands

Power (Daily ✦ Radiant): Free Action. Use this power to change the damage type dealt by your next divine power to radiant. On a hit, deal an extra 1d6 radiant damage. If the power doesn't normally deal damage, no extra damage is dealt. Also, you deal an extra 1 radiant damage on successful attacks with the radiant keyword until the end of the encounter.

If you've reached at least one milestone today, instead deal an extra 2 radiant damage on successful attacks with the radiant keyword until the end of the encounter.

Level 18: 2d6 radiant damage, extra 3 radiant damage (4 after milestone).

Level 28: 3d6 radiant damage, extra 5 radiant damage (6 after milestone).

Gloves of the Healer — Level 12+

Your healing is enhanced by this elegant handwear.

Lvl 12	13,000 gp	Lvl 22	325,000 gp

Item Slot: Hands

Property: When you use a power that has the healing keyword, one target regains an extra 1d6 hit points.
Level 22: 2d6 hit points.

Power (Daily ✦ Healing): Standard Action. Spend a healing surge. An adjacent ally regains hit points equal to the value of the healing surge you lost.

Gloves of Transference — Level 14

You can bestow powers upon others with these gossamer gloves.

Item Slot: Hands 21,000 gp

Property: The ranges of your ranged utility powers are increased by 2.

Power (Daily): Free Action. Use this power on your turn when you use a power that has a personal range. The power affects an ally adjacent to you instead of you, as if that ally had used the power. This power does not function on powers that have the stance keyword, and if the power can be sustained, the ally must spend the action to sustain it.

Knifethrower's Gloves — Level 6

Knives become even more deadly when you hands are wrapped in these fingerless, suede sheaths.

Item Slot: Hands 1,800 gp

Property: You can draw and attack with a dagger as part of the same standard action.

Power (Daily): Free Action. Use this power when you hit with a thrown weapon attack. Add a +5 power bonus to the damage roll.

Lancing Gloves — Level 7

These supple brown leather riding gloves grip well and true.

Item Slot: Hands 2,600 gp

Property: Gain an extra 2 damage on melee attacks while mounted.

Lightning Reflex Gloves — Level 19

These tight, black gloves grip your arms, making you twitch with nervous energy.

Item Slot: Hands 105,000 gp

Property: Gain a +2 item bonus to opportunity attacks.

Power (Daily): Free Action. Use this power when an enemy provokes an opportunity attack. Take an opportunity attack, even if you've already used an opportunity attack this turn.

Longshot Gloves — Level 11+

Long range shots are eased by these fingerless gloves.

Lvl 11	9,000 gp	Lvl 21	225,000 gp

Item Slot: Hands

Power (Encounter): Minor Action. Your ranged attacks ignore the –2 penalty for long range until the end of your turn.

Level 21: This power becomes an at-will power.

Luckbender Gloves — Level 6+

Avandra favors the wearer of these gloves, each of which has a golden shamrock stitched on the back.

Lvl 6	1,800 gp	Lvl 16	45,000 gp

Item Slot: Hands

Power (Encounter): Free Action. Use this power after you make a damage roll for a melee weapon attack. Reroll one damage die, using the second result even if it's lower.

Level 16: Reroll any two damage dice.

Parry Gauntlets — Level 5

With these thickly armored gauntlets, you are more secure when you take a breather.

Item Slot: Hands 1,000 gp

Property: When you take the total defense or second wind actions, gain a +2 item bonus to all defenses until the beginning of your next turn.

Lightning reflex gloves

Spell Anchors — Level 9

When you transfer control of a spell to these fine broadcloth gloves, the arcane rune on the back of each glove glows cheerily.

Item Slot: Hands 4,200 gp

Power (Daily): Free Action. Sustain one of your powers that normally requires a minor action to sustain.

Storm Gauntlets — Level 10+

The gold and iron plates bolted to the back of these gauntlets crackle with energy.

Lvl 10	5,000 gp	Lvl 30	3,125,000 gp
Lvl 20	125,000 gp		

Item Slot: Hands

Power (Daily ✦ Thunder): Free Action. Use this power when you make a melee attack. Change the damage type dealt by that attack to thunder. On a hit, deal an extra 1d6 thunder damage. Also, deal an extra 1 thunder damage on successful melee attacks until the end of your next turn.

If you've reached at least one milestone today, instead deal an extra 2 thunder damage on successful melee attacks until the end of your next turn.

Level 20: 2d6 thunder damage, extra 3 thunder damage (4 after milestone).

Level 30: 3d6 thunder damage, extra 5 thunder damage (6 after milestone).

Strikebacks — Level 10

Backed with spikes, these vicious gauntlets hurt those who hurt you.

Item Slot: Hands 5,000 gp

Property: Gain a +1 item bonus to opportunity attacks.

Power (Encounter): Immediate Reaction. Use this power when an adjacent enemy hits you. Make a melee basic attack against that enemy.

ED COX

Vampiric Gauntlets — Level 16

These dark gauntlets pulse with necrotic energy and appear to draw in the light around them.

Item Slot: Hands 45,000 gp

Power (Encounter ✦ Healing, Necrotic): Standard Action. Make a melee attack: Dexterity + 4 vs. Reflex; on a hit, the target takes necrotic damage equal to your healing surge value, and you regain hit points equal to that amount.

Venom Gloves — Level 16+

The embroidered serpents on the back of these snakeskin garments writhe when you use them.

| Lvl 6 | 1,800 gp | Lvl 26 | 1,125,000 gp |

Item Slot: Hands

Power (Daily ✦ Poison, Sleep): Minor Action. Change the damage type of your next one-handed weapon melee attack to poison. On a hit, the target is also slowed (save ends). After three failed saves, the target is unconscious (save ends).

Level 26: After two failed saves, the target is unconscious (save ends).

Wrestler's Gloves — Level 2

The palms of these rough hide wraps are coated with a tacky substance that holds fast to whatever you grasp.

Item Slot: Hands 520 gp

Property: Gain a +1 item bonus to grab attacks, to your defenses when attempting to prevent an escape from your grab, and to saving throws to catch yourself when falling.

HEAD SLOT ITEMS

Your mind is your best weapon. See that it as well equipped and protected as the rest of your body.

Head items provide benefits that relate to the mind. Characters interested in protecting their mind from penetration—or those seeking to use their mind as a weapon—will find an abundance of options here.

HEAD SLOT ITEMS

Lvl	Name	Price (gp)
1	Headband of perception	360
2	Eagle eye goggles	520
2	Gem of colloquy	520
2	Reading spectacles	520
3	Arcanist's glasses	680
3	Circlet of second chances	680
4	Casque of tactics	840
4	Helm of opportunity	840
4	Helm of the stubborn mind	840
5	Cynic's goggles	1,000
5	Goggles of aura sight	1,000
5	Skull mask	1,000

Strikebacks

Sure Shot Gloves — Level 9

These slick gloves guide your shots unerringly.

Item Slot: Hands 4,200 gp

Property: Your ranged weapon attacks ignore cover (but not superior cover).

WILLIAM O'CONNOR

Lvl	Name	Price (gp)
5	Stag helm	1,000
6	Crown of doors	1,800
6	Helm of vigilant awareness	1,800
6	Phylactery of divinity	1,800
7	Crown of leaves	2,600
7	Hunter's headband	2,600
7	Phrenic crown	2,600
8	Circlet of indomitability	3,400
8	Coif of mindiron	3,400
8	Eye of deception	3,400
8	Starlight goggles	3,400
9	Crown of infernal legacy	4,200
9	Goggles of the bone collector	4,200
10	Cap of water breathing	5,000
10	Hat of disguise	5,000
10	Headband of intellect	5,000
10	Helm of the flamewarped	5,000
10	Laurel circlet	5,000
11	Circlet of mental onslaught	9,000
11	Crown of doors	9,000
11	Headband of perception	9,000
11	Mask of slithering	9,000
12	Eagle eye goggles	13,000
12	Gem of colloquy	13,000
13	Dread helm	17,000
14	Casque of tactics	21,000
14	Factotum helm	21,000
14	Helm of opportunity	21,000
14	Mask of terror	21,000
15	Carcanet of psychic schism	25,000
15	Crown of nature's rebellion	25,000
15	Skull mask	25,000
15	Stag helm	25,000
16	Blasting circlet	45,000
16	Crown of doors	45,000
16	Crown of eyes	45,000
16	Headband of insight	45,000
16	Headband of psychic attack	45,000
16	Helm of hidden horrors	45,000
16	Inquisitor's helm	45,000
17	Circlet of rapid casting	65,000
17	Goggles of the hawk	65,000
17	Grimlock helm	65,000
17	Phrenic crown	65,000
18	Circlet of indomitability	85,000
18	Coif of mindiron	85,000
18	Crown of the world tree	85,000
18	Helm of swift punishment	85,000
19	Crown of infernal legacy	105,000
19	Eye of the earthmother	105,000
20	Crown of nature's rebellion	125,000
20	Headband of intellect	125,000
20	Laurel circlet	125,000
20	Trickster's mask	125,000

Lvl	Name	Price (gp)
21	Coif of focus	225,000
21	Eye of discernment	225,000
21	Headband of perception	225,000
21	Ioun stone of sustenance	225,000
22	Eagle eye goggles	325,000
22	Ioun stone of perfect learning	325,000
23	Eye of awareness	425,000
23	Ioun stone of steadfastness	425,000
24	Casque of tactics	525,000
24	Helm of opportunity	525,000
25	Crown of nature's rebellion	625,000
25	Ioun stone of regeneration	625,000
25	Skull mask	625,000
25	Stag helm	625,000
25	Telepathy circlet	625,000
26	Clockwork cowl	1,125,000
27	Eye of the basilisk	1,625,000
27	Phrenic crown	1,625,000
28	Circlet of indomitability	2,125,000
28	Coif of mindiron	2,125,000
29	Quickening diadem	2,625,000
30	Bronze serpent	3,125,000
30	Headband of intellect	3,125,000
30	Laurel circlet	3,125,000

Arcanist's Glasses — Level 3

These spectacles increase your sensitivity to the subtle patterns of magic.

Item Slot: Head   680 gp

Property: Gain a +3 item bonus to Arcana checks to
   detect magic.

Blasting Circlet — Level 16

The intricate silver circlet adorning your brow hums with mystical power.

Item Slot: Head   45,000 gp

Power (Daily): Minor Action. Make a ranged attack:
   Ranged 10; Dexterity + 4 vs. Reflex; on a hit, the target
   takes force damage equal to your level. If you score a critical hit with this item, you don't expend the use of this
   power and no daily use of a magic item power occurs.

Bronze Serpent — Level 30

This small bronze snake slowly orbits your head, fortifying you.

Item Slot: Head   3,125,000 gp

Property: Gain resist 15 poison and a +6 item bonus to
   Endurance and Heal checks.

Cap of Water Breathing — Level 10

You are at home in the water while wearing this wax-coated cap.

Item Slot: Head   5,000 gp

Property: You can breathe water as well as air.

Carcanet of Psychic Schism — Level 15

This ornate headband protects your mind by splitting it in two, but there's a price to pay.

Item Slot: Head   25,000 gp

Property: Gain a +1 bonus to Will defense.

Power (Daily): Immediate Interrupt. Use this power when an attack would make you stunned, dazed, or dominated. You are unaffected by that condition, and you instead take a -2 penalty to attack rolls and Will defense for the condition's normal duration.

Casque of Tactics — Level 4+

Favored by sergeants and commanders, this utilitarian helm is remarkable only for its satin inner padding.

Lvl 4	840 gp	Lvl 24	525,000 gp
Lvl 14	21,000 gp		

Item Slot: Head

Property: Gain +1 item bonus to initiative checks.
  Level 14: +2 item bonus.
  Level 24: +3 item bonus.

Power (Daily): Free Action. Use this power when initiative is rolled. Swap initiative check results with a willing ally who you can see.

Circlet of Indomitability — Level 8+

This simple golden circlet fortifies your mind.

Lvl 8	3,400 gp	Lvl 28	2,125,000 gp
Lvl 18	85,000 gp		

Item Slot: Head

Property: Gain a +1 bonus to Will defense.
  Level 18: +2 bonus to Will defense.
  Level 28: +3 bonus to Will defense.

Circlet of Mental Onslaught — Level 11

Your mental attacks strike more true while you wear this slender circlet.

Item Slot: Head   9,000 gp

Property: Gain a +1 bonus to Will defense.

Power (Daily): Minor Action. Gain a +1 power bonus to attack rolls and damage rolls when making Wisdom, Intelligence, and Charisma attacks until the end of the encounter.

Circlet of Rapid Casting — Level 17

This rune-etched silver headband speeds arcane formulas through your mind.

Item Slot: Head   65,000 gp

Power (Daily): Free Action. During your turn, use an arcane utility power that normally requires a minor action. This counts as a daily or encounter use of that power, if applicable.

Circlet of Second Chances — Level 3

Luck favors those who don this plain copper accessory.

Item Slot: Head   680 gp

Power (Daily): No Action. Use this power when you fail a saving throw. Reroll the saving throw, using the second result even if it's lower.

Clockwork Cowl — Level 26

This brass and electrum helm makes a soft ticking noise that can only be heard by its wearer.

Item Slot: Head   1,125,000 gp

Property: Gain a +4 item bonus to initiative checks.

Power (Daily): Minor Action. Gain two extra standard actions that cannot be used as attacks.

Coif of Focus — Level 21

This plain mail hood hangs close to your eyes and ears, protecting them from assault.

Item Slot: Head   225,000 gp

Property: Gain a +5 item bonus to saving throws against effects that make you dazed and/or stunned.

Power (Daily): Immediate Interrupt. Use this power when an attack would make you dazed or stunned. Spend a healing surge to not be dazed or stunned by that attack.

Coif of Mindiron

Level 8+

Your head and mind is guarded by this glistening mail hood.

Lvl 8	3,400 gp	Lvl 28	2,125,000 gp
Lvl 18	85,000 gp		

Item Slot: Head

Power (Encounter): Standard Action. Immediate Interrupt. Use this power when you would be dazed by an attack that targets your Will defense. You are not dazed by the attack.

Level 18: Use this power when you would be dazed or stunned by an attack that targets your Will defense. You are not dazed or stunned by the attack.

Level 28: Use this power when you would be dazed, dominated, or stunned by an attack that targets your Will defense. You are not dazed, dominated, or stunned by the attack.

Crown of Doors

Level 6+

Architecture holds no secrets from those wearing this wood and stone headpiece.

Lvl 6	1,800 gp	Lvl 16	45,000 gp
Lvl 11	9,000 gp		

Item Slot: Head

Property: Gain a +2 item bonus to Perception checks to find secret doors and hidden passages.

Level 11: +4 item bonus.

Level 16: +6 item bonus.

Crown of Eyes

Level 16

This circlet incorporating eyelike designs watches every angle.

Item Slot: Head   45,000 gp

Property: You do not grant combat advantage to flanking enemies.

Crown of Infernal Legacy

Level 9+

This chain cowl empowers a tiefling's anger.

Lvl 9	4,200 gp	Lvl 19	105,000 gp

Item Slot: Head

Property: If you are a tiefling, gain a +1 item bonus to any attack roll benefiting from *infernal wrath*. On a miss, you deal fire damage equal to your Charisma modifier to the target.

Level 19: +2 item bonus.

Crown of Leaves

Level 7

This halo of ever-fresh oak leaves pulses with primal energy.

Item Slot: Head   2,600 gp

Property: Gain a +2 item bonus to Nature and Insight checks.

Crown of Nature's Rebellion

Level 15+

This birch skullcap wards against death.

Lvl 15	25,000 gp	Lvl 25	625,000 gp
Lvl 20	125,000 gp		

Item Slot: Head

Property: Gain resist 10 necrotic.

Level 20: Resist 15 necrotic.

Level 25: Resist 20 necrotic.

Power (Daily): Immediate Reaction. Use this power when you are hit by an attack that deals necrotic damage. The attacker takes an amount of damage equal to the nectoric damage you took, along with any other effect from the attack.

Crown of the World Tree

Level 18

The experience of a thousand ritualists is yours when you don this crown of ash.

Item Slot: Head   85,000 gp

Property: When performing a ritual, roll twice and take the better result.

Cynic's Goggles

Level 5

With these bronze and leather eye pieces, you more easily see through illusions.

Item Slot: Head   1,000 gp

Property: Gain a +2 item bonus to Will defense against illusion attacks and to Insight and Perception checks to detect illusions.

Dread Helm

Level 13

Beneath this closed chapel de fer, your eyes become burning points and you exude palpable menace.

Item Slot: Head   17,000 gp

Property: Gain a +4 item bonus to Intimidate checks. Take a -2 item penalty to Diplomacy checks.

Power (Daily ✦ Fear): Minor Action. Make an Intimidate check against the Will defense of a target within 5 squares of you. If the attack succeeds, the target takes a -2 penalty to attack rolls and defenses until the end of your next turn.

Eagle Eye Goggles

Level 2+

Though these leather goggles have dark eye pieces, they sharpen your sight when making ranged attacks.

Lvl 2	520 gp	Lvl 22	325,000 gp
Lvl 12	13,000 gp		

Item Slot: Head

Property: Gain a +1 item bonus to ranged basic attack rolls.

Level 12: +2 item bonus.

Level 22: +3 item bonus.

Eye of Awareness — Level 23

This patch quickens your reactions and is embroidered with a giant, bloodshot eye.

Item Slot: Head 425,000 gp
Property: Gain a +2 bonus to Will defense
Property: You gain a +5 item bonus to your initiative checks.

Eye of Deception — Level 8

This copper circlet is set with a mummified eye and aids you in the ways of deception.

Item Slot: Head 3,400 gp
Property: Gain a +2 item bonus to Bluff and Stealth checks, and to saving throws against effects with the illusion or charm keywords.

Eye of Discernment — Level 21

Little escapes your notice when this astral diamond-studded velvet patch covers one eye.

Item Slot: Head 225,000 gp
Property: Gain a +4 item bonus to Insight and Perception checks. The patch does not impair the sight of the covered eye. If you are blinded, the patch allows you to see through the covered eye as normal.

Eye of discernment

Eye of the Basilisk — Level 27

This burnished silver eye patch turns aside gaze attacks.

Item Slot: Head 1,625,000 gp
Property: You are immune to the petrified condition.
Power (Daily): Immediate Reaction. Use this power when an attack that has the gaze keyword misses you. The attacker rerolls the attack against a target of your choice within 5 squares of you.

Eye of the Earthmother — Level 19

A knothole resembling an eye peers out of this fist-sized tangle of roots, which floats near your head.

Item Slot: Head 105,000 gp
Property: You know the origin, type, and keyword(s) of any creature in sight.
Power (Daily ✦ Charm): Standard Action. Make a ranged attack: Ranged sight; affects beasts only; Intelligence + 4, Wisdom + 4, or Charisma + 4 vs. Will; on a hit, the targeted beast is dominated until the end of your next turn. Sustain minor (repeat the attack roll and hit to continue dominating the target).

Factotum Helm — Level 14

With this elaborately etched helm, you gain skill mastery beyond you previously.

Item Slot: Head 21,000 gp
Power (Daily): Minor Action. Gain training in one skill until the end of the encounter, or for one hour when not in an encounter.

Gem of Colloquy — Level 2+

This jewel hovers near your head, sharpening your wit and expanding your knowledge of languages.

Lvl 2 520 gp   Lvl 12 13,000 gp
Item Slot: Head
Property: Gain a +1 item bonus to Bluff and Diplomacy checks. Understand and speak 1 additional language, chosen at the time of the gem's creation.
Level 12: +3 item bonus, 2 additional languages.

Goggles of Aura Sight — Level 5

These goggles aid in diagnosis and healing.

Item Slot: Head 1,000 gp
Property: Gain a +2 item bonus to Heal checks.
Power (Encounter): Minor Action. Choose a target within 10 squares of you. Learn the target's current and maximum hit point values, any current disease or poison conditions on the target, and any disease or poison effect the target can deal.

Goggles of the Bone Collector — Level 9

The bones of various creatures are woven into this eyewear.

Item Slot: Head 4,200 gp

Property: Gain a +3 item bonus to monster knowledge checks.

Power (Encounter): Minor Action. Learn the origin, type, and keyword(s) of one creature in sight.

Goggles of the Hawk — Level 17

These goggles greatly extend your vision.

Item Slot: Head 65,000 gp

Property: You can make Perception checks to notice or examine targets within your line of sight, with no penalty for distance.

Grimlock Helm — Level 17

An opaque visor lowers to cover your eyes, yet this helm allows you to sense your surroundings regardless.

Item Slot: Head 65,000 gp

Power (Daily): Minor Action. You become blind and gain blindsight 5. You can spend another minor action to revert to normal sight.

Hat of Disguise — Level 10

This chapeau appears as you wish, changing you and your equipment as it transforms.

Item Slot: Head 5,000 gp

Property: While using this item's power, gain a +5 item bonus to Bluff checks to pass off a disguise.

Power (At-Will ✦ Illusion): Standard Action. You gain the appearance of any humanoid race of the same size category as you. Your clothing and equipment alter appearance to reflect this change. The illusion does not alter sound or texture, so a creature listening to you or touching you might detect the illusion.

Headband of Insight — Level 16

This unremarkable-looking headband allows you to see through another's lies.

Item Slot: Head 45,000 gp

Property: Gain a +4 item bonus to Insight checks.

Power (Daily): Free Action. Gain a +6 power bonus to a single Insight check made before the start of your next turn.

Helm of opportunity

Headband of Intellect — Level 10+

This ornamental silk cord strengthens your mental retention, recall, and powers.

| Lvl 10 | 5,000 gp | Lvl 30 | 3,125,000 gp |
| Lvl 20 | 125,000 gp | | |

Item Slot: Head

Property: Gain a +2 item bonus to knowledge or monster knowledge checks, and a +1 item bonus to attack rolls on powers that have the psychic keyword.
Level 20: +4 item bonus to knowledge or monster knowledge checks.
Level 30: +6 item bonus to knowledge or monster knowledge checks.

Power (Daily): Minor Action. Gain a +2 power bonus to the next Intelligence attack that you make this turn.
Level 20: +3 power bonus.
Level 30: +4 power bonus.

Headband of Perception — Level 1+

This chiffon headwrap is stitched with eye-shaped patterns, which heighten your senses.

| Lvl 1 | 360 gp | Lvl 21 | 225,000 gp |
| Lvl 11 | 9,000 gp | | |

Item Slot: Head

Property: Gain a +1 item bonus to Perception checks.
Level 11: +3 item bonus.
Level 21: +5 item bonus.

Headband of Psychic Attack — Level 16

This leather headband has crystal shards stitched into it.

Item Slot: Head 45,000 gp

Power (Daily ✦ Psychic): Minor Action. Make an attack: Ranged 10; Intelligence + 4, Wisdom + 4, or Charisma + 4 vs. Will; on a hit, the target is dazed until the end of your next turn.

Helm of Hidden Horrors — Level 16

This leather helm is a bane to wielders of illusions and charms.

Item Slot: Head 45,000 gp

Property: Gain a +1 bonus to Will defense.

Power (Daily ✦ Psychic): Immediate Interrupt. Use this power when you are hit by an attack against Will defense. The attacker takes psychic damage equal to your level.

Helm of Opportunity — Level 4+

This simple bronze helm allows you to strike more accurately at those who let down their guard.

| Lvl 4 | 840 gp | Lvl 24 | 525,000 gp |
| Lvl 14 | 21,000 gp | | |

Item Slot: Head

Property: Gain a +1 item bonus to opportunity attack rolls.
Level 14: +2 item bonus.
Level 24: +3 item bonus.

Helm of Swift Punishment — Level 18

Your foes soon learn the error of ignoring the threat you pose when you wear this helmet.

Item Slot: Head　85,000 gp

Power (Daily): Free Action. Use this power when you make an opportunity attack. Make two melee basic attacks instead of one.

Helm of the Flamewarped — Level 10

The one who wears this slightly charred copper helm can strike a devastating blow, but at a cost.

Item Slot: Head　5,000 gp

Power (Daily): Free Action. Use this power when you make a melee basic attack or use an at-will melee attack power. You are dazed until the end of your next turn. If your attack hits, the power's damage roll deals maximum damage, and you can choose to make it fire damage.

Helm of the Stubborn Mind — Level 4

This helm fortifies you against enchanters.

Item Slot: Head　840 gp

Property: Gain a +1 item bonus to Will defense against charm attacks.

HOWARD LYON

Helm of Vigilant Awareness — Level 7

The gems mounted above the ears and eyeholes of this steel helmet flash red when a deafening noise or blinding light appears.

Item Slot: Head　2,600 gp

Power (Daily): Immediate Interrupt. Use this power when an attack would make you blinded or deafened. The blinded or deafened condition from that attack does not affect you

Hunter's Headband — Level 7

This leather headband helps you forage for food underground and in the wilderness.

Item Slot: Head　2,600 gp

Property: Gain a +5 item bonus to Dungeoneering and Nature checks when foraging.

Inquisitor's Helm — Level 16

Your mind can access the secrets of another while you wear this cuir-bouilli skullcap.

Item Slot: Head　45,000 gp

Power (Daily): Standard Action. Make an attack: Ranged 10; Intelligence + 4, Wisdom + 4, or Charisma + 4 vs. Will; on a hit, you pry the answer to one question from the target's mind. If the target doesn't know the answer to the question, you get no answer but the power is still spent.

Ioun Stone of Perfect Language — Level 22

This white and pink rhombic prism hovers about your head, making you far more adept at negotiation.

Item Slot: Head　325,000 gp

Property: Gain a +5 item bonus to Bluff, Diplomacy, Intimidate, and Streetwise checks. You also can understand all spoken languages, and when you speak all creatures hear your words in their native language.

Power (Daily): Free Action. Use this power during a skill challenge. Treat your next Insight check as though you rolled a natural 20.

Ioun Stone of Regeneration — Level 25

This tiny red ovoid orbits your head.

Item Slot: Head　625,000 gp

Power (Daily ✦ Healing): Minor Action. Gain regeneration 10 while you are bloodied until the end of the encounter.

Ioun Stone of Steadfastness — Level 23

This pale aquamarine hovering prism offers a constant reminder of your allies' support and loyalty.

Item Slot: Head　425,000 gp

Property: As long as you are adjacent to an ally, you are immune to fear effects and cannot attack your allies as a result of an effect.

Ioun Stone of Sustenance
Level 21

With this rhombic stone circling your head, you never require food or drink and rarely need to rest.

Item Slot: Head   225,000 gp

Property: You do not need to eat, drink, or breathe. You require half the amount of rest that you ordinarily need.

Laurel Circlet
Level 10+

Your social graces and force of personality are amplified while you wear this thin coronet.

Lvl 10	5,000 gp	Lvl 30	3,125,000 gp
Lvl 20	125,000 gp		

Item Slot: Head

Property: Gain a +2 item bonus to Diplomacy and Insight checks, and a +1 item bonus to attack rolls on powers that have the charm or illusion keyword.

Level 20: +4 item bonus to Diplomacy and Insight checks.

Level 30: +6 item bonus to Diplomacy and Insight checks.

Power (Daily): Minor Action. Gain a +2 power bonus to the next Charisma attack that you make this turn.

Level 20: +3 power bonus.

Level 30: +4 power bonus.

Mask of Slithering
Level 11

This serpentine mask allows you to slink out of harm's way and cause another to suffer in your stead.

Item Slot: Head   9,000 gp

Power (Daily): Immediate Interrupt. Use this power when an enemy makes a melee or ranged attack against you. Gain a +2 bonus to AC and Reflex defense. If the attack misses, then the attacker rerolls the attack against a creature adjacent to you of your choice.

Mask of Terror
Level 14

This frightful, demonic mask is formed from charred flesh and adorned with horns and fangs.

Item Slot: Head   21,000 gp

Power (Daily ✦ Fear): Minor Action. Make an attack: Close blast 5; Intelligence + 3, Wisdom +3, or Charisma + 3 vs. Will; on a hit, the target takes a -2 penalty to attack rolls until the end of your next turn.

Phrenic Crown
Level 7+

This pink coral coronet is eerily reminiscent of brain matter, yet is still bewitching.

Lvl 7	2,600 gp	Lvl 27	1,625,000 gp
Lvl 17	65,000 gp		

Item Slot: Head

Property: When you use a power against Will defense, the target (or targets) takes a -1 penalty to saving throws against any ongoing effect of that power.

Level 17: -2 penalty.

Level 27: -3 penalty.

Phylactery of Divinity
Level 6

This leather casing is strapped to the head and focuses your faith and healing powers.

Item Slot: Head   1,800 gp

Property: Gain a +2 item bonus to Heal and Religion checks.

Quickening Diadem
Level 29

A diadem of astral diamonds floats about your head, honing your mental clarity and your reflexes.

Item Slot: Head   2,625,000 gp

Property: When you are stunned or dazed, you can take a move action on your turn in addition to whatever actions you are normally allowed.

Power (Daily): Free Action. Take a move or minor action.

Reading Spectacles
Level 2

You can decipher any written passage while gazing through these unadorned copper eyeglasses.

Item Slot: Head   520 gp

Property: You can read any language while wearing this item.

Skull Mask
Level 5+

This rough iron visor is shaped in the likeness of a skull whose grim countenance saps your enemies' courage.

Lvl 5	1,000 gp	Lvl 25	625,000 gp
Lvl 15	25,000 gp		

Item Slot: Head

Property: Enemies who can see you take a -2 penalty to saving throws against fear effects.

Property: Gain resist 5 necrotic, and a +1 item bonus to Intimidate checks.

Level 15: Resist 10 necrotic, +2 item bonus.

Level 25: Resist 15 necrotic, +3 item bonus.

Stag Helm
Level 5+

This helm sports a set of antlers and makes you as alert as a stag.

Lvl 5	1,000 gp	Lvl 25	625,000 gp
Lvl 15	25,000 gp		

Item Slot: Head

Property: Gain a +2 item bonus to passive Perception checks. Also, you can take a minor action during a round when you are surprised.

Level 15: +4 item bonus, move action.

Level 25: +6 item bonus, standard action.

Starlight Goggles
Level 8

These dark leather goggles sparkle with tiny silver studs, aiding your vision in dim light.

Item Slot: Head 3,400 gp

Property: Gain low-light vision.

Telepathy Circlet
Level 25

A boon to leaders and liars, this mithral band allows you to communicate without speaking, and extract the thoughts of another.

Item Slot: Head 25,000 gp

Property: Gain a +2 item bonus to Insight checks. Also, you can speak telepathically to any creature you can see. Those willing to communicate with you can send thoughts back to you, allowing two-way communication. This telepathic communication fulfills class feature or power requirements that a target be able to hear you.

Power (Daily ✦ Psychic): Standard Action. Make an attack: Ranged 5; Charisma Modifier + 6 vs. Will; on a hit, the target is dazed (save ends). *Aftereffect:* The target is dazed (save ends).

DARRELL RICHE

Trickster's Mask
Level 20

This velvet masquerade mask is highly prized among the more shadowy worshipers of Avandra.

Item Slot: Head 125,000 gp

Property: When you make a Stealth or Thievery check, roll twice and take the better result.

Power (Daily): Free Action. Use this power before you make a Stealth or Thievery check. Treat that check as though you rolled a natural 20.

NECK SLOT ITEMS

Amulets and brooches, cloaks and capes—the prepared adventurer who appreciates fashion and values her life never leaves home without them.

After armor and weapons, neck items are perhaps the most important item for an adventurer to acquire. Every neck item provides an enhancement bonus to Fortitude, Reflex, and Will defenses. In addition, neck items offer powerful measures to protect a character from enfeebling conditions, elemental energies, and even death.

Although most neck items are protective in nature, a few do boast offensive enchantments. Some items also enhance skill checks, particularly those that are Charisma-based.

NECK SLOT ITEMS

Lvl	Name	Price (gp)
2	Amulet of mental resolve +1	520
2	Amulet of physical resolve +1	520
2	Amulet of resolution +1	520
3	Brooch of no regrets +1	680
3	Brooch of shielding +1	680
3	Cloak of the chirurgeon +1	680
3	Gloaming shroud +1	680
3	Ornament of alertness +1	680
4	Cloak of distortion +1	840
4	Cloak of the walking wounded +1	840
4	Collar of recovery +1	840
4	Healer's brooch +1	840
5	Cape of the mountebank +1	1,000
7	Amulet of mental resolve +2	2,600
7	Amulet of physical resolve +2	2,600
7	Amulet of resolution +2	2,600
7	Fireflower pendant +2	2,600
8	Brooch of no regrets +2	3,400
8	Brooch of shielding +2	3,400
8	Choker of eloquence +2	3,400
8	Cloak of the chirurgeon +2	3,400
8	Evil eye fetish +2	3,400
8	Gloaming shroud +2	3,400
8	Ornament of alertness +2	3,400
8	Peacemaker's periapt +2	3,400

Lvl	Name	Price (gp)
8	Periapt of recovery +2	3,400
8	Resilience amulet +2	3,400
8	Steadfast amulet +2	3,400
9	Cloak of distortion +2	4,200
9	Cloak of the cautious +2	4,200
9	Cloak of the walking wounded +2	4,200
9	Collar of recovery +2	4,200
9	Healer's brooch +2	4,200
9	Medallion of death deferred +2	4,200
10	Cape of the mountebank +2	5,000
12	Absence amulet +3	13,000
12	Amulet of mental resolve +3	13,000
12	Amulet of physical resolve +3	13,000
12	Amulet of resolution +3	13,000
12	Clasp of noble sacrifice +3	13,000
12	Fireflower pendant +3	13,000
13	Abyssal adornment +3	17,000
13	Brooch of no regrets +3	17,000
13	Brooch of shielding +3	17,000
13	Choker of eloquence +3	17,000
13	Cloak of arachnida +3	17,000
13	Cloak of the chirurgeon +3	17,000
13	Evil eye fetish +3	17,000
13	Gloaming shroud +3	17,000
13	Liar's trinket +3	17,000
13	Ornament of alertness +3	17,000
13	Peacemaker's periapt +3	17,000
13	Periapt of recovery +3	17,000
13	Resilience amulet +3	17,000
13	Steadfast amulet +3	17,000
14	Amulet of attenuation +3	21,000
14	Amulet of bodily sanctity +3	21,000
14	Amulet of elusive prey +3	21,000
14	Amulet of inner voice +3	21,000
14	Cloak of distortion +3	21,000
14	Cloak of the cautious +3	21,000
14	Cloak of the walking wounded +3	21,000
14	Collar of recovery +3	21,000
14	Flamewrath cape +3	21,000
14	Healer's brooch +3	21,000
14	Medallion of death deferred +3	21,000
15	Amulet of aranea +3	25,000
15	Brooch of vitality +3	25,000
15	Cape of the mountebank +3	25,000
15	Cloak of displacement +3	25,000
15	Necklace of fireballs +3	25,000
15	Torc of power preservation +3	25,000
17	Absence amulet +4	65,000
17	Amulet of mental resolve +4	65,000
17	Amulet of physical resolve +4	65,000
17	Amulet of resolution +4	65,000
17	Clasp of noble sacrifice +4	65,000
17	Fireflower pendant +4	65,000
18	Abyssal adornment +4	85,000
18	Amulet of material darkness +4	85,000

Lvl	Name	Price (gp)
18	Brooch of no regrets +4	85,000
18	Brooch of shielding +4	85,000
18	Chamber cloak +4	85,000
18	Choker of eloquence +4	85,000
18	Cloak of arachnida +4	85,000
18	Cloak of the chirurgeon +4	85,000
18	Evil eye fetish +4	85,000
18	Gloaming shroud +4	85,000
18	Liar's trinket +4	85,000
18	Moonlight lavaliere +4	85,000
18	Ornament of alertness +4	85,000
18	Peacemaker's periapt +4	85,000
18	Periapt of recovery +4	85,000
18	Resilience amulet +4	85,000
18	Steadfast amulet +4	85,000
19	Amulet of attenuation +4	105,000
19	Amulet of bodily sanctity +4	105,000
19	Amulet of elusive prey +4	105,000
19	Amulet of inner voice +4	105,000
19	Cloak of autumn's child +4	105,000
19	Cloak of distortion +4	105,000
19	Cloak of the cautious +4	105,000
19	Cloak of the walking wounded +4	105,000
19	Collar of recovery +4	105,000
19	Flamewrath cape +4	105,000
19	Healer's brooch +4	105,000
19	Medallion of death deferred +4	105,000
19	Tattered cloak +4	105,000
19	Wyrmtouched amulet +4	105,000
20	Amulet of aranea +4	125,000
20	Brooch of vitality +4	125,000
20	Cape of the mountebank +4	125,000
20	Cloak of displacement +4	125,000
20	Necklace of fireballs +4	125,000
20	Torc of power preservation +4	125,000
22	Absence amulet +5	325,000
22	Amulet of mental resolve +5	325,000
22	Amulet of physical resolve +5	325,000
22	Amulet of resolution +5	325,000
22	Clasp of noble sacrifice +5	325,000
22	Fireflower pendant +5	325,000
23	Abyssal adornment +5	425,000
23	Amulet of material darkness +5	425,000
23	Brooch of no regrets +5	425,000
23	Brooch of shielding +5	425,000
23	Chamber cloak +5	425,000
23	Choker of eloquence +5	425,000
23	Cloak of arachnida +5	425,000
23	Cloak of the chirurgeon +5	425,000
23	Evil eye fetish +5	425,000
23	Gloaming shroud +5	425,000
23	Liar's trinket +5	425,000
23	Moonlight lavaliere +5	425,000
23	Ornament of alertness +5	425,000
23	Peacemaker's periapt +5	425,000

NECK SLOT ITEMS (CONTINUED)

Lvl	Name	Price (gp)
23	Periapt of recovery +5	425,000
23	Resilience amulet +5	425,000
23	Steadfast amulet +5	425,000
24	Amulet of attenuation +5	525,000
24	Amulet of bodily sanctity +5	525,000
24	Amulet of elusive prey +5	525,000
24	Amulet of inner voice +5	525,000
24	Cloak of autumn's child +5	525,000
24	Cloak of distortion +5	525,000
24	Cloak of the cautious +5	525,000
24	Cloak of the walking wounded +5	525,000
24	Collar of recovery +5	525,000
24	Death-denying cloak +5	525,000
24	Flamewrath cape +5	525,000
24	Healer's brooch +5	525,000
24	Medallion of death deferred +5	525,000
24	Tattered cloak +5	525,000
24	Wyrmtouched amulet +5	525,000
25	Amulet of aranea +5	625,000
25	Brooch of vitality +5	625,000
25	Cape of the mountebank +5	625,000
25	Cloak of displacement +5	625,000
25	Cloak of elemental evolution +5	625,000
25	Life charm +5	625,000
25	Necklace of fireballs +5	625,000
25	Torc of power preservation +5	625,000
27	Absence amulet +6	1,625,000
27	Amulet of mental resolve +6	1,625,000
27	Amulet of physical resolve +6	1,625,000
27	Amulet of resolution +6	1,625,000
27	Clasp of noble sacrifice +6	1,625,000
27	Fireflower pendant +6	1,625,000
28	Abyssal adornment +6	2,125,000
28	Amulet of material darkness +6	2,125,000
28	Brooch of no regrets +6	2,125,000
28	Brooch of shielding +6	2,125,000
28	Chamber cloak +6	2,125,000
28	Choker of eloquence +6	2,125,000
28	Cloak of arachnida +6	2,125,000
28	Cloak of the chirurgeon +6	2,125,000
28	Evil eye fetish +6	2,125,000
28	Gloaming shroud +6	2,125,000
28	Liar's trinket +6	2,125,000
28	Moonlight lavaliere +6	2,125,000
28	Ornament of alertness +6	2,125,000
28	Peacemaker's periapt +6	2,125,000
28	Periapt of recovery +6	2,125,000
28	Resilience amulet +6	2,125,000
28	Steadfast amulet +6	2,125,000
29	Amulet of attenuation +6	2,625,000
29	Amulet of bodily sanctity +6	2,625,000
29	Amulet of elusive prey +6	2,625,000
29	Amulet of inner voice +6	2,625,000
29	Amulet of the unbroken +6	2,625,000
29	Cloak of autumn's child +6	2,625,000

NECK SLOT ITEMS (CONTINUED)

Lvl	Name	Price (gp)
29	Cloak of distortion +6	2,625,000
29	Cloak of the cautious +6	2,625,000
29	Cloak of the walking wounded +6	2,625,000
29	Collar of recovery +6	2,625,000
29	Death-denying cloak +6	2,625,000
29	Flamewrath cape +6	2,625,000
29	Healer's brooch +6	2,625,000
29	Medallion of death deferred +6	2,625,000
29	Star of the Astral Sea +6	2,625,000
29	Tattered cloak +6	2,625,000
29	Wyrmtouched amulet +6	2,625,000
30	Amulet of aranea +6	3,125,000
30	Brooch of vitality +6	3,125,000
30	Cape of the mountebank +6	3,125,000
30	Cloak of displacement +6	3,125,000
30	Cloak of elemental evolution +6	3,125,000
30	Cloak of the phoenix +6	3,125,000
30	Gorget of reciprocity +6	3,125,000
30	Life charm +6	3,125,000
30	Necklace of fireballs +6	3,125,000
30	Talisman of repulsion +6	3,125,000
30	Torc of power preservation +6	3,125,000

Absence Amulet — Level 12+

This crystal bauble has no setting and is secured by an unassuming rawhide band.

Lvl 12	+3	13,000 gp	Lvl 22	+5	325,000 gp
Lvl 17	+4	65,000 gp	Lvl 27	+6	1,625,000 gp

Item Slot: Neck

Enhancement: Fortitude, Reflex, and Will

Property: Attempts to scry upon you, your location, or objects in your possession fail, as if the target of the attempt did not exist.

Amulet of aranea

MARC SASSO

Abyssal Adornment — Level 13+

Made of charred and twisted black metal, this heavy chain broods with bridled hate.

| Lvl 13 | +3 | 17,000 gp | Lvl 23 | +5 | 425,000 gp |
| Lvl 18 | +4 | 85,000 gp | Lvl 28 | +6 | 2,125,000 gp |

Item Slot: Neck

Enhancement: Fortitude, Reflex, and Will

Power (Daily): Immediate Interrupt. Use this power when you are hit by an attack that would deal acid, cold, fire, lightning, or thunder damage. Gain resist 20 against that damage type until the end of your next turn.
Level 24 or 29: Resist 30.

Amulet of Aranea — Level 15+

Your ability to ward off poison increases while wearing this spider-shaped talisman.

| Lvl 15 | +3 | 25,000 gp | Lvl 25 | +5 | 625,000 gp |
| Lvl 20 | +4 | 125,000 gp | Lvl 30 | +6 | 3,125,000 gp |

Item Slot: Neck

Enhancement: Fortitude, Reflex, and Will

Property: Gain resist 10 poison.
Level 25 or 30: Resist 15 poison.

Power (Daily): Immediate Reaction. Use this power when you are hit by a melee attack. The attacker takes 1d10 poison damage and ongoing 10 poison (save ends). The attacker also takes a –2 penalty to saving throws against poison effects until the end of the encounter.
Level 25 or 30: 2d10 poison damage, ongoing 20 poison (save ends).

Amulet of Attenuation — Level 14+

This crude trinket has a rubbery shell that briefly toughens the skin.

| Lvl 14 | +3 | 21,000 gp | Lvl 24 | +5 | 525,000 gp |
| Lvl 19 | +4 | 105,000 gp | Lvl 29 | +6 | 2,625,000 gp |

Item Slot: Neck

Enhancement: Fortitude, Reflex, and Will

Power (Daily): Immediate Interrupt. Use this power when you are hit by an attack that deals damage. Reduce the damage by 15.
Level 24 or 29: Reduce the damage by 20.

Amulet of Bodily Sanctity — Level 14+

This heart-shaped ruby keepsafe is set in a gold cage.

| Lvl 14 | +3 | 21,000 gp | Lvl 24 | +5 | 525,000 gp |
| Lvl 19 | +4 | 105,000 gp | Lvl 29 | +6 | 2,625,000 gp |

Item Slot: Neck

Enhancement: Fortitude, Reflex, and Will

Property: Gain a +2 item bonus to saving throws against ongoing damage.

Power (Daily): Minor Action. You and all allies within a number of squares of you equal to 2 + the amulet's enhancement bonus roll a saving throw against any current ongoing damage effect.

Amulet of Elusive Prey — Level 14+

White ash, oak, and bloodwood are carved in concentric circles and scorched with an X mark to ward off attacks.

| Lvl 14 | +3 | 21,000 gp | Lvl 24 | +5 | 525,000 gp |
| Lvl 19 | +4 | 105,000 gp | Lvl 29 | +6 | 2,625,000 gp |

Item Slot: Neck

Enhancement: Fortitude, Reflex, and Will

Property: If you end your turn at least 4 squares from the square in which you began it, gain a +2 item bonus to AC and Reflex defense until the start of your next turn.

Amulet of Inner Voice — Level 14+

This clear diamond charm helps you shake off mental control.

| Lvl 14 | +3 | 21,000 gp | Lvl 24 | +5 | 525,000 gp |
| Lvl 19 | +4 | 105,000 gp | Lvl 29 | +6 | 2,625,000 gp |

Item Slot: Neck

Enhancement: Fortitude, Reflex, and Will

Property: Gain a +2 item bonus to saving throws against effects with the charm or fear keyword.

Power (Daily): Immediate Interrupt. Use this power when you would be dominated by an effect that a save can end. Make a saving throw against the effect. On a failure, you don't expend the use of this power and no daily use of a magic item power occurs.

Amulet of Material Darkness — Level 18+

Shadows congregate around the wearer of this onyx amulet.

| Lvl 18 | +4 | 85,000 gp | Lvl 28 | +6 | 2,125,000 gp |
| Lvl 23 | +5 | 425,000 gp | | | |

Item Slot: Neck

Enhancement: Fortitude, Reflex, and Will

Property: While in dim light or darkness, you are treated as having cover against area and ranged attacks. This property applies even against attackers who can see you normally or otherwise ignore concealment penalties.

Amulet of Mental Resolve — Level 2+

Your mind is guarded when wearing this cold iron talisman.

Lvl 2	+1	520 gp	Lvl 17	+4	65,000 gp
Lvl 7	+2	2,600 gp	Lvl 22	+5	325,000 gp
Lvl 12	+3	13,000 gp	Lvl 27	+6	1,625,000 gp

Item Slot: Neck

Enhancement: Fortitude, Reflex, and Will

Property: Gain a +2 item bonus to saving throws against effects with the charm, illusion, or sleep keyword.

Amulet of Physical Resolve — Level 2+

This striking amulet wards you against effects that leave you physically debilitated.

Lvl 2	+1	520 gp	Lvl 17	+4	65,000 gp
Lvl 7	+2	2,600 gp	Lvl 22	+5	325,000 gp
Lvl 12	+3	13,000 gp	Lvl 27	+6	1,625,000 gp

Item Slot: Neck

Enhancement: Fortitude, Reflex, and Will

Property: Gain a +2 item bonus to saving throws against effects with the poison keyword and effects that render you weakened, slowed, or immobilized.

Amulet of Resolution — Level 2+

Whether the affliction be of mind or body, this mithral necklace gives you a second chance to ward it off.

Lvl 2	+1	520 gp	Lvl 17	+4	65,000 gp
Lvl 7	+2	2,600 gp	Lvl 22	+5	325,000 gp
Lvl 12	+3	13,000 gp	Lvl 27	+6	1,625,000 gp

Item Slot: Neck

Enhancement: Fortitude, Reflex, and Will

Power (Daily): No Action. Use this power when you fail a saving throw. Reroll the saving throw, using the second result even if it's lower.

Amulet of the Unbroken — Level 29

Encrusted with vibrant rubies that flash when it is used, this magnificent amulet proves that some heroes never say die.

Item Slot: Neck   2,625,000 gp

Enhancement: Fortitude, Reflex, and Will

Power (Daily ✦ Healing): Immediate Interrupt. Use this power when you would be reduced to 0 or fewer hit points. Expend any number of healing surges and regain hit points as normal for each surge spent.

Brooch of No Regrets — Level 3+

This ornate golden shield pin bolsters your allies even in dire circumstances.

Lvl 3	+1	680 gp	Lvl 18	+4	85,000 gp
Lvl 8	+2	3,400 gp	Lvl 23	+5	425,000 gp
Lvl 13	+3	17,000 gp	Lvl 28	+6	2,125,000 gp

Item Slot: Neck

Enhancement: Fortitude, Reflex, and Will

Power (Daily): Free Action. Use this power when an ally within 10 squares of you fails a saving throw. That ally rerolls that saving throw with a +2 power bonus and must use the second result, even if it's lower.
Level 13 or 18: An ally within 20 squares.
Level 23 or 28: An ally within line of sight.

Brooch of Shielding — Level 3+

This ornate silver shield pin absorbs force attacks against you.

Lvl 3	+1	680 gp	Lvl 18	+4	85,000 gp
Lvl 8	+2	3,400 gp	Lvl 23	+5	425,000 gp
Lvl 13	+3	17,000 gp	Lvl 28	+6	2,125,000 gp

Item Slot: Neck

Enhancement: Fortitude, Reflex, and Will

Property: Gain resist 10 force.
Level 13 or 18: Resist 15 force.
Level 23 or 28: Resist 20 force.

Power (Daily): Immediate Interrupt. Use this power when you are hit by an area, close, or ranged attack. Gain resist to all damage equal to the brooch's resist force value against that attack.

Brooch of Vitality — Level 15+

This warm, redwood, heart-shaped brooch beats softly and represents the durability of life.

Lvl 15	+3	25,000 gp	Lvl 25	+5	625,000 gp
Lvl 20	+4	125,000 gp	Lvl 30	+6	3,125,000 gp

Item Slot: Neck

Enhancement: Fortitude, Reflex, and Will

Property: Increase your maximum hit points by 5.
Level 20: By 10 hit points.
Level 25: By 15 hit points.
Level 30: By 20 hit points.

Cape of the Mountebank — Level 5+

With a flourish of this silk-hemmed garment, you transport out of harm's way.

Lvl 5	+1	1,000 gp	Lvl 20	+4	125,000 gp
Lvl 10	+2	5,000 gp	Lvl 25	+5	625,000 gp
Lvl 15	+3	25,000 gp	Lvl 30	+6	3,125,000 gp

Item Slot: Neck

Enhancement: Fortitude, Reflex, and Will

Power (Daily ✦ Teleportation): Immediate Reaction. Use this power when you are hit by an attack. Teleport 5 squares and gain combat advantage against the attacker until the end of your next turn.

DREW BAKER

Chamber Cloak   Level 18+

This voluminous garment envelops you when you're hurt, giving you a safe place to recover.

Lvl 18	+4	85,000 gp	Lvl 28	+6	2,125,000 gp
Lvl 23	+5	425,000 gp			

Item Slot: Neck

Enhancement: Fortitude, Reflex, and Will

Power (Daily): Free Action. Use this power when you take damage from an enemy or trap. You disappear from the world, stepping through your cloak into a secure place on another plane. At the start of your next turn, you reappear within 5 squares of your original location.

Choker of Eloquence   Level 8+

This damask neck wrap quickens the tongue and finds favor with diplomats and aristocrats.

Lvl 8	+1	3,400 gp	Lvl 23	+4	425,000 gp
Lvl 13	+2	17,000 gp	Lvl 28	+5	2,125,000 gp
Lvl 18	+3	85,000 gp			

Item Slot: Neck

Enhancement: Fortitude, Reflex, and Will

Property: Gain an item bonus to Bluff and Diplomacy checks equal to the item's enhancement bonus.

Power (Daily): Free Action. Use this power after you roll a Bluff or Diplomacy check. Reroll that check, using the second result even if it's lower.

Clasp of Noble Sacrifice   Level 12+

This gold cloak buckle protects your friends with your life force.

Lvl 12	+3	13,000 gp	Lvl 22	+5	325,000 gp
Lvl 17	+4	65,000 gp	Lvl 27	+6	1,625,000 gp

Item Slot: Neck

Enhancement: Fortitude, Reflex, and Will

Power (Daily): Minor Action. Until the end of the encounter, any time an ally within 5 squares of you spends a healing surge, it is deducted from your total instead of the ally's. Each time an ally spends one of your healing surges in this way, gain temporary hit points equal to the clasp's enhancement bonus.

Cloak of Arachnida   Level 13+

This soft cloak is traced in spiderweb patterns.

Lvl 13	+3	17,000 gp	Lvl 23	+5	425,000 gp
Lvl 18	+4	85,000 gp	Lvl 28	+6	2,125,000 gp

Item Slot: Neck

Enhancement: Fortitude, Reflex, and Will

Property: Gain a +2 item bonus to saving throws against effects that immobilize or restrain you.

Level 23 or 28: Also gain resist 15 poison.

Power (Daily): Immediate Interrupt. Use this power when an adjacent enemy attacks you or moves away from you. Make an attack: Melee 1; Intelligence, Wisdom, or Charisma vs. Reflex; on a hit, the target is immobilized (save ends).

Cloak of Autumn's Child   Level 19+

Woven from exotic Feywild leaves, this cloak whisks you to a soothing pocket of peace where afflictions are less severe.

Lvl 19	+4	105,000 gp	Lvl 29	+6	2,625,000 gp
Lvl 24	+5	525,000 gp			

Item Slot: Neck

Enhancement: Fortitude, Reflex, and Will

Power (Daily ✦ Teleportation): Move Action. You disappear from the world into a safe pocket of the Feywild. While you are gone, all effects on you are suppressed (you don't take ongoing damage, for example). You roll saving throws at the end of each turn as normal, except you gain a +2 power bonus. Also, while gone, you remain as aware of your surroundings as if you were standing in your last position. At the start of each turn thereafter, you can choose to return to any space within 5 squares of your last position. Line of sight between the two positions must exist (you can't reappear on the other side of a wall, for example).

Cloak of Displacement   Level 15+

This shimmering cloak conceals your precise location.

Lvl 15	+3	25,000 gp	Lvl 25	+5	625,000 gp
Lvl 20	+4	125,000 gp	Lvl 30	+6	3,125,000 gp

Item Slot: Neck

Enhancement: Fortitude, Reflex, and Will

Property: Each encounter, you gain a +2 item bonus to AC and Reflex defenses until an attack hits you.

Power (Daily ✦ Teleportation): Immediate Interrupt. Use this power when you would be hit with a melee or ranged attack. The attacker must reroll the attack, using the second result even if it's lower. If the attacker misses you, you can teleport 1 square.

Cloak of the phoenix

Cloak of Distortion — Level 4+

This cloak roils about you like the rippling air of a scorching desert.

Lvl 4	+1	840 gp	Lvl 19	+4	105,000 gp
Lvl 9	+2	4,200 gp	Lvl 24	+5	525,000 gp
Lvl 14	+3	21,000 gp	Lvl 29	+6	2,625,000 gp

Item Slot: Neck

Enhancement: Fortitude, Reflex, and Will

Property: A ranged attack against you from more than 5 squares away takes a -5 penalty to the attack roll.

Cloak of Elemental Evolution — Level 25+

Stitched with the material forms of the elements, this cloak adopts the form of the element it is set to resist.

Lvl 25	+4	625,000 gp	Lvl 30	+5	3,125,000 gp

Item Slot: Neck

Enhancement: Fortitude, Reflex, and Will

Power (Daily): Minor Action. Choose a damage type from the following list: acid, cold, fire, lightning, or thunder. Gain resist 10 against that damage type until the end of the encounter.

Power (At-Will): Immediate Interrupt. Use this power when you would take damage from an attack while you are under the effect of this item's daily power. Change the resistance provided by this cloak to any other damage type listed above. This lasts until the start of your next turn, at which point the damage type reverts to the type chosen when the item's daily power was activated.

Cloak of the Cautious — Level 9+

Dragonborn refer to this slick garment as the "cloak of the craven" because it facilitates hasty retreats.

Lvl 9	+2	4,200 gp	Lvl 24	+5	525,000 gp
Lvl 14	+3	21,000 gp	Lvl 29	+6	2,625,000 gp
Lvl 19	+4	105,000 gp			

Item Slot: Neck

Enhancement: Fortitude, Reflex, and Will

Power (Daily): Minor Action. Gain a +5 power bonus to speed until the end of your next turn. If you attack any target while this power is active, this effect ends and you are stunned until the end of your next turn.

Cloak of the Chirurgeon — Level 3+

This garment gives you the confidence and knowledge to assuage an ally's pain.

Lvl 3	+1	680 gp	Lvl 18	+4	85,000 gp
Lvl 8	+2	3,400 gp	Lvl 23	+5	425,000 gp
Lvl 13	+3	17,000 gp	Lvl 28	+6	2,125,000 gp

Item Slot: Neck

Enhancement: Fortitude, Reflex, and Will

Property: Gain an item bonus to Heal checks equal to the enhancement bonus of this cloak.

Power (Daily): Minor Action. An adjacent ally regains 1 healing surge already spent today.

Cloak of the Phoenix — Level 30

This elegant mantle is woven with elemental fire.

Lvl 30 +6 3,125,000 gp

Item Slot: Neck

Enhancement: Fortitude, Reflex, and Will

Power (Daily ✦ Fire, Healing): No Action. Use this power when you are reduced to 0 or fewer hit points. Deal 3d10 fire damage to all enemies within 3 squares of you, then disappear from the world in a plume of smoke. At the start of your next turn, you reappear in the same space, or the nearest unoccupied space if that space is taken. You are restored to full hit points, and all effects previously on you are eliminated. You lose all remaining healing surges (if any).

Cloak of the Walking Wounded — Level 4+

Thin red veins form across the fabric of this handsome cloak when its healing properties are evoked.

Lvl 4	+1	840 gp	Lvl 19	+4	105,000 gp
Lvl 9	+2	4,200 gp	Lvl 24	+5	525,000 gp
Lvl 14	+3	21,000 gp	Lvl 29	+6	2,625,000 gp

Item Slot: Neck

Enhancement: Fortitude, Reflex, and Will

Property: If you use your second wind while bloodied, you can expend two healing surges instead of one (gaining hit points from both).

Collar of Recovery — Level 4+

Inset with a bloodstone, this neckpiece aids healing.

Lvl 4	+1	840 gp	Lvl 19	+4	105,000 gp
Lvl 9	+2	4,200 gp	Lvl 24	+5	525,000 gp
Lvl 14	+3	21,000 gp	Lvl 29	+6	2,625,000 gp

Item Slot: Neck

Enhancement: Fortitude, Reflex, and Will

Property: Gain extra hit points equal to this item's enhancement bonus when you spend a healing surge to regain hit points.

Death-Defying Cloak — Level 24+

This voluminous mantle lets you cheat death.

Lvl 24	+5	525,000 gp	Lvl 29	+6	2,625,000 gp

Item Slot: Neck

Enhancement: Fortitude, Reflex, and Will

Power (Daily ✦ Illusion): Immediate Interrupt. Use this power when you would be reduced to 0 or fewer hit points. Instead, you are reduced to 1 hit point. You also become invisible until the end of your next turn or until you attack (whichever comes first). Until you become visible, an illusion of your deceased body appears on the ground where you would have fallen. Anyone who touches or otherwise manipulates the body sees through the illusion automatically. Otherwise a Perception check (DC 20 + the cloak's level) is required to discern the illusion.

Flamewrath Cape — Level 14+

Intermittent wisps of smoke rise from this garment, which can burst into flame upon your command.

| Lvl 14 | +3 | 21,000 gp | Lvl 24 | +5 | 525,000 gp |
| Lvl 19 | +4 | 105,000 gp | Lvl 29 | +6 | 2,625,000 gp |

Item Slot: Neck

Enhancement: Fortitude, Reflex, and Will

Property: Gain an item bonus to Intimidate checks equal to the cloak's enhancement bonus.

Power (Daily ✦ Fire): Minor Action. Until the end of your next turn, your melee attacks deal extra fire damage equal to the cloak's enhancement bonus. Also, until the end of your next turn, an enemy that hits you with a melee attack takes 3d6 fire damage.
Level 19: 4d6 fire damage.
Level 24: 5d6 fire damage.
Level 29: 6d6 fire damage.

Gloaming Shroud — Level 3+

This billowing cloak drinks in the light around it.

Lvl 3	+1	680 gp	Lvl 18	+4	85,000 gp
Lvl 8	+2	3,400 gp	Lvl 23	+5	425,000 gp
Lvl 13	+3	17,000 gp	Lvl 28	+6	2,125,000 gp

Item Slot: Neck

Enhancement: Fortitude, Reflex, and Will

Property: Gain an item bonus to Stealth checks in dim light or darkness equal to the shroud's enhancement bonus.

Power (Daily ✦ Zone): Minor Action. Create a zone of dim light (close burst 10) that lasts until the end of the encounter. Bright light created or brought into the zone is reduced to dim light while within the zone.

Gorget of Reciprocity — Level 30

Runic symbols meaning "an eye for an eye" adorn this decorative platinum neck armor.

Item Slot: Neck   3,125,000 gp

Enhancement: Fortitude, Reflex, and Will

Power (Daily): Immediate Reaction. Use this power when you are hit by an attack. The attacker is also hit by the attack (no attack roll required); the damage roll and effects are identical to the attack against you.

Healer's Brooch — Level 4+

This innocuous adornment boosts your healing powers.

Lvl 4	+1	840 gp	Lvl 19	+4	105,000 gp
Lvl 9	+2	4,200 gp	Lvl 24	+5	525,000 gp
Lvl 14	+3	21,000 gp	Lvl 29	+6	2,625,000 gp

Item Slot: Neck

Enhancement: Fortitude, Reflex, and Will

Property: When you use a power that enables you or an ally to regain hit points, add the brooch's enhancement bonus to the hit points gained.

Evil Eye Fetish — Level 8+

The vile bloodshot eye attached to this rawhide collar punishes those who seek to take advantage of you.

Lvl 8	+2	3,400 gp	Lvl 23	+5	425,000 gp
Lvl 13	+3	17,000 gp	Lvl 28	+6	2,125,000 gp
Lvl 18	+4	85,000 gp			

Item Slot: Neck

Enhancement: Fortitude, Reflex, and Will

Property: An enemy with combat advantage against you that hits you takes necrotic damage equal to this item's enhancement bonus.

Fireflower Pendant — Level 7+

Formed from a string of fire opals, this ornament unleashes fiery retribution.

Lvl 7	+2	2,600 gp	Lvl 22	+5	325,000 gp
Lvl 12	+3	13,000 gp	Lvl 27	+6	1,625,000 gp
Lvl 17	+4	65,000 gp			

Item Slot: Neck

Enhancement: Fortitude, Reflex, and Will

Property: If you take fire damage from an enemy attack, the first attack you make before the end of your next turn deals extra fire damage equal to the pendant's enhancement bonus.

Liar's Trinket
Level 13+

No two of these adornments look alike, but all appear to be mundane necklaces of little value.

| Lvl 13 | +3 | 17,000 gp | Lvl 23 | +5 | 425,000 gp |
| Lvl 18 | +4 | 85,000 gp | Lvl 28 | +6 | 2,125,000 gp |

Item Slot: Neck

Enhancement: Fortitude, Reflex, and Will

Property: Gain an item bonus to Bluff checks equal to the trinket's enhancement bonus. While you wear the trinket, it appears nonmagical unless an observer succeeds on an Arcana check (DC 20 + the trinket's level).

Property: Whenever you are subject to a divination or scrying ritual, such as Discern Lies or Observe Creature, the ritualist must succeed on an Arcana check opposed by your Bluff check. If the ritualist's check fails, the ritual doesn't work on you, the ritualist cannot discern the source of the failure, and resources are expended as normal to perform the ritual.

Life Charm
Level 25+

This small, heart-shaped pendant beats softly after you fall in battle, drawing your fleeting spirit back from death's door.

| Lvl 25 | +5 | 625,000 gp | Lvl 30 | +6 | 3,125,000 gp |

Item Slot: Neck

Enhancement: Fortitude, Reflex, and Will

Property: Automatically succeed on death saving throws.

Medallion of Death Deferred
Level 9+

This distinctive talisman holds the icy grip of death in check.

Lvl 9	+2	4,200 gp	Lvl 24	+5	525,000 gp
Lvl 14	+3	21,000 gp	Lvl 29	+6	2,625,000 gp
Lvl 19	+4	105,000 gp			

Item Slot: Neck

Enhancement: Fortitude, Reflex, and Will

Power (Daily): No Action. Use this power when you are reduced to 0 hit points or fewer. You regain hit points equal to 3 per plus of this item.

Moonlight Lavaliere
Level 18+

This pendant sheds a soft moonlight glow when you are attacked, dazing enemies that hit you.

| Lvl 18 | +4 | 85,000 gp | Lvl 28 | +6 | 2,125,000 gp |
| Lvl 23 | +5 | 425,000 gp | | | |

Item Slot: Neck

Enhancement: Fortitude, Reflex, and Will

Power (Daily): Minor Action. Until the end of the encounter or until you make an attack, you gain a +2 bonus to all defenses, and any creature that hits you is dazed until the start of your next turn.

Necklace of Fireballs
Level 15+

A star ruby, glowing with inner fire, hangs from an iron chain.

| Lvl 15 | +3 | 25,000 gp | Lvl 25 | +5 | 625,000 gp |
| Lvl 20 | +4 | 125,000 gp | Lvl 30 | +6 | 3,125,000 gp |

Item Slot: Neck

Enhancement: Fortitude, Reflex, and Will

Power (Daily ✦ Fire): Standard Action. Pull the ruby from the necklace and throw it. Make an attack: Area burst 2 within 10 squares; Intelligence or Dexterity vs. Reflex (add the necklace's enhancement bonus to the attack roll); on a hit, the target takes fire damage equal to 5d6 + the necklace's enhancement bonus (half damage on a miss). After an extended rest, the necklace regrows a new ruby and can be used again.
Level 20: 6d6 + enhancement bonus fire damage.
Level 25: 7d6 + enhancement bonus fire damage.
Level 30: 8d6 + enhancement bonus fire damage.

Ornament of Alertness
Level 3+

This small amulet or token is etched with an eye and sharpens your senses.

Lvl 3	+1	680 gp	Lvl 18	+4	85,000 gp
Lvl 8	+2	3,400 gp	Lvl 23	+5	425,000 gp
Lvl 13	+3	17,000 gp	Lvl 28	+6	2,125,000 gp

Item Slot: Neck

Enhancement: Fortitude, Reflex, and Will

Property: Gain an item bonus to Perception checks equal to the ornament's enhancement bonus.

Power (Daily): Minor Action. Until the end of the encounter, enemies don't gain the normal +2 bonus to attack rolls when you grant them combat advantage. They still gain any other benefit of combat advantage.

Peacemaker's Periapt
Level 8+

Carved from alabaster and shaped into the stylized likeness of a dove, this amulet enhances your charm.

Lvl 8	+2	3,400 gp	Lvl 23	+5	425,000 gp
Lvl 13	+3	17,000 gp	Lvl 28	+6	2,125,000 gp
Lvl 18	+4	85,000 gp			

Item Slot: Neck

Enhancement: Fortitude, Reflex, and Will

Property: Gain an item bonus to Diplomacy checks equal to the periapt's enhancement bonus.

Power (Daily ✦ Charm): Minor Action. Choose a target within 10 squares of you. That target takes a –2 penalty to melee and ranged attack rolls against you for the remainder of the encounter or until you attack it (whichever comes first).

Periapt of Recovery
Level 8+

Ward off death's grasp with this small pendant.

Lvl 8	+2	3,400 gp	Lvl 23	+5	425,000 gp
Lvl 13	+3	17,000 gp	Lvl 28	+6	2,125,000 gp
Lvl 18	+4	85,000 gp			

Item Slot: Neck

Enhancement: Fortitude, Reflex, and Will

Property: Gain a +2 item bonus to death saving throws.

Resilience Amulet — Level 8+

A platinum disk overlaid with a crystalline star, this amulet repels lasting injuries.

Lvl 8	+2	3,400 gp	Lvl 23	+5	425,000 gp
Lvl 13	+3	17,000 gp	Lvl 28	+6	2,125,000 gp
Lvl 18	+4	85,000 gp			

Item Slot: Neck

Enhancement: Fortitude, Reflex, and Will

Power (Daily): Immediate Reaction. Use this power when you are hit by an attack that deals ongoing damage. Make a saving throw against the ongoing damage. On a failure, you don't expend the use of this power and no daily use of a magic item power occurs.

1. Resilience amulet; 2. Steadfast amulet

Star of the Astral Sea — Level 29

This immense blue star sapphire glows when your allies approach death and allows you to use your own life force to rejuvenate them.

Lvl 29 +6 2,625,000 gp

Item Slot: Neck

Enhancement: Fortitude, Reflex, and Will

Power (Daily): Free Action. Use this power when an ally in line of sight is reduced to 0 or fewer hit points. Spend a healing surge. The ally regains hit points as if he or she had spent a healing surge.

Steadfast Amulet — Level 8+

The crystal set in this amulet helps to focus your mind.

Lvl 8	+2	3,400 gp	Lvl 23	+5	425,000 gp
Lvl 13	+3	17,000 gp	Lvl 28	+6	2,125,000 gp
Lvl 18	+4	85,000 gp			

Item Slot: Neck

Enhancement: Fortitude, Reflex, and Will

Power (Daily): Immediate Interrupt. Use this power when you are dazed or stunned by an attack. Make a saving throw against the condition. On a failure, you don't expend the use of this power and no daily use of a magic item power occurs.

Talisman of Repulsion — Level 30

This platinum talisman is inset with astral diamonds that flash brightly and unleash a burst of force when you are threatened.

Lvl 30 +6 3,125,000 gp

Item Slot: Neck

Enhancement: Fortitude, Reflex, and Will

Power (Daily): Immediate Reaction. Use this power when you are hit by a melee attack. Make an attack against the enemy that attacked you: Melee 1; +35 vs. Fortitude; on a hit, the target slides 5 squares and is immobilized until the end of your next turn.

Tattered Cloak — Level 19+

This ragged cloak holds a secret defense.

Lvl 19	+4	105,000 gp	Lvl 29	+6	2,625,000 gp
Lvl 24	+5	525,000 gp			

Item Slot: Neck

Enhancement: Fortitude, Reflex, and Will

Power (Daily ✦ Charm): Minor Action. Make an attack: Close burst 5; targets each enemy in burst; item's level + 3 vs. Will defense; the target cannot attack you (save ends).

Torc of Power Preservation — Level 15+

This platinum and gold neckband contains a reservoir of energy that you can tap.

Lvl 15	+3	25,000 gp	Lvl 25	+5	625,000 gp
Lvl 20	+4	125,000 gp	Lvl 30	+6	3,125,000 gp

Item Slot: Neck

Enhancement: Fortitude, Reflex, and Will

Power (Daily): Free Action. Use this power after you use an encounter power of the torc's level or lower. Roll 1d20 + the torc's enhancement bonus. If the result is 10 or higher, that power renews as if you had taken a short rest. If the result is lower than 10, you don't expend the use of this power and no daily use of a magic item power occurs.

ANNE STOKES

Wyrmtouched Amulet

Level 19+

Shaped in the likeness of a dragon and adorned with Draconic runes, this handsome amulet is a boon to dragonborn.

Lvl 19	+4	105,000 gp	Lvl 29	+6	2,625,000 gp
Lvl 24	+5	525,000 gp			

Item Slot: Neck

Enhancement: Fortitude, Reflex, and Will

Property: If you are a dragonborn, gain resist 10 to the same type of damage dealt by your *dragon breath* power. After you use your *dragon breath* power, the resistance increases to 20 until the end of your next turn.

Level 24: Resist 15, resist 30 after using *dragon breath*

Level 29: Resist 20, resist 40 after using *dragon breath*

Power (Daily): Immediate Reaction. Use this power when you become bloodied. If you have the *dragon breath* power, you can use it even if you have already expended it this encounter.

RINGS

These symbols of power adorn the hands of mighty kings and legendary heroes alike.

Because of the energy invested in magic rings, only those who attain significant power can create them. As such, characters might not see their first magic ring until they have already attained paragon level.

RINGS

Lvl	Name	Price (gp)
14	Cherished ring	21,000
14	Magician's ring	21,000
14	Ring of brotherhood	21,000
14	Ring of calling	21,000
14	Ring of feather fall	21,000
14	Ring of fireblazing	21,000
14	Ring of perfect grip	21,000
15	Premonition ring	25,000
15	Ring of aquatic ability	25,000
15	Ring of shadow travel	25,000
15	Ring of the dragonborn emperor	25,000
16	Chameleon ring	45,000
16	Cognizance ring	45,000
16	Ring of forgetful touch	45,000
16	Ring of personal gravity	45,000
16	War ring	45,000
17	Banquet ring	65,000
17	Ring of arcane information	65,000
17	Ring of retreat	65,000
17	Ring of vigilant defense	65,000
18	Bone ring of better fortune	85,000
18	Face-stealing ring	85,000
18	Ring of dread	85,000
18	Ring of ramming	85,000
18	Ring of shadow guard	85,000
18	Ring of the protector	85,000

RINGS (CONTINUED)

Lvl	Name	Price (gp)
19	Amethyst band of invisible eyes	105,000
19	Bone ring of preservation	105,000
19	Ring of the spectral hand	105,000
19	Star ruby ring	105,000
20	Ring of spell storing	125,000
21	Ring of heroic insight	225,000
21	Ring of tenacious will	225,000
22	Blink ring	325,000
22	Luminary ring	325,000
22	Ring of fey travel	325,000
23	Ring of adaptation	425,000
24	Ritualist's ring	525,000
25	Gargoyle ring	625,000
25	Sorrowsworn ring	625,000
27	Ring of the phoenix	1,625,000
27	Shadow band	1,625,000
29	Opal ring of remembrance	2,625,000
30	Nullifying ring	3,125,000
30	Ring of spell storing, greater	3,125,000

Amethyst Band of Invisible Eyes

Level 19

This band of pristine amethyst is favored by spellcasters seeking indirect targeting capability.

Item Slot: Ring   105,000 gp

Property: Determine line of sight from the square you occupy or any square adjacent to you. Determine cover from the square you occupy as normal.

Power (Daily): Minor Action. Choose a square within 10 squares of you. Determine line of sight from this square until the end of your next turn.

If you've reached at least one milestone today, you also gain darkvision until the end of your next turn.

Banquet Ring

Level 17

Monarchs, and those who fear what might be in their food, treasure these gaudy, gem-encrusted baubles.

Item Slot: Ring   65,000 gp

Property: You gain a +5 item bonus to Fortitude defense against attacks with the poison keyword.

Power (Daily): Minor Action. You are immune to ingested poisons until the end of the encounter.

If you've reached at least one milestone today, you can extend this protection to a number of people within your line of sight equal to your level.

Blink Ring — Level 22

This adamantine ring moves from finger to finger, much in the same way that you can move from place to place while wearing it.

Item Slot: Ring   325,000 gp

Property: You gain a +3 item bonus to Thievery checks.

Power (Daily ✦ Teleportation): Minor Action. Teleport 1d4 squares.

Sustain Minor: Teleport 1d4 squares at the start of your turn.

If you've reached at least one milestone today, you do not need to use a minor action to sustain the item's effect.

Bone Ring of Better Fortune — Level 18

Formed from coated bones cleverly entwined, this tiny circlet fortifies your life force.

Item Slot: Ring   85,000 gp

Property: Reduce by half the necrotic damage you take.

Power (Daily): Immediate Interrupt. Use this power when you are hit by an attack with the necrotic keyword. After applying any resistance, choose either to take no damage or to ignore an effect imposed by that attack, but not both.

If you've reached at least one milestone today, you take no damage and ignore any effects imposed by that attack.

Bone Ring of Preservation — Level 19

This plain, bone ring protects its wearer from life-draining effects.

Item Slot: Ring   105,000 gp

Property: You gain resist 15 necrotic.

Power (Daily): Free Action. Use this power when an effect would make you lose a healing surge. You do not lose the healing surge.

If you've reached at least one milestone today, the source of the effect takes 3d10 damage.

Chameleon Ring — Level 16

This lizard skin band is barely visible against your skin and makes you equally hard to discern.

Item Slot: Ring   45,000 gp

Property: Gain a +2 item bonus to Stealth checks. Gain a +4 item bonus instead if you have not moved since the start of your last turn.

Power (Daily): Minor Action. You do not require cover or concealment to make Stealth checks until the end of your next turn.

If you've reached at least one milestone today, this power lasts until the end of the encounter.

Cherished Ring — Level 14

You and your words are more alluring when you wear this simple loop of burnished gold.

Item Slot: Ring   21,000 gp

Property: Gain a +2 item bonus to Diplomacy checks.

Power (Daily ✦ Charm): Standard Action. Make an attack: Ranged 10; Charisma vs. Will; on a hit, the target moves its speed toward you.

If you've reached at least one milestone today, the target must spend one move action on each of its turns to move closer to you (save ends).

Cognizance Ring — Level 16

Inlaid with tourmaline gems, this electrum trinket strengthens your mind and spirit.

Item Slot: Ring   45,000 gp

Property: Gain a +1 item bonus to saving throws against conditions with the charm, fear, illusion, or psychic keyword.

Power (Daily): Minor Action. Gain a +5 power bonus to saving throws against conditions with the charm, fear, illusion, or psychic keyword until the end of the encounter.

If you've reached at least one milestone today, you also gain a +2 power bonus to Will defense against powers with those keywords.

Face-Stealing Ring — Level 18

This wearer of this ivory ring sees the faces of others as potential disguises.

Item Slot: Ring   85,000 gp

Property: You gain a +2 item bonus to Insight checks.

Power (Daily ✦ Illusion): Standard Action. You assume the exact appearance of an adjacent humanoid creature. You also gain the creature's mannerisms, voice, and speech patterns. This effect lasts for 1 hour or until you dismiss it (a free action). You gain a +5 power bonus to Bluff checks to pass yourself off as the creature you're imitating.

If you've reached at least one milestone today, the effect lasts for one day and you can use a standard action to recall the effect after dismissing it.

Gargoyle Ring — Level 25

Wearing this ring of rough stone allows you to adopt a rocky form.

Item Slot: Ring   625,000 gp

Property: While you are petrified, you can make a saving throw at the end of your turn to remove the effect.

Power (Daily): Standard Action. You become a stone statue, gaining resist 25 to all damage and tremorsense 10. You lose all other senses and can take no actions in this form other than a minor action to resume your normal form.

If you've reached at least one milestone today, you can spend a healing surge to regain hit points equal to your surge value at the same time you turn into a statue or resume your normal form.

Luminary Ring — Level 22

You are more able to aid your allies with this gold ring, which bears a faintly glowing sigil signifying your ideals.

Item Slot: Ring   325,000 gp

Property: Increase the range of powers that restore hit points or provide a bonus to your allies by a number of squares equal to your Charisma modifier.

Power (Daily): Free Action. Use this power when you grant one or more allies a power bonus. Increase that bonus by 1 for all targets for the duration of that power.

If you've reached at least one milestone today, increase the affected bonus by 2.

Magician's Ring — Level 14

Tricksters and hedge wizards everywhere love this cheap-looking gold ring.

Item Slot: Ring   21,000 gp

Property: Double the ranges of your *ghost sound* and *prestidigitation* powers.

Power (At-Will): Standard Action. Use *ghost sound* as the wizard's power (*PH* 158).

Power (At-Will): Standard Action. Use *prestidigitation* as the wizard's power (*PH* 159).

If you've reached at least one milestone today, double the duration of effects created using this ring.

Nullifying Ring — Level 30

Formed from a metal as black as a starless night, this band counters attacks made against you.

Item Slot: Ring   3,125,000 gp

Property: Gain a +3 item bonus to saving throws.

Power (Daily): Immediate Interrupt. Use this power when you would be hit by an attack. Gain a +6 power bonus to all defenses against that attack. A critical hit scored against you with that attack is instead considered a normal hit.

If you've reached at least one milestone today, the attack automatically misses and you take no damage from it.

Opal Ring of Remembrance — Level 29

The large fire opal set into this bauble flares brightly when it bestows mental clarity.

Item Slot: Ring   2,625,000 gp

Property: Gain a +2 item bonus to Intelligence attacks, and a +4 item bonus to Intelligence checks and Intelligence-based skill checks.

Power (Daily): Minor Action. Regain the use of an arcane encounter utility power that you have already used (as if you hadn't used it this encounter).

If you've reached at least one milestone today, you can instead regain the use of an arcane daily utility power (as if you hadn't used it today).

Premonition Ring — Level 15

With this dark obsidian ring on your finger, you act quickly when faced with danger.

Item Slot: Ring   25,000 gp

Property: Gain a +2 item bonus to initiative and passive Perception checks.

Power (Daily): No Action. Use this power when you are surprised. You are not surprised.

If you've reached at least one milestone today, you also move 3 squares and take a minor action.

Ring of Adaptation — Level 23

This silvery metal loop is engraved with Primordial runes, protecting you from elemental effects.

Item Slot: Ring   425,000 gp

Property: Gain a +5 item bonus to Endurance checks to endure extreme weather.

Power (Daily): Immediate Interrupt. Use this power when you would take acid, cold, fire, lightning, or thunder damage. Take half damage from that damage type until the end of your next turn.

If you've reached at least one milestone today, this power lasts until the end of the encounter.

Ring of Aquatic Ability — Level 15

While you wear this aquamarine jeweled band, breathing and moving underwater comes as naturally to you as breathing air and walking on land.

Item Slot: Ring   25,000 gp

Property: Gain a swim speed equal to your speed. You can breathe underwater.

If you've reached at least one milestone today, gain a swim speed equal to twice your speed.

Ring of Arcane Information — Level 17

This ring helps you discern the nature of arcane phenomena.

Item Slot: Ring   65,000 gp

Property: You gain a +5 item bonus to Arcana checks made to detect magic.

Power (Daily): Minor Action. You detect magic within 20 squares of you in every direction, and you can ignore any sources of magical energy you're already aware of. Ignore all barriers; you can detect magic through walls, doors, and such.

If you've reached at least one milestone today, you also learn the name, power source, and keywords of any magical effects in the area.

Ring of Brotherhood — Level 14

These platinum rings come in pairs and are shared only by the closest companions.

Item Slot: Ring   21,000 gp

Property: Each of these rings is part of a set of two. As a minor action, a ring wearer can ascertain the following information:

✦ The current hit points and general status (alive, dying, or dead) of the other ring wearer

✦ The number of healing surges the other ring wearer has remaining

✦ Any effects currently affecting the other ring wearer

✦ The current emotional state of the other ring wearer

✦ The straight-line distance to the other ring wearer. If the other ring wearer is on a different plane, neither the distance nor the specific plane can be ascertained.

Special: These rings come in pairs. If one ring is disenchanted, the other loses all its magic. The cost covers a set of rings.

Power (Daily): Free Action. Transfer a single healing surge to the wearer of the other ring. This cannot bring the recipient above his or her total healing surges.

If you've reached at least one milestone today, transfer two healing surges.

Ring of Calling — Level 14

This mithral ring brings you and your allies closer together in times of need.

Item Slot: Ring   21,000 gp

Property: When an ally adjacent to you uses a teleport power, he or she can increase the distance teleported by 4 squares.

Power (Daily ✦ Teleportation): Minor Action. Choose one ally within 20 squares of you and within line of sight. That ally is teleported to any unoccupied square adjacent to you.

If you've reached at least one milestone today, you can instead teleport to a square adjacent to an ally within 20 squares of you.

Ring of calling

Ring of Dread — Level 18

This rough iron ring heightens your enemies' fears and weakens their defenses.

Item Slot: Ring   85,000 gp

Property: Gain a +2 item bonus to Intimidate checks.

Power (Daily ✦ Fear): Standard Action. Make an Intimidate check against an enemy within 5 squares of you, and compare the result to each of the target's defenses (AC, Fortitude, Reflex, and Will). The target takes a -2 penalty to any defense your check equals or exceeds (save ends all).

If you've reached at least one milestone today, the target must make a separate saving throw for each defense penalized.

Ring of Feather Fall — Level 14

With this airy mithral filigree band, you and sometimes your allies need not fear a fall even from the highest cliff.

Item Slot: Ring   21,000 gp

Property: You take no damage from a fall and always land on your feet.

Power (Daily): Minor Action. Allies within 5 squares of you also benefit from this ring's property until the end of the encounter.

If you've reached at least one milestone today, allies within 10 squares of you also benefit.

Ring of Fey Travel — Level 22

Wearing this shimmering feywood ring, you move with other-worldly speed, seemingly out of phase at times.

Item Slot: Ring   325,000 gp

Property: Gain a +1 item bonus to speed while wearing light armor or no armor.

Power (Daily ✦ Teleportation): Minor Action. Teleport your speed.

If you've reached at least one milestone today, this power lasts until the end of your next turn.

Ring of Fireblazing — Level 14

Fire springs from the hand that bears this red steel ring.

Item Slot: Ring   21,000 gp

Property: As a standard action, ignite any unattended combustible object (such as cloth, oil, paper, tinder, or a torch) that you touch.

Power (Daily ✦ Fire): Standard Action. Make an attack: Close blast 3; Constitution + 4 or Charisma + 4 vs. Reflex; on a hit, the target takes 1d10 + Constitution modifier or Charisma modifier fire damage and ongoing 5 fire damage (save ends); on a miss, the target takes half damage and no ongoing damage.

If you've reached at least one milestone today, a hit deals 1d10 + Constitution modifier or Charisma modifier fire damage and ongoing 10 fire damage (save ends). On a miss, deal half damage and ongoing 5 fire damage (save ends).

Ring of Forgetful Touch — Level 16

This unassuming copper band makes your words more convincing, and even temporarily erases the memory of an unwitting target.

Item Slot: Ring   45,000 gp

Property: Gain a +1 item bonus to Bluff checks.

Power (Daily ✦ Charm): Standard Action. Make an attack: Melee 1; Dexterity + 4 vs. Will; on a hit, the target forgets everything that took place in the last minute and is surprised until the end of your next turn.

If you've reached at least one milestone today, the subject does not notice the memory loss and does not regain the memory until 1 minute has passed.

Ring of Heroic Insight — Level 21

While wearing this scored adamantine trinket, you more easily notice weaknesses—mental, physical, or social.

Item Slot: Ring   225,000 gp

Property: Gain a +3 item bonus to Insight checks.

Power (Daily): Minor Action. Choose a target. Gain a +2 power bonus to attack rolls and a +6 power bonus to damage rolls against that target until the end of your next turn. If the target is an object, instead apply a +6 power bonus to Strength checks to break it.

If you've reached at least one milestone today, instead gain a +3 power bonus to attack rolls, and a +8 bonus to damage rolls, or to Strength checks to break.

Ring of Perfect Grip — Level 14

This rough alloy band gives you a grip of steel when you are about to fall.

Item Slot: Ring   21,000 gp

Property: Gain a +5 item bonus to saving throws to catch yourself from falling.

Power (Daily): Immediate Interrupt. Use this power when you would be forced over a precipice or into a pit. You automatically succeed on the saving throw to catch yourself from falling.

If you've reached at least one milestone today, you do not fall prone when you catch yourself from falling.

Ring of Personal Gravity — Level 16

This gray metal band keeps your enemies within reach.

Item Slot: Ring   45,000 gp

Property: When an effect forces you to move—through a pull, a push, or a slide—you can move 1 square less than the effect specifies.

Power (Daily): Minor Action. You and enemies adjacent to you or marked by you are either slowed or immobilized (your choice). For marked enemies, save ends. For adjacent enemies, no saving throw is allowed. As a free action, you can end the effect of this power on you and all affected creatures.

If you've reached at least one milestone today, while you are under the effect of this power's condition, any newly marked enemies or enemies that move adjacent to you are also affected by the chosen condition.

Ring of Ramming — Level 18

This iron ring is inlaid with the image of a ram's head.

Item Slot: Ring   85,000 gp

Property: When you push a target, you can increase the distance pushed by 1 square.

Power (Daily ✦ Force): Standard Action. Make an attack: Ranged 10; +21 vs. Fortitude; on a hit, the target takes 3d10 force damage and is pushed 1 square (this distance can be increased by the ring's property). You can instead use this power to make a Strength attack to break down a door or other object using the same attack bonus.

If you've reached at least one milestone today, a hit deals 5d10 force damage and pushes the target 3 squares (which can be increased by the ring's property).

Ring of Retreat — Level 17

This silver ring allows you to teleport farther. It can also transport you and your allies to a distant redoubt.

Item Slot: Ring   65,000 gp

Property: When you use a teleport power, you can increase the distance teleported by 1 square.

Power (Daily ✦ Teleportation): Standard Action. You teleport to a predetermined location, set into the ring at its creation. This location cannot be determined through examination of the ring. For up to ten hours after, you can spend another standard action to teleport back to your original location. You can reset a ring's target location with the Enchant Magic Item ritual. The component cost to perform the ritual for this purpose is 32,500 gp.

If you've reached at least two milestones today, teleport yourself and up to 7 allies.

Ring of Shadow Guard — Level 18

While wearing this dark iron ring, your shadow is infused with black tendrils from the Shadowfell.

Item Slot: Ring   85,000 gp

Property: Gain resist 10 cold and resist 10 necrotic.

Power (Daily ✦ Cold, Necrotic): Standard Action. You infuse your shadow with the essence of the Shadowfell. Until the end of your next turn, any enemy that starts its turn or moves adjacent to you takes 2d10 cold and necrotic damage.

If you've reached at least one milestone today, you also gain 15 temporary hit points. This benefit lasts until none of these temporary hit points remain or until you take an extended rest.

Ring of Shadow Travel — Level 15

This dark iron ring lets you disappear into the shadows.

Item Slot: Ring   25,000 gp

Property: Gain a +2 item bonus to Stealth checks.

Power (Daily ✦ Teleportation): Move Action. Teleport 4 squares. If the space you teleport from is not brightly lit, you can teleport 8 squares. You cannot teleport to a brightly lit space. If you've reached at least one milestone today, double all teleport distances of this power.

Ring of ramming

Ring of Spell Storing   Level 20

This intricate wooden ring stores a measure of arcane power that can be unlocked in a time of need.

Item Slot: Ring   125,000 gp

Property: During an extended rest, you can store one at-will or encounter arcane power in this ring for future use. You can place a power that you know into the ring as long as the power's level is no higher than the ring's level. The name of the power currently contained in the ring appears in etched Elven script on the inside of the band.

Power (Daily ✦ Arcane): Standard Action. Use the arcane power stored in the ring as long as the stored power's level is no higher than your level. If the stored arcane power is an encounter power, you must expend an action point to unlock it. Use the stored arcane power as normal, but replace any required implement and its enhancement bonus with this ring and a +4 enhancement bonus.

Once the stored arcane power is used, another arcane power must be stored in the ring before it can be used again. If a new arcane power is stored before a previously stored one is used, the previously stored power is lost. If you've reached at least one milestone today, gain a +1 bonus to the attack roll of the stored power.

Ring of Spell Storing, Greater   Level 30

This handsome gold ring contains a measure of arcane power that can be unlocked in a time of need.

Item Slot: Ring   3,125,000 gp

Property: During an extended rest, you can store one at-will or encounter arcane power that you know in this ring for future use. The name of the power currently contained in the ring appears in luminous Elven script on the inside of the band.

Power (Daily ✦ Arcane): Standard Action. Use the arcane power stored in the ring as long as the stored power's level is no higher than your level. If the stored arcane power is an encounter power, you must expend an action point to unlock it. Use the stored arcane power as normal, but replace any required implement and its enhancement bonus with this ring and a +6 enhancement bonus.

Once the stored arcane power is used, another arcane power must be stored in the ring before it can be used again. If a new arcane power is stored before a previously stored one is used, the previously stored power is lost. If you've reached at least one milestone today, gain a +1 bonus to the attack roll of the stored power.

Ring of Tenacious Will — Level 21

Striped with platinum and amber, this band allows you to survive on force of personality rather than toughness of body.

Item Slot: Ring   225,000 gp

Property: Use Charisma instead of Constitution to determine the number of healing surges you possess.

Power (Daily ✦ Healing): No Action. Use this power when you would be reduced to 0 hit points or fewer. You are reduced to 1 hit point instead.

    If you've reached at least one milestone today, you also regain a number of hit points equal to your level.

Ring of the Dragonborn Emperor — Level 15

Modelled after the signet rings worn by the dragonborn emperors of Arkhosia, this item enhances your attacks, particularly if you are a dragonborn.

Item Slot: Ring   25,000 gp

Property: Gain a +3 item bonus to damage rolls with close attacks. If you are dragonborn, gain a +5 item bonus to damage rolls with your *dragon breath*.

Power (Daily): Immediate Reaction. Use this power when you become bloodied. Use one of your encounter powers. If you've reached at least one milestone today, you can use an encounter power that you have already expended. If you use a power that has not already been expended, you don't expend the use of that power.

Ring of the Phoenix — Level 27

This red and gold ring is etched with the symbol of a fiery bird.

Item Slot: Ring   1,625,000 gp

Property: You gain resist 15 fire.

Power (Daily ✦ Fire): No Action. Use this power when you die or when you are dying. Your body burns away to ash. On the start of your next turn, you appear in a burst of flame within 5 squares of your last location with a number of hit points equal to your healing surge value.

    If you've reached at least one milestone today, the burst of flame surrounding your return is treated as an attack: Close burst 2; Constitution + 6 or Charisma + 6 vs. Reflex; the target takes 4d10 + Constitution modifier or Charisma modifier fire damage on a hit, or half damage on a miss.

Ring of the Protector
Level 18

Creations of the eladrin, these paired mithral and jade rings bond you to another.

Item Slot: Ring   85,000 gp

Property: Each of these rings is part of a set of two. As a minor action, a ring wearer can ascertain the following information:

✦ The current hit points and general status (alive, dying, or dead) of the other ring wearer

✦ The number of healing surges the other ring wearer has remaining

✦ Any effects currently affecting the other ring wearer

✦ The current emotional state of the other ring wearer

✦ The straight-line distance to the other ring wearer. If the other ring wearer is on a different plane, neither the distance nor the specific plane can be ascertained.

Special: These rings come in pairs. If one ring is disenchanted, the other loses all its magic. The cost covers a set of rings.

Power (Daily ✦ Teleportation): Standard Action. Teleport to a square adjacent to the wearer of the other ring, regardless of distance.

If you've reached at least one milestone today, this power uses a minor action.

Ring of the Spectral Hand
Level 19

With a silent command, this onyx band conjures a translucent hand, and sometimes a spectral eye as well.

Item Slot: Ring   105,000 gp

Property: Gain resist 10 radiant.

Power (Daily ✦ Conjuration): Free Action. A spectral hand appears in any square you can see within 6 squares of you and casts a power with the implement keyword that you know. Use the square occupied by the spectral hand to determine line of effect and cover for your attack. You expend the power as normal.

If you've reached at least one milestone today, a spectral eye also appears in the same square. Use that square to determine line of sight and concealment for your attack.

Ring of Vigilant Defense
Level 17

This large ring is composed of overlapping miniature iron, steel, mithral, and adamantine shields.

Item Slot: Ring   65,000 gp

Property: Gain a +4 item bonus to all defenses when using total defense.

Power (Daily): Minor Action. Gain a +2 bonus to all defenses until the start of your next turn.

If you've reached at least one milestone today, gain a +3 power bonus to all defenses until the end of your next turn.

Ritualist's Ring
Level 24

This engraved mahogany ring allows you to cast rituals more quickly and easily.

Item Slot: Ring   525,000 gp

Property: Gain a +2 item bonus to checks to perform rituals.

Power (Daily): Free Action. Reduce by half the time necessary to perform a ritual.

If you've reached at least one milestone today, also reduce the component cost by half.

Shadow Band
Level 27

This smoky obsidian ring envelops you in shadows, making you difficult to discern.

Item Slot: Ring   1,625,000 gp

Property: Gain concealment.

Power (Daily): Minor Action. Gain total concealment until the end of your next turn.

If you've reached at least one milestone today, this benefit lasts until the end of the encounter.

Sorrowsworn Ring
Level 25

You can siphon life force from those you kill using this loop of black feathers bearing two gleaming jet gems.

Item Slot: Ring   625,000 gp

Property: Gain darkvision and a +4 item bonus to Intimidate checks.

Power (Daily): Immediate Reaction. Use this power when you reduce a creature to 0 or fewer hit points. That creature dies and you gain a number of temporary hit points equal to your healing surge value.

If you've reached at least one milestone today, this power can be used as an immediate interrupt when you would be reduced to 0 or fewer hit points. Gain a number of temporary hit points equal to your healing surge value.

Star Ruby Ring
Level 19

This handsome ruby ring is favored by courtiers who rise and fall by the favor they earn with their honeyed words.

Item Slot: Ring   105,000 gp

Property: Gain a +2 item bonus to Diplomacy checks.

Power (Daily): Free Action. Use this power when making a Charisma-based skill check during a skill challenge. You can roll twice and take the better result.

If you've reached at least one milestone today, a successful roll on the skill challenge counts for two victories.

War Ring Level 16

This steel band, emblazoned with a stylized sword, makes your attacks even more lethal.

Item Slot: Ring   45,000 gp

Property: When you score a critical hit, deal 1 extra die of critical hit damage, based on the weapon or implement you wield. If your weapon or implement deals no extra damage when you score a critical hit, deal an extra 1d6 damage when you score a critical hit.

Power (Daily): Free Action. Use this power when you score a critical hit with a weapon or implement. Add 2 extra dice of critical hit damage based on the weapon or implement. If your weapon or implement deals no extra damage when you score a critical hit, deal an extra 2d6 damage when you score a critical hit.

If you've reached at least one milestone today, instead of rolling the extra dice of critical hit damage, deal extra damage equal to the maximum value of those dice.

WAIST SLOT ITEMS

Magic belts are great utility items. Wear one, and you'll never get caught with your pants down.

Waist slot items augment healing, defenses, and one's ability to face physical challenges, such as escaping a grab, carrying a heavy load, or resisting a bull rush. Although waist items might seem to be oriented toward defenders and characters who use martial powers, many spellcasters learn to appreciate the healing or resistance afforded by a magic belt, girdle, or baldric.

WAIST SLOT ITEMS

Lvl	Name	Price (gp)
1	Belt of resilience	360
2	Muleback harness	520
3	Belt of the brawler	680
4	Viper belt	840
5	Barbed baldric	1,000
5	Girdle of the oxen	1,000
6	Belt of endurance	1,800
6	Cincture of the dragon spirit	1,800
6	Stalwart belt	1,800
7	Belt of fitness	2,600
7	Belt of recovery	2,600
7	Contortionist's cord	2,600
7	Rope of slave fighting	2,600
8	Baldric of tactical positioning	3,400
8	Belt of vim	3,400
8	Centering cincture	3,400
8	Sash of ensnarement	3,400
8	Swimtide harness	3,400
9	Goliath's belt	4,200
9	Reinforcing belt	4,200

WAIST SLOT ITEMS (CONTINUED)

Lvl	Name	Price (gp)
10	Belt of blood	5,000
10	Shielding girdle	5,000
11	Backbone belt	9,000
11	Belt of resilience	9,000
11	Healer's sash	9,000
11	Rogue's belt	9,000
11	Survivor's belt	9,000
11	Totemic belt	9,000
12	Cingulum of combat rushing	13,000
12	Muleback harness	13,000
13	Cord of divine favor	17,000
14	Cincture of vivacity	21,000
15	Barbed baldric	25,000
15	Girdle of the umber hulk	25,000
15	Reality cord	25,000
16	Belt of endurance	45,000
16	Girdle of the dire bear	45,000
16	Stalwart belt	45,000
17	Rope of slave fighting	65,000
18	Baldric of tactical positioning	85,000
18	Belt of vim	85,000
18	Cord of foresight	85,000
18	Swimtide harness	85,000
21	Baldric of valor	225,000
21	Belt of resilience	225,000
21	Healer's sash	225,000
22	Muleback harness	325,000
23	Belt of vitality	425,000
23	Vengeance sash	425,000
25	Barbed baldric	625,000
25	Girdle of the umber hulk	625,000
26	Belt of endurance	1,125,000
26	Girdle of the dire bear	1,125,000
26	Stalwart belt	1,125,000
28	Belt of vim	2,125,000
28	Swimtide harness	2,125,000

Backbone Belt Level 11

Coupled with your second wind, this belt helps you stay in the fight longer.

Item Slot: Waist   9,000 gp

Property: Gain a +4 bonus (instead of the normal +2 bonus) to all defenses until the start of your next turn after using your second wind.

Baldric of Tactical Positioning Level 8+

This belt gives you greater command of the battlefield by helping you keep your enemies off-balance.

Lvl 8	3,400 gp	Lvl 18	85,000 gp

Item Slot: Waist

Power (Encounter): Minor Action. Choose one square adjacent to you. That square counts as an ally for the purpose of flanking until the end of your next turn.

Level 18: You can use this power twice per encounter.

Baldric of Valor — Level 21

This handsome belt rewards decisive action.

Item Slot: Waist   225,000 gp

Property: When you spend an action point, gain a +3 item bonus to saving throws, a +1 item bonus to attack rolls, and a +1 item bonus to all defenses. This benefit lasts until the end of your next turn.

Barbed Baldric — Level 5+

Hooked metal barbs spring from this belt on command, making it dangerous for anyone to grab you.

Lvl 5	1,000 gp	Lvl 25	625,000 gp
Lvl 15	25,000 gp		

Item Slot: Waist

Property: Enemies that are grabbing you take 1d8 damage at the start of your turn.
   Level 15: 2d8 damage.
   Level 25: 3d8 damage.

Belt of Blood — Level 10

This bloodstained belt helps you recover from serious injuries.

Item Slot: Waist   5,000 gp

Property: Your healing surge value increases by your Constitution modifier while you are bloodied.

Belt of Endurance — Level 6+

Stitched from the hides of various animals, this belt gives you a beastly endurance.

Lvl 6	1,800 gp	Lvl 26	1,125,000 gp
Lvl 16	45,000 gp		

Item Slot: Waist

Property: Gain a +2 item bonus to Endurance checks.
   Level 16: +4 item bonus.
   Level 26: +6 item bonus.

Power (Daily): Free Action. Use this power before you make a Endurance check. Treat that check as though you rolled a natural 20.

Belt of Fitness — Level 7

This well-made champion's belt lets you use your endurance to resist bodily harm.

Item Slot: Waist   2,600 gp

Power (Daily): Immediate Interrupt. Use this power when you would be hit by an attack against Fortitude defense. Make an Endurance check and use that result in place of your Fortitude defense.

Belt of Recovery — Level 7

When you suffer a telling blow, this belt bolsters your defenses, giving you a moment to recover.

Item Slot: Waist   2,600 gp

Property: When a critical hit is scored against you, gain a +2 item bonus to AC until the end of your next turn.

Belt of Resilience — Level 1+

This common and well-worn belt aids those who aid you.

Lvl 1	360 gp	Lvl 21	225,000 gp
Lvl 11	9,000 gp		

Item Slot: Waist

Property: Heal checks made to aid you gain a +2 item bonus.
   Level 11: +4 item bonus.
   Level 21: +6 item bonus.

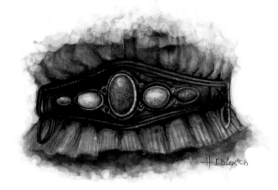

Belt of the Brawler — Level 3

Your punch packs a wallop when this belt is about your waist.

Item Slot: Waist   680 gp

Property: Make improvised attacks (included unarmed attacks) as if you were armed with a club.

Belt of Vim — Level 8+

You feel hale and hearty while wearing this wide belt.

Lvl 8	3,400 gp	Lvl 28	2,125,000 gp
Lvl 18	85,000 gp		

Item Slot: Waist

Property: Gain a +1 bonus to Fortitude defense.
   Level 18: +2 bonus to Fortitude defense.
   Level 28: +3 bonus to Fortitude defense.

Belt of Vitality — Level 23

This belt helps you keep death at bay.

Item Slot: Waist   425,000 gp

Property: Gain a +2 bonus to Fortitude defense.

Power (Daily ✦ Healing): No Action. Use this power when you make a death saving throw. Spend a healing surge.

Centering Cincture — Level 8

With this simple sash, you fend off attacks against your body.

Item Slot: Waist   3,400 gp

Power (Daily): Immediate Interrupt. Use this power when you are hit by an attack. Gain a +4 power bonus to your Fortitude defense until the end of your next turn.

Cincture of the Dragon Spirit — Level 6

This scaly belt infuses you with the ferocity of a dragon.

Item Slot: Waist   1,800 gp

Property: You can use your Strength modifier instead of your Charisma modifier when making Intimidate checks.

Cincture of Vivacity — Level 14

Wearing this heavy damask wrap, you can exceed your body's normal recuperative ability.

Item Slot: Waist   21,000 gp

Property: When you spend a healing surge and regain hit points above your maximum hit points, you can keep the extra hit points as temporary hit points until the end of the encounter.

Cingulum of Combat Rushing — Level 12

This heavily decorated belt pushes you straight through your foes.

Item Slot: Waist   13,000 gp

Power (Daily): Minor Action. You can move into squares occupied by enemies until the end of your next turn. Your movement provokes opportunity attacks as normal, and you cannot end your move in an occupied space.

Contortionist's Cord — Level 7

This extremely flexible snakeskin binding allows you to quickly squeeze through even the tightest spots.

Item Slot: Waist   2,600 gp

Property: While squeezing, you move at full speed and do not take penalties to attack rolls, but you still grant combat advantage.

Cord of Divine Favor — Level 13

A healer's garment, this cinch lets you tend to yourself as you aid others.

Item Slot: Waist   17,000 gp

Power (Encounter ✦ Healing): Free Action. Use this power when you use *healing word* on an ally or use another power that grants an ally the use of a healing surge. You can spend a healing surge as well and regain hit points equal to your healing surge value.

Cord of Foresight — Level 18

With the insight provided by this woven silk belt, you brace your body for physical danger.

Item Slot: Waist   85,000 gp

Property: After each extended rest, deduct 1 healing surge and gain temporary hit points equal to your healing surge value. These temporary hit points remain until lost, or until you take an extended rest.

Girdle of the Dragon — Level 16+

The translucent visage of a young dragon surrounds your body as you unleash the draconic spirit embodied in this magic item.

| Lvl 16 | 45,000 gp | Lvl 26 | 1,125,000 gp |

Item Slot: Waist

Property: Gain a +2 bonus to Fortitude defense.

Power (Daily): Standard Action. Make two attack rolls: Melee 1; Strength + 3 vs. AC; on a hit, the target takes 3d6 + Strength modifier damage. If both attacks hit the same target, the target is grabbed (until escape).

Level 26: Strength + 6 vs. AC, 3d10 + Strength modifier damage.

Girdle of the Oxen — Level 5

With this belt, you can bull rush enemies farther than normal.

Item Slot: Waist   1,000 gp

Property: When you bull rush a target, you push it 1 additional square.

Girdle of the Umber Hulk — Level 15+

This belt, cut from the carapace of an umber hulk, grants you the power to tunnel through the ground.

| Lvl 15 | 25,000 gp | Lvl 25 | 625,000 gp |

Item Slot: Waist

Property: Gain a +2 bonus to Fortitude defense.

Power (Daily): Minor Action. Gain a burrow speed equal to half your speed. You cannot dig through solid rock or shift while burrowing. Sustain minor.

Level 25: Gain a burrow speed equal to your speed. You can dig through solid rock at half your burrow speed.

Goliath's Belt — Level 9

This hide belt makes it easier for you to push people around.

Item Slot: Waist   4,200 gp

Property: You gain a +2 item bonus on Strength attacks to bull rush or grab a target. In addition, you can attempt to bull rush or grab a target up to two sizes larger than you.

Healer's Sash — Level 11+

With this white homespun wrap, you can keep your allies going long after they have exhausted their healing resources.

Lvl 11	9,000 gp	Lvl 21	225,000 gp

Item Slot: Waist

Property: This sash can have no more than 5 charges at one time and resets to 1 charge after an extended rest.

Power (At-Will): Standard Action. You or an adjacent ally expends a healing surge but does not regain hit points as normal. Instead, add 1 charge to this sash.

Power (Encounter ✦ Healing): Immediate Reaction. Use this power when an ally within 5 squares of you takes damage. Expend 1 charge from the belt. The ally regains hit points as though he or she had spent a healing surge, and regains an extra 1d6 hit points.

Level 21: +2d6 hit points.

Muleback Harness — Level 2+

This unadorned leather harness allows you to carry and drag heavier loads.

Lvl 2	520 gp	Lvl 22	325,000 gp
Lvl 12	13,000 gp		

Item Slot: Waist

Property: When determining your normal load, heavy load, or maximum drag load (*PH* 222), treat your Strength score as 5 points higher.

Level 12: 10 points higher.

Level 22: 15 points higher.

Reality Cord — Level 15

First crafted by the gith races, this waistband roots you in a reality that doesn't recognize the place of aberrant creatures.

Item Slot: Waist   25,000 gp

Property: Gain a +1 item bonus to damage rolls, Fortitude defense, and Will defense against aberrant creatures.

Power (Daily): Free Action. Use this power when you fail a saving throw against an effect placed on you by an aberrant creature. Reroll the saving throw with a +5 power bonus, using the second result even if it's lower.

Reinforcing Belt — Level 9

This sturdy belt offers magical protection when you need it most.

Item Slot: Waist   4,200 gp

Property: Only the wearer of this belt can remove it. If the wearer is dead, anyone else can remove the belt as a standard action.

Property: Enemies cannot perform a coup de grace against you while you are helpless.

Rogue's Belt — Level 11

No one can hold you, no chains can restrain you, and no bars can contain you while you wear this slick belt.

Item Slot: Waist   9,000 gp

Property: You can attempt to escape a grab or restraints as a minor action.

Rope of Slave Fighting — Level 7+

You fight as well on your back as on your feet while wearing this frayed rope belt.

Lvl 7	2,600 gp	Lvl 17	65,000 gp

Item Slot: Waist

Property: You do not take the −2 penalty to attack rolls while prone.

Level 17: You also do not grant combat advantage while prone.

Sash of Ensnarement — Level 8

While wearing this long braided wrap, your reach rarely exceeds your grasp.

Item Slot: Waist   3,400 gp

Property: Gain reach 2 for purposes of grab attacks. Also, you do not need a free hand to make a grab attack.

Power (Daily): Free Action. Use this power when you would spend a minor action to sustain a grab. The sash detaches from you and sustains the grab for you. You no longer need to sustain the grab or remain adjacent to the creature. During this time, you do not benefit from the sash's property. The sash uses your Fortitude and Reflex defenses for resisting the creature's escape. It holds the creature in place until you command it to cease or the creature escapes, at which time the sash returns to you.

Reinforcing belt

ED COX

Shielding girdle

Swimtide Harness

Level 8+

More than a few sea captains who have lost their ships in storms have survived due to these blue oilskin straps.

Lvl 8	3,400 gp	Lvl 28	2,125,000 gp
Lvl 18	85,000 gp		

Item Slot: Waist

Property: Gain a +2 item bonus to Athletics checks made to swim, and to Endurance checks made to hold your breath, swim, or tread water.

Level 18: +4 item bonus.

Level 28: +6 item bonus.

Shielding Girdle

Level 10

This item helps you turn away physical attacks.

Item Slot: Waist   5,000 gp

Power (Daily): Immediate Interrupt. Use this power when you would be hit by an attack. Gain a +4 power bonus to AC until the end of your next turn.

Totemic Belt

Level 11

This colorful hide belt infuses you with the ferocity of a wild beast, augmenting your attacks.

Item Slot: Waist   9,000 gp

Power (Daily): Minor Action. Use this power when you charge. Gain a +1 power bonus to all Strength, Constitution, and Dexterity attack rolls and the subsequent damage rolls until the end of the encounter.

Stalwart Belt

Level 6+

Each time you deal a grievous wound to an enemy, you feel the invigorating power of this belt.

Lvl 6	1,800 gp	Lvl 26	1,125,000 gp
Lvl 16	45,000 gp		

Item Slot: Waist

Property: When you score a critical hit, gain temporary hit points equal to your Constitution modifier.

Level 16: Equal to twice your Constitution modifier.

Level 26: Equal to three times your Constitution modifier.

Vengeance Sash

Level 23

This dark binding allows you to vent your wrath against those who defeat you in battle.

Item Slot: Waist   425,000 gp

Power (Daily): Immediate Interrupt. Use this power when you are reduced to 0 or fewer hit points. Use any attack power you can perform as a standard action.

Viper Belt

Level 4

This snakeskin belt provides modest protection against poison.

Item Slot: Waist   840 gp

Property: Gain resist 5 poison.

Power (Encounter): No Action. Use this power when making a saving throw against ongoing poison damage. Gain a +2 power bonus to the saving throw.

Survivor's Belt

Level 11

This belt gives you the ability to stabilize even when near death.

Item Slot: Waist   9,000 gp

Property: You roll two death saving throws, taking the higher result.

Sash of ensnarement

WONDROUS ITEMS

Welcome to the bazaar of the bizarre! Sometimes the most useful items are also the most peculiar.

Wondrous items include a hodgepodge of trinkets, devices, and oddities that can't be placed within the normal equipment slots.

WONDROUS ITEMS

Lvl	Name	Price (gp)
1	Eternal chalk	360
1	Restful bedroll	360
2	Hunter's flint	520
2	Shroud of protection	520
2	Silent tool	520
3	Floating lantern	680
4	Bridle of conjuration	840
4	Chime of awakening	840
5	Enchanted reins	1,000
5	Instant campsite	1,000
5	Lamp of discerning	1,000
5	Pouch of platinum	1,000
5	Power jewel	1,000
5	Ruby scabbard	1,000
6	Polyglot gem	1,800
6	Solitaire (cinnabar)	1,800
6	Watchful ruby eye	1,800
7	Enshrouding candle	2,600
7	Horn of summons	2,600
7	Jar of steam	2,600
7	Lens of reading	2,600
7	Phantom soldier	2,600
7	Shroud of revival	2,600
7	Stylus of the translator	2,600
8	Death rattle	3,400
8	Dust of arcane insight	3,400
8	Fan of the four winds	3,400
9	Darkskull	4,200
9	Endless canteen	4,200
9	Endless quiver	4,200
9	Harmonious harp	4,200
9	Map of orienteering	4,200
9	Pouch of frozen passage	4,200
10	Bowl of purity	5,000
10	Chime of warding	5,000
10	Crystal ball of spying	5,000
10	Dust of disenchantment	5,000
10	Lens of discernment	5,000
10	Salve of power	5,000
10	Scabbard of sacred might	5,000
10	Skeleton key	5,000
10	Spymaster's quill	5,000
11	Solitaire (citrine)	9,000
11	Unfettered thieves' tools	9,000
12	Exodus knife	13,000

WONDROUS ITEMS (CONTINUED)

Lvl	Name	Price (gp)
12	Foe stone	13,000
12	Fragrance of authority	13,000
12	Immovable shaft	13,000
13	Drum of panic	17,000
14	Golden spade	21,000
14	Sail of winds	21,000
15	Flying hook	25,000
15	Invulnerable case	25,000
15	Pouch of shared acquisition	25,000
15	Sapphire scabbard	25,000
15	Talisman of fortune	25,000
16	Gem of auditory recollection	45,000
16	Lantern of revelation	45,000
16	Solitaire (aquamarine)	45,000
17	Bottled smoke	65,000
17	Horn of blasting	65,000
17	Horn of undead enmity	65,000
18	Dust of creation	85,000
18	Earthbind lodestone	85,000
19	Deadblast bone	105,000
20	Crystal ball of spying	125,000
20	Mirror of opposition	125,000
21	Solitaire (cerulean)	225,000
25	Chime of opening	625,000
25	Diamond scabbard	625,000
25	Dust of banishment	625,000
26	Solitaire (violet)	1,125,000
27	Mummified hand	1,625,000
28	Charm of abundant action	2,125,000

Bottled Smoke — Level 17

This brass bottle is hot to the touch, spewing forth a cloud of ash and smoke when opened.

Wondrous Item   65,000 gp

Power (Daily ✦ Fire, Zone): Standard Action. When you uncork the bottle, hot smoke fills a close burst 3 until the end of your next turn. This zone of smoke provides concealment to all creatures within it. Any creature other than you that starts its turn within the smoke takes 2d6 fire damage.

Sustain Minor: You must be within 10 squares of the zone to sustain it.

Bowl of Purity — Level 10

This plain earthenware bowl can purify food and drink.

Wondrous Item   5,000 gp

Power (Daily): Standard Action. When you place food or drink within the *bowl of purity*, it is cleansed of poison and diseases of 10th level or lower.

Bridle of Conjuration — Level 4

This simple leather bridle conjures a magical mount for your use.

Wondrous Item   840 gp

Power (Daily ✦ Conjuration): As a standard action, you conjure a riding horse (*MM* 159) in a space adjacent to you. The bridle transforms into the mount's tack and saddle. The horse serves you, obeying your spoken commands to the best of its ability, though it does not attack even in defense. The horse disappears after 12 hours or if reduced to 0 hit or fewer points.

Charm of Abundant Action — Level 28

This plain metal charm allows you to outrun or outfight your foes.

Wondrous Item   2,125,000 gp

Power (Encounter): Free Action. Use this power on your turn to spend an action point (assuming you have one available). You can spend the action point even if you spent an action point earlier in the encounter. You must be holding the charm when you spend the second action point.

Chime of Awakening — Level 4

This silver chime sounds an alarm in the minds of you and your resting allies.

Wondrous Item   840 gp

Power (Daily): Standard Action. You set the *chime of awakening* to ring when a specific trigger occurs within 10 squares of it. Example triggers include the presence of anyone other than you and your allies, the light of the sun touching the area, or the appearance of a specific character or type of creature. The chime rings in the minds of you and all allies within 10 squares of it. You and affected allies are instantly awoken (if asleep) and alert.

The *chime of awakening* can be fooled by creatures in disguise. It makes active Perception checks with a +10 modifier.

Chime of Opening — Level 25

The subtle tone of this fluted mithral chime can overcome traps, wards, and the toughest locks.

Wondrous Item   625,000 gp

Power (Daily): Standard Action. When you strike the chime, you direct it to open a single locked or trapped door, chest, gate, or other object within 5 squares of you. Make a single Thievery check with a +30 modifier against the DCs required to open the object and disable any traps on it. Depending on the DCs, it is possible for the chime to unlock an object but not disable the traps on it (or vice versa), or to disable some traps but leave others intact.

Chime of Warding — Level 10

The air around you shimmers with protective force when you strike this golden chime.

Wondrous Item   5,000 gp

Power (Daily ✦ Zone): As a standard action, strike this chime to create a close burst 2 that lasts until the end of your next turn. Any enemy that enters the zone is attacked: +15 vs. Fortitude. A hit pushes the target 1 square away from the center of the burst and immobilizes it until the start of its next turn. If you or any ally makes an attack while in the zone, the effect ends. Sustain standard.

Crystal Ball of Spying — Level 10+

This clear crystal orb flickers with the hazy images of distant people and places.

Lvl 10	5,000 gp	Lvl 20	125,000 gp

Wondrous Item

Property: When you use this crystal ball as a focus for a scrying ritual, gain a +2 item bonus to Arcana checks made during that ritual. The value of this crystal ball must meet the focus cost requirement for the ritual, as normal.
Level 20: +4 item bonus.

Darkskull — Level 9

Darkness swells around this menacing onyx skull.

Wondrous Item   4,200 gp

Power (Encounter ✦ Illusion): As a minor action, you cause all active light sources within 10 squares of you to be suppressed until the end of the encounter. Light sources activated after you use this power function normally.

Deadblast Bone — Level 19

This rune-scarred bone has the power to temporarily stun undead.

Wondrous Item   105,000 gp

Power (Daily): Standard Action. Make an attack: Close burst 5; targets undead creatures; +22 vs. Will; on a hit, the target is stunned until the end of your next turn or until it is attacked, whichever comes first.

Death Rattle — Level 8

Bone shards clatter within this black-beaded rattle, making your necrotic attacks more potent.

Wondrous Item   3,400 gp

Power (Daily ✦ Necrotic): Minor Action. You and all allies within 10 squares of you gain a +1 power bonus to attack rolls and damage rolls with powers that have the necrotic keyword. This effect lasts until the end of your next turn. Sustain minor.

Diamond Scabbard
Level 25

A blade drawn from this diamond-studded scabbard is granted an incomparable magical edge.

Wondrous Item 625,000 gp

Property: This scabbard resizes to fit any light blade or heavy blade. You can draw a weapon from this scabbard as part of the same action used to make an attack with that weapon.

Power (Encounter): Free Action. Use this power when you attack with the weapon most recently sheathed in the scabbard. Gain a +5 power bonus to the next damage roll you make with that weapon before the end of your next turn.

The weapon must have been sheathed in the scabbard within the past 24 hours to gain this power.

Drum of Panic
Level 13

Covered with the hide of a cacklefiend hyena, this drum strikes fear into the hearts of your enemies.

Wondrous Item 17,000 gp

Power (Daily ✦ Fear): Minor Action. When you strike the drum, you and each ally within 10 squares of you gain a +2 power bonus to attack rolls and damage rolls with powers that have the fear keyword. This effect lasts until the end of your next turn. Sustain minor.

Dust of Arcane Insight
Level 8

This foil pouch periodically renews a supply of metallic dust that attunes you to arcane effects.

Wondrous Item 3,400 gp

Power (3/Day): Standard Action. Pull out and toss a pinch of dust into the air above you. You gain the ability to detect magic for 5 minutes even if you are not trained in the Arcana skill. You also gain a +2 power bonus to Arcana checks made to identify a conjuration or zone, identify a magical effect, or sense the presence of magic (see the Arcana skill entry, *PH* 181).

A pouch of *dust of arcane insight* can be used three times per day.

Dust of Banishment
Level 25

The crimson powder periodically renewed by this red leather pouch can banish a creature to a fiery prison.

Wondrous Item 625,000 gp

Power (Daily): Standard Action. You sprinkle a handful of this dust on an adjacent creature. Make an attack: Melee 1; +28 vs. Will; on a hit, the target is banished to a fiery corner of the Elemental Chaos, where it is stunned and takes ongoing 10 fire damage. A save ends both effects and returns the target to its original location or the closest unoccupied space.

Dust of Creation
Level 18

This clear bottle periodically renews a supply of golden sand that can transform into any object.

Wondrous Item 85,000 gp

Power (Daily ✦ Conjuration): Standard Action. When you toss a handful of this dust into the air, it settles in the form of any mundane nonmagical object with a weight of up to 25 pounds. The fully functional object glows faintly and radiates magic that can be detected with a DC 24 Arcana check. The object lasts for 24 hours or until you will it back to dust (a minor action).

Dust of Disenchantment
Level 10

The sparkling silver dust periodically renewed within this leather pouch can suppress the effects of magic.

Wondrous Item 5,000 gp

Power (Daily): Standard Action. Sprinkle a pinch of this dust on an adjacent object or magical effect. Make an attack: Dexterity vs. Reflex. If you are targeting a held item, make the attack against the creature holding it. If you are targeting an unattended magic item or magical effect, use a Reflex defense of 10 + the level of the object or effect. A hit renders that object or effect inert (save ends). An inert magic item loses any properties and enhancement bonus, and its powers cannot be activated. An inert magical effect is suppressed.

Special: You can use a dose of *dust of disenchantment* in place of the required component cost for a Disenchant Magic Item ritual.

Earthbind Lodestone
Level 18

When thrown to the ground, this smooth metallic stone hits with such force that it knocks airborne creatures from the sky.

Wondrous Item 85,000 gp

Power (Daily): Standard Action. Throw this stone to the ground in your square and make an attack: Close burst 5; affects creatures with a fly speed; +23 vs. Fortitude; on a hit, the target loses the ability to fly or hover until the start of its next turn. If a target is airborne when it is hit, it falls.

Enchanted Reins
Level 5

Made of woven silver and black leather, these reins can help tame even the most savage beast.

Wondrous Item 1,000 gp

Property: These reins resize to fit any Small, Medium, or Large natural beast. All Nature checks made to handle a natural beast fitted with the *enchanted reins* gain a +2 item bonus.

Endless Canteen — Level 9

This mundane-looking canteen pours forth water in a seemingly limitless stream.

Wondrous Item 4,200 gp

Power (At-Will): Standard Action. When you open its stopper, the *endless canteen* pours out up to 1 pint of cool, clean water. Any water that has not been consumed within 1 hour of its creation disappears.

Endless Quiver — Level 9

This elven-styled quiver can create an endless supply of normal arrows or bolts.

Wondrous Item 4,200 gp

Power (At-Will ✦ Conjuration): Free Action. Use this power as part of your action when you attack with a bow or crossbow. When you reach into the *endless quiver*, it automatically produces a single arrow or bolt, as appropriate. Ammunition created by the quiver that is not used within 1 round of its creation disappears.

Enshrouding Candle — Level 7

This everburning candle creates a dim corona of light that helps conceal you from foes.

Wondrous Item 2,600 gp

Property: This candle sheds dim light in a 2-square radius, but it never burns down. Bright light within the candle's radius is reduced to dim light.

Power (Daily ✦ Illusion): Standard Action. When the *enshrouding candle* is lit, it generates an illusion within the area of its illumination. Creatures within the area are invisible to those outside the area, though other features within the area appear as normal. Sound (including speech) within the area is likewise inaudible to those outside. Creatures within the area are unaffected by the illusion and can perceive each other normally.

Other senses are unaffected by the *enshrouding candle*. For example, a creature with tremorsense could locate characters in the area normally. Likewise, if characters within the area move objects around them, those moving objects can be seen.

The candle burns for 8 hours or until it is moved or extinguished (a minor action). If any character within the area of the illusion attacks, the candle is automatically extinguished.

Eternal Chalk — Level 1

Vandals, scholars, and explorers alike appreciate the magical longevity of this short stick of chalk.

Wondrous Item 360 gp

Property: A stick of *eternal chalk* never breaks or wears down with normal use. Any writing or drawing made with this chalk cannot be erased for one week by anyone except the original artist or author.

A stick of *eternal chalk* can be created in any color.

Exodus Knife — Level 12

This insubstantial silver blade appears to cut through solid walls.

Wondrous Item 13,000 gp

Power (Daily): Standard Action. When you use the *exodus knife* to trace a doorway onto a solid object, it opens a portal into an empty extradimensional space 4 squares wide, 4 squares high, and 4 squares long.

While the door is open, anyone can enter, see into, or affect the extradimensional space. Only creatures inside the space can open or close the door (a minor action). Once closed, the door becomes invisible to anyone outside the extradimensional space. Creatures on the inside of the closed door can see out, but those outside can't see in. Creatures on one side of the closed door cannot affect creatures on the other side.

The extradimensional space lasts for 8 hours. Any creatures still in the space when the effect ends reappear in the closest unoccupied squares outside the door.

Fan of the Four Winds — Level 8

A wave of this fan sends a blast of air against a foe.

Wondrous Item 3,400 gp

Power (Daily): Standard Action. Sweep this fan through the air and make an attack against a Large or smaller creature: Ranged 5; +13 vs. Fortitude; on a hit, you push the target 2 squares. Until the start of your next turn, each time the target moves a square closer to you, it must pay 1 extra square of movement. Sustain standard. If you end your turn more than 5 squares from the target, the effect ends.

Floating Lantern — Level 3

This silver lantern floats in midair under your control.

Wondrous Item 680 gp

Property: This lantern never needs lighting or refilling. When you let go of the lantern, it continues to hang in the air where you leave it. If weight in excess of 1 pound is applied to the lantern, it falls to the ground.

Power (At-Will): Minor Action. While you hold the *floating lantern* or are adjacent to it, you can set its light to be bright (10-square radius), dim (5-square radius), or off.

Power (At-Will): Move Action. The last creature to hold the lantern can mentally command it to move up to 10 squares in any direction, but not more than 10 squares from it.

Flying Hook
Level 15

This grappling hook flies through the air and can latch onto almost anything.

Wondrous Item 25,000 gp

Power (At-Will): Minor Action. You command the flying hook to fly 10 squares (up to a maximum distance of 20 squares from you) and magically latch onto the surface of any unattended object in your line of sight. Once secured, the flying hook extends a thin rope back to your hands. The rope can be climbed with an Athletics check, or it can be used to pull the object toward you with a Strength check. The hook and rope can support up to 3,000 pounds before the hook detaches from the surface. The rope cannot be tied or knotted in any way, nor can it be used to attack or affect a creature.

Power (At-Will): Minor Action. On your command, the hook detaches from a surface and returns to your hand. This causes the rope to retract.

Foe Stone
Level 12

This lodestone is set into a chain, and when aimed toward an enemy, it grants you understanding of your foes' weaknesses.

Wondrous Item 13,000 gp

Power (At-Will): Minor Action. Choose one creature you can see. You learn all the target's vulnerabilities, as well as which of its defenses is lowest.

Fragrance of Authority
Level 12

This opaque alabaster bottle periodically renews a subtle perfume that can influence the reactions of others.

Wondrous Item 13,000 gp

Power (Daily): Standard Action. Apply the perfume to yourself or an adjacent ally. The target gains a +2 power bonus to Bluff, Diplomacy, or Intimidate checks (the target's choice) for 1 hour.

Gem of Auditory Recollection
Level 16

This rough-cut quartz gemstone echoes with faint voices when held to the ear.

Wondrous Item 45,000 gp

Power (At-Will): Standard Action. Use this power to record all words spoken by one creature within 20 squares of you. You can end the transcription as a free action. The gem can record 12 hours of speech before becoming full.

Power (At-Will): Standard Action. Use this power to make the gem repeat a section of recorded text aloud in the exact voice and language of the original speaker. The gem continues its recitation until the section is finished or until you use a free action to stop it.

Power (At-Will): Standard Action. Erase all speech recorded by the gem.

Golden Spade
Level 14

This magic shovel instantly clears away a section of earth, ice, or sand to create a deep trench.

Wondrous Item 21,000 gp

Power (Daily): Standard Action. Plunge the golden spade into the ground to create a pit that fills squares in a close burst 2, 3, or 4 (your choice). The pit is 2 squares deep. The pit can only form in an area of earth, ice, or sand. Any creature on the ground whose space is entirely within the bounds of the pit falls into the pit unless it makes a saving throw to catch itself (see Falling, *PH* 284).

Harmonious Harp
Level 9

The melodious tones of this harp fortify your senses and your mind.

Wondrous Item 4,200 gp

Power (Daily): Standard Action. When you strum this harp, you and every ally within 10 squares of you can make a saving throw against an effect with the charm or fear keyword that a save can end. You and affected allies also gain resist 10 psychic until the end of your next turn.

Foe stone

Horn of Blasting — Level 17

This adamantine-trimmed hunting horn unleashes a powerful blast of thunder when blown.

Wondrous Item 65,000 gp

Power (Daily ✦ Thunder): Standard Action. When you sound the horn, make an attack: Close blast 5; +19 vs. Fortitude; on a hit, the target takes 2d10 thunder damage and is dazed and deafened until the end of your next turn; on a miss, the target takes half damage and is deafened until the end of your next turn. On a critical hit, the target is also pushed 1 square and knocked prone.

Horn of Summons — Level 7

This steel battle horn alerts even those allies you cannot see.

Wondrous Item 2,600 gp

Power (Encounter): Standard Action. When you sound the horn, all creatures within 1 mile hear its call. Allies within that range are awakened if they are sleeping, and instantly know your current location, hit point total, and any effects currently affecting you.

Horn of Undead Enmity — Level 17

The haunting sound of this bone horn forces undead to turn against their own allies.

Wondrous Item 65,000 gp

Power (Daily ✦ Charm): Standard Action. When you sound the horn, make an attack: Close blast 5; targets undead only; +20 vs. Will. On a hit, the target makes its next attack against one of its adjacent allies. If it has no adjacent allies, it charges its nearest ally. If the target can't attack or charge, it moves its speed away from you.

Hunter's Flint — Level 2

This chunk of flint strikes sparks that can ignite a magical blaze.

Wondrous Item 520 gp

Power (Daily ✦ Illusion): Standard Action. Use this flint to light a campfire. The fire burns without smoke or sound. The light of this magic campfire is invisible from outside its 10-square radius, though creatures and objects within that radius can be seen normally with darkvision or if existing light allows. The campfire is a normal fire in all other respects. The fire lasts for 12 hours (requiring no additional fuel) or until extinguished normally. The flint can be used to light lanterns and other fires as normal, but such fires gain no magical effect.

Immovable Shaft — Level 12

This 1-foot-long black metal rod can defy gravity, supporting weight and resisting manipulation.

Wondrous Item 13,000 gp

Power (At-Will): Minor Action. Place the *immovable shaft* into position. It remains in that spot even if such placement defies gravity. You can reposition the *immovable shaft* using another minor action, but any other creature seeking to move it must succeed on a DC 25 Strength check and spend a standard action to move it 1 square.

Instant Campsite — Level 5

This tightly packed satchel expands into a complete campsite that can automatically pack up again.

Wondrous Item 1,000 gp

Power (Daily): Standard Action. You open the satchel and it magically expands into a complete campsite, including a campfire and four two-person tents with bedrolls. The campfire lasts for up to 12 hours (requiring no fuel) or until you spend another standard action to pack the campsite back into the satchel once more.

Invulnerable Case — Level 15

This smooth metal case protects its contents from all but the most devastating damage.

Wondrous Item 25,000 gp

Property: The *invulnerable case* can hold one item the size of a large book. It opens easily to the touch of one wanting to access its contents, but otherwise stays closed despite any external forces acting on it. The case has resist 30 to all damage and 100 hit points, and it regenerates 10 hit points per hour. As long as the case has at least 1 hit point, any item held within it is immune to damage.

Jar of Steam
Level 7

This clay jar is warm to the touch. When opened, it creates a cloud of steam that fills the area around it.

Wondrous Item   2,600 gp

Power (Daily ✦ Zone): Standard Action. When you pull the lid off the jar, hot steam fills a close burst 1 until the end of your next turn. This zone of steam provides concealment to all creatures within it. Any creature other than you that starts its turn within the zone takes 1d6 fire damage. Sustain minor; you must be within 10 squares of the zone.

Lamp of Discerning
Level 5

This plain-looking lantern grants those in its light the ability to see through deception.

Wondrous Item   1,000 gp

Property: This lantern sheds light in a 10-square radius as normal, but it never needs lighting or refilling. You and all allies within the area of illumination gain a +1 power bonus to Insight and Perception checks.

Lantern of Revelation
Level 16

Light from this lantern reveals even the most well-hidden foes.

Wondrous Item   45,000 gp

Property: This lantern sheds light in a 10-square radius as normal, but it never needs lighting or refilling.

Power (Daily): Minor Action. This power creates a close burst 10 that coats all creatures in the area with glowing motes of light (save ends). Affected creatures gain no benefit from concealment or invisibility.

Lens of Discernment
Level 10

This lens reveals useful information regarding a creature you observe.

Wondrous Item   5,000 gp

Power (Encounter): Minor Action. Hold the lens up to a creature that you can see. You gain a +10 power bonus to monster knowledge checks made to identify the creature until the start of your next turn.

Lens of Reading — Level 7

Holding this lens to your eye allows you to read even the most complex scripts and obscure languages.

Wondrous Item   2,600 gp

Power (Daily): Standard Action. Use this power while perusing text written in a language you do not know. For 1 hour, you can read that language as long as you hold the *lens of reading*.

Special: You can activate the *lens of reading* in place of the required component cost for a Comprehend Languages ritual.

Map of Orienteering — Level 9

As you unfold this sheet of parchment, sepia ink spreads across its surface to depict your immediate surroundings.

Wondrous Item   4,200 gp

Property: As long as it is opened, this map automatically and continuously reproduces the area within 100 feet in all directions. It can reproduce only what you have seen personally, so invisible objects, undiscovered traps or secret doors, and unknown areas around the next corner do not appear on the map. Illusions are faithfully reproduced unless you have previously recognized them as false. Creatures are not shown on the map unless they take the form of objects (for example, a gargoyle in *stone form* or an earthwind ravager disguised as a pile of rocks) and have not been recognized for what they are.

The map shows the area within 100 feet by default, but you can mentally command it to zoom in or out to display any areas explored within the last 24 hours (a minor action).

The *map of orienteering* automatically erases and begins redrawing after you take an extended rest, unless you command it to do otherwise.

Mirror of Opposition — Level 20

This small, ornately framed mirror briefly reverses your opponent's loyalties.

Wondrous Item   125,000 gp

Power (Daily ✦ Charm): Standard Action. Hold this mirror up to an enemy within 5 squares of you and make an attack against that enemy: Ranged 5; +23 vs. Will; on a hit, the target treats its allies as enemies and its enemies as allies until the end of your next turn. It takes opportunity attacks against its former allies but not against you and your allies. As a free action on the target's turn, you can command the target to make a basic attack (using its standard action for its turn) against any other target or targets of your choice. However, you cannot command the target to use any of its other powers.

Mummified Hand — Level 27

This gnarled hand allows you to gain the benefit of a third ring.

Wondrous Item   1,625,000 gp

Property: The *mummified hand* has one ring item slot that you can use in addition to your own ring item slots. As long as you hold the *mummified hand*, you gain the benefit and can use the powers of any ring placed on one of its fingers. If two or more rings are placed on the *mummified hand*, none of the rings function. You cannot benefit from more than one *mummified hand*.

Phantom Soldier — Level 7

This tiny figurine is carved in the shape of a warrior and can be used summon a life-sized illusion of the depicted warrior to distract your enemies in battle.

Wondrous Item   2,600 gp

Power (Daily ✦ Illusion): Minor Action. You must have the figurine in your hand to use this power. An illusory soldier appears in an unoccupied square adjacent to you or an enemy within 5 squares of you. The soldier is treated as one of your allies and can be used to flank enemies, but it does not make attacks.

The illusory soldier has the same defenses as you and 1 hit point. It never takes damage on a miss. Once per round, you can use a minor action to move the soldier up to your speed. The illusory soldier remains until the end of the encounter or for 5 minutes.

Polyglot Gem — Level 6

This intricately carved gemstone holds the secrets of language within its many facets.

Wondrous Item   1,800 gp

Property: Each *polyglot gem* contains the knowledge of one language, chosen when the item is created. As long as you carry the gem on your person, you are able to speak, read, and write that language fluently.

If you carry more than one *polyglot gem* on your person, none of them function.

Special: If you create a *polyglot gem*, you can imbue it only with a language you know.

Pouch of Frozen Passage — Level 9

This pouch periodically renews a flurry of ice crystals that can freeze any liquid surface.

Wondrous Item   4,200 gp

Power (Daily): Standard Action. You fling ice crystals from the pouch onto an area of open liquid, freezing up to 20 contiguous squares of the liquid's surface. The frozen surface is normal terrain and can support the weight of up to twenty Medium creatures, five Large creatures, or one Huge creature.

The *pouch of frozen passage* can solidify any sort of liquid, from water to lava. The frozen surface has the following statistics: AC 3, Fortitude 15, Reflex 3, hp 20 per square. It lasts for 4 hours or until destroyed.

Pouch of Platinum
Level 5

This platinum-embossed leather pouch can convert gems and coins into platinum pieces.

Wondrous Item   1,000 gp

Property: Normal gemstones and coins of any denomination placed into the pouch are converted to an equal value of platinum pieces. Coins or gems that cannot be evenly converted to platinum pieces are unaffected.

Pouches of Shared Acquisition
Level 15

These simple leather pouches share a bond of powerful magic.

Wondrous Item   25,000 gp

Property: These two matched leather pouches magically share the same interior space. Whatever is placed in one pouch (to a maximum weight of 3 pounds) can be accessed from the other pouch regardless of the distance between them, as long as both pouches are on the same plane. If the pouches are on different planes, neither pouch can access the interior space. Only one pouch can be accessed at a time.

Power Jewel
Level 5

Magical energy pulses within this stunning red jewel, allowing you to use a power you have already expended.

Wondrous Item   1,000 gp

Power (Daily): Minor Action. This power allows you to regain the use of an encounter power of 1st or 3rd level.

Special: You must have reached at least one milestone today to activate this item.

Restful Bedroll
Level 1

An extended rest in this magic bedroll grants you extra vitality.

Wondrous Item   360 gp

Power (Daily): Standard Action. Use this power when you complete an extended rest in the *restful bedroll*. Gain 1d8 temporary hit points that last until you take another rest (short or extended).

Ruby Scabbard
Level 5

Blood-red rubies adorn this scabbard, their magic granting your blade an extra edge.

Wondrous Item   1,000 gp

Property: This scabbard resizes to fit any light blade or heavy blade. You can draw a weapon from this scabbard as part of the same action used to make an attack with that weapon.

Power (Encounter): Free Action. Use this power when you attack with the weapon most recently sheathed in the scabbard. Gain a +1 power bonus to the next damage roll you make with that weapon before the end of your next turn.

The weapon must have been sheathed in the scabbard within the past 24 hours to gain this power.

Sail of Winds
Level 14

Elemental runes run the length of this fine sail of blue cloth, which fills with its own wind as it is raised.

Wondrous Item   21,000 gp

Property: This sail grants a +2 item bonus to the miles-per-hour speed of any sailing ship it is installed on.

Salve of Power
Level 10

This stoneware jar periodically renews a potent unguent that can restore a character's power.

Wondrous Item   5,000 gp

Power (Daily): Minor Action. When *salve of power* is applied to a creature, the target can expend one healing surge to regain the use of one daily power of 5th level or lower (instead of regaining hit points). If the target has no healing surges remaining, it cannot benefit from the salve.

Sapphire Scabbard
Level 15

This scabbard bears a matched pair of azure sapphires whose magic imbues your blade with deadly sharpness.

Wondrous Item   25,000 gp

Property: This scabbard resizes to fit any light blade or heavy blade. You can draw a weapon from this scabbard as part of the same action used to make an attack with that weapon.

Power (Encounter): Free Action. Use this power when you attack with the weapon most recently sheathed in the scabbard. Gain a +3 power bonus to the next damage roll you make with that weapon before the end of your next turn.

The weapon must have been sheathed in the scabbard within the past 24 hours to gain this power.

Scabbard of Sacred Might — Level 10

The blade drawn from this simple leather scabbard glows with a sacred radiance.

Wondrous Item 5,000 gp

Property: This scabbard resizes to fit any light blade or heavy blade. You can draw a weapon from this scabbard as part of the same action used to make an attack with that weapon.

Power (Encounter ✦ Radiant): Free Action. Use this power when you attack with the weapon most recently sheathed in the scabbard. The next attack you make with that weapon before the end of your next turn deals radiant damage instead of its normal damage. The weapon must have been sheathed in the scabbard within the past 24 hours to gain this power.

Shroud of Protection — Level 2

This diaphanous shroud appears insubstantial. Yet when laid over a dying ally, it provides a defense stronger than steel.

Wondrous Item 520 gp

Power (Daily): Standard Action. When you place the *shroud of protection* over an adjacent dying creature, that creature gains resist 20 to all damage. This effect lasts until the creature regains consciousness or dies, or until the shroud is removed (a standard action), whichever comes first.

Shroud of Revival — Level 7

This white gossamer shroud grants protection and bodily strength to a dying ally.

Wondrous Item 2,600 gp

Power (Daily): Standard Action. When you place the *shroud of revival* over an adjacent dying creature, that creature gains resist 20 to all damage and a +2 power bonus to death saving throws. This effect lasts until the creature regains consciousness or dies, or until the shroud is removed (a standard action), whichever comes first.

Silent Tool — Level 2

This mundane-looking tool muffles the noise you make while you work.

Wondrous Item 520 gp

Property: When used to do the work it was designed for, a *silent tool* grants the user a +5 power bonus to Stealth checks made while using the tool. Any individual mundane tool—a woodcutter's axe, a crowbar, a grappling hook, a hammer, a shovel, and so on—can be made silent. For example, a *silent crowbar* could aid attempts to open a locked door without alerting the sleeping monster on the other side, while a *silent grappling hook* has less chance of being heard by nearby guards.

This property can be applied only to mundane tools. It cannot be placed on weapons, clothing, jewelry, or other mundane objects.

Skeleton Key — Level 10

This ornate ivory key opens locks with ease.

Wondrous Item 5,000 gp

Power (Daily): Standard Action. When you touch the key to a locked door, chest, gate, or other object, make a Thievery check with a +20 bonus against the DC required to open the lock.

Solitaire (Aquamarine) — Level 16

This jagged blue-green crystal lets you intensify your attacks against your foes.

Wondrous Item 45,000 gp

Power (Encounter): Free Action. Use this power when you score a critical hit on your turn. Make a basic attack against the same target struck by your critical hit.

Special: You cannot use more than one *solitaire* in an encounter.

Solitaire (Cerulean) — Level 21

This rough blue crystal grants you the ability to shake off lingering effects in the thick of combat.

Wondrous Item 225,000 gp

Power (Encounter): Free Action. Use this power when you score a critical hit on your turn. Roll a saving throw against each effect on you that a save can end.

Special: You cannot use more than one *solitaire* in an encounter.

Solitaire (Cinnabar) — Level 6

This jagged red crystal boosts your resilience when you hit your foes hard.

Wondrous Item 1,800 gp

Power (Encounter): Free Action. Use this power when you score a critical hit on your turn. Roll a saving throw against an effect that a save can end.

Special: You cannot use more than one *solitaire* in an encounter.

Solitaire (Citrine) — Level 11

This irregular yellow crystal channels healing power to you in battle.

Wondrous Item 9,000 gp

Power (Encounter ✦ Healing): Free Action. Use this power when you score a critical hit on your turn. You spend a healing surge.

Special: You cannot use more than one *solitaire* in an encounter.

Solitaire (Violet) — Level 26

This jagged purple crystal lets you follow up on a successful attack.

Wondrous Item   1,125,000 gp

Power (Encounter): Free Action. Use this power when you score a critical hit on your turn. Gain 1 action point, which you must spend before the end of your turn. This does not count against the normal limit of spending an action point no more than once per encounter.

Special: You cannot use more than one *solitaire* in an encounter.

Spymaster's Quill — Level 10

This ornate quill pen can magically record and reproduce any text or illustration.

Wondrous Item   5,000 gp

Power (At-Will): Standard Action. Pass the *spymaster's quill* over an amount of text or an illustration equivalent to a single parchment page. The image or text is magically recorded for later reproduction. Recording another page with the quill erases the page already recorded.

Power (At-Will): Standard Action. You point the *spymaster's quill* at a sheet of parchment or paper and mentally command it to reproduce the illustration or text recorded within it. No matter what the medium of the original (charcoal on paper, runes scribed in stone, and so on), the reproduction is rendered in normal ink.

Special: The reproduction created by the quill is of perfect quality, but the quill cannot record magical properties. For example, you cannot perform a ritual from a ritual scroll recorded and copied by the *spymaster's quill*, nor can the quill copy powers or rituals from a wizard's spellbook.

Stylus of the Translator — Level 7

This writing implement allows you to scribe in translation.

Wondrous Item   2,600 gp

Power (At-Will): Free Action. Whenever you write with the stylus, your writing is automatically translated into another language. Each stylus can translate into only one language, chosen when the item is created.

Special: You must be fluent in the language that you are writing for the stylus to function. For example, you could not copy text in an unknown language and have the stylus translate it into a known language.

Talisman of Fortune — Level 15

This small gold talisman renews a magic item or strengthens your health, attacks, and defenses in turn.

Wondrous Item   25,000 gp

Power (Daily): Minor Action. You must spend an action point to use this power. When you do, roll 1d20 and add +1 to the result for each milestone you've reached today. The total result determines the power's effect(s):

1-9: Lose 1 healing surge, or take damage equal to one-quarter of your maximum hit point total if you have no healing surges remaining. Gain one extra daily use of a magic item in your possession (your choice, not including the *talisman of fortune*) until the end of the encounter. You also renew the power of the talisman.

10-19: Recover one expended healing surge and gain a +1 power bonus to attack rolls and all defenses until the end of your next turn.

20 or higher: As 10-19, and you renew the power of the talisman.

Unfettered Thieves' Tools — Level 11

The picks, keys, tweezers, and tongs that comprise this set of thieves' tools move through the air and operate under your mental command.

Wondrous Item   9,000 gp

Property: Like a normal set of thieves' tools, *unfettered thieves' tools* grant a +2 bonus to Thievery checks made to open locks or disable traps.

Power (Daily): As part of the action required to make a Thievery check, you can make the check on an object up to 5 squares away. You must have line of sight to the object.

Watchful Ruby Eye — Level 6

This crimson gem set in gold and silver enhances your warding rituals.

Wondrous Item   1,800 gp

Property: While grasping this gem, any skill check you make as part of a warding ritual gains a +2 power bonus.

Special: The *watchful ruby eye* can be used as a focus in warding rituals that allow a focus (such as *eye of alarm*). The value of a *watchful ruby eye* must meet the focus cost requirement for the ritual, as normal.

BATTLE STANDARDS

A battle standard is a magic flag flown during combat. The zone of mystical energy created by a battle standard grants a benefit to allies or hinders your foes. A battle standard's magic allows it to be set into any solid surface that is not difficult terrain, even rocky ground or a stone floor. You and your allies can deploy any number of battle standards at one time, and any number of battle standards can be placed in a square, though the standards do not occupy a square.

While deployed, a battle standard has resist 50 to all damage.

BATTLE STANDARDS

Lvl	Name	Price (gp)
2	Battle standard of honor	520
3	Battle standard of healing	680
4	Battle standard of might	840
16	Battle standard of the fiery legion	45,000
17	Battle standard of shadow	65,000
18	Battle standard of tactics	85,000
19	Battle standard of the stalwart	105,000
20	Battle standard of the vanguard	125,000

Battle Standard of Honor — Level 2

This blood-red banner weakens the resolve of those who fight against you.

Wondrous Item   520 gp

Power (Encounter ✦ Zone): Standard Action. When you plant the battle standard in your space or an adjacent square, it creates a zone of protective energy in a close burst 5. Enemies within the zone that are marked take a –1 penalty to damage rolls against any creature other than the one that marked them.

This effect lasts until the end of the encounter or until the battle standard is removed from the ground. Any character in or adjacent to a battle standard's square can remove it from the ground as a standard action.

Battle Standard of Might — Level 4

This flag is marked with martial runes that inspire strength in you and your allies.

Wondrous Item   840 gp

Power (Encounter ✦ Zone): Standard Action. When you plant the battle standard in your space or an adjacent square, it creates a zone in a close burst 5. While within the zone, you and your allies gain a +1 power bonus on damage rolls.

This effect lasts until the end of the encounter or until the battle standard is removed from the ground. Any character in or adjacent to a battle standard's square can remove it from the ground as a standard action.

Battle Standard of Shadow — Level 17

This silky black flag becomes insubstantial as you raise it, a field of shadow spreading out from it to cover the battlefield.

Wondrous Item   65,000 gp

Power (Encounter ✦ Illusion, Zone): Standard Action. When you plant the battle standard in your space or an adjacent square, it creates a zone of shadow in a close burst 10. Within the zone, all bright light is reduced to dim light, and you and your allies gain low-light vision and a +2 power bonus to Stealth checks.

This effect lasts until the end of the encounter or until the battle standard is removed from the ground. Any character in or adjacent to a battle standard's square can remove it from the ground as a standard action.

Battle Standard of Tactics — Level 18

This long pennant swirls even in still air as it carries your thoughts to your allies.

Wondrous Item   85,000 gp

Power (Encounter ✦ Zone): Standard Action. When you plant the battle standard in your space or an adjacent square, it creates a zone in a close burst 10. You and each ally in the zone gain the ability to communicate telepathically, with no chance of foes hearing your thoughts. You and your allies automatically know each other's positions even if you cannot see one another, and can target one another with powers even without line of sight.

This effect lasts until the end of the encounter or until the battle standard is removed from the ground. Any character in or adjacent to a battle standard's square can remove it from the ground as a standard action.

Battle Standard of the Fiery Legion — Level 16

Swirling with animated flames, this flag lets you and your allies draw on the power of fire.

Wondrous Item   45,000 gp

Power (Encounter ✦ Fire, Zone): Standard Action. When you plant the battle standard in your space or an adjacent square, it creates a zone in a close burst 10. You and each ally in the zone gain resist 10 fire and can choose to have any attack you make deal fire damage instead of its normal damage type.

This effect lasts until the end of the encounter or until the battle standard is removed from the ground. Any character in or adjacent to a battle standard's square can remove it from the ground as a standard action.

Battle Standard of Healing — Level 3

This white flag is emblazoned with sigils of healing that restore the vitality of you and your allies.

Wondrous Item 680 gp

Power (Encounter ✦ Healing, Zone): Standard Action. When you plant the battle standard in your space or an adjacent square, it creates a zone of healing energy in a close burst 5. Whenever you or an ally spends a healing surge while in the zone, you and all allies in the zone regain 1 hit point.

This effect lasts until the end of the encounter or until the battle standard is removed from the ground. Any character in or adjacent to a battle standard's square can remove it from the ground as a standard action.

Battle Standard of the Stalwart — Level 19

This silver and blue banner heightens both courage and resilience.

Wondrous Item 105,000 gp

Power (Encounter ✦ Zone): Standard Action. When you plant the battle standard in your space or an adjacent square, it creates a zone in a close burst 10. While within the zone, you and your allies gain a +1 power bonus to all defenses.

This effect lasts until the end of the encounter or until the battle standard is removed from the ground. Any character in or adjacent to a battle standard's square can remove it from the ground as a standard action.

Battle Standard of the Vanguard — Level 20

The martial runes emblazoned on this bold banner grant combat prowess to those who rally beneath it.

Wondrous Item 125,000 gp

Power (Encounter ✦ Zone): Standard Action. When you plant the battle standard in your space or an adjacent square, it creates a zone in a close burst 10. While within the zone, you and your allies gain a +1 power bonus on attack rolls.

This effect lasts until the end of the encounter or until the battle standard is removed from the ground. Any character in or adjacent to a battle standard's square can remove it from the ground as a standard action.

FIGURINE OF WONDROUS POWER

These tiny animal statuettes are fashioned from a variety of materials and can be used to conjure the creatures they depict.

When you activate a figurine, the conjured creature appears in a space adjacent to you, provided the space is large enough to contain the creature without squeezing. The creature obeys only you, responding to commands spoken in any language. The creature remains for up to 8 hours or until you use a minor action to dismiss it. The conjured creature acts on the same initiative count as you. Every action it takes costs you a minor action (which you use to issue commands), and a conjured creature cannot exceed its normal allotment of actions (a standard, a move, and a minor action) during its turn. If you spend no minor actions on your turn to command the creature, it remains where it is without taking any actions on its turn.

A conjured creature has hit points, defenses, and attacks as indicated in its statistics block. It has no healing surges and cannot be healed, though it can still benefit from temporary hit points. When reduced to 0 hit points or fewer, the conjured creature disappears and cannot be conjured again until after you've taken an extended rest.

Conjured creatures lack basic attacks and therefore cannot make opportunity attacks.

Mount: If the conjured creature has the mount keyword, you can ride the creature and are considered to have the Mounted Combat feat while mounted on it. While mounted, you can command the creature using free actions, though the mount is still limited to its normal allotment of actions. You can choose to be mounted on the creature when it appears.

FIGURINES OF WONDROUS POWER

Lvl	Name	Price (gp)
4	Onyx dog	840
5	Obsidian steed	1,000
8	Jade macetail	3,400
9	Ebony fly	4,200
9	Pearl sea horse	4,200
10	Marble elephant	5,000
11	Bloodstone spider	9,000
11	Ivory goat of travail	9,000
11	Golden lion	13,000

Bloodstone Spider — Level 11

This tiny spider, carved from red bloodstone, can become monstrously real at your whim.

Wondrous Item 9,000 gp

Power (Daily ✦ Conjuration): Standard Action. Use this figurine to conjure a spider made of bloodstone (see below for statistics). As a free action, you can spend a healing surge when activating this item to give the creature temporary hit points equal to your healing surge value.

Power (At-Will): Standard Action. The bloodstone spider recharges its poisoned slash power.

Bloodstone Spider
Large natural animate

Initiative as conjurer   **Senses** Perception +7; tremorsense 5

HP 16; **Bloodied** 8

AC 22; **Fortitude** 21, **Reflex** 20, **Will** 18

Immune disease, poison

Speed 6, climb 6 (spider climb)

⚔ **Bite** (standard; at-will)

   +13 vs. AC; 1d8 + 5 damage.

⚔ **Poisoned Bite** (standard; encounter) ✦ **Poison**

   +13 vs. AC; 1d8 + 5 damage, and ongoing 5 poison damage
   (save ends).

Alignment Unaligned	**Languages** –	
Skills Stealth +14		
Str 20 (+10)	**Dex** 18 (+9)	**Wis** 15 (+7)
Con 18 (+9)	**Int** 1 (+0)	**Cha** 10 (+5)

Ebony Fly   Level 9

This dark wood sculpture of a fly can be used to conjure an enormous fly that you can ride.

Wondrous Item   4,200 gp

Power (Daily ✦ Conjuration): Standard Action. Use this
figurine to conjure a giant black fly (see below for statistics). As a free action, you can spend a healing surge
when activating this item to give the creature temporary
hit points equal to your healing surge value.

The fly can carry one Medium or Small character weighing no more than 300 pounds. If more than 300 pounds
are placed on it, the creature disappears and cannot be
conjured again until after an extended rest.

Ebony Fly
Large natural animate (mount)

Initiative as conjurer   **Senses** Perception +5

HP 14; **Bloodied** 7

AC 18; **Fortitude** 16, **Reflex** 16, **Will** 14

Speed 4, fly 10, overland flight 15

⚔ **Bite** (standard; at-will)

   +12 vs. AC; 1d6 + 4 damage.

Aerial Agility (while mounted by a friendly rider of 9th level or
higher) ✦ **Mount**

   An ebony fly's rider gains a +1 bonus to all defenses while the
   ebony fly is flying.

Alignment Unaligned	**Languages** –	
Str 14 (+6)	**Dex** 17 (+7)	**Wis** 12 (+5)
Con 16 (+7)	**Int** 2 (+0)	**Cha** 6 (+2)

Golden Lion   Level 12

This burnished, gold figurine depicts a pouncing lion.

Wondrous Item   13,000 gp

Power (Daily ✦ Conjuration): Standard Action. Use this
figurine to conjure a golden-furred lion (see below for
statistics). As a free action, you can spend a healing surge
when activating this item to give the creature temporary
hit points equal to your healing surge value.

Golden Lion
Large natural animate

Initiative as conjurer   **Senses** Perception +14; low-light vision

HP 17; **Bloodied** 8

AC 23; **Fortitude** 21, **Reflex** 22, **Will** 20

Speed 8

⚔ **Claw** (standard; at-will)

   +13 vs. AC; 1d8 + 4 damage.

⚔ **Pounce** (standard; at-will)

   The golden lion moves up to 8 squares and makes two claw
   attacks against the same target. If both attacks hit, the target
   is grabbed (until escape). This power can be used as part of a
   charge.

Alignment Unaligned	**Languages** –	
Str 18 (+10)	**Dex** 20 (+11)	**Wis** 17 (+9)
Con 17 (+9)	**Int** 2 (+2)	**Cha** 10 (+6)

Ivory Goat of Travail   Level 11

*This ivory statuette depicts a goat in the midst of a headlong
charge.*

Wondrous Item   9,000 gp

Power (Daily ✦ Conjuration): Standard Action. Use this
figurine to conjure a regal white goat (see below for
statistics). As a free action, you can spend a healing surge
when activating this item to give the creature temporary
hit points equal to your healing surge value.

Ivory Goat of Travail
Medium natural animate

Initiative as conjurer   **Senses** Perception +6; low-light vision

HP 9; **Bloodied** 4

AC 21; **Fortitude** 20, **Reflex** 19, **Will** 18

Speed 6

⚔ **Ram's Charge** (standard; at-will)

   +14 vs. AC; 2d6 + 3 damage, and the target is pushed 2
   squares and knocked prone. This power can be used as part of
   a charge.

⚔ **Goat Rush** (standard; at-will)

   +11 vs. Fortitude; the target is pushed 1 square, and the ivory
   goat shifts into the vacated space.

Alignment Unaligned	**Languages** –	
Str 16 (+8)	**Dex** 14 (+7)	**Wis** 13 (+6)
Con 19 (+9)	**Int** 2 (+1)	**Cha** 10 (+5)

Jade Macetail   Level 8

*This green jade figurine depicts an armored reptilian beast with
a spiked tail.*

Wondrous Item   3,400 gp

Power (Daily ✦ Conjuration): Standard Action. Use this
figurine to conjure a macetail behemoth that appears
to be made of jade (see below for statistics). As a free
action, you can spend a healing surge when activating
this item to give the creature temporary hit points equal
to your healing surge value.

Power (At-Will): Standard Action. The jade macetail
recharges its tail sweep power.

Jade Macetail Behemeth
Large natural animate

Initiative as conjurer   **Senses** Perception +6
HP 13; **Bloodied** 6
AC 23; **Fortitude** 23, **Reflex** 20, **Will** 19
Speed 5
⳨ Tail Bludgeon (standard; at-will)
   Reach 2; +14 vs. AC; 1d10 + 6 damage.
⳦ Tail Sweep (standard; encounter)
   Close burst 1; +12 vs. Reflex; 1d10 + 6 damage, and the target
   is knocked prone if it is Medium size or smaller.

Alignment Unaligned	**Languages** –	
Str 22 (+10)	**Dex** 16 (+7)	**Wis** 14 (+6)
Con 18 (+8)	**Int** 2 (+0)	**Cha** 6 (+2)

Marble Elephant   Level 10

Made of white stone, this statuette can become a powerful elephant.

Wondrous Item   5,000 gp
Power (Daily ✦ Conjuration): Standard Action. Use this
   figurine to conjure an elephant that appears to be made
   of white marble (see below for statistics). As a free action,
   you can spend a healing surge when activating this item
   to give the creature temporary hit points equal to your
   healing surge value.
   The marble elephant can carry one or more Large or
   smaller creatures weighing no more than 1,000 pounds
   total. If more than 1,000 pounds are placed on it, the
   creature disappears and cannot be conjured again until
   after an extended rest.

Marble Elephant
Huge natural animate (mount)

Initiative as conjurer   **Senses** Perception +8
HP 15; **Bloodied** 7
AC 20; **Fortitude** 20, **Reflex** 16, **Will** 18
Speed 8
⳨ Stamp (standard; at-will)
   +11 vs. AC; 1d10 + 7 damage, and the target is knocked prone.
Trampling Charge (while mounted by a friendly rider of 10th
level or higher) **✦ Mount**
   When charging, the elephant can move through one Medium
   or smaller creature's space and make a stamp attack against
   that creature. The marble elephant must end its move in
   unoccupied squares, and the rider still attacks at the end of the
   mount's movement.

Alignment Unaligned	**Languages** –	
Str 25 (+12)	**Dex** 13 (+6)	**Wis** 16 (+8)
Con 21 (+10)	**Int** 2 (+1)	**Cha** 9 (+4)

Obsidian Steed   Level 5

This figurine of dark volcanic glass can become a sleek riding horse.

Wondrous Item   1,000 gp
Power (Daily ✦ Conjuration): Standard Action. Use this
   figurine to conjure a horse that appears to be made of
   obsidian (see below for statistics). As a free action, you
   can spend a healing surge when activating this item to
   give the creature temporary hit points equal to your
   healing surge value.

Obsidian Steed
Large natural animate (mount)

Initiative as conjurer   **Senses** Perception +9
HP 8; **Bloodied** 4
AC 17; **Fortitude** 17, **Reflex** 14, **Will** 14
Speed 8
⳨ Kick (standard; at-will)
   +6 vs. AC; 1d6 + 5 damage.
Charger (while mounted by a friendly rider of 5th level or higher)
✦ Mount
   The obsidian steed grants its rider a +5 bonus to damage rolls
   on charge attacks.

Alignment Unaligned	**Languages** –	
Str 21 (+7)	**Dex** 14 (+4)	**Wis** 14 (+4)
Con 18 (+6)	**Int** 2 (-2)	**Cha** 10 (+2)

Onyx Dog   Level 4

This figurine, sculpted of reflective onyx, depicts a barking dog.

Wondrous Item   840 gp
Power (Daily ✦ Conjuration): Standard Action. Use
   this figurine to conjure a black mastiff (see below for
   statistics). As a free action, you can spend a healing surge
   when activating this item to give the creature temporary
   hit points equal to your healing surge value.
Power (At-Will): Immediate Reaction. Use this power
   when an enemy adjacent to the onyx dog attacks you.
   The onyx dog makes a bite attack against the attacker.

Onyx Dog
Medium natural animate

Initiative as conjurer   **Senses** Perception +7; low-light vision
HP 9; **Bloodied** 4
AC 16; **Fortitude** 15, **Reflex** 14, **Will** 13
Speed 8
⳨ Bite (standard; at-will)
   +7 vs. AC; 1d6 + 3 damage.

Alignment Unaligned	**Languages** –	
Str 16 (+5)	**Dex** 14 (+4)	**Wis** 13 (+3)
Con 14 (+4)	**Int** 2 (-2)	**Cha** 10 (+2)

Pearl Sea Horse — Level 9

This figurine depicts an iridescent sea horse wearing a saddle.

Wondrous Item 4,200 gp

Power (Daily ✦ Conjuration): Standard Action. Use this figurine to conjure a Large majestic sea horse (see below for statistics). There must be a body of water adjacent to you for the sea horse to appear in; otherwise, the figurine cannot be activated. As a free action, you can spend a healing surge when activating this item to give the creature temporary hit points equal to your healing surge value.

While riding the sea horse, you breathe water as if it were air and can speak normally underwater.

The sea horse can carry one Medium or Small character weighing no more than 300 pounds. If more than 300 pounds are placed on it, the creature disappears and cannot be conjured again until after an extended rest.

Pearl Sea Horse
Large natural animate (aquatic, mount)

Initiative as conjurer	**Senses** Perception +4	
HP 14; **Bloodied** 7		
AC 17; **Fortitude** 17, **Reflex** 15, **Will** 13		
Speed swim 10		

↯ Tail Slap (standard; at-will)
Reach 2; +10 vs. AC; 2d8 + 4 damage.

Aquatic Charge (while mounted by a friendly rider of 9th level or higher; at-will) ✦ **Mount**
The sea horse's rider deals an extra 1d10 damage when he or she attacks after the sea horse charges. While in water, the rider also gains a +2 bonus to attack rolls against creatures without a swim speed..

Waterborn
While in water, the sea horse gains a +2 bonus to attack rolls against creatures without a swim speed.

Alignment Unaligned	**Languages** –	
Str 18 (+8)	**Dex** 15 (+6)	**Wis** 10 (+4)
Con 20 (+9)	**Int** 2 (+0)	**Cha** 9 (+3)

BAG OF TRICKS

These small leather bags come in a variety of colors, gray being the most common. You can use a *bag of tricks* to conjure an obedient beast. You must spend a healing surge to activate the bag's power, and you gain no other benefit for spending the healing surge.

When you use a *bag of tricks* to conjure a creature, it appears in an unoccupied space within 5 squares of you; the space must be large enough to contain the creature without squeezing. The creature obeys only you, responding to commands spoken in any language. The creature remains until the end of the encounter or for 5 minutes. The conjured creature acts on the same initiative count as you. Every action it takes costs you a minor action (which you use to issue commands), and a conjured creature cannot exceed its normal allotment of actions (a standard, a move, and a minor action) during its turn. If you spend no minor actions on your turn to command the creature, it remains where it is without taking any actions on its turn.

A conjured creature is a minion (*MM* 282). It has no healing surges and cannot be healed, and it cannot gain temporary hit points. When reduced to 0 hit points or fewer, the conjured creature disappears.

If an object is placed in the *bag of tricks*, the bag ceases to function until the object is removed. A *bag of tricks* used for simple storage holds up to 3 pounds.

BAGS OF TRICKS

Lvl	Name	Price (gp)
8	Bag of tricks, gray	3,400
18	Bag of tricks, rust	85,000
28	Bag of tricks, vermilion	2,125,000

Bag of Tricks, Gray — Level 8

This simple, leather bag produces feral critters that you can send against your enemies.

Wondrous Item 3,400 gp

Power (Daily ✦ Conjuration): Standard Action. Use this bag to conjure a Tiny minion (see below for statistics). Roll a d8 to determine which beast is produced and modify its statistics accordingly:

1: Bat; this creature also has a fly speed of 6.

2: Rat; this creature also has darkvision.

3: Cat; this creature also knocks the target prone on a hit.

4: Weasel; this creature does not provoke opportunity attacks for moving.

5: Snake; this creature also deals 2 poison damage on a hit.

6: Badger; this creature gains a +1 bonus to attack rolls.

7: Spider; this creature also has a climb speed of 6.

8: Scorpion; this creature deals ongoing 1 poison damage (save ends) on a hit.

Conjured Critter (Gray Bag) — Level 8 Minion
Tiny natural beast

Initiative as conjurer   **Senses** Perception +8; low-light vision

HP 1; a missed attack never damages a minion.

AC 18; **Fortitude** 17, **Reflex** 18, **Will** 16

Speed 6

⊕ **Bite or Claw** (standard; at-will)

+11 vs. AC; 4 damage.

Alignment Unaligned		**Languages** —
Str 6 (+2)	Dex 12 (+5)	Wis 9 (+3)
Con 11 (+4)	Int 2 (+0)	Cha 6 (+2)

Bag of Tricks, Rust — Level 18
This handsome leather bag conjures predatory beasts that obey simple commands.

Wondrous Item   85,000 gp

Power (Daily ✦ Conjuration): Standard Action. Use this bag to conjure a Large minion (see below for statistics). Roll a d8 to determine which beast is produced and modify its statistics accordingly:

1: Bear; when this creature hits with its melee basic attack, the target is grabbed (until escape).

2: Ape; when this creature hits with its melee basic attack, the target is dazed (save ends).

3: Wolf; when this creature hits with its melee basic attack, the target is knocked prone.

4: Bull; when this creature hits with its melee basic attack, the target is also pushed 2 squares.

5: Spider; when this creature hits with its melee basic attack, the target also takes ongoing 5 poison damage (save ends).

6: Warhorse; this creature's rider gains a +5 bonus to damage rolls while mounted on the creature.

7: Macetail Behemoth; this creature can make a melee basic attack with its tail: Reach 2; +21 vs. AC; 7 damage.

8: Rage Drake; this creature deals 10 damage instead of 7 damage on a hit.

Conjured Beast (Rust Bag) — Level 18 Minion
Large natural beast

Initiative as conjurer   **Senses** Perception +9; low-light vision

HP 1; a missed attack never damages a minion.

AC 28; **Fortitude** 28, **Reflex** 26, **Will** 24

Speed 6

⊕ **Bite or Claw** (standard; at-will)

+21 vs. AC; 7 damage.

Alignment Unaligned		**Languages** —
Str 18 (+13)	Dex 14 (+11)	Wis 10 (+9)
Con 14 (+11)	Int 2 (+5)	Cha 10 (+9)

Bag of Tricks, Vermilion — Level 28
This beautiful leather bag is inlaid with the images of beasts—not unlike the ones that it can summon to fight by your side.

Wondrous Item   2,125,000 gp

Power (Daily ✦ Conjuration): Standard Action. Use this bag to conjure a Large or Huge minion (see below for statistics). Roll a d8 to determine which beast is produced and modify its statistics accordingly:

1: Large Bloodspike Behemoth; when this creature hits with its melee basic attack (tail), the target also takes ongoing 5 damage (save ends) and is knocked prone.

2: Large Crushgrip Constrictor; when this creature hits with its melee basic attack (bite), the target is also grabbed (until escape).

3: Large Blade Spider; this creature's melee basic attack (claw) does not have reach but instead affects all enemies in a close burst 1.

4: Large Stone-Eye Basilisk; when this creature hits with its melee basic attack (bite), the target is also immobilized (save ends).

5: Large Wyvern; this creature has a fly speed of 8, and when the creature hits with its melee basic attack (tail), the target also takes ongoing 10 poison damage (save ends).

6: Huge Guulvorg; when this creature hits with a melee basic attack (bite), the target takes 15 damage instead of 10 damage and is knocked prone.

7: Large Iron Gorgon; when this creature hits with its melee basic attack (horns), the target is pushed 1 square. On a successful charge, it deals 20 damage instead of 10 damage, and the target is pushed 2 squares.

8: Huge Carrion Crawler; this creature's melee basic attack (bite) has reach 3, and on a hit, the target is also pulled 2 squares and slowed (save ends).

Conjured Beast (Vermilion Bag) — Level 28 Minion
Large or Huge natural beast

Initiative as conjurer   **Senses** Perception +14; low-light vision

HP 1; a missed attack never damages a minion.

AC 38; **Fortitude** 38; **Reflex** 36; **Will** 33

Speed 6

⊕ **Bite, Claw, Horns, or Tail** (standard; at-will)

Reach 2; +31 vs. AC; 10 damage.

Alignment Unaligned		**Languages** —
Str 23 (+20)	Dex 18 (+18)	Wis 10 (+14)
Con 18 (+18)	Int 2 (+10)	Cha 12 (+15)

CONSUMABLES

A proper adventurer has four slots on his or her belt: one for a potion, one for a potion, one for a potion, and one for a potion.

Although they lack the longevity of other magic items, consumables are essential to the survival of any adventuring party. Whether a party maintains an equal distribution of healing potions or keeps a supply of attack-enhancing elixirs or carries a stash of deadly reagents, all are excellent countermeasures to the inherent perils of dungeon exploration.

This section is divided into four subsections. First we have potions and elixirs, each with the power to augment a single character for a short period of time. Then come the whetstones, which provide bonuses to weapon-based attacks. The third batch includes a miscellany of items not easily categorized. Last are the reagents, which do for nonweapon attacks what whetstones do for weapon-based powers.

POTIONS AND ELIXIRS

Potions and elixirs are magical liquids contained in small vials or flasks.

A potion or elixir must be imbibed for its power to work. Drinking a potion or elixir is usually a minor action. Administering a potion or elixir to an unconscious creature is usually a standard action.

The difference between a potion and an elixir is that a potion usually requires the imbiber to expend a healing surge to use its power, whereas drinking an elixir does not. However, consuming an elixir usually counts as a use of a magic item daily power (*PH* 226); the same cannot be said for most potions.

POTIONS AND ELIXIRS

Lvl	Name	Price (gp)
4	Potion of resistance	40
5	Elixir of aptitude	50
5	Gravespawn potion	50
5	Potion of clarity	50
5	Potion of spirit	50
6	Fire beetle potion	75
7	Elixir of dragon breath	100
7	Potion of lifeshield	100
7	Potion of mimicry	100
8	Elixir of accuracy	125
8	Elixir of fortitude	125
8	Elixir of reflexes	125
8	Elixir of will	125
8	Potion of stormshield	125
9	Potion of regeneration	160
9	Potion of vigor	160
10	Kruthik potion	200
10	Potion of clarity	200

Lvl	Name	Price (gp)
10	Potion of spirit	200
11	Elixir of speed	350
13	Elixir of accuracy	650
13	Elixir of fortitude	650
13	Elixir of reflexes	650
13	Elixir of will	650
14	Potion of resistance	800
15	Cryptspawn potion	1,000
15	Elixir of aptitude	1,000
15	Potion of clarity	1,000
15	Potion of spirit	1,000
16	Elixir of invisibility	1,800
17	Elixir of dragon breath	2,600
17	Potion of lifeshield	2,600
17	Potion of mimicry	2,600
18	Elixir of accuracy	3,400
18	Elixir of fortitude	3,400
18	Elixir of reflexes	3,400
18	Elixir of will	3,400
18	Potion of stormshield	3,400
19	Potion of regeneration	4,200
19	Potion of vigor	4,200
20	Potion of clarity	5,000
20	Potion of spirit	5,000
20	Spider potion	5,000
21	Elixir of flying	9,000
23	Elixir of accuracy	17,000
23	Elixir of fortitude	17,000
23	Elixir of reflexes	17,000
23	Elixir of will	17,000
24	Potion of resistance	21,000
25	Deathspawn potion	25,000
25	Elixir of aptitude	25,000
25	Potion of clarity	25,000
25	Potion of spirit	25,000
27	Elixir of dragon breath	65,000
27	Potion of lifeshield	65,000
27	Potion of mimicry	65,000
28	Elixir of accuracy	85,000
28	Elixir of fortitude	85,000
28	Elixir of reflexes	85,000
28	Elixir of will	85,000
28	Potion of stormshield	85,000
29	Potion of regeneration	105,000
29	Potion of vigor	105,000
30	Potion of clarity	125,000
30	Potion of spirit	125,000

Cryptspawn Potion — Level 15

This viscous liquid smells faintly of death, yet it invigorates you against diseases and poisons.

Potion 1,000 gp

Power (Consumable): Minor Action. Consume this potion and spend a healing surge. You do not regain hit points as normal. Instead, gain resist 10 necrotic and resist 10 poison until the end of the encounter. You also gain a +5 power bonus to your next Endurance check against any disease of level 15 or lower.

Deathspawn Potion — Level 25

Dark gray and odorless, this liquid wards off diseases and poisons.

Potion 25,000 gp

Power (Consumable): Minor Action. Consume this potion and spend a healing surge. You do not regain hit points as normal. Instead, gain resist 15 necrotic and resist 15 poison until the end of the encounter. You also gain a +5 power bonus to your next Endurance check against any disease of level 25 or lower.

Elixir of Accuracy — Level 8+

You strike true after quaffing this sour, azure liquid.

Lvl 8	125 gp	Lvl 23	17,000 gp
Lvl 13	800 gp	Lvl 28	85,000 gp
Lvl 18	3,400 gp		

Elixir

Power (Consumable): Minor Action. Use this power after your drink the elixir. Once during this encounter, you can use a free action to gain a power bonus to a single attack roll equal to 5 minus one-half your level.
Level 13: 8 minus one-half your level.
Level 18: 10 minus one-half your level.
Level 23: 13 minus one-half your level.
Level 28: 15 minus one-half your level.

Special: Consuming this elixir counts as a use of a magic item daily power.

Elixir of Aptitude — Level 5+

This sweet amber broth enhances your innate talents.

Lvl 5	50 gp	Lvl 25	25,000 gp
Lvl 15	1,000 gp		

Elixir

Power (Consumable): Minor Action. For 1 hour, gain a +1 power bonus to checks using one skill of your choice.
Level 15: +3 power bonus.
Level 25: +5 power bonus.

Special: Consuming this elixir counts as a use of a magic item daily power.

Elixir of Dragon Breath — Level 7+

Whether frigid, acidic, or crackling with energy, this liquid grants you a potent blast of dragon breath.

Lvl 7	100 gp	Lvl 27	65,000 gp
Lvl 17	2,600 gp		

Elixir

Power (Consumable ✦ Acid, Cold, Fire, Lightning, or Poison): Minor Action. Use this power after your drink the elixir. Until the end of the encounter, you gain an at-will attack power that requires a standard action to use: Close blast 3; +10 vs. Reflex; on a hit, deal 2d6 + Constitution modifier damage of a type determined when the elixir is created: acid, cold, fire, lightning, or poison.
Level 17: +20 vs. Reflex; 3d6 + Constitution modifier damage.
Level 27: +30 vs. Reflex; 4d6 + Constitution modifier damage.

Special: Consuming this elixir counts as a use of a magic item daily power.

Elixir of Flying — Level 21

Your feet leave the ground after imbibing this fluorescent, effervescent draught.

Elixir 9,000 gp

Power (Consumable): Minor Action. Gain a fly speed of 8 (hover) until the end of the encounter or for 5 minutes, whichever comes first. When the duration ends, you float 100 feet toward the ground. If you are not on a horizontal surface sufficient to bear your weight at the end of this distance, you fall to the nearest such surface, taking damage accordingly.

Special: Consuming this elixir counts as a use of a magic item daily power.

Elixir of Fortitude — Level 8+

Your body grows tougher after imbibing this viscous fuchsia liquid.

Lvl 8	125 gp	Lvl 23	17,000 gp
Lvl 13	650 gp	Lvl 28	85,000 gp
Lvl 18	3,400 gp		

Elixir

Power (Consumable): Minor Action. Use this power after your drink the elixir. Once during this encounter, you can use an immediate interrupt action when you would be hit by an attack to gain a Fortitude defense of 25 against a single attack. This replaces your normal Fortitude defense for that attack.
Level 13: Fortitude defense of 30.
Level 18: Fortitude defense of 35.
Level 23: Fortitude defense of 40.
Level 28: Fortitude defense of 45.

Special: Consuming this elixir counts as a use of a magic item daily power.

Elixir of Invisibility — Level 16

With a sip of this ivory, scentless liquid, you fade from view.

Elixir 1,800 gp

Power (Consumable): Minor Action. You drink the elixir and become invisible until the end of the encounter or for 5 minutes, whichever comes first. The effect ends if you make an attack.

Special: Consuming this elixir counts as a use of a magic item daily power.

Elixir of Reflexes — Level 8+

You become quicker after imbibing this thin rose liquid.

Lvl 8	125 gp	Lvl 23	17,000 gp
Lvl 13	650 gp	Lvl 28	85,000 gp
Lvl 18	3,400 gp		

Elixir

Power (Consumable): Minor Action. Use this power after your drink the elixir. Once during this encounter, you can use an immediate interrupt action when you would be hit by an attack to gain a Reflex defense of 25 against a single attack. This replaces your normal Reflex defense value for that attack.
Level 13: Reflex defense of 30.
Level 18: Reflex defense of 35.
Level 23: Reflex defense of 40.
Level 28: Reflex defense of 45.

Special: Consuming this elixir counts as a use of a magic item daily power.

Elixir of Speed — Level 11

This sapphire brew crackles with energy and increases your speed.

Elixir 350 gp

Power (Consumable): Minor Action. Drink the elixir and gain a +2 power bonus to your speed for 1 hour.

Special: Consuming this elixir counts as a use of a magic item daily power.

Elixir of Will — Level 8+

Your mind becomes more resilient after imbibing this bubbling white liquid.

Lvl 8	125 gp	Lvl 23	17,000 gp
Lvl 13	650 gp	Lvl 28	85,000 gp
Lvl 18	3,400 gp		

Elixir

Power (Consumable): Minor Action. Use this power after your drink the elixir. Once during this encounter, you can use an immediate interrupt action when you would be hit by an attack to gain a Will defense of 25 against a single attack. This replaces your normal Will defense value for that attack.
Level 13: Will defense of 30.
Level 18: Will defense of 35.
Level 23: Will defense of 40.
Level 28: Will defense of 45.

Special: Consuming this elixir counts as a use of a magic item daily power.

Fire Beetle Potion — Level 6

Your eyes glow faintly and your skin darkens and takes on a chitinous texture when you imbibe this red, smoky potion.

Potion 75 gp

Power (Consumable): Minor Action. Drink this potion and spend a healing surge. You do not regain hit points as normal. Instead, gain 5 temporary hit points and resist 5 fire until the end of the encounter.

Gravespawn Potion — Level 5

This deep purple, putrescent liquid fends off diseases and poisons.

Potion 50 gp

Power (Consumable): Minor Action. Drink this potion and spend a healing surge. You do not regain hit points as normal. Instead, gain resist 5 necrotic and resist 5 poison until the end of the encounter. You also gain a +5 power bonus to your next Endurance check against any disease of level 5 or lower.

Kruthik Potion — Level 10

This foul concoction bestows a burst of health and coats you in fine, silvery plates that protect against acid.

Potion 200 gp

Power (Consumable): Minor Action. Drink this potion and spend a healing surge. You do not regain hit points as normal. Instead, gain 15 temporary hit points and resist 5 acid until the end of the encounter.

Potion of Clarity
Level 5+

This cool cyan liquid hones your physical and mental acuity at a critical moment.

Lvl 5	50 gp	Lvl 20	5,000 gp
Lvl 10	200 gp	Lvl 25	25,000 gp
Lvl 15	1,000 gp	Lvl 30	125,000 gp

Potion

Power (Consumable): Minor Action. Drink this potion and spend a healing surge. You do not regain hit points as normal. Instead, once during this encounter as a free action, you can reroll a d20 roll you just made, gaining a +1 bonus on the reroll. You must use the result of the reroll.
Level 10: +2 bonus.
Level 15: +3 bonus.
Level 20: +4 bonus.
Level 25: +5 bonus.
Level 30: +6 bonus.

Potion of Lifeshield
Level 7+

This lemony potion shields you from necrotic energy.

Lvl 7	100 gp	Lvl 27	65,000 gp
Lvl 17	2,600 gp		

Potion

Power (Consumable): Minor Action. Drink this potion and spend a healing surge. You do not gain hit points as normal. Instead, once during this encounter, you can use an immediate interrupt action to gain resist 15 necrotic against a single attack.
Level 17: Resist 25 necrotic.
Level 27: Resist 35 necrotic.

Potion of Mimicry
Level 7+

This bitter orange liquid has the consistency of honey and allows you to adopt an instant disguise.

Lvl 7	100 gp	Lvl 27	65,000 gp
Lvl 17	2,600 gp		

Potion

Power (Consumable ✦ Illusion): Minor Action. Drink this potion and spend a healing surge. You do not gain hit points as normal. Instead, you alter your appearance through illusion, appearing as a specific humanoid creature within your line of sight. You also gain the creature's attire, mannerisms, voice, and speech patterns. This effect lasts for 5 minutes or until you dismiss it (a free action). You gain a +5 power bonus to Bluff checks to pass yourself off as the creature you're imitating.
Level 17: +10 bonus.
Level 27: +15 bonus.

Potion of Regeneration
Level 9+

If you are sufficiently wounded after having quaffed this russet, copper-scented potion, you heal quickly.

Lvl 9	160 gp	Lvl 29	105,000 gp
Lvl 19	4,200 gp		

Potion

Power (Consumable ✦ Healing): Minor Action. Drink this potion and spend a healing surge. You do not gain hit points as normal. Instead, gain regeneration 5 until the end of the encounter. If you aren't bloodied at the start of your turn while this power is in effect, you don't regain any hit points and the regeneration is suppressed until the start of your next turn.
Level 19: Gain regeneration 10.
Level 29: Gain regeneration 15.

Potion of Resistance
Level 4+

The color and smell of this potion varies with the protection it provides.

Lvl 4	40 gp	Lvl 24	21,000 gp
Lvl 14	800 gp		

Potion

Power (Consumable): Minor Action. Drink this potion and spend a healing surge. You do not gain hit points as normal. Instead, gain resist 5 to damage of a specific type until the end of the encounter. The damage type (acid, cold, fire, lightning, necrotic, poison, psychic, or thunder) is determined when the potion is created. Only one *potion of resistance* can be in effect on you at once.
Level 14: Gain resist 10 to damage of the specified type.
Level 24: Gain resist 15 to damage of the specified type.

Potion of Spirit
Level 5+

This lavender-scented potion helps keep the spirit alive within you.

Lvl 5	50 gp	Lvl 20	5,000 gp
Lvl 10	200 gp	Lvl 25	25,000 gp
Lvl 15	1,000 gp	Lvl 30	125,000 gp

Potion

Power (Consumable): Minor Action. Drink this potion and spend a healing surge. You do not regain hit points as normal. Instead, you gain a +1 power bonus to death saving throws until the end of the encounter.
Level 10: +2 power bonus.
Level 15: +3 power bonus.
Level 20: +4 power bonus.
Level 25: +5 power bonus.
Level 30: +6 power bonus.

Potion of lifeshield

Potion of Stormshield — Level 8+

Your skin takes on a metallic sheen when you consume this slate gray, ozone-smelling drink.

| Lvl 8 | 125 gp | Lvl 28 | 85,000 gp |
| Lvl 18 | 3,400 gp | | |

Potion

Power (Consumable): Minor Action. Drink this potion and spend a healing surge. You do not gain hit points as normal. Instead, once during this encounter, you can use an immediate interrupt action to gain resist 15 lightning or resist 15 thunder against a single attack.
Level 18: Resist 25 lightning or resist 25 thunder.
Level 28: Resist 35 lightning or resist 35 thunder.

Potion of Vigor — Level 9+

This vermilion liquid invigorates you, at least temporarily.

| Lvl 9 | 160 gp | Lvl 29 | 105,000 gp |
| Lvl 19 | 4,200 gp | | |

Potion

Power (Consumable): Minor Action. Drink this potion and spend a healing surge. You do not gain hit points as normal. Instead, gain 15 temporary hit points.
Level 19: Gain 25 temporary hit points.
Level 29: Gain 35 temporary hit points.

Spider Potion — Level 20

This pungent-smelling, sepia-colored concoction grants a spider's resilience against damage and poison.

Potion 5,000 gp

Power (Consumable): Minor Action. Drink this potion and spend a healing surge. You do not regain hit points as normal. Instead, gain 20 temporary hit points and resist 10 poison until the end of the encounter.

WHETSTONES

You can use a magic whetstone on any melee or ranged weapon you hold. Doing so is a minor action and destroys the whetstone.

Using a magic whetstone counts as a use of a daily magic item power. Using a second whetstone on the same weapon removes any previous whetstone effect on that weapon.

WHETSTONES

Lvl	Name	Price (gp)
6	Augmenting whetstone	75
7	Frozen whetstone	100
9	Whetstone of venom	160
10	Caustic whetstone	200
10	Tempest whetstone	200
10	Whetstone of combustion	200
11	Augmenting whetstone	350
16	Augmenting whetstone	1,800
17	Frozen whetstone	2,600
19	Whetstone of venom	4,200
20	Caustic whetstone	5,000
20	Tempest whetstone	5,000
20	Whetstone of combustion	5,000
21	Augmenting whetstone	9,000
26	Augmenting whetstone	45,000
27	Frozen whetstone	65,000
29	Whetstone of venom	105,000
30	Caustic whetstone	125,000
30	Tempest whetstone	125,000
30	Whetstone of combustion	125,000

WILLIAM O'CONNOR

Augmenting Whetstone
Level 6+

This rough sharpening stone temporarily grants your weapon a magical enhancement.

Lvl 6	75 gp	Lvl 21	9,000 gp
Lvl 11	350 gp	Lvl 26	45,000 gp
Lvl 16	1,800 gp		

Whetstone

Power (Consumable): Minor Action. Touch this whetstone to a melee or ranged weapon you hold. The weapon gains a +2 enhancement bonus on attack rolls and damage rolls until the end of the encounter. This has no effect on the extra damage dice or other special effect applied when the weapon scores a critical hit.
Level 11: +3 enhancement bonus.
Level 16: +4 enhancement bonus.
Level 21: +5 enhancement bonus.
Level 26: +6 enhancement bonus.

Caustic Whetstone
Level 10+

This metallic green sharpener drips acid when touched to a weapon.

Lvl 10	200 gp	Lvl 30	125,000 gp
Lvl 20	5,000 gp		

Whetstone

Power (Consumable ✦ Acid): Minor Action. Touch this whetstone to a melee or ranged weapon you hold. Until the end of the encounter, any successful attack with the weapon deals ongoing 2 acid damage (save ends).
Level 20: Ongoing 4 acid damage (save ends).
Level 30: Ongoing 6 acid damage (save ends).

Frozen Whetstone
Level 7+

A weapon honed with this blue-white crystalline whetstone becomes icy cold to the touch.

Lvl 7	100 gp	Lvl 27	65,000 gp
Lvl 17	2,600 gp		

Whetstone

Power (Consumable ✦ Cold): Minor Action. Touch this whetstone to a melee or ranged weapon you hold. Until the end of the encounter, any successful attack with the weapon deals an extra 2 cold damage.
Level 17: Extra 4 cold damage.
Level 27: Extra 6 cold damage.

Tempest Whetstone
Level 10+

This unfinished iron whetstone lends your weapon a spark.

Lvl 10	200 gp	Lvl 30	125,000 gp
Lvl 20	5,000 gp		

Whetstone

Power (Consumable ✦ Lightning): Minor Action. Touch this whetstone to a melee or ranged weapon you hold. Until the end of the encounter, any successful attack with the weapon deals an extra 2 lightning damage to each enemy within 2 squares of the target; the target of the attack does not take this damage.
Level 20: Extra 4 lightning damage.
Level 30: Extra 6 lightning damage.

Whetstone of Combustion
Level 10+

Your weapon gains an oily residue when you run it across this obsidian sharpening stone.

Lvl 10	200 gp	Lvl 30	125,000 gp
Lvl 20	5,000 gp		

Whetstone

Power (Consumable): Minor Action. Touch this whetstone to a melee or ranged weapon you hold. Until the end of the encounter, any creature hit with an attack from this weapon gains vulnerable 5 fire against the next attack that deals fire damage to it.
Level 20: Vulnerable 10 fire.
Level 30: Vulnerable 15 fire.

Whetstone of Venom
Level 9+

This sickly green whetstone coats a weapon in toxin.

Lvl 9	160 gp	Lvl 29	105,000 gp
Lvl 19	4,200 gp		

Whetstone

Power (Consumable ✦ Poison): Minor Action. Touch this whetstone to a melee or ranged weapon you hold. The next creature successfully attacked by the weapon takes ongoing 5 poison damage (save ends).
Level 19: Ongoing 10 poison damage (save ends).
Level 29: Ongoing 15 poison damage (save ends).

Other Consumables

If an item is exhausted after one use, but it's not a potion, an elixir, a reagent, or a whetstone, you'll find it here. This section includes an assortment of one-use items that any adventurer would be prudent to carry.

OTHER CONSUMABLES

Lvl	Name	Price (gp)
3	Stonemeal biscuit	30
4	Life shroud	40
4	Nail of sealing	40
6	Vision sand	75
10	Glowstone	200
10	Oil of flesh returned	200
11	Unguent of darkvision	350
13	Feybread biscuit	650
20	Gem of valor	5,000
21	Unguent of blindsight	9,000
23	Astral mead	17,000

Astral Mead — Level 23

This sweet sparkling beverage infuses and restores your body.

Other Consumable　17,000 gp

Property: A single flask of *astral mead* weighs half of a pound and has the nutritional value of a full day's worth of food and water.

Power (Consumable ✦ Healing): Standard Action. You drink the flask of *astral mead*. For the next 12 hours, you gain a +2 power bonus on Endurance checks and regain an extra 2 hit points whenever you spend a healing surge.

Feybread Biscuit — Level 13

This hard but tasty biscuit enhances your recuperative powers for the rest of the day.

Other Consumable　650 gp

Property: A single *feybread biscuit* weighs one-tenth of a pound and has the nutritional value of a full day's worth of food.

Power (Consumable ✦ Healing): Standard Action. You eat a *feybread biscuit*. For the next 12 hours, you gain a +1 power bonus on Endurance checks and regain an extra 1 hit point whenever you spend a healing surge.

Gem of Valor — Level 20

This brilliant sapphire promises great rewards to the bold.

Other Consumable　5,000 gp

Power (Consumable): Free Action. Use this power when you spend an action point. Roll 1d20 to determine the result, adding 1 to the result for each milestone you've reached today. Regardless of the result, using the gem consumes it and turns it to dust.

1-9: Gain a +1 power bonus to all defenses until the end of your next turn.

10-19: Gain a +1 power bonus to all attack rolls until the end of your next turn.

20: Gain 1 action point. You must spend this action point before the end of this turn, or it is lost. You can spend it even if you've already spent an action point during this encounter.

Special: Using this item counts as a use of a magic item daily power.

Glowstone — Level 10

This fist-sized stone glows faintly and can be used to create a bright burst of radiant light that harms undead creatures.

Other Consumable　200 gp

Property: A *glowstone* radiates dim light in a 2-square radius.

Power (Consumable ✦ Radiant, Zone): Standard Action. Use the *glowstone* to creates a zone of bright illumination in an area burst 2 within 5 squares of you. Any undead creature that is vulnerable to radiant damage that enters or starts its turn within the zone is affected as if it had taken radiant damage. For example, a skeleton that has vulnerable 5 radiant takes 5 radiant damage if it enters or starts its turn in the zone. The zone remains until the end of the encounter or for 5 minutes, whichever comes first. Using this power turns the *glowstone* to dust.

Life Shroud — Level 4

This clean linen wrap protects a corpse from the ravages of time and the blasphemies of necromancers.

Other Consumable　40 gp

Property: A corpse wrapped in this shroud does not decay, can't be touched by an undead creature, and can't become undead. Once wrapped about a body, a shroud turns to dust after 1 week.

Nail of Sealing — Level 4

This thick iron nail is adorned with warding symbols and can hold shut any portal or container.

Other Consumable　40 gp

Power (Consumable): Standard Action. When you push this nail into a door, chest, or other closeable object, it magically sinks into the material of that object and seals it shut. Treat this as if you had used an Arcane Lock ritual with an Arcana check result of 25.

Special: You can use this item in place of the required component cost for an Arcane Lock ritual. In that case, use your own Arcana check instead of that of the nail.

Oil of Flesh Returned — Level 10+

This milky-white oil returns petrified creatures to flesh.

Lvl 10   200 gp

Other Consumable

Power (Consumable): Minor Action. An adjacent target who is petrified can spend a healing surge to remove the petrified condition. If the target has no healing surges remaining, he or she can instead take damage equal to his or her healing surge value to remove the condition. The resistance granted by the petrified condition does not reduce this damage.

Stonemeal Biscuit — Level 3

This coarse dwarven fare tastes foul but keeps you going throughout the day.

Other Consumable   30 gp

Property: A single *stonemeal biscuit* weighs one-tenth of a pound and has the nutritional value of a full day's worth of food.

Power (Consumable ✦ Healing): Standard Action. You eat the *stonemeal biscuit*. You gain a +1 power bonus on Endurance checks for 12 hours. In addition, you regain an extra 1 hit point the next time you spend a healing surge this day.

Nail of sealing

Unguent of Blindsight — Level 21

You can perceive visible and invisible dangers alike with this white cream.

Other Consumable   9,000 gp

Power (Consumable): Standard Action. Rub this unguent on your closed eyelids. You gain blindsight 10 until the end of the encounter.

Unguent of Darkvision — Level 11

Darkness is less impenetrable with this black ointment.

Other Consumable   350 gp

Power (Consumable): Standard Action. Rub this unguent on your closed eyelids. You gain darkvision for 1 hour.

Vision Sand — Level 6

Blessed by Ioun's clergy, this sparkling crystalline sand enhances divinations.

Other Consumable   75 gp

Property: When added to the normal components for casting a divination ritual, *vision sand* grants a +2 power bonus to any one skill check required by the ritual.

REAGENTS

Reagents enhance the use of a power of a specified type and level. When used in conjunction with an attack power, a reagent's effect typically applies only to one target hit by the power. Only one reagent can be used to enhance any given power. You must be holding a reagent to use it (which might require a minor action to retrieve the item). A reagent is consumed during the power's action.

Each reagent affects powers up to a specified maximum level. In some cases, more refined or concentrated versions of a reagent can be used, with an increased maximum level for the power it can affect. These versions are listed as having higher levels.

REAGENTS

Lvl	Name	Price (gp)
7	Desert rose	100
7	Glassteel shard	100
8	Brightleaf	125
8	Dark clover	125
9	Black dragon bile	160
9	Terror ichor	160
10	Creeping gatevine	200
10	Flame rose	200
10	Fundamental ice	200
14	Black cave pearl	800
15	Dread nightshade	1,000
15	Mind dust	1,000
17	Desert rose	2,600
17	Glassteel shard	2,600
18	Brightleaf	3,400
18	Dark clover	3,400

REAGENTS (CONTINUED)

Lvl	Name	Price (gp)
19	Black dragon bile	4,200
19	Terror ichor	4,200
20	Creeping gatevine	5,000
20	Flame rose	5,000
20	Fundamental ice	5,000
24	Black cave pearl	21,000
25	Dread nightshade	25,000
25	Mind dust	25,000
27	Desert rose	65,000
27	Glassteel shard	65,000
28	Brightleaf	85,000
28	Dark clover	85,000
29	Black dragon bile	105,000
29	Terror ichor	105,000
30	Creeping gatevine	125,000
30	Flame rose	125,000
30	Fundamental ice	125,000

Black Cave Pearl — Level 14+

This rare black pearl is found in subterranean lakes and favored by mesmerists and hypnotists.

Lvl 14	800 gp	Lvl 24	21,000 gp

Reagent

Power (Consumable): Free Action. Expend this reagent when you use of a power with the charm keyword of up to 7th level. Roll twice for the power's attack roll and take the better of the two results.
Level 24: Power up to 17th level.

Black Dragon Bile — Level 9+

Distilled from the gullet of a black dragon, this caustic substance makes your foes more vulnerable to acid.

Lvl 9	160 gp	Lvl 29	105,000 gp
Lvl 19	4,200 gp		

Reagent

Power (Consumable): Free Action. Expend this reagent when you use a power with the acid keyword of up to 5th level. One target hit by the attack (chosen by you) gains vulnerable 5 acid until the end of your next turn.
Level 19: Power up to 15th level, vulnerable 10 acid.
Level 29: Power up to 25th level, vulnerable 15 acid.

Brightleaf — Level 8+

These leaves, which sprout from old growth forests, never fall even in the deep winter. When used, they explode with stored light and energy.

Lvl 8	125 gp	Lvl 28	85,000 gp
Lvl 18	3,400 gp		

Reagent

Power (Consumable): Free Action. Expend this reagent when you use a power with the radiant keyword of up to 5th level. One target hit by the attack (chosen by you) gains vulnerable 5 radiant until the end of your next turn.
Level 18: Power up to 13th level, vulnerable 10 radiant.
Level 28: Power up to 23th level, vulnerable 15 radiant.

Creeping Gatevine — Level 10+

This red-flowering vine grows on the stones of magical gates and menhirs.

Lvl 10	200 gp	Lvl 30	125,000 gp
Lvl 20	5,000 gp		

Reagent

Power (Consumable ✦ Teleportation): Free Action. Expend this reagent when you use a power with the teleport keyword of up to 10th level. Increase the distance teleported by 2 squares.
Level 20: Power up to 20th level, increase by 5 squares.
Level 30: Power up to 30th level, increase by 10 squares.

Dark Clover — Level 8+

These clovers are identical in shape to the garden variety, but their connection to the Shadowfell aids necrotic powers.

Lvl 8	125 gp	Lvl 28	85,000 gp
Lvl 18	3,400 gp		

Reagent

Power (Consumable): Free Action. Expend this reagent when you use a power with the necrotic keyword of up to 5th level. One target hit by the attack (chosen by you) gains vulnerable 5 necrotic until the end of your next turn.
Level 18: Power up to 15th level, vulnerable 10 necrotic.
Level 28: Power up to 25th level, vulnerable 15 necrotic.

Desert Rose — Level 7+

Growing only in remote desert oases, this yellow flower helps to maintain arcane and divine powers.

Lvl 7	100 gp	Lvl 27	65,000 gp
Lvl 17	2,600 gp		

Reagent

Power (Consumable): Free Action. Expend this reagent when you use a arcane or divine power of up to 5th level. You do not need to use an action on the following round to sustain that power (sustaining it for subsequent rounds does require the appropriate action).
Level 17: Power up to 15th level.
Level 27: Power up to 25th level.

WAYNE ENGLAND

Dread Nightshade
Level 15+

This poisonous relative of the eggplant is cultivated to empower poison effects.

Lvl 15	1000 gp	Lvl 25	25,000 gp

Reagent

Power (Consumable): Free Action. Expend this reagent when you use a power with the poison keyword of up to 7th level. Roll twice for the power's attack roll and take the better of the two results.
Level 25: Power up to 17th level.

Flame Rose
Level 10+

Your fire magic is augmented by this beautiful crimson rose.

Lvl 10	200 gp	Lvl 30	125,000 gp
Lvl 20	5,000 gp		

Reagent

Power (Consumable ✦ Fire): Free Action. Expend this reagent when you use a power with the fire keyword of up to 7th level. Each target takes ongoing 5 fire damage (save ends).
Level 20: Power up to 17th level, ongoing 10 fire damage (save ends).
Level 30: Power up to 27th level, ongoing 15 fire damage (save ends).

Fundamental Ice
Level 10+

Immobilize your enemies with powers enhanced by this unmelting ice from the Elemental Chaos.

Lvl 10	200 gp	Lvl 30	125,000 gp
Lvl 20	5,000 gp		

Reagent

Power (Consumable): Free Action. Expend this reagent when you use a power with the cold keyword of up to 7th level. One target hit is also immobilized (save ends). This reagent has no effect if the power already immobilizes the target.
Level 20: Power up to 17th level.
Level 30: Power up to 27th level.

Glassteel Shard
Level 7+

Strong as steel, this tempered glass shard enhances the force with which a power strikes.

Lvl 7	100 gp	Lvl 27	65,000 gp
Lvl 17	2,600 gp		

Reagent

Power (Consumable): Free Action. Expend this reagent when you use a power with the force keyword of up to 7th level. Slide each target 1 square.
Level 17: Power up to 17th level, slide 3 squares.
Level 27: Power up to 27th level, slide 5 squares.

Mind Dust
Level 15+

Psychic attacks are deadlier when you use the powdered brain of a mind flayer.

Lvl 15	1000 gp	Lvl 25	25,000 gp

Reagent

Power (Consumable): Free Action. Expend this reagent when you use a power with the psychic keyword of up to 7th level. Roll twice for the power's attack roll and take the better of the two results.
Level 25: Power up to 17th level.

Terror Ichor
Level 9+

With this vial of bewitching pixie blood, you can terrorize your foes with greater efficacy.

Lvl 9	160 gp	Lvl 29	105,000 gp
Lvl 19	4,200 gp		

Reagent

Power (Consumable): Free Action. Expend this reagent when you use a power with the fear keyword of up to 5th level. Each target takes a -2 penalty to saving throws to end any effect of the power that a save can end.
Level 19: Power up to 15th level.
Level 29: Power up to 25th level.

APPENDIX 1

MAGIC ITEMS are the most tangible signs of a character's adventuring success. The PCs' enchanted weapons, armor, and implements tell the tale of how far they've come, the challenges they've faced, and, most importantly, that they've survived those challenges and lived to brag about them.

However, as characters advance in level, they can accumulate a surplus of magic items that become increasingly less relevant, less useful, and less distinctive. Surplus items can be sold or disenchanted easily enough, but a player might want an item his character earns at 1st level to stay with him throughout his career. Another might want to alter or increase an existing item's power rather than claiming a brand-new item and abandoning the old. Yet another character might desire an item with a special history, or one that provides a built-in roleplaying hook.

The rules in this chapter allow DMs and players to place and use magic items with greater ease—not just employing them as treasure and tools, but as memorable elements of the game world.

UNIQUE ITEMS

One of the most time-honored ways of customizing a magic item in a D&D game is to give it a unique history. By working together, players and DMs can create magic items specifically suited for the campaign, giving them an inimitable quality that no standard rulebook can match. The deeds of the PCs then become part of the ongoing history of these items—possibly even the most important chapter in their storied existence.

Such an approach to shared storytelling works best with care and moderation, however. Giving a notable backstory or a complicated array of unfolding powers to a select few of the items the PCs acquire can increase the fun. On the other hand, making every item a relic with a detailed history and a host of secrets behind it serves only to make none of those items particularly special. Make customization choices count by letting a small number of unique items add to the PCs' reputation, rather than filling a campaign with items that compete with the PCs for importance.

HISTORY

As with a character, an item's past can help create a strong sense of its place in the world. Every campaign is unique, and magic items tied to people, places, and myths within the game world can't help but be distinctive. When the item's history becomes relevant to the campaign narrative, it adds depth to the game.

The history of an item claimed at the climax of one adventure can provide the impetus for further adventures. An item that is out of place in its current setting or in the hands of its former owner can also serve as a campaign hook. PCs that recover a magic shield of Pelor from an orc king are likely to wonder how it got there—and might have a mystery on their hands that could take the campaign in new directions.

Characters can uncover fragments of the history and legends surrounding a unique magic item with skill checks (most commonly Arcana or History knowledge checks) or even a skill challenge. Alternatively, an NPC might recognize the item and relate its history to a new owner. An account of the item might be found in lore uncovered during, after, or even before the adventure in which the item appears. Sometimes an item's history is recorded on the item, and powerful relics and artifacts can convey their own sagas.

The more common and low-level an item is, the less likely it is to have an exceptional history. Unless magic items are rare in your world, it's fine for a *+1 dagger* to be just that most of the time.

PERSONALITY AND CHARACTER

Even the most common magic items can have personality. Magic is a strange and wondrous force, and the arcane energy at loose in the world can change the people and objects it touches. As such, magic items—especially those created in ancient times or found in magic-rich environments—can develop quirks.

For instance, the surface of a magic shield might darken as if bruised or glow an angry red when it is struck in battle. A weapon might shout out curses against its wielder's enemies in the first round of combat. Gloves made for a healer might become noticeably warm whenever the wearer enters combat.

Such quirks serve the same function as the quirks and mannerisms given to NPCs by the DM. They add minor narrative color to an item and to the campaign as a whole. Be careful how you apply and use them, however. A quirk can involve a minor negative drawback, but it should never hinder or affect an item's usefulness, especially in combat.

PC INFLUENCE

The PCs are the game's focus. Any magic items they carry—whatever their history and character—should reflect this fact. The actions of a PC can have an impact on the items he or she carries, causing those items to take on specific characteristics as a result of being wielded by a character of power and destiny.

Giving out item levels as treasure (discussed later in this chapter) is one way to give the PCs a degree of influence over the magic they carry. Another way is to create quirks not as a reflection of an item's history but as an example of a PC's influence. This is particularly appropriate when a player chooses to use an item as a roleplaying hook, rewarding player and character alike for interacting with the game world in a meaningful way. For example, a fighter's prized axe might start to echo its wielder's battle cry whenever it scores a critical hit. A paladin's shield might glow brightly as a symbol of her virtue when she fights sworn enemies.

Such character-inspired items can even be reused in a new campaign after epic characters pass into myth and immortality. When new PCs discover these legendary relics, the players whose characters were the item's original owners can have the satisfaction of seeing their roleplaying efforts live on.

ALIGNMENT

Magic items can be strongly attuned to good or evil. An item with an alignment might impose a minor penalty or drawback on a wielder of different alignment. A magic weapon or implement might withhold some of its full enhancement bonus, or a magic item's powers could fail at a critical moment. (In the most extreme cases, an item simply might not function in the hands of a differently aligned character. However, such limitations are typically useful only as plot hooks.)

Alignment incompatibilities should never be allowed to become a permanent hindrance to a character's ability to use a magic item. (See Level Scaling, below, for suggestions on withholding a magic item's powers in a more balanced way.) Characters should always be given the chance to earn an item's full power. For example, a PC might be able to redeem a partially functioning evil item by using it for good. Such an undertaking makes an excellent minor quest, or it could become a hook for an entire campaign.

DAVID GRIFFITH

ITEM LEVEL

The default assumption in the *Player's Handbook* is that each magic item has a level that equates to both its cost and its suitability as part of a PC's equipment. However, an item's level doesn't restrict its use by the PCs. A 1st-level fighter can freely use a +6 *vorpal greatsword* if he can somehow manage to acquire one.

Alternatively, relative level can play a stronger part in how magic items function in your campaign. Although level doesn't have a narrative equivalent in the game world, it does suggest a certain degree of inherent power within characters and their magic items alike. As such, any imbalance between the level of a character and the magic he or she wields can have repercussions in the game.

LEVEL-BASED PENALTIES

DMs should feel free to place restrictions on the way magic items function, according to their level. The standard treasure rules (which assume that PCs can find an item up to four levels higher than their own level) are a good place to start.

It's entirely reasonable to say that items five or more levels higher than a character simply don't function in that character's hands. Alternatively, limitations or penalties for powerful items used by lower-level characters can be assigned on an ad-hoc basis. For example, a powerful magic weapon might function at its normal level but impose a penalty to the wielder's defenses. Likewise, a defensive item might penalize attack rolls, damage rolls, or both. An item that grants a bonus on a certain skill check might penalize other skill checks as its power overwhelms its user.

More extreme penalties might function in the same manner as the behavior of artifacts (see Chapter 9 of the *Dungeon Master's Guide*). A character wielding high-level magic might be inspired (or even forced) to take up an item's goals or purpose in the short term. For example, a 2nd-level character might feel the urge to give her excess wealth to charity under the influence of a +3 *symbol of hope*, while a 10th-level paladin might be driven to seek revenge on the elder red dragon that killed the former owner of his +5 *greatsword*.

DMs should use this technique sparingly, however, and only in the interest of advancing the campaign. It can be fun for a character to try to deal with the unexpected side effects of magic beyond his or her ability to effectively use. It's typically less fun for the PCs' magic items to limit their ability to choose their own path.

LEVEL SCALING

In the interest of entertaining game play, sometimes a DM will want to place a magic item as treasure that is too high for the party's current level. Other times, bravery and fortune sees the PCs defeat a foe and gain access to magic that the DM never intended them to have. In either case, an advanced magic item can have its power scaled back to a level usable by the PCs, with its additional power revealed over time. This technique works particularly well for items that have lower-level versions, but single-level items can be reworked to lower levels as well.

For example, your world's histories might speak of the legendary *Travic's Blade*—a 25th-level *holy avenger*. If the DM decides to introduce the sword into the campaign when the PCs are lower level, he or she can do so by introducing a story hook that speaks of the blade's powers being suppressed until certain conditions are met.

If first found when the PCs are 12th level, the sword could function as a basic +3 *sword*—perhaps one that deals radiant damage on critical hits as a hint of its latent power. When its wielder is 15th level or so, the sword can increase its enhancement bonus to +4 and add a +2 item bonus to damage rolls done with radiant powers through the weapon.

When the PCs ascend to a level suitable for the appearance of a *holy avenger* (21st level or higher), the blade finally attains the full power wielded by mighty Travic in the annals of history. It might even scale up again to become a 30th-level *holy avenger* when its wielder reaches 26th or 27th level, allowing its wielder to transcend the sword's mythic past.

ITEM LEVELS AS TREASURE

Sometimes a magic item enters the campaign at the correct level, but a player wants her character to hold onto that item at higher levels rather than replacing it with a newer, higher-level item. The DM can allow the PC to invest monetary treasure in Enchant Magic Item rituals to increase the item's power (see Enchanting Items, below). Alternatively, item level increases can be given out as treasure.

Item levels granted as treasure follow the same guidelines as normal magic item placement. An increase in an item's enhancement bonus should be given out only when the PCs have attained an appropriate level to earn magic items with the improved bonus.

MAGIC ITEM SCALING

Item Level	Enhancement Bonus
1-5	+1
6-10	+2
11-15	+3
16-20	+4
21-25	+5
26-30	+6

The value of an item's enhancement bonus increase equals the difference in cost between the item's lower-level form and its higher-level form. This value should be primarily subtracted from the magic items given out in an adventure, with only a small portion coming from gold or other monetary treasure.

For example, a PC with *+1 delver's armor* wants to increase the effectiveness of that armor rather than seek another set of more powerful armor. According to the table, that PC should be of a level suitable for using 6th-level items before such an increase can occur. The difference in cost between *+1 delver's armor* and *+2 delver's armor* in the *Player's Handbook* is 2,720 gp—roughly the cost of a 7th-level magic item (2,600 gp). The item level can thus replace a 7th-level item normally placed as treasure (see Treasure Parcels in Chapter 7 of the *Dungeon Master's Guide*), with the additional 120 gp taken out of monetary treasure. Likewise, the increase in the armor's enhancement bonus could partially take the place of an 8th-level treasure (worth 3,400 gp), with the difference (680 gp) made up by a 3rd-level magic item of use to the party.

This system can even be used to turn mundane items into magic items. A PC's nonmagical heirloom longsword might be empowered by exposure to magic or a heroic deed to become a signature magic weapon.

EMPOWERING EVENTS

Whether a magic item increases its power through level scaling or the granting of item levels as treasure, the nature of that increase should be tied to an empowering event. The transition points where new item powers are revealed should be triumphant moments for the wielder and the party as a whole— the defeat of a significant foe, the completion of a major quest, and so on.

Such events should let the players and the characters know that something about the affected item has changed. A being from another plane might show up to reward the PCs for service, imbuing the item in question with newfound power. Perhaps the death of a mighty enemy suffuses the party with supernatural energy that coalesces in the weapon that slew the foe. An eldritch font uncovered at the climax of an adventure could instill a single item with greater potency. Whatever the case, the effect of increasing a magic item's level should be both impressive and apparent.

ENCHANTING ITEMS

The use of the Enchant Magic Item ritual is straightforward enough, allowing characters to make magic items of their level or lower. However, the ritual can also be used to place a property in a magic item that has no property, or to upgrade a magic item to a more powerful version 5 levels higher. This use of the ritual follows the same rules for enchanting a magic item from a mundane item but reduces the cost. The ritual caster must still be high enough level to create the final item, but the caster pays only the difference in cost between the final version and the item in its current form.

For example, a 5th-level ritual caster wishing to imbue a *+1 longsword* (1st level, 360 gp) with the properties of a *+1 flaming longsword* (5th level, 1,000 gp) needs to pay a component cost of only 640 gp. Likewise, a 6th-level ritual caster could spend 1,440 gp to make a *+1 wand* (360 gp) into a *+2 wand* (1,800 gp), while a 10th-level ritual caster could spend 4,640 gp to make a suit of *+1 chainmail* (360 gp) into *+2 exalted chainmail* (5,000 gp), a huge leap in the armor's potency.

The Enchant Magic Item ritual cannot convert one item property into another. For example, a character could not use the ritual to turn a *+1 flaming longsword* into a *+2 lifedrinker longsword*. However, at the DM's option, a character can upgrade a magic item to another item with similar properties. For example, a *thundering bow* might be upgraded to a *thunderburst bow* in this way.

As normal, this use of the Enchant Magic Item ritual does not allow a character to ignore restrictions on the creation of magic items. A ranged weapon cannot be given a property restricted to melee weapons, nor can the ritual imbue a pair of boots with an enchantment normally given to a hands slot item. Likewise, magic item properties and powers cannot be stacked, so that a character cannot imbue a suit of *sylvan armor* with the property and power of *sunleaf armor* as well.

MOVING MAGIC

A rogue might find potent hide armor in an ogre's horde, but she wears leather. The holy symbol taken from a fallen foe has formidable power, but the party's cleric of Pelor doesn't feel like clutching a symbol of Vecna as he prays. The Transfer Enchantment ritual helps you to customize magic items by moving enchantments from one magic item to another.

TRANSFER ENCHANTMENT

With great care and concentration, you carefully strip magical power from one object to imbue it in another.

Level: 4   **Component Cost:** 25 gp
Category: Creation   **Market Price:** 175 gp
Time: 1 hour   **Key Skill:** Arcana (no check)
Duration: Permanent

You transfer the magical qualities (properties, powers, and enhancement bonus) of an enchanted item into another object. You must maintain physical contact with both items for the duration of the ritual. The receiving item must occupy the same magic item slot (head, waist, armor, and so on) and be the same type (wand, rod, weapon, and so on) as the original item. The enchantment to be moved must be valid for the receiving item, so that you cannot transfer ranged weapon properties to melee weapons, cloth-only armor properties to chainmail, and so on.

You can transfer an enchantment to an item that already contains a lower-level enchantment, but the receiving item's previous magic is lost. For example, the enhancement bonus and power of a suit of *+1 barkskin hide* (5th level) could be placed into a suit of *+1 curseforged scale* (3rd level), but the scale armor's existing power is lost in doing so. You cannot transfer an enchantment to an item that already has a higher-level enchantment.

APPENDIX 2: MAGIC ITEMS

The following section includes a master table of all magic items in *Adventurer's Vault*. Items are sorted by level and alphabetized by name. An entry on the table includes an item's level, its name, and the slot it occupies.

LEVEL 1

Lvl	Name	Slot	Pg
1	Belt of resilience	Waist	164
1	Distance +1	Weapon	68
1	Eternal chalk	Wondrous Item	171
1	Floating shield	Arms	117
1	Headband of perception	Head	142
1	Impenetrable barding	Mount Item	123
1	Restful bedroll	Wondrous Item	176

LEVEL 2

Lvl	Name	Slot	Pg
2	Amulet of mental resolve +1	Neck	148
2	Amulet of physical resolve +1	Neck	148
2	Amulet of resolution +1	Neck	149
2	Armor of resistance +1	Armor	41
2	Battle standard of honor	Wondrous Item	179

2	Bloodclaw +1	Weapon	65
2	Bloodguard shield	Arms	114
2	Boots of adept charging	Feet	126
2	Bracers of respite	Arms	115
2	Darkleaf shield	Arms	116
2	Defensive +1	Weapon	67
2	Defensive staff +1	Staff	104
2	Eagle eye goggles	Head	140
2	Feyleaf sandals	Feet	129
2	Flesh seeker +1	Weapon	69
2	Gambler's +1	Weapon	69
2	Gem of colloquy	Head	141
2	Holy healer's +1	Weapon	70
2	Hunter's flint	Wondrous Item	173
2	Immunizing +1	Armor	46
2	Jester shoes	Feet	129
2	Jousting shield	Arms	118
2	Mage's +1	Weapon	72
2	Martyr's +1	Armor	47
2	Mirrored comparison	Mount Item	124
2	Mnemonic staff +1	Staff	104
2	Muleback harness	Waist	166
2	Orb of debilitating languor +1	Orb	93

2	Pact hammer +1	Weapon	74
2	Pact sword +1	Weapon	74
2	Parrying +1	Weapon	74
2	Pinning +1	Weapon	74
2	Prime shot +1	Weapon	76
2	Quickcurse rod +1	Rod	99
2	Reading spectacles	Head	144
2	Reproachful +1	Weapon	76
2	Repulsion +1	Armor	49
2	Robe of eyes +1	Armor	50
2	Robe of scintillation +1	Armor	50
2	Rod of cursed honor +1	Rod	99
2	Screaming +1	Armor	51
2	Shield of the guardian	Arms	120
2	Shroud of protection	Wondrous Item	177
2	Silent tool	Wondrous Item	177
2	Slick +1	Armor	52
2	Staff of missile mastery +1	Staff	106
2	Staggering +1	Weapon	78
2	Symbol of divinity +1	Holy Symbol	88
2	Symbol of good fortune +1	Holy Symbol	88
2	Symbol of reproach +1	Holy Symbol	90
2	Symbol of resilience +1	Holy Symbol	90
2	Utility staff +1	Staff	107
2	Veteran's +1	Armor	55
2	Wrestler's gloves	Hands	137

LEVEL 3

Lvl	Name	Slot	Pg
3	Addergrease +1	Armor	39
3	Arcanist's glasses	Head	138
3	Armor of cleansing +1	Armor	40
3	Armor of exploits +1	Armor	41
3	Battle standard of healing	Wondrous Item	180
3	Belt of the brawler	Waist	164
3	Bestial +1	Armor	42
3	Boots of stealth	Feet	126
3	Breaching +1	Armor	43
3	Brooch of no regrets +1	Neck	149
3	Brooch of shielding +1	Neck	149
3	Circlet of second chances	Head	139
3	Cloak of the chirurgeon +1	Neck	151
3	Earthroot staff +1	Staff	104
3	Flame bracers	Arms	117
3	Flame wand +1	Wand	109
3	Floating lantern	Wondrous Item	171
3	Force staff +1	Staff	104
3	Force wand +1	Wand	109
3	Gloaming shroud +1	Neck	152
3	Heartening +1	Armor	46
3	Hellfire wand +1	Wand	109
3	Horseshoes of speed	Mount Item	123
3	Inescapable +1	Weapon	70
3	Inspiring +1	Weapon	71
3	Lifegiving +1	Armor	47
3	Luckblade +1	Weapon	71
3	Master's wand of cloud of daggers +1	Wand	109

3	Master's wand of dire radiance +1	Wand	110
3	Master's wand of eldritch blast +1	Wand	110
3	Master's wand of eyebite +1	Wand	110
3	Master's wand of hellish rebuke +1	Wand	110
3	Master's wand of magic missile +1	Wand	110
3	Master's wand of ray of frost +1	Wand	110
3	Master's wand of scorching burst +1	Wand	110
3	Master's wand of thunderwave +1	Wand	110
3	Meliorating +1	Armor	47
3	Orb of far seeing +1	Orb	93
3	Orb of insurmountable force +1	Orb	95
3	Orb of judicious conjuration +1	Orb	95
3	Orb of sweet sanctuary +1	Orb	96
3	Orb of unlucky exchanges +1	Orb	96
3	Ornament of alertness +1	Neck	153
3	Paired +1	Weapon	74
3	Point blank +1	Weapon	75
3	Quick +1	Weapon	76
3	Reckless +1	Weapon	76
3	Robe of quills +1	Armor	50
3	Rod of blasting +1	Rod	99
3	Rod of malign conveyance +1	Rod	100
3	Saddle of strength	Mount Item	124
3	Scalebane +1	Weapon	77
3	Serpentskin +1	Armor	51
3	Skewering +1	Weapon	77
3	Staff of ruin +1	Staff	106
3	Staff of the spectral hands +1	Staff	107
3	Staff of ultimate defense +1	Staff	107
3	Stoneborn +1	Armor	53
3	Stonemeal Biscuit	Consumable	192
3	Stoneskin robes +1	Armor	53
3	Strongheart +1	Weapon	79
3	Subtle +1	Weapon	79
3	Swiftshot +1	Weapon	79
3	Symbol of confrontation +1	Holy Symbol	88
3	Symbol of divine reach +1	Holy Symbol	88
3	Thunder wand +1	Wand	111
3	Vanguard +1	Weapon	81
3	Versatile +1	Armor	54
3	Vicious rod +1	Rod	102
3	Wand of cold +1	Wand	111
3	Wand of psychic ravaging +1	Wand	111
3	Wand of radiance +1	Wand	112
3	Wand of swarming force +1	Wand	112
3	Whiteflame +1	Armor	55

LEVEL 4

Lvl	Name	Slot	Pg
4	Acidic +1	Weapon	62
4	Armor of durability +1	Armor	40
4	Battle standard of might	Wondrous Item	179
4	Battlecrazed +1	Weapon	64
4	Battleforged shield	Arms	114
4	Bloodcurse rod +1	Rod	98
4	Bloodthirst bracers	Arms	114
4	Bridle of conjuration	Wondrous Item	169

4	Casque of tactics	Head	139
4	Chime of awakening	Wondrous Item	169
4	Climbing claws	Hands	133
4	Cloak of distortion +1	Neck	151
4	Cloak of the walking wounded +1	Neck	151
4	Collar of recovery +1	Neck	151
4	Communal +1	Weapon	66
4	Counterstrike guards	Arms	116
4	Crystal +1	Armor	43
4	Deathstalker +1	Weapon	67
4	Feyleaf vambraces	Arms	117
4	Feyswarm staff +1	Staff	104
4	Flaying gloves	Hands	133
4	Fortification +1	Armor	45
4	Friend's gift	Companion Item	122
4	Frozen +1	Armor	46
4	Ghost bridle	Mount Item	123
4	Healer's brooch +1	Neck	152
4	Hedge wizard's gloves	Hands	135
4	Helm of opportunity	Head	142
4	Helm of the stubborn mind	Head	143
4	Life shroud	Consumable	191
4	Lullaby +1	Weapon	72
4	Medic's +1	Weapon	72
4	Mithral +1	Armor	48
4	Mountain shield	Arms	118
4	Nail of sealing	Consumable	191
4	Oathblade +1	Weapon	73
4	Onyx dog	Wondrous Item	182
4	Opportunistic +1	Weapon	73
4	Orb of fickle fate +1	Orb	93
4	Orb of harmonic agony +1	Orb	94
4	Pelaurum +1	Armor	48
4	Potion of resistance	Consumable	188
4	Reinforcing +1	Armor	48
4	Rending +1	Weapon	76
4	Robe of contingency +1	Armor	49
4	Rod of the dragonborn +1	Rod	101
4	Rod of the shadow walker +1	Rod	101
4	Salubrious +1	Armor	51
4	Shield of eyes	Arms	120
4	Shimmering +1	Armor	51
4	Staff of light +1	Staff	105
4	Sunblade +1	Weapon	79
4	Symbol of astral might +1	Holy Symbol	87
4	Symbol of mortality +1	Holy Symbol	89
4	Symbol of vengeance +1	Holy Symbol	91
4	Verve +1	Armor	54
4	Viper belt	Waist	167
4	Wildrunners	Feet	131
4	Wounding +1	Weapon	82

LEVEL 5

Lvl	Name	Slot	Pg
5	Agile +1	Armor	39
5	Architect's staff +1	Staff	103
5	Armor of sacrifice +1	Armor	41
5	Barbed baldric	Waist	164
5	Breach bracers	Arms	116
5	Bridle of rapid action	Mount Item	123
5	Cape of the mountebank +1	Neck	149
5	Cat paws	Hands	132
5	Cold iron shield	Arms	116
5	Companion's defender	Companion Item	122
5	Couters of second chances	Arms	116
5	Cynic's goggles	Head	140
5	Direbeast shield	Arms	117
5	Elixir of aptitude	Consumable	186
5	Enchanted reins	Wondrous Item	170
5	Girdle of the oxen	Waist	165
5	Gloves of agility	Hands	134
5	Goggles of aura sight	Head	141
5	Gravespawn potion	Consumable	187
5	Instant campsite	Wondrous Item	173
5	Lamp of discerning	Wondrous Item	174
5	Obsidian steed	Wondrous Item	182
5	Parry gauntlets	Hands	136
5	Poisoned +1	Weapon	75
5	Potion of clarity	Consumable	188
5	Potion of spirit	Consumable	188
5	Pouch of platinum	Wondrous Item	176
5	Power jewel	Wondrous Item	176
5	Quickhit bracers	Arms	118
5	Ruby scabbard	Wondrous Item	176
5	Shared suffering +1	Armor	51
5	Shimmerlight shield	Arms	120
5	Skull mask	Head	144
5	Skybound +1	Armor	52
5	Staff of unparalleled vision +1	Staff	107
5	Stag helm	Head	145
5	Surefoot boots	Feet	130
5	Symbol of dire fate +1	Holy Symbol	88
5	Tactician's +1	Armor	54
5	Thieving +1	Weapon	80
5	Vengeful +1	Weapon	81

LEVEL 6

Lvl	Name	Slot	Pg
6	Augmenting whetstone	Consumable	190
6	Belt of endurance	Waist	164
6	Boots of equilibrium	Feet	126
6	Boots of free movement	Feet	126
6	Bracers of archery	Arms	115
6	Bracers of mental might	Arms	115
6	Bracers of tactical blows	Arms	116
6	Breaching gauntlets	Hands	132
6	Burning gauntlets	Hands	132
6	Caustic gauntlets	Hands	133
6	Cincture of the dragon spirit	Waist	165

6	Cold iron bracers	Arms	116
6	Crown of doors	Head	140
6	Distance +2	Weapon	68
6	Dynamic + 2	Weapon	68
6	Fire beetle potion	Consumable	187
6	Flamedrinker shield	Arms	117
6	Goblin stompers	Feet	129
6	Grasping +2	Weapon	70
6	Helm of vigilant awareness	Head	143
6	Imposter's +2	Armor	46
6	Iron armbands of power	Arms	117
6	Knifethrower's gloves	Hands	136
6	Luckbender gloves	Hands	136
6	Martyr's saddle	Mount Item	124
6	Mercurial rod +2	Rod	99
6	Orb of impenetrable escape +2	Orb	94
6	Orb of mental dominion +2	Orb	95
6	Phylactery of divinity	Head	144
6	Polyglot gem	Wondrous Item	175
6	Sacrificial +2	Weapon	77
6	Sandals of precise stepping	Feet	130
6	Sigil of companionship	Companion Item	123
6	Solitaire (cinnabar)	Wondrous Item	177
6	Stalwart belt	Waist	167
6	Summoned +2	Armor	53
6	Throwing shield	Arms	121
6	Vision sand	Consumable	192
6	Watchful ruby eye	Wondrous Item	178

LEVEL 7

Lvl	Name	Slot	Pg
7	Amulet of mental resolve +2	Neck	148
7	Amulet of physical resolve +2	Neck	148
7	Amulet of resolution +2	Neck	149
7	Armor of resistance +2	Armor	41
7	Belt of fitness	Waist	164
7	Belt of recovery	Waist	164
7	Bloodclaw +2	Weapon	65
7	Boots of the fencing master	Feet	127
7	Contortionist's cord	Waist	165
7	Crown of leaves	Head	140
7	Defensive +2	Weapon	67
7	Defensive staff +2	Staff	104
7	Desert rose	Consumable	193
7	Elixir of dragon breath	Consumable	186
7	Enshrouding candle	Wondrous Item	171
7	Fireflower pendant +2	Neck	152
7	Flesh seeker +2	Weapon	69
7	Frost gauntlets	Hands	133
7	Frozen whetstone	Consumable	190
7	Gambler's +2	Weapon	69
7	Glassteel shard	Consumable	194
7	Holy Healer's +2	Weapon	70
7	Horn of summons	Wondrous Item	173
7	Hunter's Headband	Head	143
7	Immunizing +2	Armor	46
7	Irrefutable +2	Armor	47

7	Jar of steam	Wondrous Item	174
7	Lancing gloves	Hands	136
7	Lens of reading	Wondrous Item	175
7	Mage's +2	Weapon	72
7	Martyr's +2	Armor	47
7	Mnemonic staff +2	Staff	104
7	Orb of debilitating languor +2	Orb	93
7	Orb of spatial contortion +2	Orb	95
7	Pact hammer +2	Weapon	74
7	Pact sword +2	Weapon	74
7	Parrying +2	Weapon	74
7	Pelaurum shield	Arms	118
7	Phantom soldier	Wondrous Item	175
7	Phrenic crown	Head	144
7	Piercing +2	Weapon	74
7	Pinning +2	Weapon	74
7	Potion of lifeshield	Consumable	188
7	Potion of mimicry	Consumable	188
7	Prime shot +2	Weapon	76
7	Quickcurse rod +2	Rod	99
7	Razor bracers	Arms	119
7	Reproachful +2	Weapon	76
7	Repulsion +2	Armor	49
7	Retribution +2	Weapon	76
7	Robe of eyes +2	Armor	50
7	Robe of scintillation +2	Armor	50
7	Rod of cursed honor +2	Rod	99
7	Rod of feythorns +2	Rod	100
7	Rope of slave fighting	Waist	166
7	Rushing cleats	Feet	130
7	Screaming +2	Armor	51
7	Shroud of revival	Wondrous Item	177
7	Skull bracers	Arms	120
7	Slick +2	Armor	52
7	Splitting +2	Weapon	78
7	Staff of elemental prowess +2	Staff	105
7	Staff of missile mastery +2	Staff	106
7	Staff of the serpent +2	Staff	106
7	Staggering +2	Weapon	78
7	Stylus of the translator	Wondrous Item	178
7	Symbol of divinity +2	Holy Symbol	88
7	Symbol of freedom +2	Holy Symbol	88
7	Symbol of good fortune +2	Holy Symbol	88
7	Symbol of perseverance +2	Holy Symbol	89
7	Symbol of reproach +2	Holy Symbol	90
7	Symbol of resilience +2	Holy Symbol	90
7	Symbol of shielding +2	Holy Symbol	90
7	Transference +2	Weapon	81
7	Trauma bracers	Arms	121
7	Utility staff +2	Staff	107
7	Veteran's +2	Armor	55
7	Wildleaf +2	Armor	55
7	Wrestler's gloves	Hands	137

LEVEL 8

Lvl	Name	Slot	Pg
8	Adamantine +2	Weapon	63
8	Addergrease +2	Armor	39
8	Armor of cleansing +2	Armor	40
8	Armor of exploits +2	Armor	41
8	Assassin's +2	Weapon	63
8	Bag of tricks, gray	Wondrous Item	183
8	Baldric of tactical positioning	Waist	163
8	Beastlord +2	Armor	41
8	Belt of vim	Waist	164
8	Bestial +2	Armor	42
8	Black feather of the Raven Queen +2	Holy Symbol	85
8	Bloodiron +2	Armor	42
8	Boots of quickness	Feet	126
8	Bracers of bold maneuvering	Arms	115
8	Bracers of rejuvenation	Arms	115
8	Breaching +2	Armor	43
8	Briartwine +2	Armor	43
8	Brightleaf	Consumable	193
8	Bronzewood +2	Weapon	65
8	Brooch of no regrets +2	Neck	149
8	Brooch of shielding +2	Neck	149
8	Cat tabi	Feet	127
8	Centering cincture	Waist	165
8	Choker of eloquence +2	Neck	150
8	Circlet of indomitability	Head	139
8	Cloak of the chirurgeon +2	Neck	151
8	Cloaked +2	Weapon	66
8	Cog of Erathis +2	Holy Symbol	85
8	Coif of mindiron	Head	140
8	Cold iron +2	Weapon	66
8	Controlling +2	Weapon	66
8	Cunning +2	Weapon	67
8	Dark clover	Consumable	193
8	Death rattle	Wondrous Item	169
8	Decerebrating +2	Weapon	67
8	Determined +2	Weapon	67
8	Dragonscale of Bahamut +2	Holy Symbol	85
8	Dread +2	Weapon	68
8	Dust of arcane insight	Wondrous Item	170
8	Earthbreaker +2	Weapon	68
8	Earthroot staff +2	Staff	104
8	Elixir of accuracy	Consumable	186
8	Elixir of fortitude	Consumable	187
8	Elixir of reflexes	Consumable	187
8	Elixir of will	Consumable	187
8	Evil eye fetish +2	Neck	152
8	Eye of deception	Head	141
8	Eye of Ioun +2	Holy Symbol	86
8	Fan of the four winds	Wondrous Item	171
8	Fist of Kord +2	Holy Symbol	86
8	Flame wand +2	Wand	109
8	Flanking +2	Weapon	68
8	Force +2	Weapon	69
8	Force staff +2	Staff	104
8	Force wand +2	Wand	109
8	Gem of colloquy	Head	141
8	Gloaming shroud +2	Neck	152
8	Gloves of eldritch admixture	Hands	134
8	Gloves of the bounty hunter	Hands	134
8	Graceful +2	Weapon	70
8	Heartening +2	Armor	46
8	Hellfire wand +2	Wand	109
8	Holy gauntlets	Hands	135
8	Inescapable +2	Weapon	70
8	Inspiring +2	Weapon	71
8	Jade macetail	Wondrous Item	181
8	Lifegiving +2	Armor	47
8	Luckblade +2	Weapon	71
8	Mace of healing +2	Weapon	72
8	Manticore shield	Arms	118
8	Mask of Melora +2	Holy Symbol	86
8	Master's wand of cloud of daggers +2	Wand	109
8	Master's wand of dire radiance +2	Wand	110
8	Master's wand of eldritch blast +2	Wand	110
8	Master's wand of eyebite +2	Wand	110
8	Master's wand of hellish rebuke +2	Wand	110
8	Master's wand of magic missile +2	Wand	110
8	Master's wand of ray of frost +2	Wand	110
8	Master's wand of scorching burst +2	Wand	110
8	Master's wand of thunderwave +2	Wand	110
8	Mauling +2	Weapon	72
8	Meliorating +2	Armor	47
8	Mindiron vambraces	Arms	118
8	Mithral shield	Arms	118
8	Moon disk of Sehanine +2	Holy Symbol	86
8	Moradin's indestructible anvil +2	Holy Symbol	86
8	Orb of crystalline terror +2	Orb	93
8	Orb of far seeing +2	Orb	93
8	Orb of inescapable consequences +2	Orb	94
8	Orb of insurmountable force +2	Orb	95
8	Orb of judicious conjuration +2	Orb	95
8	Orb of sweet sanctuary +2	Orb	96
8	Orb of unlucky exchanges +2	Orb	96
8	Ornament of alertness +2	Neck	153
8	Paired +2	Weapon	74
8	Peacemaker's periapt +2	Neck	153
8	Periapt of recovery +2	Neck	153
8	Point blank +2	Weapon	75
8	Potion of stormshield	Consumable	189
8	Quick +2	Weapon	76
8	Quickling boots	Feet	129
8	Rat form +2	Armor	48
8	Recalling harness	Companion Item	123
8	Reckless +2	Weapon	76
8	Resilience amulet +2	Neck	154
8	Robe of quills +2	Armor	50
8	Rod of blasting +2	Rod	99
8	Rod of malign conveyance +2	Rod	100
8	Rod of the Feywild +2	Rod	101
8	Rod of the hidden star +2	Rod	101
8	Rod of the infernal +2	Rod	101

Lvl	Name	Slot	Pg
8	Sash of ensnarement	Waist	166
8	Scalebane +2	Weapon	77
8	Serpentskin +2	Armor	51
8	Skewering +2	Weapon	77
8	Snakefang +2	Armor	52
8	Staff of ruin +2	Staff	106
8	Staff of the spectral hands +2	Staff	107
8	Staff of ultimate defense +2	Staff	107
8	Star of Corellon +2	Holy Symbol	86
8	Starlight goggles	Head	145
8	Steadfast amulet +2	Neck	154
8	Steadfast boots	Feet	130
8	Steadfast saddle	Mount Item	124
8	Stone of Avandra +2	Holy Symbol	87
8	Stoneborn +2	Armor	53
8	Stoneskin robes +2	Armor	53
8	Storm shield	Arms	121
8	Stout +2	Weapon	78
8	Strongheart +2	Weapon	79
8	Subtle +2	Weapon	79
8	Sun disk of Pelor +2	Holy Symbol	87
8	Swiftshot +2	Weapon	79
8	Swimtide harness	Waist	167
8	Symbol of confrontation +2	Holy Symbol	88
8	Symbol of divine reach +2	Holy Symbol	88
8	Thunder wand +2	Wand	111
8	Tigerclaw gauntlets +2	Weapon	80
8	Tyrant's +2	Weapon	81
8	Vanguard +2	Weapon	81
8	Versatile +2	Armor	54
8	Vicious rod +2	Rod	102
8	Wand of cold +2	Wand	111
8	Wand of psychic ravaging +2	Wand	111
8	Wand of radiance +2	Wand	112
8	Wand of swarming force +2	Wand	112
8	Waterbane +2	Weapon	82
8	Whiteflame +2	Armor	55
8	Wyrmguard shield	Arms	122

LEVEL 9

Lvl	Name	Slot	Pg
9	Acidic +2	Weapon	62
9	Angelsteel shield	Arms	114
9	Armor of durability +2	Armor	40
9	Battlecrazed +2	Weapon	64
9	Black dragon bile	Consumable	193
9	Bloodcurse rod +2	Rod	98
9	Bloodshored shield	Arms	114
9	Bloodsoaked shield	Arms	114
9	Boots of eagerness	Feet	126
9	Boots of furious speed	Feet	126
9	Boots of many tricks	Feet	126
9	Champion's +2	Armor	43
9	Cloak of distortion +2	Neck	151
9	Cloak of the cautious +2	Neck	151
9	Cloak of the walking wounded +2	Neck	151
9	Collar of recovery +2	Neck	151
9	Communal +2	Weapon	66
9	Crown of infernal legacy	Head	140
9	Crusader's +2	Weapon	66
9	Crystal +2	Armor	43
9	Darkskull	Wondrous Item	169
9	Deathstalker +2	Weapon	67
9	Demonbane +2	Weapon	67
9	Diamond bracers	Arms	116
9	Ebony fly	Wondrous Item	181
9	Endless canteen	Wondrous Item	171
9	Endless quiver	Wondrous Item	171
9	Feyslaughter +2	Weapon	68
9	Feyswarm staff +2	Staff	104
9	Fortification +2	Armor	45
9	Frozen +2	Armor	46
9	Gloves of storing	Hands	134
9	Goggles of the bone collector	Head	142
9	Goliath's belt	Waist	165
9	Green thumbs	Hands	135
9	Harmonious harp	Wondrous Item	172
9	Healer's brooch +2	Neck	152
9	Laughing death +2	Armor	47
9	Lifesapper rod +2	Rod	99
9	Loamweave +2	Armor	47
9	Lullaby +2	Weapon	72
9	Map of orienteering	Wondrous Item	175
9	Medic's +2	Weapon	72
9	Mirrorsheen coat +2	Armor	48
9	Mithral +2	Armor	48
9	Pearl sea horse	Wondrous Item	183
9	Oathblade +2	Weapon	73
9	Opportunistic +2	Weapon	73
9	Orb of fickle fate +2	Orb	93
9	Orb of harmonic agony +2	Orb	94
9	Pelaurum +2	Armor	48
9	Potion of regeneration	Consumable	188
9	Potion of vigor	Consumable	189
9	Pouch of frozen passage	Wondrous Item	175
9	Recoil shield	Arms	119
9	Reflexive +2	Armor	48
9	Reinforcing +2	Armor	48
9	Reinforcing belt	Waist	166
9	Rending +2	Weapon	76
9	Righteous +2	Armor	49
9	Robe of contingency +2	Armor	49
9	Rod of brutality +2	Rod	99
9	Rod of the dragonborn +2	Rod	101
9	Rod of the shadow walker +2	Rod	101
9	Salubrious +2	Armor	51
9	Shadowflow shield	Arms	119
9	Shapechanger's sorrow +2	Weapon	77
9	Shimmering +2	Armor	51
9	Skyrender +2	Weapon	78
9	Solar +2	Armor	52
9	Spell anchors	Hands	136
9	Staff of light +2	Staff	105
9	Sunblade +2	Weapon	79
9	Sure shot gloves	Hands	137
9	Survivor's +2	Armor	54

APPENDIX 2| *Magic Items*

Lvl	Name	Slot	Pg
9	Symbol of astral might +2	Holy Symbol	87
9	Symbol of mortality +2	Holy Symbol	89
9	Symbol of penitence +2	Holy Symbol	89
9	Symbol of vengeance +2	Holy Symbol	91
9	Terror ichor	Consumable	194
9	Thoughtstealer +2	Weapon	80
9	Thunderhead +2	Armor	54
9	Vampiric +2	Weapon	81
9	Verve +2	Armor	54
9	Whetstone of venom	Consumable	190
9	Wounding +2	Weapon	82
9	Zephyr horseshoes	Mount Item	124

LEVEL 10

Lvl	Name	Slot	Pg
10	Agile +2	Armor	39
10	Antipathy gloves	Hands	132
10	Architect's staff +2	Staff	103
10	Armor of sacrifice +2	Armor	41
10	Belt of blood	Waist	164
10	Blackshroud +2	Weapon	64
10	Bloodsoaked bracers	Arms	114
10	Boots of sand and sea	Feet	126
10	Bowl of purity	Wondrous Item	168
10	Branchrunners	Feet	127
10	Cap of water breathing	Head	138
10	Cape of the mountebank +2	Neck	149
10	Caustic whetstone	Consumable	190
10	Chime of warding	Wondrous Item	169
10	Creeping gatevine	Consumable	193
10	Crystal ball of spying	Wondrous Item	169
10	Dust of disenchantment	Wondrous Item	170
10	Dwarven throwers	Hands	133
10	Flame rose	Consumable	194
10	Footpad's friend + 2	Weapon	69
10	Fundamental ice	Consumable	194
10	Gauntlets of brilliance	Hands	133
10	Glowstone	Consumable	191
10	Guardian's collar	Companion Item	122
10	Hat of disguise	Head	142
10	Headband of intellect	Head	142
10	Healer's shield	Arms	117
10	Helm of the flamewarped	Head	143
10	Kruthik potion	Consumable	187
10	Laurel circlet	Head	144
10	Lens of discernment	Wondrous Item	174
10	Marble elephant	Wondrous Item	182
10	Oil of flesh returned	Consumable	192
10	Poisoned +2	Weapon	75
10	Potion of clarity	Consumable	188
10	Potion of spirit	Consumable	188
10	Precise wand of color spray +2	Wand	111
10	Righteous +2	Weapon	77
10	Rod of mindbending +2	Rod	100
10	Rod of starlight +2	Rod	100
10	Salve of power	Wondrous Item	176
10	Scabbard of sacred might	Wondrous Item	177
10	Shared suffering +2	Armor	51

Lvl	Name	Slot	Pg
10	Shielding girdle	Waist	167
10	Skeleton key	Wondrous Item	177
10	Skybound +2	Armor	52
10	Spymaster's quill	Wondrous Item	178
10	Staff of acid and flame +2	Staff	105
10	Staff of gathering +2	Staff	105
10	Staff of unparalleled vision +2	Staff	107
10	Storm gauntlets	Hands	136
10	Strikebacks	Hands	136
10	Symbol of dire fate +2	Holy Symbol	88
10	Tactician's +2	Armor	54
10	Tempest whetstone	Consumable	190
10	Thieving +2	Weapon	80
10	Vengeful +2	Weapon	81
10	Wallwalkers	Feet	131
10	Warsheath +2	Armor	55
10	Whetstone of combustion	Consumable	190

LEVEL 11

Lvl	Name	Slot	Pg
11	Assassin's slippers	Feet	125
11	Augmenting whetstone	Consumable	190
11	Backbone belt	Waist	163
11	Battering +3	Weapon	63
11	Belt of resilience	Waist	164
11	Blacksmelt +3	Weapon	64
11	Bloodstone spider	Wondrous Item	180
11	Boots of dancing	Feet	126
11	Bracers of infinite blades	Arms	115
11	Circlet of mental onslaught	Head	139
11	Crown of doors	Head	140
11	Distance +3	Weapon	68
11	Dynamic + 3	Weapon	68
11	Elixir of speed	Consumable	187
11	Gauntlets of blinding strikes	Hands	133
11	Grasping +3	Weapon	70
11	Headband of perception	Head	142
11	Healer's sash	Waist	166
11	Impenetrable barding	Mount Item	123
11	Imposter's +3	Armor	46
11	Ivory goat of travail	Wondrous Item	181
11	Longshot gloves	Hands	136
11	Mask of slithering	Head	144
11	Mercurial rod +3	Rod	99
11	Orb of impenetrable escape +3	Orb	94
11	Orb of mental dominion +3	Orb	95
11	Ricochet +3	Weapon	76
11	Rogue's belt	Waist	166
11	Sacrificial +3	Weapon	77
11	Solitaire (citrine)	Wondrous Item	177
11	Summoned +3	Armor	53
11	Survivor's belt	Waist	167
11	Totemic belt	Waist	167
11	Tumbler's shoes	Feet	131
11	Unfettered thieves' tools	Wondrous Item	178
11	Unguent of darkvision	Consumable	192
11	Warlock's bracers	Arms	121

LEVEL 12

Lvl	Name	Slot	Pg
12	Absence amulet +3	Neck	147
12	Amulet of mental resolve +3	Neck	148
12	Amulet of physical resolve +3	Neck	148
12	Amulet of resolution +3	Neck	149
12	Armor of resistance +3	Armor	41
12	Assault boots	Feet	125
12	Blade of night +3	Weapon	65
12	Bloodclaw +3	Weapon	65
12	Bloodguard shield	Arms	114
12	Bracers of respite	Arms	115
12	Butterfly sandals	Feet	127
12	Cingulum of combat rushing	Waist	165
12	Clasp of noble sacrifice +3	Neck	150
12	Darkforged +3	Armor	43
12	Darkleaf shield	Arms	116
12	Defensive +3	Weapon	67
12	Defensive staff +3	Staff	104
12	Dragonborn greaves	Feet	128
12	Dwarven boots	Feet	128
12	Eagle eye goggles	Head	140
12	Elukian clay +3	Weapon	68
12	Exodus knife	Wondrous Item	171
12	Feystep lacings	Feet	129
12	Fireflower pendant +3	Neck	152
12	Flesh seeker +3	Weapon	69
12	Flickersight +3	Armor	45
12	Foe stone	Wondrous Item	172
12	Fragrance of authority	Wondrous Item	172
12	Gem of colloquy	Head	141
12	Gambler's +3	Weapon	69
12	Gloves of the healer	Hands	135
12	Golden lion	Wondrous Item	181
12	Holy Healer's +3	Weapon	70
12	Immovable shaft	Wondrous Item	173
12	Immunizing +3	Armor	46
12	Irrefutable +3	Armor	47
12	Jagged +3	Weapon	71
12	Jousting shield	Arms	118
12	Mage's +3	Weapon	72
12	Martyr's +3	Armor	47
12	Mnemonic staff +3	Staff	104
12	Muleback harness	Waist	166
12	Orb of augmented stasis +3	Orb	92
12	Orb of debilitating languor +3	Orb	93
12	Orb of spatial contortion +3	Orb	95
12	Orb of sudden insanity +3	Orb	96
12	Pact hammer +3	Weapon	74
12	Pact sword +3	Weapon	74
12	Parrying +3	Weapon	74
12	Piercing +3	Weapon	74
12	Pinning +3	Weapon	74
12	Prime shot +3	Weapon	76
12	Quickcurse rod +3	Rod	99
12	Razor shield	Arms	119
12	Reproachful +3	Weapon	76

Lvl	Name	Slot	Pg
12	Repulsion +3	Armor	49
12	Retribution +3	Weapon	76
12	Ricochet shield	Arms	119
12	Robe of eyes +3	Armor	50
12	Robe of scintillation +3	Armor	50
12	Rod of cursed honor +3	Rod	99
12	Rod of feythorns +3	Rod	100
12	Rod of the churning inferno +3	Rod	100
12	Screaming +3	Armor	51
12	Shield of the guardian	Arms	120
12	Slick +3	Armor	52
12	Splitting +3	Weapon	78
12	Staff of elemental prowess +3	Staff	105
12	Staff of missile mastery +3	Staff	106
12	Staff of searing death +3	Staff	106
12	Staff of the serpent +3	Staff	106
12	Staggering +3	Weapon	78
12	Stormbolt +3	Weapon	78
12	Symbol of divinity +3	Holy Symbol	88
12	Symbol of freedom +3	Holy Symbol	88
12	Symbol of good fortune +3	Holy Symbol	88
12	Symbol of lifebonding +3	Holy Symbol	89
12	Symbol of perseverance +3	Holy Symbol	89
12	Symbol of reproach +3	Holy Symbol	90
12	Symbol of resilience +3	Holy Symbol	90
12	Symbol of shielding +3	Holy Symbol	90
12	Tauran shield	Arms	121
12	Thornwalker slippers	Feet	130
12	Transference +3	Weapon	81
12	Transposition harness	Companion Item	123
12	Utility staff +3	Staff	107
12	Veteran's +3	Armor	55
12	Wildleaf +3	Armor	55
12	Wrestler's gloves	Hands	137

LEVEL 13

Lvl	Name	Slot	Pg
13	Abyssal adornment +3	Neck	148
13	Adamantine +3	Weapon	63
13	Addergrease +3	Armor	39
13	Armor of cleansing +3	Armor	40
13	Armor of exploits +3	Armor	41
13	Armor of starlight +3	Armor	41
13	Assassin's +3	Weapon	63
13	Beastlord +3	Armor	41
13	Bestial +3	Armor	42
13	Black feather of the Raven Queen +3	Holy Symbol	85
13	Bloodfire +3	Armor	42
13	Bloodiron +3	Weapon	65
13	Bloodiron +3	Armor	42
13	Bloodthirsty +3	Weapon	65
13	Boots of stealth	Feet	126
13	Boots of swimming	Feet	127
13	Bracers of wound closure	Arms	116
13	Breaching +3	Armor	43
13	Briartwine +3	Armor	43

13	Bronzewood +3	Weapon	65
13	Brooch of no regrets +3	Neck	149
13	Brooch of shielding +3	Neck	149
13	Chaos weave +3	Weapon	65
13	Choker of eloquence +3	Neck	150
13	Cloak of arachnida +3	Neck	150
13	Cloak of the chirurgeon +3	Neck	151
13	Cloaked +3	Weapon	66
13	Cog of Erathis +3	Holy Symbol	85
13	Cold iron +3	Weapon	66
13	Controlling +3	Weapon	66
13	Coral +3	Armor	43
13	Cord of divine favor	Waist	165
13	Cunning +3	Weapon	67
13	Decerebrating +3	Weapon	67
13	Desiccating +3	Weapon	67
13	Determined +3	Weapon	67
13	Dragonscale of Bahamut +3	Holy Symbol	85
13	Dread +3	Weapon	68
13	Dread helm	Head	140
13	Drum of panic	Wondrous Item	170
13	Earthbreaker +3	Weapon	68
13	Earthroot staff +3	Staff	104
13	Elixir of accuracy	Consumable	186
13	Elixir of fortitude	Consumable	187
13	Elixir of reflexes	Consumable	187
13	Elixir of will	Consumable	187
13	Elukian clay +3	Armor	45
13	Evil eye fetish +3	Neck	152
13	Eye of Ioun +3	Holy Symbol	86
13	Farslayer +3	Weapon	68
13	Feybread biscuit	Consumable	191
13	Fist of Kord +3	Holy Symbol	86
13	Flame bracers	Arms	117
13	Flame wand +3	Wand	109
13	Flanking +3	Weapon	68
13	Force +3	Weapon	69
13	Force staff +3	Staff	104
13	Force wand +3	Wand	109
13	Giant gloves	Hands	133
13	Giantdodger +3	Armor	46
13	Gloaming shroud +3	Neck	152
13	Gloves of missile deflection	Hands	134
13	Graceful +3	Weapon	70
13	Heartening +3	Armor	46
13	Hellfire wand +3	Wand	109
13	Inescapable +3	Weapon	70
13	Inspiring +3	Weapon	71
13	Liar's trinket +3	Neck	153
13	Lifegiving +3	Armor	47
13	Luckblade +3	Weapon	71
13	Mace of healing +3	Weapon	72
13	Mask of Melora +3	Holy Symbol	86
13	Master's wand of cloud of daggers +3	Wand	109
13	Master's wand of dire radiance +3	Wand	110
13	Master's wand of eldritch blast +3	Wand	110
13	Master's wand of eyebite +3	Wand	110
13	Master's wand of hellish rebuke +3	Wand	110
13	Master's wand of magic missile +3	Wand	110
13	Master's wand of ray of frost +3	Wand	110
13	Master's wand of scorching burst +3	Wand	110
13	Master's wand of thunderwave +3	Wand	110
13	Mauling +3	Weapon	72
13	Meliorating +3	Armor	47
13	Moon disk of Sehanine +3	Holy Symbol	86
13	Moradin's indestructible anvil +3	Holy Symbol	86
13	Necrotic +3	Weapon	73
13	Orb of crystalline terror +3	Orb	93
13	Orb of far seeing +3	Orb	93
13	Orb of indefatigable concentration +3	Orb	94
13	Orb of inescapable consequences +3	Orb	94
13	Orb of insurmountable force +3	Orb	95
13	Orb of judicious conjuration +3	Orb	95
13	Orb of karmic resonance +3	Orb	95
13	Orb of sweet sanctuary +3	Orb	96
13	Orb of unlucky exchanges +3	Orb	96
13	Ornament of alertness +3	Neck	153
13	Paired +3	Weapon	74
13	Paralyzing +3	Weapon	74
13	Peacemaker's periapt +3	Neck	153
13	Periapt of recovery +3	Neck	153
13	Point blank +3	Weapon	75
13	Predatory +3	Weapon	75
13	Quick +3	Weapon	76
13	Rat form +3	Armor	48
13	Reckless +3	Weapon	76
13	Reliable staff +3	Staff	104
13	Resilience amulet +3	Neck	154
13	Robe of defying flames +3	Armor	49
13	Robe of defying frost +3	Armor	49
13	Robe of quills +3	Armor	50
13	Robe of stars +3	Armor	50
13	Rod of blasting +3	Rod	99
13	Rod of malign conveyance +3	Rod	100
13	Rod of the Feywild +3	Rod	101
13	Rod of the hidden star +3	Rod	101
13	Rod of the infernal +3	Rod	101
13	Scalebane +3	Weapon	77
13	Serpentskin +3	Armor	51
13	Skewering +3	Weapon	77
13	Snakefang +3	Armor	52
13	Sniper's +3	Weapon	78
13	Staff of ruin +3	Staff	106
13	Staff of the spectral hands +3	Staff	107
13	Staff of ultimate defense +3	Staff	107
13	Star of Corellon +3	Holy Symbol	86
13	Steadfast amulet +3	Neck	154
13	Stone of Avandra +3	Holy Symbol	87
13	Stoneborn +3	Armor	53
13	Stoneskin robes +3	Armor	53
13	Stonewall shield	Arms	120
13	Stout +3	Weapon	78
13	Strongheart +3	Weapon	79
13	Subtle +3	Weapon	79

Lvl	Name	Slot	Pg
13	Sun disk of Pelor +3	Holy Symbol	87
13	Surge +3	Armor	53
13	Swiftshot +3	Weapon	79
13	Symbol of confrontation +3	Holy Symbol	88
13	Symbol of divine reach +3	Holy Symbol	88
13	Thunder wand +3	Wand	111
13	Thunderbolt +3	Weapon	80
13	Thundergod +3	Weapon	80
13	Tigerclaw gauntlets +3	Weapon	80
13	Tyrant's +3	Weapon	81
13	Vanguard +3	Weapon	81
13	Versatile +3	Armor	54
13	Vicious rod +3	Rod	102
13	Wand of cold +3	Wand	111
13	Wand of psychic ravaging +3	Wand	111
13	Wand of radiance +3	Wand	112
13	Wand of swarming force +3	Wand	112
13	Waterbane +3	Weapon	82
13	Whiteflame +3	Armor	55
13	Withering +3	Weapon	82

LEVEL 14

Lvl	Name	Slot	Pg
14	Acidic +3	Weapon	62
14	Adamantine rod +3	Rod	98
14	Amulet of attenuation +3	Neck	148
14	Amulet of bodily sanctity +3	Neck	148
14	Amulet of elusive prey +3	Neck	148
14	Amulet of inner voice +3	Neck	148
14	Aqueous +3	Armor	40
14	Armor of attraction +3	Armor	40
14	Armor of durability +3	Armor	40
14	Armor of night +3	Armor	41
14	Assured wand of frostburn +3	Wand	109
14	Assured wand of howl of doom +3	Wand	109
14	Battlecrazed +3	Weapon	64
14	Battleforged shield	Arms	114
14	Battlemaster's +3	Weapon	64
14	Bilethorn +3	Weapon	64
14	Black cave pearl	Consumable	193
14	Bloodcurse rod +3	Rod	98
14	Bloodiron rod +3	Rod	98
14	Bloodthirst bracers	Arms	114
14	Bonegrim +3	Armor	42
14	Bracers of iron arcana	Arms	115
14	Casque of tactics	Head	139
14	Champion's +3	Armor	43
14	Chaos weave +3	Armor	43
14	Cherished ring	Ring	156
14	Cincture of vivacity	Waist	165
14	Cloak of distortion +3	Neck	151
14	Cloak of the cautious +3	Neck	151
14	Cloak of the walking wounded +3	Neck	151
14	Collar of recovery +3	Neck	151
14	Communal +3	Weapon	66
14	Counterstrike guards	Arms	116
14	Crusader's +3	Weapon	66

Lvl	Name	Slot	Pg
14	Crystal +3	Armor	43
14	Deathstalker +3	Weapon	67
14	Demonbane +3	Weapon	67
14	Displacer +3	Armor	44
14	Earthstriders	Feet	128
14	Factotum helm	Head	141
14	Feymind +3	Armor	45
14	Feyslaughter +3	Weapon	68
14	Feyswarm staff +3	Staff	104
14	Fireburst boots	Feet	129
14	Flamewrath cape +3	Neck	152
14	Flaring shield	Arms	117
14	Flaying gloves	Hands	133
14	Forbidding +3	Weapon	69
14	Fortification +3	Armor	45
14	Friend's gift	Companion Item	122
14	Frostburn +3	Armor	45
14	Frozen +3	Armor	46
14	Gloves of dimensional repulsion	Hands	134
14	Gloves of transference	Hands	135
14	Golden spade	Wondrous Item	172
14	Healer's brooch +3	Neck	152
14	Healing +3	Weapon	70
14	Helm of opportunity	Head	142
14	Hypnotic shield	Arms	117
14	Laughing death +3	Armor	47
14	Lifesapper rod +3	Rod	99
14	Loamweave +3	Armor	47
14	Lullaby +3	Weapon	72
14	Magician's ring	Ring	157
14	Mask of terror	Head	144
14	Medic's +3	Weapon	72
14	Mindiron +3	Weapon	72
14	Mirrorsheen coat +3	Armor	48
14	Mithral +3	Armor	48
14	Mountain shield	Arms	118
14	Oathblade +3	Weapon	73
14	Oceanstrider boots	Feet	129
14	Opportunistic +3	Weapon	73
14	Orb of crimson commitment +3	Orb	92
14	Orb of draconic majesty +3	Orb	93
14	Orb of fickle fate +3	Orb	93
14	Orb of harmonic agony +3	Orb	94
14	Pelaurum +3	Armor	48
14	Potion of resistance	Consumable	188
14	Quickening staff +3	Staff	104
14	Reflexive +3	Armor	48
14	Reinforcing +3	Armor	48
14	Rending +3	Weapon	76
14	Righteous +3	Armor	49
14	Ring of brotherhood	Ring	158
14	Ring of calling	Ring	158
14	Ring of feather fall	Ring	158
14	Ring of fireblazing	Ring	158
14	Ring of perfect grip	Ring	159
14	Robe of contingency +3	Armor	49
14	Rod of brutality +3	Rod	99

Lvl	Name	Slot	Pg
14	Rod of the dragonborn +3	Rod	101
14	Rod of the shadow walker +3	Rod	101
14	Rod of the sorrowsworn +3	Rod	101
14	Sail of winds	Wondrous Item	176
14	Salubrious +3	Armor	51
14	Shapechanger's sorrow +3	Weapon	77
14	Shimmering +3	Armor	51
14	Skyrender +3	Weapon	78
14	Solar +3	Armor	52
14	Spellshield	Arms	120
14	Staff of light +3	Staff	105
14	Staff of transposition +3	Staff	107
14	Sunblade +3	Weapon	79
14	Survivor's +3	Armor	54
14	Symbol of astral might +3	Holy Symbol	87
14	Symbol of censure +3	Holy Symbol	87
14	Symbol of mortality +3	Holy Symbol	89
14	Symbol of penitence +3	Holy Symbol	89
14	Symbol of vengeance +3	Holy Symbol	91
14	Thoughtstealer +3	Weapon	80
14	Thunderhead +3	Armor	54
14	Transposing +3	Weapon	81
14	Vampiric +3	Weapon	81
14	Verve +3	Armor	54
14	Voidcrystal +3	Weapon	82
14	Voidcrystal +3	Armor	55
14	Wounding +3	Weapon	82

LEVEL 15

Lvl	Name	Slot	Pg
15	Agile +3	Armor	39
15	Amulet of aranea +3	Neck	148
15	Antipathy gloves	Hands	132
15	Architect's staff +3	Staff	103
15	Armor of negation +3	Armor	41
15	Armor of sacrifice +3	Armor	41
15	Assassinbane +3	Armor	41
15	Barbed baldric	Waist	164
15	Blackshroud +3	Weapon	64
15	Breach bracers	Arms	116
15	Brooch of vitality +3	Neck	149
15	Cape of the mountebank +3	Neck	149
15	Carcanet of psychic schism	Head	139
15	Cat paws	Hands	132
15	Cloak of displacement +3	Neck	150
15	Cold iron shield	Arms	116
15	Companion's defender	Companion Item	122
15	Couters of second chances	Arms	116
15	Crown of nature's rebellion	Head	140
15	Cryptspawn potion	Consumable	186
15	Direbeast shield	Arms	117
15	Dread nightshade	Consumable	194
15	Elixir of aptitude	Consumable	186
15	Flanker's boots	Feet	129
15	Floorfighter straps	Feet	129
15	Flying hook	Wondrous Item	172
15	Footpad's friend + 3	Weapon	69

Lvl	Name	Slot	Pg
15	Girdle of the umber hulk	Waist	165
15	Illithid robes +3	Armor	46
15	Invulnerable case	Wondrous Item	173
15	Mind dust	Consumable	194
15	Necklace of fireballs +3	Neck	153
15	Orb of mighty retort +3	Orb	95
15	Orb of weakness intensified +3	Orb	97
15	Poisoned +3	Weapon	75
15	Potion of clarity	Consumable	188
15	Potion of spirit	Consumable	188
15	Pouch of shared acquisition	Wondrous Item	176
15	Precise wand of color spray +3	Wand	111
15	Premonition ring	Ring	157
15	Quickhit bracers	Arms	118
15	Radiant +3	Weapon	76
15	Rapidstrike bracers	Arms	118
15	Reality cord	Waist	166
15	Righteous +3	Weapon	77
15	Ring of aquatic ability	Ring	157
15	Ring of shadow travel	Ring	159
15	Ring of the dragonborn emperor	Ring	161
15	Robe of defying storms +3	Armor	49
15	Rod of mindbending +3	Rod	100
15	Rod of starlight +3	Rod	100
15	Rod of vulnerability +3	Rod	102
15	Saddle of the nightmare	Mount Item	124
15	Saddle of the shark	Mount Item	124
15	Sapphire scabbard	Wondrous Item	176
15	Shared suffering +3	Armor	51
15	Shimmerlight shield	Arms	120
15	Skull mask	Head	144
15	Skybound +3	Armor	52
15	Spiritlink +3	Armor	53
15	Staff of acid and flame +3	Staff	105
15	Staff of gathering +3	Staff	105
15	Staff of unparalleled vision +3	Staff	107
15	Stag helm	Head	145
15	Stormlord +3	Armor	53
15	Striking staff +3	Staff	107
15	Symbol of brilliance +3	Holy Symbol	87
15	Symbol of dire fate +3	Holy Symbol	88
15	Symbol of renewal +3	Holy Symbol	89
15	Symbol of the warpriest +3	Holy Symbol	90
15	Tactician's +3	Armor	54
15	Talisman of fortune	Wondrous Item	178
15	Thieving +3	Weapon	80
15	Torc of power preservation +3	Neck	154
15	Vengeful +3	Weapon	81
15	Wand of erupting flame +3	Wand	111
15	Warsheath +3	Armor	55
15	Zealot's +3	Armor	55

LEVEL 16

Lvl	Name	Slot	Pg
16	Augmenting whetstone	Consumable	190
16	Battering +4	Weapon	63
16	Battle standard of the fiery legion	Wondrous Item	179
16	Belt of endurance	Waist	164
16	Blacksmelt +4	Weapon	64
16	Blasting circlet	Head	138
16	Boots of withdrawal	Feet	127
16	Bracers of archery	Arms	115
16	Bracers of infinite blades	Arms	115
16	Bracers of tactical blows	Arms	116
16	Breaching gauntlets	Hands	132
16	Burning gauntlets	Hands	132
16	Caustic gauntlets	Hands	133
16	Chameleon ring	Ring	156
16	Cognizance ring	Ring	156
16	Cold iron bracers	Arms	116
16	Crown of doors	Head	140
16	Crown of eyes	Head	140
16	Distance +4	Weapon	68
16	Dynamic + 4	Weapon	68
16	Elixir of invisibility	Consumable	187
16	Flamedrinker shield	Arms	117
16	Forceful +4	Weapon	69
16	Gem of auditory recollection	Wondrous Item	172
16	Girdle of the dragon	Waist	165
16	Gloves of accuracy	Hands	134
16	Grasping +4	Weapon	70
16	Headband of insight	Head	142
16	Headband of psychic attack	Head	142
16	Helm of hidden horrors	Head	142
16	Imposter's +4	Armor	46
16	Inquisitor's helm	Head	143
16	Iron armbands of power	Arms	117
16	Lantern of revelation	Wondrous Item	174
16	Luckbender gloves	Hands	136
16	Mercurial rod +4	Rod	99
16	Orb of impenetrable escape +4	Orb	94
16	Orb of mental dominion +4	Orb	95
16	Ricochet +4	Weapon	76
16	Ring of forgetful touch	Ring	159
16	Ring of personal gravity	Ring	159
16	Sacrificial +4	Weapon	77
16	Sandals of precise stepping	Feet	130
16	Sigil of companionship	Companion Item	123
16	Solitaire (aquamarine)	Wondrous Item	177
16	Stalwart belt	Waist	167
16	Summoned +4	Armor	53
16	Throwing shield	Arms	121
16	Vampiric gauntlets	Hands	137
16	Venom gloves	Hands	137
16	War ring	Ring	163

LEVEL 17

Lvl	Name	Slot	Pg
17	Absence amulet +4	Neck	147
17	Amulet of mental resolve +4	Neck	148
17	Amulet of physical resolve +4	Neck	148
17	Amulet of resolution +4	Neck	149
17	Armor of resistance +4	Armor	41
17	Avandra's whisper +4	Weapon	63
17	Banquet ring	Ring	155
17	Battle standard of shadow	Wondrous Item	179
17	Blade of night +4	Weapon	65
17	Bloodclaw +4	Weapon	65
17	Bottled smoke	Wondrous Item	168
17	Circlet of rapid casting	Head	139
17	Clasp of noble sacrifice +4	Neck	150
17	Darkforged +4	Armor	43
17	Defensive +4	Weapon	67
17	Defensive staff +4	Staff	104
17	Desert rose	Consumable	193
17	Earthreaver stompers	Feet	128
17	Elixir of dragon breath	Consumable	186
17	Elukian clay +4	Weapon	68
17	Fireflower pendant +4	Neck	152
17	Flesh seeker +4	Weapon	69
17	Flickersight +4	Armor	45
17	Frost gauntlets	Hands	133
17	Frozen whetstone	Consumable	190
17	Gambler's +4	Weapon	69
17	Glassteel shard	Consumable	194
17	Goggles of the hawk	Head	142
17	Grimlock helm	Head	142
17	Holy Healer's +4	Weapon	70
17	Horn of blasting	Wondrous Item	173
17	Horn of undead enmity	Wondrous Item	173
17	Immunizing +4	Armor	46
17	Irrefutable +4	Armor	47
17	Jagged +4	Weapon	71
17	Mage's +4	Weapon	72
17	Martyr's +4	Armor	47
17	Mnemonic staff +4	Staff	104
17	Moradin's +4	Weapon	73
17	Orb of augmented stasis +4	Orb	92
17	Orb of debilitating languor +4	Orb	93
17	Orb of revenant magic +4	Orb	95
17	Orb of spatial contortion +4	Orb	95
17	Orb of sudden insanity +4	Orb	96
17	Pact hammer +4	Weapon	74
17	Pact sword +4	Weapon	74
17	Parrying +4	Weapon	74
17	Pelaurum shield	Arms	118
17	Phrenic crown	Head	144
17	Piercing +4	Weapon	74
17	Pinning +4	Weapon	74
17	Potion of lifeshield	Consumable	188
17	Potion of mimicry	Consumable	188
17	Prime shot +4	Weapon	76
17	Quickcurse rod +4	Rod	99

17	Razor bracers	Arms	119
17	Reproachful +4	Weapon	76
17	Repulsion +4	Armor	49
17	Retribution +4	Weapon	76
17	Ring of arcane information	Ring	157
17	Ring of retreat	Ring	159
17	Ring of vigilant defense	Ring	162
17	Robe of bloodwalking +4	Armor	49
17	Robe of eyes +4	Armor	50
17	Robe of sapping +4	Armor	50
17	Robe of scintillation +4	Armor	50
17	Rod of cursed honor +4	Rod	99
17	Rod of feythorns +4	Rod	100
17	Rod of the bloodthorn +4	Rod	100
17	Rod of the churning inferno +4	Rod	100
17	Rope of slave fighting	Waist	166
17	Screaming +4	Armor	51
17	Shield of blocking	Arms	119
17	Skull bracers	Arms	120
17	Slick +4	Armor	52
17	Splitting +4	Weapon	78
17	Staff of elemental prowess +4	Staff	105
17	Staff of missile mastery +4	Staff	106
17	Staff of searing death +4	Staff	106
17	Staff of the serpent +4	Staff	106
17	Staggering +4	Weapon	78
17	Stormbolt +4	Weapon	78
17	Symbol of dedication +4	Holy Symbol	88
17	Symbol of divinity +4	Holy Symbol	88
17	Symbol of freedom +4	Holy Symbol	88
17	Symbol of good fortune +4	Holy Symbol	88
17	Symbol of lifebonding +4	Holy Symbol	89
17	Symbol of perseverance +4	Holy Symbol	89
17	Symbol of reproach +4	Holy Symbol	90
17	Symbol of resilience +4	Holy Symbol	90
17	Symbol of shielding +4	Holy Symbol	90
17	Symbol of sustenance +4	Holy Symbol	90
17	Transference +4	Weapon	81
17	Utility staff +4	Staff	107
17	Veteran's +4	Armor	55
17	Wildleaf +4	Armor	55
17	Wrestler's gloves	Hands	137

LEVEL 18

Lvl	Name	Slot	Pg
18	Abyssal adornment +4	Neck	148
18	Adamantine +4	Weapon	63
18	Addergrease +4	Armor	39
18	Amulet of material darkness +4	Neck	148
18	Armor of cleansing +4	Armor	40
18	Armor of exploits +4	Armor	41
18	Armor of starlight +4	Armor	41
18	Assassin's +4	Weapon	63
18	Bag of tricks, rust	Wondrous Item	184
18	Baldric of tactical positioning	Waist	163
18	Battle standard of tactics	Wondrous Item	179
18	Beastlord +4	Armor	41

18	Belt of vim	Waist	164
18	Bestial +4	Armor	42
18	Black feather of the Raven Queen +4	Holy Symbol	85
18	Bloodfire +4	Armor	42
18	Bloodiron +4	Weapon	65
18	Bloodiron +4	Armor	42
18	Bloodthirsty +4	Weapon	65
18	Bone ring of better fortune	Ring	156
18	Boots of quickness	Feet	126
18	Bracers of bold maneuvering	Arms	115
18	Breaching +4	Armor	43
18	Briartwine +4	Armor	43
18	Brightleaf	Consumable	193
18	Bronzewood +4	Weapon	65
18	Brooch of no regrets +4	Neck	149
18	Brooch of shielding +4	Neck	149
18	Cat tabi	Feet	127
18	Chamber cloak +4	Neck	150
18	Chaos weave +4	Weapon	65
18	Choker of eloquence +4	Neck	150
18	Circlet of indomitability	Head	139
18	Cloak of arachnida +4	Neck	150
18	Cloak of the chirurgeon +4	Neck	151
18	Cloaked +4	Weapon	66
18	Cog of Erathis +4	Holy Symbol	85
18	Coif of mindiron	Head	140
18	Cold iron +4	Weapon	66
18	Controlling +4	Weapon	66
18	Coral +4	Armor	43
18	Cord of foresight	Waist	165
18	Crown of the world tree	Head	140
18	Cunning +4	Weapon	67
18	Dark clover	Consumable	193
18	Decerebrating +4	Weapon	67
18	Defiant boots	Feet	128
18	Desiccating +4	Weapon	67
18	Determined +4	Weapon	67
18	Dimensional stride boots	Feet	128
18	Dragonscale of Bahamut +4	Holy Symbol	85
18	Dragonscale, black +4	Armor	44
18	Dragonscale, white +4	Armor	45
18	Dread +4	Weapon	68
18	Dust of creation	Wondrous Item	170
18	Dwarfstride boots	Feet	128
18	Earthbind lodestone	Wondrous Item	170
18	Earthbreaker +4	Weapon	68
18	Earthroot staff +4	Staff	104
18	Elixir of accuracy	Consumable	186
18	Elixir of fortitude	Consumable	187
18	Elixir of reflexes	Consumable	187
18	Elixir of will	Consumable	187
18	Elukian clay +4	Armor	45
18	Evil eye fetish +4	Neck	152
18	Eye of Ioun +4	Holy Symbol	86
18	Face-stealing ring	Ring	156
18	Farslayer +4	Weapon	68

18	Feyrod +4	Rod	98
18	Fist of Kord +4	Holy Symbol	86
18	Flame wand +4	Wand	109
18	Flanking +4	Weapon	68
18	Force +4	Weapon	69
18	Force staff +4	Staff	104
18	Force wand +4	Wand	109
18	Giantdodger +4	Armor	46
18	Gloaming shroud +4	Neck	152
18	Gloves of eldritch admixture	Hands	134
18	Graceful +4	Weapon	70
18	Greatreach gauntlets	Hands	135
18	Heartening +4	Armor	46
18	Hellfire wand +4	Wand	109
18	Hellrod +4	Rod	98
18	Helm of swift punishment	Head	143
18	Holy gauntlets	Hands	135
18	Impaling +4	Weapon	70
18	Inescapable +4	Weapon	70
18	Inspiring +4	Weapon	71
18	Liar's trinket +4	Neck	153
18	Lifegiving +4	Armor	47
18	Luckblade +4	Weapon	71
18	Mace of healing +4	Weapon	72
18	Manticore shield	Arms	118
18	Mask of Melora +4	Holy Symbol	86
18	Master's wand of cloud of daggers +4	Wand	109
18	Master's wand of dire radiance +4	Wand	110
18	Master's wand of eldritch blast +4	Wand	110
18	Master's wand of eyebite +4	Wand	110
18	Master's wand of hellish rebuke +4	Wand	110
18	Master's wand of magic missile +4	Wand	110
18	Master's wand of ray of frost +4	Wand	110
18	Master's wand of scorching burst +4	Wand	110
18	Master's wand of thunderwave +4	Wand	110
18	Mauling +4	Weapon	72
18	Meliorating +4	Armor	47
18	Mindiron vambraces	Arms	118
18	Mithral shield	Arms	118
18	Moon disk of Sehanine +4	Holy Symbol	86
18	Moonlight lavaliere +4	Neck	153
18	Moradin's indestructible anvil +4	Holy Symbol	86
18	Necrotic +4	Weapon	73
18	Orb of crystalline terror +4	Orb	93
18	Orb of far seeing +4	Orb	93
18	Orb of indefatigable concentration +4	Orb	94
18	Orb of inescapable consequences +4	Orb	94
18	Orb of insurmountable force +4	Orb	95
18	Orb of judicious conjuration +4	Orb	95
18	Orb of karmic resonance +4	Orb	95
18	Orb of sweet sanctuary +4	Orb	96
18	Orb of unintended solitude +4	Orb	96
18	Orb of unlucky exchanges +4	Orb	96
18	Ornament of alertness +4	Neck	153
18	Paired +4	Weapon	74
18	Paralyzing +4	Weapon	74
18	Peacemaker's periapt +4	Neck	153
18	Periapt of recovery +4	Neck	153
18	Phantom chaussures	Feet	129
18	Point blank +4	Weapon	75
18	Potion of stormshield	Consumable	189
18	Predatory +4	Weapon	75
18	Quick +4	Weapon	76
18	Rat form +4	Armor	48
18	Recalling harness	Companion Item	123
18	Reckless +4	Weapon	76
18	Reliable staff +4	Staff	104
18	Resilience amulet +4	Neck	154
18	Ring of ramming	Ring	159
18	Ring of shadow guard	Ring	159
18	Ring of the protector	Ring	162
18	Robe of defying flames +4	Armor	49
18	Robe of defying frost +4	Armor	49
18	Robe of quills +4	Armor	50
18	Robe of stars +4	Armor	50
18	Rod of blasting +4	Rod	99
18	Rod of malign conveyance +4	Rod	100
18	Rod of the Feywild +4	Rod	101
18	Rod of the hidden star +4	Rod	101
18	Rod of the infernal +4	Rod	101
18	Sandals of arcane transposition	Feet	130
18	Scalebane +4	Weapon	77
18	Serpentskin +4	Armor	51
18	Shadowsteppers	Feet	130
18	Skewering +4	Weapon	77
18	Skystrider horseshoes	Mount Item	124
18	Snakefang +4	Armor	52
18	Sniper's +4	Weapon	78
18	Staff of corrosion +4	Staff	105
18	Staff of ruin +4	Staff	106
18	Staff of the spectral hands +4	Staff	107
18	Staff of ultimate defense +4	Staff	107
18	Stalker's +4	Armor	53
18	Star of Corellon +4	Holy Symbol	86
18	Star rod +4	Rod	102
18	Steadfast amulet +4	Neck	154
18	Stone of Avandra +4	Holy Symbol	87
18	Stoneborn +4	Armor	53
18	Stoneskin robes +4	Armor	53
18	Storm shield	Arms	121
18	Stout +4	Weapon	78
18	Strongheart +4	Weapon	79
18	Subtle +4	Weapon	79
18	Sun disk of Pelor +4	Holy Symbol	87
18	Surge +4	Armor	53
18	Swiftshot +4	Weapon	79
18	Swimtide harness	Waist	167
18	Symbol of confrontation +4	Holy Symbol	88
18	Symbol of divine reach +4	Holy Symbol	88
18	Symbol of sacrifice +4	Holy Symbol	90
18	Thunder wand +4	Wand	111
18	Thunderbolt +4	Weapon	80
18	Thundergod +4	Weapon	80
18	Tigerclaw gauntlets +4	Weapon	80

18	Tyrant's +4	Weapon	81
18	Vanguard +4	Weapon	81
18	Versatile +4	Armor	54
18	Vicious rod +4	Rod	102
18	Wand of cold +4	Wand	111
18	Wand of psychic ravaging +4	Wand	111
18	Wand of radiance +4	Wand	112
18	Wand of swarming force +4	Wand	112
18	Waterbane +4	Weapon	82
18	Whiteflame +4	Armor	55
18	Withering +4	Weapon	82
18	Wyrmguard shield	Arms	122

LEVEL 19

Lvl	Name	Slot	Pg
19	Acidic +4	Weapon	62
19	Adamantine rod +4	Rod	98
19	Amethyst band of invisible eyes	Ring	155
19	Amulet of attenuation +4	Neck	148
19	Amulet of bodily sanctity +4	Neck	148
19	Amulet of elusive prey +4	Neck	148
19	Amulet of inner voice +4	Neck	148
19	Angelsteel shield	Arms	114
19	Anklets of opportunity	Feet	125
19	Aqueous +4	Armor	40
19	Armor of attraction +4	Armor	40
19	Armor of durability +4	Armor	40
19	Armor of night +4	Armor	41
19	Assured wand of frostburn +4	Wand	109
19	Assured wand of howl of doom +4	Wand	109
19	Battle standard of the stalwart	Wondrous Item	180
19	Battlecrazed +4	Weapon	64
19	Battlemaster's +4	Weapon	64
19	Bilethorn +4	Weapon	64
19	Black dragon bile	Consumable	193
19	Blade of Bahamut +4	Weapon	64
19	Bloodcurse rod +4	Rod	98
19	Bloodiron rod +4	Rod	98
19	Bloodshored shield	Arms	114
19	Bloodsoaked shield	Arms	114
19	Bloodtheft +4	Armor	42
19	Bonegrim +4	Armor	42
19	Bone ring of preservation	Ring	156
19	Champion's +4	Armor	43
19	Chaos weave +4	Armor	43
19	Cloak of autumn's child +4	Neck	150
19	Cloak of distortion +4	Neck	151
19	Cloak of the cautious +4	Neck	151
19	Cloak of the walking wounded +4	Neck	151
19	Collar of recovery +4	Neck	151
19	Communal +4	Weapon	66
19	Crown of infernal legacy	Head	140
19	Crusader's +4	Weapon	66
19	Crystal +4	Armor	43
19	Deadblast bone	Wondrous Item	169
19	Deathstalker +4	Weapon	67
19	Demonbane +4	Weapon	67

19	Diamond bracers	Arms	116
19	Displacer +4	Armor	44
19	Dragonscale, blue +4	Armor	44
19	Dragonscale, green +4	Armor	44
19	Eye of the earthmother	Head	141
19	Feymind +4	Armor	45
19	Feyslaughter +4	Weapon	68
19	Feyswarm staff +4	Staff	104
19	Flamewrath cape +4	Neck	152
19	Forbidding +4	Weapon	69
19	Fortification +4	Armor	45
19	Frostburn +4	Armor	45
19	Frozen +4	Armor	46
19	Healer's brooch +4	Neck	152
19	Healing +4	Weapon	70
19	Laughing death +4	Armor	47
19	Lifesapper rod +4	Rod	99
19	Lightning reflex gloves	Hands	136
19	Loamweave +4	Armor	47
19	Lullaby +4	Weapon	72
19	Medic's +4	Weapon	72
19	Mindiron +4	Weapon	72
19	Mirrorsheen coat +4	Armor	48
19	Mithral +4	Armor	48
19	Oathblade +4	Weapon	73
19	Opportunistic +4	Weapon	73
19	Orb of coercive dementia +4	Orb	92
19	Orb of crimson commitment +4	Orb	92
19	Orb of draconic majesty +4	Orb	93
19	Orb of fickle fate +4	Orb	93
19	Orb of harmonic agony +4	Orb	94
19	Pelaurum +4	Armor	48
19	Potion of regeneration	Consumable	188
19	Potion of vigor	Consumable	189
19	Prismatic robe +4	Armor	48
19	Quickening staff +4	Staff	104
19	Reflexive +4	Armor	48
19	Reinforcing +4	Armor	48
19	Rending +4	Weapon	76
19	Righteous +4	Armor	49
19	Ring of the spectral hand	Ring	162
19	Robe of contingency +4	Armor	49
19	Rod of brutality +4	Rod	99
19	Rod of the dragonborn +4	Rod	101
19	Rod of the shadow walker +4	Rod	101
19	Rod of the sorrowsworn +4	Rod	101
19	Salubrious +4	Armor	51
19	Shadowflow shield	Arms	119
19	Shapechanger's sorrow +4	Weapon	77
19	Shimmering +4	Armor	51
19	Skeletal +4	Armor	52
19	Skyrender +4	Weapon	78
19	Solar +4	Armor	52
19	Staff of light +4	Staff	105
19	Staff of transposition +4	Staff	107
19	Star ruby ring	Ring	162
19	Sunblade +4	Weapon	79

19	Survivor's +4	Armor	54
19	Symbol of astral might +4	Holy Symbol	87
19	Symbol of censure +4	Holy Symbol	87
19	Symbol of mortality +4	Holy Symbol	89
19	Symbol of penitence +4	Holy Symbol	89
19	Symbol of vengeance +4	Holy Symbol	91
19	Tattered cloak +4	Neck	154
19	Tenacious +4	Weapon	80
19	Terror ichor	Consumable	194
19	Thoughtstealer +4	Weapon	80
19	Thunderhead +4	Armor	54
19	Transposing +4	Weapon	81
19	Trollhide bracers	Arms	121
19	Vampiric +4	Weapon	81
19	Vaporform +4	Armor	54
19	Verve +4	Armor	54
19	Voidcrystal +4	Weapon	82
19	Voidcrystal +4	Armor	55
19	Whetstone of venom	Consumable	190
19	Wounding +4	Weapon	82
19	Wyrmtouched amulet +4	Neck	155

LEVEL 20

Lvl	Name	Slot	Pg
20	Agile +4	Armor	39
20	Amulet of aranea +4	Neck	148
20	Antipathy gloves	Hands	132
20	Architect's staff +4	Staff	103
20	Armor of negation +4	Armor	41
20	Armor of sacrifice +4	Armor	41
20	Assassinbane +4	Armor	41
20	Battle standard of the vanguard	Wondrous Item	180
20	Blackshroud +4	Weapon	64
20	Bloodsoaked bracers	Arms	114
20	Brooch of vitality +4	Neck	149
20	Cape of the mountebank +4	Neck	149
20	Caustic whetstone	Consumable	190
20	Cloak of displacement +4	Neck	150
20	Creeping gatevine	Consumable	193
20	Crown of nature's rebellion	Head	140
20	Crystal ball of spying	Wondrous Item	169
20	Dragonscale, red +4	Armor	45
20	Flame rose	Consumable	194
20	Footpad's friend + 4	Weapon	69
20	Fundamental ice	Consumable	194
20	Gem of valor	Consumable	191
20	Headband of intellect	Head	142
20	Healer's shield	Arms	117
20	Illithid robes +4	Armor	46
20	Jarring +4	Weapon	71
20	Laurel circlet	Head	144
20	Lucklender +4	Weapon	71
20	Mirror of opposition	Wondrous Item	175
20	Necklace of fireballs +4	Neck	153
20	Orb of mighty retort +4	Orb	95
20	Orb of weakness intensified +4	Orb	97

20	Poisoned +4	Weapon	75
20	Potion of clarity	Consumable	188
20	Potion of spirit	Consumable	188
20	Precise wand of color spray +4	Wand	111
20	Radiant +4	Weapon	76
20	Righteous +4	Weapon	77
20	Ring of spell storing	Ring	160
20	Robe of defying storms +4	Armor	49
20	Robe of the archfiend +4	Armor	50
20	Rod of mindbending +4	Rod	100
20	Rod of starlight +4	Rod	100
20	Rod of vulnerability +4	Rod	102
20	Shared suffering +4	Armor	51
20	Skybound +4	Armor	52
20	Spider potion	Consumable	189
20	Spiritlink +4	Armor	53
20	Staff of acid and flame +4	Staff	105
20	Staff of gathering +4	Staff	105
20	Staff of unparalleled vision +4	Staff	107
20	Storm gauntlets	Hands	136
20	Stormlord +4	Armor	53
20	Striking staff +4	Staff	107
20	Symbol of brilliance +4	Holy Symbol	87
20	Symbol of dire fate +4	Holy Symbol	88
20	Symbol of renewal +4	Holy Symbol	89
20	Symbol of the warpriest +4	Holy Symbol	90
20	Tactician's +4	Armor	54
20	Tempest whetstone	Consumable	190
20	Thieving +4	Weapon	80
20	Torc of power preservation +4	Neck	154
20	Trickster's mask	Head	145
20	Vengeful +4	Weapon	81
20	Wand of erupting flame +4	Wand	111
20	Warsheath +4	Armor	55
20	Whetstone of combustion	Consumable	190
20	Zealot's +4	Armor	55

LEVEL 21

Lvl	Name	Slot	Pg
21	Augmenting whetstone	Consumable	190
21	Baldric of valor	Waist	164
21	Battering +5	Weapon	63
21	Belt of resilience	Waist	164
21	Blacksmelt +5	Weapon	64
21	Coif of focus	Head	139
21	Distance +5	Weapon	68
21	Dynamic + 5	Weapon	68
21	Elixir of flying	Consumable	186
21	Eye of discernment	Head	141
21	Forceful +5	Weapon	69
21	Gloves of camaraderie	Hands	134
21	Grasping +5	Weapon	70
21	Headband of perception	Head	142
21	Healer's sash	Waist	166
21	Impenetrable barding	Mount Item	123
21	Imposter's +5	Armor	46
21	Ioun stone of sustenance	Head	144

21	Lightstep slippers	Feet	129
21	Longshot gloves	Hands	136
21	Mercurial rod +5	Rod	99
21	Orb of impenetrable escape +5	Orb	94
21	Orb of mental dominion +5	Orb	95
21	Ricochet +5	Weapon	76
21	Ring of heroic insight	Ring	159
21	Ring of tenacious will	Ring	161
21	Sacrificial +5	Weapon	77
21	Skygliders	Feet	130
21	Solitaire (cerulean)	Wondrous Item	177
21	Summoned +5	Armor	53
21	Unguent of blindsight	Consumable	192

LEVEL 22

Lvl	Name	Slot	Pg
22	Absence amulet +5	Neck	147
22	Amulet of mental resolve +5	Neck	148
22	Amulet of physical resolve +5	Neck	148
22	Amulet of resolution +5	Neck	149
22	Armor of resistance +5	Armor	41
22	Avandra's whisper +5	Weapon	63
22	Blade of night +5	Weapon	65
22	Blink ring	Ring	156
22	Bloodclaw +5	Weapon	65
22	Bloodguard shield	Arms	114
22	Boots of speed	Feet	126
22	Bracers of respite	Arms	115
22	Clasp of noble sacrifice +5	Neck	150
22	Darkforged +5	Armor	43
22	Darkleaf shield	Arms	116
22	Defensive +5	Weapon	67
22	Defensive staff +5	Staff	104
22	Deflection +5	Armor	436
22	Eagle eye goggles	Head	140
22	Elukian clay +5	Weapon	68
22	Fireflower pendant +5	Neck	152
22	Flesh seeker +5	Weapon	69
22	Flickersight +5	Armor	45
22	Gambler's +5	Weapon	69
22	Gloves of the healer	Hands	135
22	Holy Healer's +5	Weapon	70
22	Immunizing +5	Armor	46
22	Ioun stone of perfect learning	Head	143
22	Irrefutable +5	Armor	47
22	Jagged +5	Weapon	71
22	Jousting shield	Arms	118
22	Luminary ring	Ring	157
22	Mage's +5	Weapon	72
22	Martyr's +5	Armor	47
22	Mnemonic staff +5	Staff	104
22	Moradin's +5	Weapon	73
22	Muleback harness	Waist	166
22	Orb of augmented stasis +5	Orb	92
22	Orb of debilitating languor +5	Orb	93
22	Orb of revenant magic +5	Orb	95
22	Orb of spatial contortion +5	Orb	95

22	Orb of sudden insanity +5	Orb	96
22	Pact hammer +5	Weapon	74
22	Pact sword +5	Weapon	74
22	Parrying +5	Weapon	74
22	Piercing +5	Weapon	74
22	Pinning +5	Weapon	74
22	Prime shot +5	Weapon	76
22	Quickcurse rod +5	Rod	99
22	Razor shield	Arms	119
22	Reproachful +5	Weapon	76
22	Repulsion +5	Armor	49
22	Retribution +5	Weapon	76
22	Ring of fey travel	Ring	158
22	Robe of bloodwalking +5	Armor	49
22	Robe of eyes +5	Armor	50
22	Robe of sapping +5	Armor	50
22	Robe of scintillation +5	Armor	50
22	Rod of cursed honor +5	Rod	99
22	Rod of feythorns +5	Rod	100
22	Rod of the bloodthorn +5	Rod	100
22	Rod of the churning inferno +5	Rod	100
22	Rod of the star spawn +5	Rod	101
22	Screaming +5	Armor	51
22	Shadow spike +5	Weapon	77
22	Shield of the guardian	Arms	120
22	Slick +5	Armor	52
22	Splitting +5	Weapon	78
22	Staff of elemental prowess +5	Staff	105
22	Staff of missile mastery +5	Staff	106
22	Staff of searing death +5	Staff	106
22	Staff of the iron tower +5	Staff	106
22	Staff of the serpent +5	Staff	106
22	Staggering +5	Weapon	78
22	Stormbolt +5	Weapon	78
22	Symbol of dedication +5	Holy Symbol	88
22	Symbol of divinity +5	Holy Symbol	88
22	Symbol of freedom +5	Holy Symbol	88
22	Symbol of good fortune +5	Holy Symbol	88
22	Symbol of lifebonding +5	Holy Symbol	89
22	Symbol of perseverance +5	Holy Symbol	89
22	Symbol of reproach +5	Holy Symbol	90
22	Symbol of resilience +5	Holy Symbol	90
22	Symbol of shielding +5	Holy Symbol	90
22	Symbol of sustenance +5	Holy Symbol	90
22	Transference +5	Weapon	81
22	Transposition harness	Companion Item	123
22	Utility staff +5	Staff	107
22	Veteran's +5	Armor	55
22	Wildleaf +5	Armor	55
22	Wrestler's gloves	Hands	137

LEVEL 23

Lvl	Name	Slot	Pg
23	Abyssal adornment +5	Neck	148
23	Adamantine +5	Weapon	63
23	Addergrease +5	Armor	39
23	Amulet of material darkness +5	Neck	148
23	Armor of cleansing +5	Armor	40
23	Armor of exploits +5	Armor	41
23	Armor of starlight +5	Armor	41
23	Assassin's +5	Weapon	63
23	Astral mead	Consumable	191
23	Beastlord +5	Armor	41
23	Belt of vitality	Waist	164
23	Bestial +5	Armor	42
23	Black feather of the Raven Queen +5	Holy Symbol	85
23	Bloodfire +5	Armor	42
23	Bloodiron +5	Weapon	65
23	Bloodiron +5	Armor	42
23	Bloodthirsty +5	Weapon	65
23	Boots of stealth	Feet	126
23	Breaching +5	Armor	43
23	Briartwine +5	Armor	43
23	Bronzewood +5	Weapon	65
23	Brooch of no regrets +5	Neck	149
23	Brooch of shielding +5	Neck	149
23	Chamber cloak +5	Neck	150
23	Chaos weave +5	Weapon	65
23	Choker of eloquence +5	Neck	150
23	Cloak of arachnida +5	Neck	150
23	Cloak of the chirurgeon +5	Neck	151
23	Cloaked +5	Weapon	66
23	Cog of Erathis +5	Holy Symbol	85
23	Cold iron +5	Weapon	66
23	Controlling +5	Weapon	66
23	Coral +5	Armor	43
23	Cunning +5	Weapon	67
23	Decerebrating +5	Weapon	67
23	Desiccating +5	Weapon	67
23	Determined +5	Weapon	67
23	Dragonscale of Bahamut +5	Holy Symbol	85
23	Dragonscale, black +5	Armor	44
23	Dragonscale, white +5	Armor	45
23	Dread +5	Weapon	68
23	Earthbreaker +5	Weapon	68
23	Earthroot staff +5	Staff	104
23	Elixir of accuracy	Consumable	186
23	Elixir of fortitude	Consumable	187
23	Elixir of reflexes	Consumable	187
23	Elixir of will	Consumable	187
23	Elukian clay +5	Armor	45
23	Evil eye fetish +5	Neck	152
23	Eye of awareness	Head	141
23	Eye of Ioun +5	Holy Symbol	86
23	Farslayer +5	Weapon	68
23	Feyrod +5	Rod	98
23	Fist of Kord +5	Holy Symbol	86
23	Flame bracers	Arms	117
23	Flame wand +5	Wand	109
23	Flanking +5	Weapon	68
23	Force +5	Weapon	69
23	Force staff +5	Staff	104
23	Force wand +5	Wand	109
23	Giantdodger +5	Armor	46
23	Gloaming shroud +5	Neck	152
23	Graceful +5	Weapon	70
23	Heartening +5	Armor	46
23	Hellfire wand +5	Wand	109
23	Hellrod +5	Rod	98
23	Impaling +5	Weapon	70
23	Inescapable +5	Weapon	70
23	Inspiring +5	Weapon	71
23	Ioun stone of steadfastness	Head	143
23	Liar's trinket +5	Neck	153
23	Lifegiving +5	Armor	47
23	Luckblade +5	Weapon	71
23	Mace of healing +5	Weapon	72
23	Mask of Melora +5	Holy Symbol	86
23	Master's wand of cloud of daggers +5	Wand	109
23	Master's wand of dire radiance +5	Wand	110
23	Master's wand of eldritch blast +5	Wand	110
23	Master's wand of eyebite +5	Wand	110
23	Master's wand of hellish rebuke +5	Wand	110
23	Master's wand of magic missile +5	Wand	110
23	Master's wand of ray of frost +5	Wand	110
23	Master's wand of scorching burst +5	Wand	110
23	Master's wand of thunderwave +5	Wand	110
23	Mauling +5	Weapon	72
23	Meliorating +5	Armor	47
23	Moon disk of Sehanine +5	Holy Symbol	86
23	Moonlight lavaliere +5	Neck	153
23	Moradin's indestructible anvil +5	Holy Symbol	86
23	Necrotic +5	Weapon	73
23	Orb of crystalline terror +5	Orb	93
23	Orb of far seeing +5	Orb	93
23	Orb of indefatigable concentration +5	Orb	94
23	Orb of inescapable consequences +5	Orb	94
23	Orb of insurmountable force +5	Orb	95
23	Orb of judicious conjuration +5	Orb	95
23	Orb of karmic resonance +5	Orb	95
23	Orb of sweet sanctuary +5	Orb	96
23	Orb of unintended solitude +5	Orb	96
23	Orb of the usurper +5	Orb	96
23	Orb of unlucky exchanges +5	Orb	96
23	Ornament of alertness +5	Neck	153
23	Paired +5	Weapon	74
23	Paralyzing +5	Weapon	74
23	Peacemaker's periapt +5	Neck	153
23	Periapt of recovery +5	Neck	153
23	Point blank +5	Weapon	75
23	Predatory +5	Weapon	75
23	Quick +5	Weapon	76
23	Rat form +5	Armor	48
23	Reckless +5	Weapon	76

23	Reliable staff +5	Staff	104
23	Resilience amulet +5	Neck	154
23	Ring of adaptation	Ring	157
23	Robe of defying flames +5	Armor	49
23	Robe of defying frost +5	Armor	49
23	Robe of quills +5	Armor	50
23	Robe of stars +5	Armor	50
23	Rod of blasting +5	Rod	99
23	Rod of malign conveyance +5	Rod	100
23	Rod of the Feywild +5	Rod	101
23	Rod of the hidden star +5	Rod	101
23	Rod of the infernal +5	Rod	101
23	Scalebane +5	Weapon	77
23	Serpentskin +5	Armor	51
23	Skewering +5	Weapon	77
23	Snakefang +5	Armor	52
23	Sniper's +5	Weapon	78
23	Staff of corrosion +5	Staff	105
23	Staff of ruin +5	Staff	106
23	Staff of the spectral hands +5	Staff	107
23	Staff of ultimate defense +5	Staff	107
23	Stalker's +5	Armor	53
23	Star of Corellon +5	Holy Symbol	86
23	Star rod +5	Rod	102
23	Steadfast amulet +5	Neck	154
23	Stone of Avandra +5	Holy Symbol	87
23	Stoneborn +5	Armor	53
23	Stoneskin robes +5	Armor	53
23	Stonewall shield	Arms	120
23	Stout +5	Weapon	78
23	Strongheart +5	Weapon	79
23	Subtle +5	Weapon	79
23	Sun disk of Pelor +5	Holy Symbol	87
23	Surge +5	Armor	53
23	Swiftshot +5	Weapon	79
23	Symbol of confrontation +5	Holy Symbol	88
23	Symbol of divine reach +5	Holy Symbol	88
23	Symbol of sacrifice +5	Holy Symbol	90
23	Thunder wand +5	Wand	111
23	Thunderbolt +5	Weapon	80
23	Thundergod +5	Weapon	80
23	Tigerclaw gauntlets +5	Weapon	80
23	Tyrant's +5	Weapon	81
23	Vanguard +5	Weapon	81
23	Vengeance sash	Waist	167
23	Versatile +5	Armor	54
23	Vicious rod +5	Rod	102
23	Wand of cold +5	Wand	111
23	Wand of psychic ravaging +5	Wand	111
23	Wand of radiance +5	Wand	112
23	Wand of swarming force +5	Wand	112
23	Waterbane +5	Weapon	82
23	Whiteflame +5	Armor	55
23	Withering +5	Weapon	82

LEVEL 24

Lvl	Name	Slot	Pg
24	Acidic +5	Weapon	62
24	Adamantine rod +5	Rod	98
24	Amulet of attenuation +5	Neck	148
24	Amulet of bodily sanctity +5	Neck	148
24	Amulet of elusive prey +5	Neck	148
24	Amulet of inner voice +5	Neck	148
24	Aqueous +5	Armor	40
24	Armor of attraction +5	Armor	40
24	Armor of durability +5	Armor	40
24	Armor of night +5	Armor	41
24	Assured wand of frostburn +5	Wand	109
24	Assured wand of howl of doom +5	Wand	109
24	Backtrack bindings	Feet	125
24	Battlecrazed +5	Weapon	64
24	Battleforged shield	Arms	114
24	Battlemaster's +5	Weapon	64
24	Bilethorn +5	Weapon	64
24	Black cave pearl	Consumable	193
24	Blade of Bahamut +5	Weapon	64
24	Bloodcurse rod +5	Rod	98
24	Bloodiron rod +5	Rod	98
24	Bloodtheft +5	Armor	42
24	Bloodthirst bracers	Arms	114
24	Bonegrim +5	Armor	42
24	Casque of tactics	Head	139
24	Champion's +5	Armor	43
24	Chaos weave +5	Armor	43
24	Cloak of autumn's child +5	Neck	150
24	Cloak of distortion +5	Neck	151
24	Cloak of the cautious +5	Neck	151
24	Cloak of the walking wounded +5	Neck	151
24	Collar of recovery +5	Neck	151
24	Communal +5	Weapon	66
24	Crusader's +5	Weapon	66
24	Crystal +5	Armor	43
24	Death-denying cloak +5	Neck	151
24	Deathstalker +5	Weapon	67
24	Demonbane +5	Weapon	67
24	Displacer +5	Armor	44
24	Dragonscale, blue +5	Armor	44
24	Dragonscale, green +5	Armor	44
24	Feymind +5	Armor	45
24	Feyslaughter +5	Weapon	68
24	Feyswarm staff +5	Staff	104
24	Flamewrath cape +5	Neck	152
24	Flaying gloves	Hands	133
24	Forbidding +5	Weapon	69
24	Fortification +5	Armor	45
24	Friend's gift	Companion Item	122
24	Frostburn +5	Armor	45
24	Frozen +5	Armor	46
24	Healer's brooch +5	Neck	152
24	Healing +5	Weapon	70
24	Helm of opportunity	Head	142
24	Laughing death +5	Armor	47

24	Lifesapper rod +5	Rod	99
24	Loamweave +5	Armor	47
24	Lullaby +5	Weapon	72
24	Medic's +5	Weapon	72
24	Mindiron +5	Weapon	72
24	Mirrorsheen coat +5	Armor	48
24	Mithral +5	Armor	48
24	Oathblade +5	Weapon	73
24	Opportunistic +5	Weapon	73
24	Orb of arcane generosity +5	Orb	92
24	Orb of coercive dementia +5	Orb	92
24	Orb of crimson commitment +5	Orb	92
24	Orb of draconic majesty +5	Orb	93
24	Orb of fickle fate +5	Orb	93
24	Orb of harmonic agony +5	Orb	94
24	Pelaurum +5	Armor	48
24	Potion of resistance	Consumable	188
24	Prismatic robe +5	Armor	48
24	Quickening staff +5	Staff	104
24	Reflexive +5	Armor	48
24	Reinforcing +5	Armor	48
24	Rending +5	Weapon	76
24	Righteous +5	Armor	49
24	Ritualist's ring	Ring	162
24	Robe of contingency +5	Armor	49
24	Robe of forbearance +5	Armor	50
24	Rod of brutality +5	Rod	99
24	Rod of the dragonborn +5	Rod	101
24	Rod of the shadow walker +5	Rod	101
24	Rod of the sorrowsworn +5	Rod	101
24	Salubrious +5	Armor	51
24	Shapechanger's sorrow +5	Weapon	77
24	Shimmering +5	Armor	51
24	Skeletal +5	Armor	52
24	Skyrender +5	Weapon	78
24	Solar +5	Armor	52
24	Soulwarding +5	Armor	53
24	Staff of light +5	Staff	105
24	Staff of transposition +5	Staff	107
24	Sunblade +5	Weapon	79
24	Survivor's +5	Armor	54
24	Symbol of astral might +5	Holy Symbol	87
24	Symbol of censure +5	Holy Symbol	87
24	Symbol of mortality +5	Holy Symbol	89
24	Symbol of penitence +5	Holy Symbol	89
24	Symbol of vengeance +5	Holy Symbol	91
24	Tattered cloak +5	Neck	154
24	Tenacious +5	Weapon	80
24	Thoughtstealer +5	Weapon	80
24	Thunderhead +5	Armor	54
24	Transposing +5	Weapon	81
24	Vampiric +5	Weapon	81
24	Vaporform +5	Armor	54
24	Verve +5	Armor	54
24	Voidcrystal +5	Weapon	82
24	Voidcrystal +5	Armor	55
24	Wounding +5	Weapon	82

24	Wyrmtouched amulet +5	Neck	155
24	Zephyr boots	Feet	131

LEVEL 25

Lvl	Name	Slot	Pg
25	Agile +5	Armor	39
25	Airstriders	Feet	125
25	Amulet of aranea +5	Neck	148
25	Antipathy gloves	Hands	132
25	Architect's staff +5	Staff	103
25	Armor of negation +5	Armor	141
25	Armor of sacrifice +5	Armor	141
25	Assassinbane +5	Armor	141
25	Barbed baldric	Waist	164
25	Blackshroud +5	Weapon	64
25	Bolstering +5	Armor	42
25	Breach bracers	Arms	116
25	Brilliant energy +5	Weapon	65
25	Brooch of vitality +5	Neck	149
25	Cape of the mountebank +5	Neck	149
25	Cat paws	Hands	132
25	Chime of opening	Wondrous Item	169
25	Cloak of displacement +5	Neck	150
25	Cloak of elemental evolution +5	Neck	151
25	Cold iron shield	Arms	116
25	Companion's defender	Companion Item	122
25	Couters of second chances	Arms	116
25	Crown of nature's rebellion	Head	140
25	Deathspawn potion	Consumable	186
25	Destiny staff +5	Staff	104
25	Diamond scabbard	Wondrous Item	170
25	Direbeast shield	Arms	117
25	Dragonscale, red +5	Armor	45
25	Dread nightshade	Consumable	194
25	Dust of banishment	Wondrous Item	170
25	Elixir of aptitude	Consumable	186
25	Footpad's friend + 5	Weapon	69
25	Gargoyle ring	Ring	156
25	Ghost chain +5	Weapon	70
25	Girdle of the umber hulk	Waist	165
25	Illithid robes +5	Armor	46
25	Ioun stone of regeneration	Head	143
25	Jarring +5	Weapon	71
25	Legendary +5	Weapon	71
25	Life charm +5	Neck	71
25	Lucklender +5	Weapon	71
25	Mind dust	Consumable	194
25	Necklace of fireballs +5	Neck	153
25	Orb of mighty retort +5	Orb	95
25	Orb of weakness intensified +5	Orb	97
25	Overreaching +5	Weapon	73
25	Poisoned +5	Weapon	75
25	Potion of clarity	Consumable	188
25	Potion of spirit	Consumable	188
25	Precise wand of color spray +5	Wand	111
25	Quickhit bracers	Arms	118
25	Radiant +5	Weapon	76

25	Righteous +5	Weapon	77
25	Robe of defying storms +5	Armor	49
25	Robe of the archfiend +5	Armor	50
25	Rod of mindbending +5	Rod	100
25	Rod of starlight +5	Rod	100
25	Rod of vulnerability +5	Rod	102
25	Sandals of Avandra	Feet	130
25	Shared suffering +5	Armor	51
25	Shimmerlight shield	Arms	120
25	Skull mask	Head	144
25	Skybound +5	Armor	52
25	Sorrowsworn ring	Ring	162
25	Spiritlink +5	Armor	53
25	Staff of acid and flame +5	Staff	105
25	Staff of gathering +5	Staff	105
25	Staff of unparalleled vision +5	Staff	107
25	Stag helm	Head	145
25	Stormlord +5	Armor	53
25	Striking staff +5	Staff	107
25	Symbol of brilliance +5	Holy Symbol	87
25	Symbol of damnation +5	Holy Symbol	88
25	Symbol of dire fate +5	Holy Symbol	88
25	Symbol of radiant vengeance +5	Holy Symbol	89
25	Symbol of renewal +5	Holy Symbol	89
25	Symbol of the warpriest +5	Holy Symbol	90
25	Tactician's +5	Armor	54
25	Telepathy circlet	Head	145
25	Thieving +5	Weapon	80
25	Torc of power preservation +5	Neck	154
25	Trespasser's bane +5	Weapon	81
25	Vengeful +5	Weapon	81
25	Wand of erupting flame +5	Wand	111
25	Warsheath +5	Armor	55
25	Zealot's +5	Armor	55

LEVEL 26

Lvl	Name	Slot	Pg
26	Augmenting whetstone	Consumable	190
26	Battering +6	Weapon	63
26	Belt of endurance	Waist	164
26	Blacksmelt +6	Weapon	64
26	Bracers of archery	Arms	115
26	Bracers of tactical blows	Arms	116
26	Breaching gauntlets	Hands	132
26	Burning gauntlets	Hands	132
26	Caustic gauntlets	Hands	133
26	Clockwork owl	Head	139
26	Cold iron bracers	Arms	116
26	Distance +6	Weapon	68
26	Dynamic + 6	Weapon	68
26	Flamedrinker shield	Arms	117
26	Forceful +6	Weapon	69
26	Girdle of the dragon	Waist	165
26	Grasping +6	Weapon	70
26	Imposter's +6	Armor	46
26	Iron armbands of power	Arms	117
26	Mercurial rod +6	Rod	99

26	Orb of mental dominion +6	Orb	95
26	Ricochet +6	Weapon	76
26	Sacrificial +6	Weapon	77
26	Sandals of precise stepping	Feet	130
26	Sigil of companionship	Companion Item	123
26	Solitaire (violet)	Wondrous Item	178
26	Stalwart belt	Waist	167
26	Summoned +6	Armor	53
26	Throwing shield	Arms	121
26	Venom gloves	Hands	137

LEVEL 27

Lvl	Name	Slot	Pg
27	Absence amulet +6	Neck	147
27	Amulet of mental resolve +6	Neck	148
27	Amulet of physical resolve +6	Neck	148
27	Amulet of resolution +6	Neck	149
27	Armor of resistance +6	Armor	41
27	Avandra's whisper +6	Weapon	63
27	Blade of night +6	Weapon	65
27	Bloodclaw +6	Weapon	65
27	Clasp of noble sacrifice +6	Neck	150
27	Darkforged +6	Armor	43
27	Defensive +6	Weapon	67
27	Defensive staff +6	Staff	104
27	Deflection +6	Armor	43
27	Desert rose	Consumable	193
27	Earthreaver stompers	Feet	128
27	Elixir of dragon breath	Consumable	186
27	Elukian clay +6	Weapon	68
27	Eye of the basilisk	Head	141
27	Fireflower pendant +6	Neck	152
27	Flesh seeker +6	Weapon	69
27	Flickersight +6	Armor	45
27	Frost gauntlets	Hands	133
27	Frozen whetstone	Consumable	190
27	Gambler's +6	Weapon	69
27	Glassteel shard	Consumable	194
27	Holy Healer's +6	Weapon	70
27	Immunizing +6	Armor	46
27	Irrefutable +6	Armor	47
27	Jagged +6	Weapon	71
27	Mage's +6	Weapon	72
27	Martyr's +6	Armor	47
27	Mnemonic staff +6	Staff	104
27	Moradin's +6	Weapon	73
27	Mummified hand	Wondrous Item	175
27	Orb of augmented stasis +6	Orb	92
27	Orb of debilitating languor +6	Orb	93
27	Orb of revenant magic +6	Orb	95
27	Orb of spatial contortion +6	Orb	95
27	Orb of sudden insanity +6	Orb	96
27	Pact hammer +6	Weapon	74
27	Pact sword +6	Weapon	74
27	Parrying +6	Weapon	74
27	Pelaurum shield	Arms	118
27	Phrenic crown	Head	144

Lvl	Name	Slot	Pg
27	Piercing +6	Weapon	74
27	Pinning +6	Weapon	74
27	Potion of lifeshield	Consumable	188
27	Potion of mimicry	Consumable	188
27	Prime shot +6	Weapon	76
27	Quickcurse rod +6	Rod	99
27	Razor bracers	Arms	119
27	Reflective shield	Arms	119
27	Reproachful +6	Weapon	76
27	Repulsion +6	Armor	49
27	Retribution +6	Weapon	76
27	Ring of the phoenix	Ring	161
27	Robe of bloodwalking +6	Armor	49
27	Robe of eyes +6	Armor	50
27	Robe of sapping +6	Armor	50
27	Robe of scintillation +6	Armor	50
27	Rod of cursed honor +6	Rod	99
27	Rod of feythorns +6	Rod	100
27	Rod of the bloodthorn +6	Rod	100
27	Rod of the churning inferno +6	Rod	100
27	Rod of the star spawn +6	Rod	101
27	Screaming +6	Armor	51
27	Shadow band	Ring	162
27	Shadow spike +6	Weapon	77
27	Shield of blocking	Arms	119
27	Shocking +6	Armor	51
27	Skull bracers	Arms	120
27	Slick +6	Armor	52
27	Splitting +6	Weapon	78
27	Staff of elemental prowess +6	Staff	105
27	Staff of missile mastery +6	Staff	106
27	Staff of searing death +6	Staff	106
27	Staff of the iron tower +6	Staff	106
27	Staff of the serpent +6	Staff	106
27	Staggering +6	Weapon	78
27	Stormbolt +6	Weapon	78
27	Symbol of dedication +6	Holy Symbol	88
27	Symbol of divinity +6	Holy Symbol	88
27	Symbol of freedom +6	Holy Symbol	88
27	Symbol of good fortune +6	Holy Symbol	88
27	Symbol of lifebonding +6	Holy Symbol	89
27	Symbol of perseverance +6	Holy Symbol	89
27	Symbol of reproach +6	Holy Symbol	90
27	Symbol of resilience +6	Holy Symbol	90
27	Symbol of shielding +6	Holy Symbol	90
27	Symbol of sustenance +6	Holy Symbol	90
27	Transference +6	Weapon	81
27	Trauma bracers	Arms	121
27	Utility staff +6	Staff	107
27	Veteran's +6	Armor	55
27	Wildleaf +6	Armor	55
27	Wrestler's gloves	Hands	137

LEVEL 28

Lvl	Name	Slot	Pg
28	Abyssal adornment +6	Neck	148
28	Adamantine +6	Weapon	63
28	Addergrease +6	Armor	39
28	Amulet of material darkness +6	Neck	148
28	Armor of cleansing +6	Armor	40
28	Armor of exploits +6	Armor	41
28	Armor of starlight +6	Armor	41
28	Assassin's +6	Weapon	63
28	Bag of tricks, vermilion	Wondrous Item	184
28	Beastlord +6	Armor	41
28	Belt of vim	Waist	164
28	Bestial +6	Armor	42
28	Black feather of the Raven Queen +6	Holy Symbol	85
28	Bloodfire +6	Armor	42
28	Bloodiron +6	Weapon	65
28	Bloodiron +6	Armor	42
28	Bloodthirsty +6	Weapon	65
28	Boots of quickness	Feet	126
28	Boots of teleportation	Feet	127
28	Breaching +6	Armor	43
28	Briartwine +6	Armor	43
28	Brightleaf	Consumable	193
28	Bronzewood +6	Weapon	65
28	Brooch of no regrets +6	Neck	149
28	Brooch of shielding +6	Neck	149
28	Cat tabi	Feet	127
28	Chamber cloak +6	Neck	150
28	Chaos weave +6	Weapon	65
28	Charm of abundant action	Wondrous Item	169
28	Choker of eloquence +6	Neck	150
28	Circlet of indomitability	Head	139
28	Cloak of arachnida +6	Neck	150
28	Cloak of the chirurgeon +6	Neck	151
28	Cloaked +6	Weapon	66
28	Cog of Erathis +6	Holy Symbol	85
28	Coif of mindiron	Head	140
28	Cold iron +6	Weapon	66
28	Controlling +6	Weapon	66
28	Coral +6	Armor	43
28	Cunning +6	Weapon	67
28	Dark clover	Consumable	193
28	Decerebrating +6	Weapon	67
28	Desiccating +6	Weapon	67
28	Determined +6	Weapon	67
28	Dragonscale of Bahamut +6	Holy Symbol	85
28	Dragonscale, black +6	Armor	44
28	Dragonscale, white +6	Armor	45
28	Dread +6	Weapon	68
28	Earthbreaker +6	Weapon	68
28	Earthroot staff +6	Staff	104
28	Elixir of accuracy	Consumable	186
28	Elixir of fortitude	Consumable	187
28	Elixir of reflexes	Consumable	187
28	Elixir of will	Consumable	187

28	Elukian clay +6	Armor	45
28	Evil eye fetish +6	Neck	152
28	Eye of Ioun +6	Holy Symbol	86
28	Farslayer +6	Weapon	68
28	Feyrod +6	Rod	98
28	Fist of Kord +6	Holy Symbol	86
28	Flame wand +6	Wand	109
28	Flanking +6	Weapon	68
28	Force +6	Weapon	69
28	Force staff +6	Staff	104
28	Force wand +6	Wand	109
28	Giantdodger +6	Armor	46
28	Gloaming shroud +6	Neck	152
28	Gloves of eldritch admixture	Hands	134
28	Graceful +6	Weapon	70
28	Heartening +6	Armor	46
28	Hellfire wand +6	Wand	109
28	Hellrod +6	Rod	98
28	Holy gauntlets	Hands	135
28	Impaling +6	Weapon	70
28	Inescapable +6	Weapon	70
28	Inspiring +6	Weapon	71
28	Liar's trinket +6	Neck	153
28	Lifegiving +6	Armor	47
28	Luckblade +6	Weapon	71
28	Mace of healing +6	Weapon	72
28	Manticore shield	Arms	118
28	Mask of Melora +6	Holy Symbol	86
28	Master's wand of cloud of daggers +6	Wand	109
28	Master's wand of dire radiance +6	Wand	110
28	Master's wand of eldritch blast +6	Wand	110
28	Master's wand of eyebite +6	Wand	110
28	Master's wand of hellish rebuke +6	Wand	110
28	Master's wand of magic missile +6	Wand	110
28	Master's wand of ray of frost +6	Wand	110
28	Master's wand of scorching burst +6	Wand	110
28	Master's wand of thunderwave +6	Wand	110
28	Mauling +6	Weapon	72
28	Meliorating +6	Armor	47
28	Mindiron vambraces	Arms	118
28	Mithral shield	Arms	118
28	Moon disk of Sehanine +6	Holy Symbol	86
28	Moonlight lavaliere +6	Neck	153
28	Moradin's indestructible anvil +6	Holy Symbol	86
28	Necrotic +6	Weapon	73
28	Orb of crystalline terror +6	Orb	93
28	Orb of far seeing +6	Orb	93
28	Orb of impenetrable escape +6	Orb	94
28	Orb of indefatigable concentration +6	Orb	94
28	Orb of inescapable consequences +6	Orb	94
28	Orb of insurmountable force +6	Orb	95
28	Orb of judicious conjuration +6	Orb	95
28	Orb of karmic resonance +6	Orb	95
28	Orb of sweet sanctuary +6	Orb	96
28	Orb of the usurper +6	Orb	96
28	Orb of unintended solitude +6	Orb	96
28	Orb of unlucky exchanges +6	Orb	96

28	Ornament of alertness +6	Neck	153
28	Paired +6	Weapon	74
28	Paralyzing +6	Weapon	74
28	Peacemaker's periapt +6	Neck	153
28	Periapt of recovery +6	Neck	153
28	Point blank +6	Weapon	75
28	Potion of stormshield	Consumable	189
28	Predatory +6	Weapon	75
28	Quick +6	Weapon	76
28	Rat form +6	Armor	48
28	Recalling harness	Companion Item	123
28	Reckless +6	Weapon	76
28	Reliable staff +6	Staff	104
28	Resilience amulet +6	Neck	154
28	Robe of defying flames +6	Armor	49
28	Robe of defying frost +6	Armor	49
28	Robe of quills +6	Armor	50
28	Robe of stars +6	Armor	50
28	Rod of blasting +6	Rod	99
28	Rod of malign conveyance +6	Rod	100
28	Rod of the Feywild +6	Rod	101
28	Rod of the hidden star +6	Rod	101
28	Rod of the infernal +6	Rod	101
28	Scalebane +6	Weapon	77
28	Serpentskin +6	Armor	51
28	Skewering +6	Weapon	77
28	Snakefang +6	Armor	52
28	Sniper's +6	Weapon	78
28	Staff of corrosion +6	Staff	105
28	Staff of ruin +6	Staff	106
28	Staff of the spectral hands +6	Staff	107
28	Staff of ultimate defense +6	Staff	107
28	Stalker's +6	Armor	53
28	Star of Corellon +6	Holy Symbol	86
28	Star rod +6	Rod	102
28	Steadfast amulet +6	Neck	154
28	Stone of Avandra +6	Holy Symbol	87
28	Stoneborn +6	Armor	53
28	Stoneskin robes +6	Armor	53
28	Storm shield	Arms	121
28	Stout +6	Weapon	78
28	Strongheart +6	Weapon	79
28	Subtle +6	Weapon	79
28	Sun disk of Pelor +6	Holy Symbol	87
28	Surge +6	Armor	53
28	Swiftshot +6	Weapon	79
28	Swimtide harness	Waist	167
28	Symbol of confrontation +6	Holy Symbol	88
28	Symbol of divine reach +6	Holy Symbol	88
28	Symbol of sacrifice +6	Holy Symbol	90
28	Thunder wand +6	Wand	111
28	Thunderbolt +6	Weapon	80
28	Thundergod +6	Weapon	80
28	Tigerclaw gauntlets +6	Weapon	80
28	Tyrant's +6	Weapon	81
28	Vanguard +6	Weapon	81
28	Versatile +6	Armor	54

Lvl	Name	Slot	Pg
28	Vicious rod +6	Rod	102
28	Wand of cold +6	Wand	111
28	Wand of psychic ravaging +6	Wand	111
28	Wand of radiance +6	Wand	112
28	Wand of swarming force +6	Wand	112
28	Waterbane +6	Weapon	82
28	Whiteflame +6	Armor	55
28	Withering +6	Weapon	82

LEVEL 29

Lvl	Name	Slot	Pg
29	Acidic +6	Weapon	62
29	Adamantine rod +6	Rod	98
29	Amulet of attenuation +6	Neck	148
29	Amulet of bodily sanctity +6	Neck	148
29	Amulet of elusive prey +6	Neck	148
29	Amulet of inner voice +6	Neck	148
29	Amulet of the unbroken +6	Neck	149
29	Angelsteel shield	Arms	114
29	Aqueous +6	Armor	40
29	Armor of attraction +6	Armor	40
29	Armor of durability +6	Armor	40
29	Armor of night +6	Armor	41
29	Assured wand of frostburn +6	Wand	109
29	Assured wand of howl of doom +6	Wand	109
29	Battlecrazed +6	Weapon	64
29	Battlemaster's +6	Weapon	64
29	Bilethorn +6	Weapon	64
29	Black dragon bile	Consumable	193
29	Blade of Bahamut +6	Weapon	64
29	Bloodcurse rod +6	Rod	98
29	Bloodiron rod +6	Rod	98
29	Bloodshored shield	Arms	114
29	Bloodsoaked shield	Arms	114
29	Bloodtheft +6	Armor	42
29	Bonegrim +6	Armor	42
29	Champion's +6	Armor	43
29	Chaos weave +6	Armor	43
29	Cloak of autumn's child +6	Neck	150
29	Cloak of distortion +6	Neck	151
29	Cloak of the cautious +6	Neck	151
29	Cloak of the walking wounded +6	Neck	151
29	Collar of recovery +6	Neck	151
29	Communal +6	Weapon	66
29	Crusader's +6	Weapon	66
29	Crystal +6	Armor	43
29	Death-denying cloak +6	Neck	151
29	Deathstalker +6	Weapon	67
29	Demonbane +6	Weapon	67
29	Diamond bracers	Arms	116
29	Displacer +6	Armor	44
29	Dragonscale, blue +6	Armor	44
29	Dragonscale, green +6	Armor	44
29	Feymind +6	Armor	45
29	Feyslaughter +6	Weapon	68
29	Feyswarm staff +6	Staff	104
29	Flamewrath cape +6	Neck	152

Lvl	Name	Slot	Pg
29	Forbidding +6	Weapon	69
29	Fortification +6	Armor	45
29	Frostburn +6	Armor	45
29	Frozen +6	Armor	46
29	Healer's brooch +6	Neck	152
29	Healing +6	Weapon	70
29	Laughing death +6	Armor	47
29	Lifesapper rod +6	Rod	99
29	Loamweave +6	Armor	47
29	Lullaby +6	Weapon	72
29	Medic's +6	Weapon	72
29	Mindiron +6	Weapon	72
29	Mirrorsheen coat +6	Armor	48
29	Mithral +6	Armor	48
29	Oathblade +6	Weapon	73
29	Opal ring of remembrance	Ring	157
29	Opportunistic +6	Weapon	73
29	Orb of arcane generosity +6	Orb	92
29	Orb of coercive dementia +6	Orb	92
29	Orb of crimson commitment +6	Orb	92
29	Orb of draconic majesty +6	Orb	93
29	Orb of fickle fate +6	Orb	93
29	Orb of harmonic agony +6	Orb	94
29	Pelaurum +6	Armor	48
29	Potion of regeneration	Consumable	188
29	Potion of vigor	Consumable	189
29	Prismatic robe +6	Armor	48
29	Quickening diadem	Head	144
29	Quickening staff +6	Staff	104
29	Reflexive +6	Armor	48
29	Reinforcing +6	Armor	48
29	Rending +6	Weapon	76
29	Righteous +6	Armor	49
29	Robe of contingency +6	Armor	49
29	Robe of forbearance +6	Armor	50
29	Rod of brutality +6	Rod	99
29	Rod of the dragonborn +6	Rod	101
29	Rod of the shadow walker +6	Rod	101
29	Rod of the sorrowsworn +6	Rod	101
29	Salubrious +6	Armor	51
29	Shapechanger's sorrow +6	Weapon	77
29	Shimmering +6	Armor	51
29	Skeletal +6	Armor	52
29	Skyrender +6	Weapon	78
29	Solar +6	Armor	52
29	Soulwarding +6	Armor	53
29	Staff of light +6	Staff	105
29	Staff of transposition +6	Staff	107
29	Star of the Astral Sea +6	Neck	154
29	Sunblade +6	Weapon	79
29	Survivor's +6	Armor	54
29	Symbol of astral might +6	Holy Symbol	87
29	Symbol of censure +6	Holy Symbol	87
29	Symbol of mortality +6	Holy Symbol	89
29	Symbol of penitence +6	Holy Symbol	89
29	Symbol of vengeance +6	Holy Symbol	91
29	Tattered cloak +6	Neck	154

Lvl	Name	Slot	Pg
29	Tenacious +6	Weapon	80
29	Terror ichor	Consumable	194
29	Thoughtstealer +6	Weapon	80
29	Thunderhead +6	Armor	54
29	Transposing +6	Weapon	81
29	Trollhide bracers	Arms	121
29	Vampiric +6	Weapon	81
29	Vaporform +6	Armor	54
29	Verve +6	Armor	54
29	Voidcrystal +6	Weapon	82
29	Voidcrystal +6	Armor	55
29	Whetstone of venom	Consumable	190
29	Wounding +6	Weapon	82
29	Wyrmtouched amulet +6	Neck	155

LEVEL 30

Lvl	Name	Slot	Pg
30	Agile +6	Armor	39
30	Amulet of aranea +6	Neck	148
30	Antipathy gloves	Hands	132
30	Architect's staff +6	Staff	103
30	Armor of negation +6	Armor	41
30	Armor of sacrifice +6	Armor	41
30	Assassinbane +6	Armor	41
30	Blackshroud +6	Weapon	64
30	Bloodsoaked bracers	Arms	114
30	Bolstering +6	Armor	42
30	Brilliant energy +6	Weapon	65
30	Bronze serpent	Head	138
30	Brooch of vitality +6	Neck	149
30	Cape of the mountebank +6	Neck	149
30	Caustic whetstone	Consumable	190
30	Cloak of displacement +6	Neck	150
30	Cloak of elemental evolution +6	Neck	151
30	Cloak of the phoenix +6	Neck	151
30	Creeping gatevine	Consumable	193
30	Destiny staff +6	Staff	104
30	Dragonscale, red +6	Armor	45
30	Flame rose	Consumable	194
30	Footpad's friend + 6	Weapon	69
30	Fundamental ice	Consumable	194
30	Ghost chain +6	Weapon	70
30	Gorget of reciprocity +6	Neck	152
30	Headband of intellect	Head	142
30	Healer's shield	Arms	117
30	Illithid robes +6	Armor	46
30	Jarring +6	Weapon	71
30	Laurel circlet	Head	144
30	Legendary +6	Weapon	71
30	Life charm +6	Neck	153
30	Lucklender +6	Weapon	71
30	Necklace of fireballs +6	Neck	153
30	Nullifying ring	Ring	157
30	Orb of mighty retort +6	Orb	95
30	Orb of weakness intensified +6	Orb	97
30	Overreaching +6	Weapon	73
30	Poisoned +6	Weapon	75

Lvl	Name	Slot	Pg
30	Potion of clarity	Consumable	188
30	Potion of spirit	Consumable	188
30	Precise wand of color spray +6	Wand	111
30	Radiant +6	Weapon	76
30	Righteous +6	Weapon	77
30	Ring of spell storing, greater	Ring	160
30	Robe of defying storms +6	Armor	49
30	Robe of the archfiend +6	Armor	50
30	Rod of mindbending +6	Rod	100
30	Rod of starlight +6	Rod	100
30	Rod of vulnerability +6	Rod	102
30	Shared suffering +6	Armor	51
30	Skybound +6	Armor	52
30	Spiritlink +6	Armor	53
30	Staff of acid and flame +6	Staff	105
30	Staff of gathering +6	Staff	105
30	Staff of unparalleled vision +6	Staff	107
30	Storm gauntlets	Hands	136
30	Stormlord +6	Armor	53
30	Striking staff +6	Staff	107
30	Symbol of brilliance +6	Holy Symbol	87
30	Symbol of damnation +6	Holy Symbol	88
30	Symbol of dire fate +6	Holy Symbol	88
30	Symbol of radiant vengeance +6	Holy Symbol	89
30	Symbol of renewal +6	Holy Symbol	89
30	Symbol of revivification +6	Holy Symbol	90
30	Symbol of the warpriest +6	Holy Symbol	90
30	Tactician's +6	Armor	54
30	Talisman of repulsion +6	Neck	154
30	Tempest whetstone	Consumable	190
30	Thieving +6	Weapon	80
30	Torc of power preservation +6	Neck	154
30	Trespasser's bane +6	Weapon	81
30	Vengeful +6	Weapon	81
30	Wand of erupting flame +6	Wand	111
30	Warsheath +6	Armor	55
30	Whetstone of combustion	Consumable	190
30	Zealot's +6	Armor	55

SHARE YOUR ADVENTURES.
SHAPE YOUR WORLD.

Explore Faerûn with a band of adventurers gathered from around the globe and make a *real* impact on the world of Toril.

The RPGA's Living Forgotten Realms campaign offers dozens of official D&D® adventures every year—adventures that will help guide how the Realms will continue to evolve.

And best of all, you can do it wherever you play D&D—at home, your favorite game store, conventions—anywhere.

GET MORE INFORMATION AT: WIZARDS.COM/RPGA

DUNGEONS & DRAGONS®
LIVING FORGOTTEN REALMS

RPGA NETWORK